Exploring the

INNER HEBRIDES

Written and illustrated by

MARY E. GILLHAM MBE

HALSGROVE

First published in Great Britain in 2008
Copyright © 2008 Dr Mary E. Gillham

Front cover: *Columnar Basalt on Staffa*
Back cover: *Roseroot*

British Library Cataloguing-in-Publication Data
A CIP record for this title is available from the British Library

ISBN 978 1 84114 755 0

HALSGROVE
Halsgrove House
Ryelands Industrial Estate
Bagley Road, Wellington, Somerset TA21 9PZ
Tel: 01823 653777   Fax: 01823 216796
email: sales@halsgrove.com
website: www.halsgrove.com

Printed and bound by
The Short Run Press Ltd, Exeter

Contents

Acknowledgements

My sincere thanks go to Sandy Mitchell and to all the island folk who gave so generously of their time on the domestic and travel fronts and as guides to their special local wildlife. Our reception was the warmest possible, wherever we went. My special gratitude goes to my mentor, Clive Thomas, who helped me through the many pitfalls of the new computer age and made possible the production of the script.

Introduction

This book records the impressions of a southern-based naturalist exploring northwards along the island dotted Minch.

Islay, the most southerly island, was visited in early winter, when spectacular hosts of geese, whooper swans and northern ducks, divers and grebes were flying in from the Arctic for the winter foraging. Also notable were the little auk, which seldom strays this far south, and the evocative sight and sound of the resident choughs. The sister island of Jura, where red deer roaming over the Paps outnumber the human population of two hundred by three hundred to one, was shrouded in low cloud, but eerily memorable, nevertheless.

Colonsay, with its satellite Oronsay beyond tidal flats, enjoys a wide range of habitats, from peaceful bluebell woods and undulating cattle pastures to rockscapes where formidable dykes cross the land as upstanding walls and the sandy bays as linear reefs. This, too, is a land of raised beaches formed before and after the Ice Age.

The Slate Islands of Nether Lorn, accessible from the mainland over the old arched Atlantic Bridge, have an industrial rather than a crofting past. Large open lagoons mark the sites of old slate quarries flooded by the sea, the surviving land surface seemingly held together by the intrusive Great Dyke.

Children of my generation used to snigger over the names of Muck, Eigg and Rum for the images they conjured up in our imaginative minds. These, comprising the Parish of the Small Islands, are, in fact delightful, Muck for its gentle charm and Rum for its austere mountain supporting upland shearwaters and red deer. Eigg we found most alluring, with its mighty dolomitic extrusion of the Sgurr rising abruptly from an older landscape bordered by a remarkable collection of 'giant's marbles' in the form of calcareous concretions along the shore below.

The next trio, Iona, Staffa and Treshnish, present three different aspects. Iona, with its spreading, flowery machair, is a holy site, modern as well as ancient. Staffa's columnar basalt, featuring the much publicised Fingal's Cave, is rivalled only by Northern Ireland's Giant's Causeway. The wealth of sea fowl in depressions of the Treshnish cliffs must be almost unique for their approachability.

Coll and Tiree, one predominantly rocky and one sandy, are blessed by spring sunshine but are almost treeless because of high winds, and are bounded by spectacular cliffs and beaches. Black Orkney sheep forage over hills of precambrian Gneiss while fat beef cattle chew the cud among the buttercups of modern deposits of blown shell sands. They are peopled by some of Britain's most hospitable folk.

Mighty columns of organ pipe basalt form five hundred foot high cliffs on the lonely Shiants, some crowded with sea-birds. Humans no longer live on its formidable slopes where abandoned lazy beds tell of a harsh crofting past.

Handa, almost as far north as the tip of the mainland, is perhaps the most spectacular of all with its vertical cliffs and stacks of pre Cambrian Dalradian Sandstone. Once again, sea-birds abound, and there are no permanent human inhabitants. A truly northern touch is supplied by the great and Arctic Skuas which nest on the brown sweeps of moorland.

There is much diversity from south to north with natural habitats ranging from true wilderness to sophisticated human communities earning a living from whisky production and tourism, including special activities such as wind and kite surfing. Recent finds in the richness of marine life offshore could lead to a future development of scuba diving opportunities.

BY THE SAME AUTHOR

SEA BIRD ISLANDS

Sea Birds, Museum Press, London, 1963

A Naturalist in New Zealand, Museum Press, London and Reeds, New Zealand, 1966

Sub-Antarctic Sanctuary: Summertime on Macquarie Island, Gollancz and Reeds, 1967

Islands of the Trade Winds, An Indian Ocean Odyssey, Minerva Press, London, 1999

Island Hopping in Tasmania's Roaring Forties, Stockwell, Devon, 2000

Memories of Welsh Islands, Dinefwr, Wales, 2004

Salt Wind from the Cape (South Africa), Lazy Cat, Cardiff, 2005

A Naturalist on Lundy, Halsgrove, Somerset, 2007

This Island Life, Halsgrove, Somerset, 2007

WELSH COUNTRYSIDE

The Natural History of Gower Edns.1 & 2.Browns, Wales, 1977, 1979

Swansea Bay's Green Mantle, Browns, Wales, 1982

Glamorgan Heritage Coast, I. Sand Dunes, South Glamorgan Co.Ccl.,1987

Glamorgan Heritage Coast, II. Rivers, Glamorgan Wildlife Trust, 1989

Glamorgan Heritage Coast, III. Limestone Downs, Glamorgan Wildlife Trust, 1991

Glamorgan Heritage Coast, IV. Coastal Downs, Glamorgan Wildlife Trust, 1993

Glamorgan Heritage Coast, V. Cliffs and Beaches, Glamorgan Wildlife Trust, 1994

The Garth Countryside: Part of Cardiff's Green Mantle, Lazy Cat, Cardiff, 2001

A Natural History of Cardiff, Exploring along the River Taff, Lazy Cat, Cardiff, 2002

A Natural History of Cardiff, Exploring along the Rhymney and Roath, Dinefwr, 2006

I
Islay and Jura

ISLAY

1. TO ISLAY VIA ARRAN AND CAMPBELTOWN

It was 26th October, 2006 and wintry sunshine coaxed a gleam of light from the wet tarmac of Glasgow Airport. I had enjoyed many visits to the Hebrides in past summers, when sea-birds and water fowl were arrayed in their breeding splendour. This time things would be different.

Most of the avian stars of former visits were now well out to sea enjoying months of freedom before domestic chores forced them ashore once more. Now I was to be seeing others, freed from the responsibilities of bringing up young and arriving here on vacation to this often far distant and more welcoming land where they could enjoy a respite from the harsh conditions of their Arctic breeding colonies. Birds remaining here in little Britain would be wearing different plumages, or may, indeed, have been replaced by other individuals of the same kind.

Three years earlier in 2003, I had visited Caerlaverock and adjacent bird reserves on the Scottish side of the Solway Firth to witness the dramatic arrival of geese and swans from northern lands. Now I was to experience a repeat of that awesome migration in a more evocative setting of coast and mountain.

In my anxiety to get to the islands as soon as possible after a pre-dawn start from a monster Glasgow hotel, I almost boarded the plane to Benbecula. Ours left a quarter of an hour later, or so we thought. An hour after boarding the aisle carpet was still rolled back, with three workmen grovelling under the floorboards and the emergency lighting system as non-functional as before.

The technicians gave up, luggage was transferred and we were put on the plane to Campbeltown. This remote settlement, surrounded by a lot of air and sea but a long way from anywhere by road, lies near the end of the dangling Kintyre peninsula. It had figured in a family holiday for me back in the early 1930s, but I remembered little more than the name.

It would be interesting to view the spot again briefly from another angle, but there was more. This route would enable me to get a bird's eye view of Scotland's Arran Island. Having come off Ireland's Aran Islands only a few months before, this other of similar name had been a subject for conjecture. I would be able to compare the two. Even so superficial a glimpse confirmed that they could not have been more different.

While the Irish cluster was composed of bald slabs of pale limestone pavement, criss-crossed with dry stone walls, the Scottish island presented itself

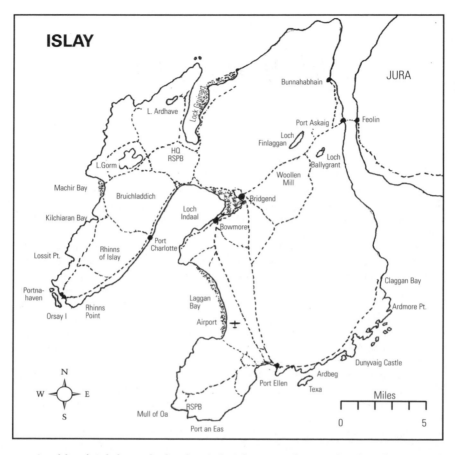

ISLAY

JURA

Bunnahabhain

L. Ardhave

Loch Gruinart

Port Askaig

Feolin

Loch
Finlaggan

HQ
RSPB

Loch
Ballygrant

L.Gorm

Woollen
Mill

Machir Bay

Bruichladdich

Bridgend

Kilchiaran Bay

Loch
Indaal

Bowmore

Port
Charlotte

Lossit Pt.

Rhinns
of Islay

Claggan Bay

Portna-
haven

Laggan
Bay

Ardmore Pt.

Orsay I

Rhinns
Point

Airport

Dunyvaig Castle

N

W — E

S

Ardbeg

Port Ellen

Texa

Miles

Mull of Oa

RSPB

0   5

Port an Eas

as a jumble of tightly packed volcanic heights, round-topped rather than jagged and said to be almost unscalable, their flanks dark with unwalled peat bog and heather moor. The island's twelve square miles thrusts ten peregrine haunted peaks up to more than two thousand feet, Goat fell rises to 2,866 feet and the summits generally are respected by professional mountaineers familiar with mightier ranges.

Our last sighting was of a less fearsome looking southern plain with little clusters of buildings in Lamlash and Brodick with its pier. A road runs right around the coast and there were scattered conifer plantations encompassed by russet rolls of bracken.

Then we were out over the sea again and dipping down to Campbeltown, to land among golfing greens tucked among yellow sandhills. To the left, bordering the Atlantic, was the long golden sweep of the Machrihanish Sands. These fronted an altogether gentler pastoral landscape. All around were green paddocks with placidly grazing cattle, sheltered by irregular plots of conifers. Revolving sails of wind farms broke the skyline. There were no other planes on the airfield and we taxied around to a small reception building snuggled in a hollow to swap passengers. Such outposts, as in the Australian Outback, are more conveniently reached by air than by land or sea. One gent, evidently a habitual traveller and on good terms with the stewardess, was helped aboard on crutches.

"What, no sweeties?" "Oh, they stopped that long ago."

Soon the propellor outside my window started to turn in slow motion, the blades clearly visible and remaining so for a while as they speeded up before whirring into a blur and becoming invisible as we took off. I wondered how the big planes managed to gain speed without them.

We lifted over sharply ridged marram grass dunes, getting good views of the undulating coast of Northern Ireland away to the south as we swung north. Islay, pronounced Isla is the most southerly of Scotland's Inner Isles and is only ten minutes away by air. It loomed dark and steep-ended as we approached over the Mull of Oa, which forms the southern end of the main island block.

Soon we were above the harbour of Port Ellen with its long pier, where we would have landed had we come by sea. First came a cluster of small islets, then a huddle of little boats and a row of white walled houses lining the shore. Again there were irregular but angular blocks of conifers patterning the landscape. The rest was a mosaic of yellow moor grass and rushy pastures with glistening pools and dark ditches following the lines of old peat cuttings.

Once more we were landing among sand dunes on a west facing coast after passing over the inevitable Scottish golf course. The bordering beach of yellow sand ran almost straight for five miles bounding Laggan Bay at the entrance to Loch Indaal. This was Traigh a'Mhachaire, the machair beach with the little rocky cluster of Knockangle Point at the end of one of the runways the only interruption shown on the map to the pristine stretch of shore. The plane turned back towards the hills to land, but by now the sun had sneaked behind the clouds and I had lost my sense of direction.

Six of us were arriving on this flight to meet our resident ornithological guide, Peter Roberts, who had little difficulty in picking us out from the small crowd. There is something about bird watchers, or is it just what they wear? We relied on Peter for the telescopes and tripods, so it was not the gear we carried which labelled us.

Our group consisted of a couple of musicians from the South of England, a mother and daughter, medical practitioner and gardener, from the Midlands, a tax man from Liverpool and myself, thirty years their senior and retired, from South Wales. Peter gathered us into his mini-bus and we set off up the coast of Laggan Bay to have the mysteries of his adopted island unfolded for our delight.

2. INTRODUCTION TO THE HUB OF THE ISLAND
AROUND THE HEAD OF LOCH INDAAL

Islay is approximately twenty by twenty five miles in extent and is shaped like an upside down U with the older, pre-cambrian rocks forming the smaller arm to the west and newer Dalradian sandstones, slates and phyllites some six hundred million years old making up the main block to the east.

The divide is caused by a major fault running from north to south, parallel to the Sound of Islay which separates Islay from Jura to its east. Disturbed ground along the fault line has been worn down by erosion and scoured out by ice to form two elongated sea lochs separated by low-lying land and dividing the two mountain blocks.

Loch Indaal is the long inlet in the south, Loch Gruinart the smaller one in the north. The airport is well down Indaal's eastern flank and our hotel, the Port Charlotte, is half way down the opposite side. Nobody was in any hurry to move in. The sun had exhausted its stint for the day by the time we landed, but there was no rain and the sea was calm, just right for duck viewing. The forecast was dire, time must be used to the full in case the heavens opened.

Our route round the head of the main loch passed through Islay's two largest towns, Bowmore and Bridgend, but these were on the sea front and the myriad sea birds that we stopped to watch were untroubled by human artefacts, revelling rather in the extra shelter afforded by piers and groynes.

We were travelling inland at first, past Duich Moss, to meet the coast where the Bowmore pier serves the rambling, white-walled whisky distillery. Next came the

1. Mew or Common Gulls

spacious saltings at the head of the loch- a gathering ground of the vast flocks of barnacle geese which were arriving all the week, to build up to awe inspiring numbers.

From here the road ran close to the coast, with handy lay-byes from which to scan the offshore waters, the winter domain of myriad sea ducks. Bowmore and Bridgend held none of the rowdy mobs of herring and black-backed gulls that haunt so many seaside towns. Most of the few gulls present were mews, which live up to their more usual name of common gull here in the North, although we southerners usually see them only as winter flocks and dispute the common epithet. They seem altogether gentler than the rubbish tip gulls of our towns, with their dark eyes, yellow-green legs and streaky head. Not much smaller were the black-headed gulls with which they consorted, those, of course, without the chocolate-black caps that they wear so proudly through the breeding season.

A bonus beyond the wide variety of ducks were grebes and divers, newly arrived family parties of whooper swans and an array of wading birds, from stately grey herons down to the pattering forms of ringed plovers. Among the expected rock and meadow pipits poking among the shoreline rocks were twites, those essentially northern finches with yellow beaks that were new to most of us.

2. Female Scaup

Mallard were present, as almost everywhere, although not usually regarded as sea-going ducks. By no means the commonest here, they were outnumbered by an impressive flock of great scaup, birds seldom seen on home waters. In some ways these were standing in for the more familiar tufted ducks, which they resembled quite closely at this time of year when the tufteds diagnostic white side patches changed to a mottled brown. Dark head, breast and tail were the same in both species, the feature to look out for being the scaup's marked white ring around the base of the beak.

Goldeneyes, here, too, in smaller numbers, were similar, the distinctive white sides and neck of summer swapped for a neutral grey in winter, but the forehead more humped and the white face patch smaller and at the side of the beak only. Both scaup and goldeneye breed in Scandinavia and Northern Europe, scaup also in Iceland, as indeed do some of the tufted duck which fly south to winter in the UK.

Shelduck retain their handsome pied, chestnut and glossy green plumage throughout the year. They are familiar estuarine birds and an enhancing feature of the Bristol Channel muds on my home patch. All black scoters were here, singly or in small flocks, appearing as distant black spots and needing the telescope to distinguish their finer points, such as the female's paler face. Most breed by lakes and rivers in Northern Europe's boreal forests, but a few do so in Scotland.

The birds most easily recognised were the muscular looking black and white eider drakes with their fat brown ducks squatting on the water like self satisfied dowagers. These are here summer and winter, although commercial gathering of eiderdown occurs mostly in Iceland. The evocative, seemingly entreating coos of the drakes always brought a smile to the face on summertime encounters. Here they peppered the sea in rafts mixed with others too far off for us to hear whether they were as talkative out of the breeding season when they have no need to impress.

A handsome flock of wigeon rode the mirror calm waters – birds that we were to see later on in vast numbers grazing as contentedly as sheep on the grassy swards beloved by the geese. Their harsher flight calls changed to a contented whistling as they settled. Again these were mostly incomers from the far North, gracing our fields with their their pied, pink, chestnut and grey plumage.

There was plenty more to see as we continued around the head of the loch. The statuesque form of a grey heron in the shallows, a young white-fronted shag wing drying on an offshore rock or a couple of ever handsome oyster catchers levering shellfish from the rocks. We lost no time in dropping our baggage at the hotel before setting off again.

3. LITTLE AUK, PRIDE OF THE SEA FOWL

We started back along the same route, giving substance to the old adage that there is often as much new to see on the way back as on the way out. Ducks were still the main feature, including a graceful, slender necked pintail, which could be said to be sharpened at both ends. Another of similar shape but with shorter beak was the handsome black and white long-tailed duck – much rarer and here from breeding grounds in Northern Norway or Iceland.

From the rather featureless grey sedimentary rocks around Port Charlotte we saw more of the pink, coarse-grained Syenite at Bruichladdich. The lighthouse here was built on an igneous dyke intruded vertically through these attractive rocks, whose colour was due to pink Felspar. It seems likely that many of the jagged black oucrops on the narrow, gravelly beach might be broken edges of the parallel swarm of volcanic dykes that run south from Mull and Iona to curve gradually around hereabouts to head off eastwards towards Northumbria's Great Whin Sill.

Here at Bruichladdich the greenish rock interleaved with the pink has been identified by geologists as a meta-gabbro. Much is overlain by new and old shoreline deposits of sand and gravel, both along the current intertidal zone and as a low cliff behind the buildings. On this and subsequent days we passed a lumpy yellow erratic dumped on the shore by moving ice somewhere along this stretch.

The pink rock was masked in places at the top of the tide by a growth of microscopic lichens resembling black paint, the blackness mirrored in the upper drift-

3. Purple Sandpipers

line of accumulated dried wrack. This may have contained sufficient kelp fly larvae or sandhoppers to satisfy the rock pipits and hoodie crows, but it was lower down, where the wracks were still olive brown and fully alive that the little flocks of dull coloured purple sandpipers and more brightly marbled turnstones with their conspicuous red legs were foraging.

Larger waders spotted hereabouts were redshanks with longer red legs, greenshanks, curlew and bar-tailed godwit. Redshanks breed on the island but are joined by others from the European mainland and Iceland in winter. Greenshank too, breed in the remote north and west of Scotland but were likely at this season to have come in from the continent, as was the godwit. Lapwings wheeling over the edge of the tide might also be from northern Europe, as residents tend to move south in hard winters.

It was in the lee of Bruichladdich Pier that we enjoyed splendid views of the week's ornithological highlight, a little auk, strayed south from the high Arctic. Only our resident and much travelled leader had set eyes on this unmistakable species before. Seldom did one of these diminutive puffin parodies venture into the comparatively mild waters of the Gulf Stream.

The stubby little black and white bird drifted about aimlessly on the inshore waters, then scrambled onto a low rock to rest. It was a long way from home and very likely sick. We learned later that another was reported that same day quite a distance away, so two might have been drifted off course together.

It was in winter plumage, with white collar and three to four horizontal white wing bars with a vertical one on the flank behind. The rest was black, including the legs, which appeared to be held vertically from the hocks down when it turned tail on the rock, this indicative of how far back they were inserted to give maximum aid when swimming.

We did not witness the rapid fluttering of the short wings because the bird did not take to the air. Nor did we see them trailing alongside as they are said to do when the bird dives. for it stayed on the surface. It was altogether too lethargic for a bird with the get up and go name of Alle alle!

Little auks nest on mountains in the high Arctic, often far from the sea, so those seemingly inadequate wings might have to carry the plump little body a long way to the sea to stock up with fish. Much as they simulate miniature penguins, they could scarcely be expected to walk or toboggan on legs set so far back, as those do to cover long distances on land.

One of our leader's bird watching buddies living closeby was out at the end of the pier on a routine watch, unaware of the treasure between him and the shore. He was called back and crept closer, with camera and sketch pad at the ready, as enchanted as the rest of us by the newcomer.

4. *Little Auk in winter plumage*

We saw few other auks and only on the first two days – two razorbills, one guillemot and a black guillemot, all in winter plumage. The black guille- mot or tystie was totally different from the completely velvet-black with snowy white wing patch of the birds I had been seeing around Ireland's Aran Islands back in June. Now the bird was predominantly white, the only pure black around the faithful white oval on the wings and the tail tip, with pale streaks on the white back and lighter mottling on the head and neck. The common guillemot and razorbill were less altered from their familiar summer garb, the main difference being the white face and throat in both instances.

An unusual bird seen in this area at the same season the previous year. was a Manx shearwater wheeling over Indaal Loch on two occasions. Although not seen here before shearwaters nest in their thousands not too many miles away, as on Rhum.

4. DUNES AT MACHIR AND RED-LEGGED DAWS

After this excitement and with our picnic lunch on board, we turned off the main highway near the Gorton Quarry and headed for the west coast at Machir Bay. To the north was Loch Gorm, a large body of fresh water which drained to the sea on both sides of the Carn Mor headland. This we would be viewing later.

Our road ended beyond Machrie between the southern lake outlet and another stream occupying the valley between two major knobs of the Northern Rhinns. The sea in Machir Bay was hidden behind the current dune ridge, but we had ample time while munching sandwiches to appreciate the height to which the sand from former dunes had been piled up against the cliffs along the southern skyline, with no doubt some more evanescent wind drift over the top in parts.

Sizable blow-outs indicated the depth of the material, whose rich shell content was at variance with the pre-Cambran acidity of the rocks beneath. The result was lush green pasture supporting happily munching cows. These were all black, with just a hint of a white Hereford? face here and there. A twittering flock of twites or northern linnets was feeding in a leafy hollow where the sand had been scoured away by a stream, the birds flipping back occasionally into stonechat territory behind.

The inner man satisfied, we set off on an elliptical walk across the slope to where the mountains abutted onto the coast and back along the pristine beach to the stream emergence. Pasture plants still in bloom at the end of the fall were predominantly the cheerful white daisy flowers of mayweed. Others were white yarrow and ox-eye, yellow ragwort and autumnal hawkbit and the ubiquitous dandelion. All were members of that most successful family traditionally known as the Compositae but newly referred to nowadays as the Asteraceae. To judge by the all-over spread of crumpled white silverweed leaves, there must have been a fine show of yellow flowers in earlier months.

Fungi were few but stable ridges of turf had thrust forth a few yellow waxcap (Hygrocybe) toadstools. One fine specimen grew horizontally from a vertical sand face, an unusual orientation. Normally the stipe bends around to align the cap horizontally, facilitating rain run-off and allowing the spores to drop from the gills to be picked up for distribution by air currents.

Blow-outs on the sand face were frequent and showed something of the history of its accumulation in the exposed soil profiles. These included narrow bands of peaty black

5. *Sea Mayweed*

humus, generated during quiet spells when no new sand was being added. It was interesting to see how the stalks of the bracken fronds often descended only to these layers, a foot or so below the surface, springing from rhizomes growing horizontally along the more stable, water and nutrient retentive horizon. The clean sand below was mostly untenanted. Why tap unprofitable substrates when needs were supplied within easier reach?

The size of these breaks in the turf were greatly increased by the efforts of a thriving rabbit population. Many of their burrows penetrated the vertical sand walls, presumably cut back from a more convenient entrance and now abandoned. On the whole shallower ones under the stabilising skin of turf were likely to prove more durable.

A major seepage soaking down from the quartz-veined rocks above harboured a few squat, rugose leaf rosettes of primroses, promising springtime elegance. Among the sogginess of mosses were the narrow winter leaves of lesser spearwort.

The underlying rocks of these Northern Rhinns are folded beds of sedimentary sandstones, some of the muddier strata changed to Phyllites. They extend out under the sea to Colonsay and Oronsay in the north and are collectively known as the Colonsay Group.

But we were an ornithological group and our attention was soon drawn to the local bird celebrities, the choughs or red-legged daws. The total count here today was twenty. Most were swooping over the rising land towards the sea cliffs in tumbling flight, emitting their mewing, uncrowlike calls as they played the fickle air currents. One was seen picking a partially ripened cow pat to pieces.

These elegant Corvids were rare in Scotland, as they were in England and Wales during the early part of the twentieth century, after suffering from nineteenth century game preservation. This persecution was not for any particular misdemeanours of their own, for they are insect eaters, but simply because they were crows and crows were regarded as evil, thieving game bird eggs and chicks. This was a parallel case to shags suffering for the sins of fishing cormorants.

As soon as they became rare they were a prime target for egg collectors. Once protected, they began to make a come-back, particularly in Scotland and Wales and, even after much manipulation of the habitat, in Cornwall.

Their elegant crimson bills were used for probing in short turf for small soil animals and in cow dung for dung beetles. Like wheatears, which do best on heavily rabbited land, they shunned long grass, so the cattle served them in two ways. Farmers were paid to keep their livestock on the ground into the winter, to produce the requisite conditions.

Our leader had spent much of his period as warden in the Welsh Bird Observatory of Bardsey Island studying their habits and had much to tell us about their feeding preferences. Among their favourites there were small dung beetles *(Aphodius contaminata)*, one of forty species of the genus which enjoys much of its life cycle in the cosy warmth of fermenting dung. Adult beetles lay their eggs in or under it just as they find it, not rolling it into balls bigger than themselves to bury elsewhere, like the more spectacular and better known Mediterranean and tropical species.

6. Choughs

Choughs also seek out the various phases of the yellow dung flies (Scatophaga or Scopeuma), adults of which were still sitting around on Islay cow pats at this late date. Yellow meadow ants *(Lasius flavus)* are taken but are usually left until last so are presumably not among their favourites. Or, more likely, they are just too wee to bother with unless hard pressed – although green woodpeckers have no problems on this score where they exist.

Cow pats here also supported little orange disc fungi *(Humaria elegans)*, but these do not interest insectivorous choughs. Thirteen pairs of these noble birds breed in this area but the size of wintering flocks may rise to sixty or seventy birds.

They prefer to roost as well as nest in caves, but not in confined holes like tawny owls, woodpeckers or starlings. A larger opening is needed to allow them to enter and leave through a free flyway and swoop up onto a ledge, as in an open cave. To provide them with more roosting sites, Islay ornithologists have rerofed some of the many derelict cottages scattered around the island and blocked up the windows apart from a twelve inch gap at the top, allowing free flight in and out.

After learning this, we spotted a number of such cottages on our drives around the island. Pampered choughs do not have things all their own way, however, having to compete for these desirable residences with barn owls, rock doves, jackdaws and starlings.

15

A larger relative, a raven, came gliding in over the piled sand as we watched the choughs and we spotted a black cat on the prowl, no doubt hoping for a baby rabbit. There are thought to be too many such on the island for the welfare of the birds and we later saw the sad, but mercifully instant, demise of a white puss which elected to cross the road at the time one of the fairly rare cars was passing.

Chaffinches and greenfinches were about and we spotted a black guillemot as we made our way down to the sea via an entrenched sand track over the dune ridge and across the slaty grey rocks that intruded minimally between dune and beach. Yellowed autumnal leaves of sea milkwort or black saltwort *(Glaux maritima)* crept over the sand at extreme high tide mark. Summer annuals had been washed away by the equinoctual springs, leaving only a few thrift tumps, and scraggy stems of curled dock. A blue-green fringe of sand couch grass bordered the tussocky marram of the dunes.

Thongweed *(Himanthalea elongata)* and bootlace weed or mermaid tresses *(Chorda filum)* had drifted in from deeper levels to lie among the displaced egg wrack and bladder wrack, all denizens of the rocks to either side of the bay. With them were a number of sea rods the woody stems of old oarweeds. Their splaying fronds were missing and we wondered if these had been collected to fertilise the fields, as on so many islands – from which the unrottable sea rods were exported for the chemical industry.

An extensive rock platform surfaced well down the beach, although still in shallow water when submerged, so flat was this delightful expanse of almost untrodden sand. Fawn rock layers protruded edgeways on, partially coated with the common inksplash lichens. They were permeated by white quartz veins four to six inches wide and considerable areas were covered by the smallest of the brown wracks – the uppermost in the tidal sequence. This, the channelled wrack *(Pelvetia canaliculata),* had a bright orange sludge of reproductive bodies oozing from the swollen receptacles at the frond tips for fertilisation in open water.

Soft green algae floated in shallow pools and the convoluted trails of grazing periwinkles wound their way across surfaces scummed with the microsopic organisms on which they feed. Sea-borne litter was no more noxious than the odd goose feather or coloured golfing tee.

The only birds seen were, rather atypically, a group of fifteen or so curlews on an offshore rock, where ring-billed or Iceland gulls have been spotted in the past. Today there were only mundane herring gulls about, but three buzzards circled overhead as we left the beach.

A brisk little stream came surging down here through dense watercress beds, these, deceptively a mixture of true and fool's watercress, the two best distinguished when in flower. Trails of flote grass emphasised the freshwater character of this spot but sea arrow grass *(Triglochin maritima)* and salt marsh rush *(Juncus gerardi)* registered a taint of salt.

Backing the stream was a small reed swamp and we moved inland through a thicket of coarse meadow plants, knapweed, sow thistle and the big leaves of coltsfoot that give the plant its name. The local twite flock moved in behind us to continue their disturbed consumption of their myriad seeds.

7. *Salt Marsh Rush, Sea Arrow Grass and Flote Grass*

Traditional machair in the Outer Hebrides is flat and scarcely above sea level. Here the blown sand was piled on mountains dipping to the coast and sometimes extending over half a mile from the sea, as at Lossit Bay further south. The spelling of this site as Machir suggested that there were no pretensions to include this with the classic type, although the root was obviously of significance.

5. GREY SEALS OFF THE SOUTHERN RHINNS

We circumnavigated the ancient mountain block of the Rhinns the next day, travelling south by the western shore of Loch Indaal and returning on the minor road along the scenically more rugged Atlantic coast. "Rhinns" translates as promontary.

Contrasting bands of coarse-grained pink Selenite brightened the blackness of the medium-grained Dolerite. On the southern point we looked out for the shear zones where rock layers had been pulled past each other, giving lines of weakness. To seaward of the highway were green paddocks. Inland were rolling brown heather heaths, poor rush-spiked grazings and a monotony of Molinia moors rolling away into hazy distances.

Our first stop was at a small freshwater loch on the seaward side near Port Caol. It was empty of birds but produced a fierce squall of rain and a long awaited burst of sunshine which spanned the landscape with the low arc of a rainbow. This was by no means the only show of these ethereal

8. *Orsay Island Lighthouse, South Rhinns*

colours experienced during our stay. The optimist in our party described these as "Days of chasing rainbows." Photographers among us would have been better pleased if we had caught up more often!

The road wound down to sea level at the end of the peninsula, to two picturesque clusters of whitewashed cottages with black slate roofs, like most on the island. The paint work conformed except on the little post office, where it was scarlet, to match the post van parked outside. These were the fisher folks' settlements of Portnahaven and Port Wemyss, the somewhat remote site at this end of the land chosen because of the two sizable offshore islands protecting their two little inlets from the force of Atlantic gales.

The southernmost island, Orsay, is crowned by an automated lighthouse, the other is Eilean Mhic Coinnich. Terns nested in good numbers on the pebble beaches there in summer, but the birds scattered across its slopes today were great black-backed gulls.

Beyond the northern bluff of the northern island the open sea was churned into a veritable mayhem. White horses tossed their manes from shore to horizon, waves not waiting to reach the shallows before toppling forwards in a frenzy of spume.

The tide was running in from the north and we watched fascinated as the unleashed current streamed through the gap between Mhic Coinnich and the mainland. Conditions can change quite rapidly in this quirky land. Yesterday the sea had been relatively still, by Hebridean standards, and a number of little boats had put to sea, but nary a one braved those vindictive waters today.

Not that there were many seamen here now, although a selection of small boats was moored on the placid waters of the main harbour and more drawn up on the grassed slope between here and the lane zig-zagging up to the higher ancient beach level where most of the cottages were sited.

The majority had recently been refurbished as holiday accommodation and at this time of year it was almost a ghost town, with probably no more than ten people in residence. Nevertheless, all the lawns were neatly mown (or grazed) and the flower beds were in good order. Renovations during the past two years had been extensive and subject to strict building regulations, maintaining their character but adding extras such as the water purification system and new sewage outlet.

9. Portnahaven Harbour and holiday cottages

Modernisation had detracted nothing from the charm of the little haven, where the old concrete jetty slept beside the pocket handkerchief sized beach. Quietened waters murmured among the boats and spoke softly between intruding arms of rock. No scene could have been more at odds with that of the breakers curling over themselves outside with that minty blue glint of winter.

A little possie of Atlantic seals had wisely chosen the harbour for their afternoon siesta, fifteen in all. In fact they were not 'bottling', with noses raised in sleep, but regarding our little party with interest. Seals have a way of staring at you with unblinking concentration until you begin to feel uncomfortable. There was, however, some interaction, with the dark, thick-necked bull nuzzling one of his paler harem members. Grey Atlantics are more commonly seen on the island than the so-called common seals which we encountered later off the Oa.

We pottered on the edge of their play pool, sorting out the hemlock, carrot and other umbellifers by their leaves and dead fruit heads near to where the stream from the mountain conifer block came tumbling down into the harbour.

On the low point itself the wind riven but ungrazed sward of red fescue grass presented the perfect example of a 'waved heath'. Wind-combed clumps of the needle-leaved grass swooped to leeward at an an angle of around forty five degrees for six to eight inches, to a tattered crest, to drop steeply on the leeward face or recede beneath the overarching fringe.

It was easy to draw a parallel with dune formation, where the gentler slope occurs on the windward side, tipping over to a steeper leeward face which can provide important shelter for invertebrates in both instances. The tumbled humps and hollows of the yielding grass blades mirrored those of the violence beyond the islands.

As we boarded our vehicle a big flock of redwings came rustling down from the slope behind, to settle on grass and fence. These, we were told, were birds of the Iceland race, moved in from the north-west, each slightly larger than their more southerly counterparts – as is the way of birds in cold climates.

10. Redwings

One perched within a few feet of the minibus, peering in through the window, its plumage ruffled by the wind to show the red flank feathers. We saw many more of their kind throughout the week but few of the fieldfares which often accompany them.

Before we left they were joined by another immigrant flock – of starlings – all headed into the wind to prevent cold air seeping in under their glossy, speckled winter finery. The odd goldfinch and chaffinch pottered in the gardens.

Our next stop, quite nearby, was to view something altogether less traditional. This was a unique, wave-powered electricity generator sponsored in 1998-9, by Greenpeace. It was a valiant attempt to harness some of the violence prevalent offshore.

We reached it through a wide metal farm gate and along a wide metalled ballast track. There was little to see apart from the concrete roof of a blocky red and white edifice built astride a gulch in the cliff below path level. There was, however, much to hear.

Each wave arrived with a thump and a whoosh, great rhyhmic roars like a giant's breath – of the sort sometimes emanating from natural cliff blow holes. Sea water did not gain entry to the turbine but pushed volumes of air through under pressure to provide the power – a giant's breath indeed. We were glad we were not down there where it was all happening. Whether the amount of power generated would make the effort of construction worth while, was open to question, but the fact that no replicas had been produced since was not encouraging.

This was one of two new devices installed on Islay exploring a programme to harness wave energy – the U K's first full scale wave power machines. Wavegen's "Limpet" is the shoreline device installed here, the other, the "Sea Snake" thought up by Ocean Power, floats on the sea surface.

They were put in place after a Greenpeace survey of the coast using side scan sonar where Limpet was installed and three D mapping of the seabed where Sea

Snake was to be anchored. Islay was selected as the ideal testing ground for the 'clean energy' hoped for as twenty first century oil power dwindles.

Experimental wave energy work had already been under way for a decade, to make the Islay community as self sufficient as possible, with home bred, renewable energy. Greenpeace was involved in a supportive role to the community-led project and to the companies manufacturing the wherewithal. Where better than Scotland, with its tradition of ship building, heavy engineering and the oil industry to find the expertise?

Our difficulty on this exposed point was to stand up at all or to make progress into the gale. No doubt that was why the apparatus was sited here. When folk chide me for not using a tripod when I photograph flowers I defend myself with "It's not me waving in the breeze but the flower." Today it would very definitely have been me – had any flower stood up to the gale long enough to be photographed.

There were few flower heads immediately behind the construction, but that was because of the rabbits which kept the sward smooth where sand had built up over the rock to a depth suitable for burrowing. A small pool among long, ungrazed grass on the walk back yielded some brookweed (*Samolus valerandi*), an uncommon plant often found near the sea, rising from a bed of lush marsh pennywort (*Hydrocotyle vulgaris*).

6. RHINNS CATTLE COUNTRY AT KILCHIARAN

From the wind blasted tip of the Rhinns opposite Frenchman's Rocks we dipped inland past the little freshwater loch at Claddach. The next grouse moor was particularly attractive, the close set heather knolls girt about with rumbustious

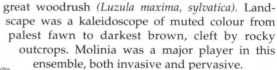

11. Brookweed and Marsh pennywort

great woodrush (*Luzula maxima, sylvatica*). Landscape was a kaleidoscope of muted colour from palest fawn to darkest brown, cleft by rocky outcrops. Molinia was a major player in this ensemble, both invasive and pervasive.

Its vernacular name of purple moor grass is applicable, like that of 'the bonnie purple heather' only in high summer. This is when the tall flower spikes splay out from each uncompromising tussock. Now, in late October, the culms were a pale orange.

Later on in winter, when the leaves of this, Britain's only deciduous grass, become detached, the scene is a pale straw colour unless completely rain sodden. This is a time of year when the withered bracken fronds retain their bright coppery sheen and the leafless boughs of birch and alder create a deep purple haze, producing a patchwork of different hues delimiting the various plant communities. Mapping their extent is a great deal easier at this season, if less physically comfortable, than at the height of summer, when all or most is green.

Outstanding on any such map hereabouts would be the irregular plots planted to conifers. Trees nearest the road appeared to be Sitka spruce rather than the native Scots pine, which we saw mainly as individual stately trees in mixed deciduous woodland.

Our route took us around the inland flank of the steep-sided 420 feet high peak of Ben Cladville. Remaining inland we crossed the deeply carved gulch of the Lossit Burn, careering down from an ancient dun or fort, to join its northern partner and go rollicking on to the golden sands of the deeply indented Lossit Bay. Material blown from the broad backing dunes here is said to penetrate half a mile from the shore, bringing much needed minerals to the hungry plants.

A brief whiff of sunshine cast a golden glow over the attractive little bay. All eyes were directed seawards, willing our driver to stop and allow us down, but he took a more practical view. The track leading that way, to Mullach Mor, ceased eight ten metre contour lines (or 260 vertical feet) above the bay!

So it came to pass that we pressed on, maps in hand, trying to spot the many marked stone circles, standing stones and duns, proving ancient usage of this unpromising looking terrain. Here and there modern man had carved out paddocks for his hardy black-faced sheep or Highland cattle. Had we lingered, we would have missed the homecoming of the big herd of cattle resident at Kilchiaran Farm. As it happened our arrival could not have been better timed.

Peter drew in beside a little sycamore spinney at the farm gate where he had spotted a chaffinch and hoped to find some accompanying bramblings. These colourful finches from the high Arctic should have arrived by now but there were none. We wandered in under the trees along a little stream to where a small tributary of clear, cider-brown water came gushing in over a little weir. One of these two must once have been the water supply for the inhabitants of the hill dun beyond Carn Mor upstream. The other drained a conifer wood. Together they skirted the farm and flowed on past an old chapel to the sea in Kilchiaran Bay.

Apparently the natural waters on this side of the great fault do not produce the fine whisky that emanates from the other side, but it looked just as palatable to me. (I am no fan of the powerful 'fire water'!)

Bramblings or not, Kilchiaran was an obligatory stop for visitors as the site of the almost unique nineteenth century semi-circular cattle steading. There is believed to be only one other such in Scotland. The main arc consisted of a half circle of stone byres, roofed with shiny black slates and with radiating walls dividing the enclosed yard, these twice the height of the cattle they restrained. Beyond was another, apparently more modern semicircle while accommodation towards the stream was on more familiar, rectangular lines.

The premises had been partially derelict when the current owner moved in, but he had renovated it, complying with strict building regulations to maintain its special character. Opposite the farm gate the land rose steeply to a soggy wet mound at the foot of the adjacent hill. We hauled ourselves up, hand over hand, along a sagging wire fence, to take aerial photographs. At which point the farmer emerged and suggested that the van be moved back as he was about to bring the herd in.

This was, indeed, a bonus, as we watched the big mob, red, roan, smooth coated and shaggy, plodding obediently down the lane ahead of their master's land rover. They were not coming in to be milked, but just for a cosy night indoors, very likely with extra provender to boot. A bulky red continental bull was already in the yard and there was a great cacaphony of greetings as his harem filed in. (The massive build of the Limousin bull is to the average cow as the motorised limousine is to the average car.)

This was a suckler herd, the shagginess of some of the calves pointing to Highland blood. We had seen tufty-coated youngsters, white as toy Polar bears, at other farms passed, these from Highland dams put to a white Shorthorn bull. Such animals served the peak of the prime beef market. We had noticed the esteem in which this meat is held when consulting the hotel dinner menu. "Six pounds extra for beef as against only four pounds extra for venison", this on top of an already generous cost.

After a less precarious detour to get down from our point of vantage – slopes that steep and that waterlogged being always more hazardous going down – I got into conversation with the herd's lord and master trudging up behind the last of his complacent brood. He, too, used a white Shorthorn bull on Highland cows, but most of the current herd were red, some roan, like the Shorthorns I had hand milked during Land Army days before Shorthorns went out of fashion in the dairy herds to make way for Friesians.

I asked if he used the Luing breed from the Slate Islands of Nether Lorn. He scoffed. "That lot thought they were producing something new. We'd been using that cross for years!"

He was benefiting from the results without the bother of getting the breed registered. (Luing Island cattle are red Shorthorn crossed with Highland.).

There is no milk production here and little anywhere on the island, most of the milk being imported from the mainland, despite all those lush green, reseeded pastures. Sadly the 1980s enterprise at Port Charlotte to convert local milk into cheese came to nought.

12. *Whooper Swans*

7. ROE DEER AND FRESHWATER DUCKS GALORE

Loch Gorm on the Northern Rhinns is the largest freshwater loch on the islands, a mile and a half wide and a mile from north to south. It yielded little in the way of bird life but about seventy whooper swans were grazing stubbles in the vicinity and may well adjourn to the safety of the open water to roost at night.

Otters and herons that we southerners tend to regard as freshwater species, are so spoiled for choice here with the intricate coastline of sea and sea loch that they have good reason to give the less bountiful fresh water a miss.

Acid mountain tarns and lochs are normally oligotrophic (poor in nutrients) and hence in water life, so it would be unfair to compare their fauna with eutrophic (fertile) lowland lakes. It was a very different kettle of fish in the freshwater marsh reclaimed from mineral rich sea level soils at the head of Loch Gruinart that we visited later in the day.

By Loch Gorm we encountered a large flock of genuine rock doves – a species not usually accepted as truly wild because of the ease with which it becomes domesticated to produce regular townees. Here they were fraternising with gulls on the farmland.

Not far off were more swans on aftermaths which had very likely been augmented with spent grain from the malting floors – as the reception areas for winter swans are augmented with grain at Slimbridge and other wildfowl reserves.

A 1980s publication stated that there were more than five hundred farms on Islay at that time. It is no doubt fewer now, with the countrywide trend to fewer, larger, more mechanised holdings. The climate is not too wet for the growing of cereal crops, barley for malting and oats, which are usually fed green, for livestock fodder.

The only crop still standing in late October was turnips, and possibly rape, their tops being eaten off green by sheep in a number of instances. Elsewhere the turnips themselves had been chopped up, presumably in the fields if, indeed, the chopping had not been achieved by the sheep themselves, as the cream coloured chunks were scattered evenly throughout.

13. Roe Deer

We headed towards Loch Gruinart along the northern road, observing goose flocks in the bordering fields, but the highlight of this drive was supplied by a roe deer. She had strayed onto the lane and evidently disliked vehicles but had forgotten that the low bounding fences were well within her capacity to jump.

She trotted up the lane ahead of us, however slowly we drove, determined not to let us by but refusing to back track past us when we stopped. Nor did she take refuge in the roadside gorse and brambles until a car came in the opposite direction, driving her back towards us. Now, surely, she would allow us by, but no. She had a way to go yet before clearing the fence in fine style, with plenty of leeway.

Graceful, long-legged and smaller than we had expected, She was dark brown, with a conspicuous white rump bobbing merrily as she cantered along. Camouflage was of no merit during movement and this was no doubt a beacon to others to flee, like the white scut of a rabbit. Roes are found mainly on this type of low-lying farmland, leaving the rougher hill grazings to the hardier red deer.

We were headed for the tract of marshland at the head of the northern sea loch reclaimed for farmland and now returned to marshland for the birds, but freshwater marsh and not saltmarsh. This was the only place on this "Island of birds" where we found ourselves in a bird hide – always a useful refuge from inclement weather.

The chief botanical treasure was spread for all to see in front of the hide and in pristine condition. This was marestail *(Hippuris vulgaris)*, an uncommon species despite the vulgaris. It thrust as a dense sward from the medium, which concealed the softly flowing underwater shoots that resemble the flowing tail of a mare in full gallop. Sub-aerial parts are smaller and neater, bearing tiny flowers in the axils of the leaf whorls.

All too often this gem is confused with the various common horsetails (Equisetum). The two are poles apart, horsetails being primitive fern allies bearing spores in terminal cones instead of flowers and fruits and with virtually no leaves, the splaying branches, stiff with silica, being photosynthetic stems.

14. *Marestail*

Little but the marestail remained fresh this late in the season, just a few tardy flowering Angelica umbels among the brittle seeding stems of purple loosestrife. Little blobs of yellow brain fungus clung to sodden timber among persicaria and dock.

Red campion was still flowering alongside the track we followed through scrub to the hide. Here too were the starry calyces of tutsan, their colourful berries shed, and disgruntled patches of yellow flags and other water plants in soggy hollows. Goldfinches and twites flipped among the flowering gorse.

But it was for bigger birds than these that we had come and there was no shortage of those. A labyrinth of waterways wove between lines and clumps of assorted vegetation and there was always something different behind the next tump.

Most numerous of the duck were teal, the smallest and arguably the most colourful. We counted group after group sheltering along the lines of rushes and still there were more idling in the shallows with mallard and shelduck. Wigeon were almost as abundant and we distinguished pintail and shoveller. Drake shovellers were every bit as handsome as the teal, their bold black and white streaking setting off the green and chestnut as they slurped the surface water with slate-coloured bills.

We had no problem with winter plumages of drakes which went into eclipse to resemble their dowdy brown partners in the summer lull of July and August. By autumn they are decked in their full breeding regalia again, ready to persuade their future mates through the drab winter months that they really were the most splendid of potential partners. Maybe this is why they are such popular additions to urban parks, to brighten the scene as the floral glory fades.

Waders are less glamorous by October than in summer when many are not to be seen in our latitude. The golden plover's magnificent white-bordered black of face, throat and belly that we see in summer if we are lucky enough to meet them on the high tops, had been moulted now. Today's birds were mottled throughout, the gold reflecting from the back less intense – or was that due to the lack of sunshine? Patterning of the lapwings with which they fraternised here was not so very different from in summer, except that the green gloss had gone from the feathers of the back and stippling had removed the spruceness from throat and face.

Throughout our sojourn in the hide, big flocks of barnacle geese were rising from the long grass to circle, chattering companionably, over their feeding patch before settling back into invisibility. We counted twenty eight white-fronted geese among them. Four mute swan cygnets paddled through the water lanes in single file, progressing in characteristic jerks as the big webbed feet pushed them on. The fourth had a job to keep up, but all finally converged on the pen and cob, hidden behind the undergrowth when they started out.

Two moorhens were spotted, but not the coots that we might have expected on so large a body of water. Apparently they are rare on Islay. As grazers, they would be in competition not only with the geese and swans but with the big, rippling flocks of wigeon and perhaps also of the many introduced pheasants. Solitary herons rose at intervals from their silent vigils and a peregrine sailed over the multitude, perhaps to see if any of the rock doves had strayed in among all these birds of inconveniently large size.

8. BROWN HARES, RED DEER AND BIRD ROOSTS

Our port of call on the west side of Loch Gruinart was the lonely little Loch Ardnave at the seaward end of the road. Although close to the shore, it was a hundred and twenty feet above current sea level, stepped back behind the raised beaches and bearing the brunt of the sea breezes.

15. Pochard

Whooper swans bobbing around on its choppy surface accorded us close views and there were tufted ducks and a couple of pochard. More remarkable were the fourteen ravens, surely normally the most solitary of all the black Corvids. We had been seeing plenty of large rook flocks, despite the paucity of the cornfields that usually attract these essentially arable birds. Their numbers had apparently increased since the hundreds of planted sycamores grew into patches of woodland lofty enough to supply suitable sites for rookeries.

Jackdaws flocked here too, as well as crows, most of which were hooded, although both types occur and are able to interbreed and produce young success-fully. A remarkable sight that few of us will forget was of several hundred large black Corvids massed on a single span of telegraph wire preparatory to moving to a roost.

Packed close together, ignoring the "individual distance" observed by most perching birds, they caused the cable to sag alarmingly between poles. It must have been the only slightly smaller numbers on the cable to either side of the main mob that prevented the poles from leaning inwards as the laden length swayed in the wind. The sight, reminiscent of grossly oversized swallows gathering for migration, caused much merriment.

After negotiating land transformed from saltmarsh to freshwater marsh, we drove along the opposite, east, coast of Loch Gruinart on the road to Killinallen. Geese were well catered for here, far more barnacles than white-fronted, as every-where else, but all having accomplished the same trek from Greenland.

We stopped short of the enticing sandy beach and dunes at the mouth of the loch. Their name, Traigh Daile Aonghais, put me in mind of our Traeth Mawr and

Traeth Bach in South Wales, the Celtic and Gaelic rendering of beach similar. While the others were spying out the wintering waders – greenshank, bar-tailed godwit and curlew – along the edge of the tide, I explored the saltings, looking in vain among the wracks for two essentially Scottish varieties of egg wrack and bladder wrack.

Where wave erosion had cut back the grassed saltings a vertical soil profile was exposed. The lower horizon was of dark, peaty loam, the upper one, up to two feet deep, of gravel, small rounded pebbles, white and yellow, in a matrix of black sand.

Upshore was a red fescue turf with scurvy grass, sea milkwort and a little thrift. Downshore was Puccinellia saltmarsh grass, grading into channelled wrack, with crowded shoots sprouting from the base and suggesting mechanical damage among shifting stones. Nitophyllum and Gracillaria had drifted up from a deeper red algal zone.

Returning from Gruinart and its hosts of geese we coincided with the time when wildlife was busy with last minute activities before settling down for the long winter night.

Never before do I remember seeing six hares within the space of a few minutes. The first attracted our attention with its leggy lollops among long grass. Stopping to view, we gradually spied three others, crouched motionless and almost invisible, despite their colour contrast against the vivid green.

16. *Brown Hares*

Immobility must surely be a greater life saver than camouflage against predators which hunt by sight, but these long leggetty beasties had the added bonus of speed at their command. Two more came to light in adjacent fields, one racing off at a speed which put the island rabbits to shame.

Where the square-cornered fields of the Gruinart Flats gave way to the heights beyond Coullabus we spotted a young red deer stag. The nearby hind remained motionless and invisible, until she moved towards him. Only when the two heads appeared above the skyline was their cover completely blown. They regarded us suspiciously before melting into the gathering twilight.

A nearby field yielded a flock of thirty one pink-footed geese, also in from Greenland. The diagnostic pink feet were hidden among the regrowth after mowing and were the only parts that we could not see. Who is it who names these birds? Here, fortunately, they co-habited with the other three species, each kind keeping themselves to themselves but with no bickering on the fringes. Did they feel some affinity, having all just accomplished the same exacting journey?

We were able to compare features other than feet. The pink feet had much darker heads and necks than the ten grey lag geese counted and the white fronts appeared uniformly pale, apart from the white forehead. The always more abundant barnacle geese were a distinct humbug mosaic of black and white and

26

much more like the Brent geese, of which we saw only eight on this day and four on another. We were exhorted to keep an eye open for the smaller version of our now resident and invasive Canada geese. These smaller birds are known as cackling geese and fly in from Canada as genuine migrants occasionally, but not for us.

A little further on was a large flock of wintering starlings from Northern Europe. Hundreds were lined up along a tall field wall. Others probed the wet grass for invertebrates or jockeyed for position on the rusting metal of an abandoned swathe turner.

By the farm gate across the road was a stunted sycamore, quite leafless, but its ultimate, wind deformed twigs blossoming with birds. Scores competed for space on these insecure perches, although they offered no cover from wind and rain.

Probably the chattering mob would move into a more suitable roost before settling for the night. Reed swamps would surely not be an option here, as they so often are, all the small plots of reeds seen consisting of puny haulms with wispy heads, widely spaced and offering neither support nor cover – presumably because of the poverty of the moorland soils where they occupied waterlogged dips. The plantations of sycamore or Sitka seemed a more appropriate haven.

9. LOCH GRUINART RSPB RESERVE

Loch Gruinart occupying the northern section of the geological fault is not only much smaller than Loch Indaal but much shallower. The O S Landrover map shows almost the entire area as yellow intertidal sand flats with a little marginal shingle and a brief deposit around a small permanent pool. Blue water remaining at low tide is almost confined to a single channel winding north to the open sea.

This is the area that the RSPB chose for their initial bird reserve, for this was the sort of terrain that called in the geese. Those vast sand flats and wide, uninterrupted skies gave optimum visibility of approaching predators. Flocks tended to settle here first to assess the situation before moving onto the grazing areas.

The RSPB HQ occupies high ground overlooking the old saltings, reclaimed originally for corn growing and now as freshwater marsh for the birds. Far below a heavy digger was moving along the parallel ditches freeing the water channels, with big gatherings of barnacle geese and Greenland whitefronts to either side.

A raised gallery in the visitor centre had two telescopes trained on the area for the benefit of viewers. Unfortunately a big new cattle shed had recently been erected by the carpark, blocking the view from there to half the goose grazing area. The cattle employed to prepare the sward for the birds had recently been brought inside and confined behind tall, solid doors, shutting out any view of the exterior. The bedlam of lowing emanating from the unseen animals within was phenomenal. Cows used here as 'ecological tools' are moved to rough grazings in the winter, the calves and bulls are kept inside.

Also cut off by the barn was the view from the gallery to the classic raised beach bordering the right hand goose grazings, with a nice example of a subsidiary raised beach carved at an intermediate stage during the sea's recession – or, to be more exact, the land's rise above it.

The marsh flats spread below were managed in spring for nesting waders – about two hundred pairs of lapwings and a hundred pairs of redshanks. Grass remained ungrazed and untrodden by cattle at this season and water levels were kept high by adjusting the network of sluices, to provide suitably damp foraging for the chicks.

17. Redshanks

When they leave the sward is grazed down to the lawn like texture preferred by the geese – its growth rate sometimes boosted by fertilisers, or by ploughing and reseeding. This accounted for the vivid green of so much of the island's grasslands when growth must be in abeyance for the winter. These flats accommodate various species of geese by day. At night the barnacle geese adjourn to the saltings to roost, the whitefronts remaining or sometimes moving to poorer, rushy pasture or moorland.

The rough grass of the slope leading up to carpark and buildings is maintained long, for corncrakes to nest in. Cutting for hay is deferred until they have left on their long flight to winter in Central Europe. To cater for late broods the grass and weed cover is mown from the centre outwards to give any late chicks the chance to escape – as opposed to the traditional trapping of rabbits in the centre to provide a free-for-all for farm hands and dogs.

Reserve lands are treated as a working farm, five wardens and five farm staff sharing the responsibility of management. A team from Scottish National Heritage counts the geese utilising different habitats throughout the winter to assess how much individual farmers should receive as compensation for the loss of grazing, which might include the young sprouts of autumn sown cereals. Additionally the paddling of so many big webbed feet can form a hard crust when the water recedes, this difficult for tender shoots to penetrate,

The annual bill is said to be of the order of a quarter of a million pounds. Nevertheless, the geese bring plenty of visitors to boost the tourist industry and the island coffers are liberally supported by the whisky trade. Formerly revenue was derived from goose shooting parties, coming often from abroad. It was in the early 1980s, when it was realised that the world populations of both barnacle and white-fronted geese from Greenland were threatened, that efforts to conserve them gained impetus.

Islay at that time was thought to house twenty per cent of the Greenland barnacle population of seventy five thousand. By late October 1985 seventeen thousand seven hundred were present, some of these moving on to other parts of Scotland so that the population levelled out at around eleven thousand. Almost all the geese pass through Islay before dispersing elsewhere.

By 2006 the number of winter residents had more than doubled, to twenty four thousand or almost half the world population. White-fronted geese have lost much of their Irish wintering territory to land drainage, one of their best sites there now being the Wexford Slobs, so their Scottish sites are increasingly important. The world population of the Greenland race of white-fronts in 1986 is recorded as sixteen to twenty thousand, five thousand of which were domiciled on Duich Moss on Islay by November.

Duich is a valuable bog ecologically, having a specially complicated pool complex in the centre with a wealth of the uncommon white beak sedge (*Rhynchospora alba*). Among the black bog rush and white bog cotton are two  mosses, very rare in England and rare in Scotland, *Sphagnum imbricatum* and *Sphagnum fuscum*.

Eleven to twelve thousand barnacle geese shared Duich Moss with the whitefronts, which are much the warier of the two and make more use of the remote, rough country than do the more choosy and tamer barnacles. Duich was also under threat in the 1980s from whisky distillers who wanted to extract peat from it, but they now dig this in less vulnerable areas.

18. White Fronted Geese

All this conservation activity on Islay coincided with the passing of the Wildlife and Countryside Bill in 1982/3 and the RSPB bought the 1,667 hectares of the Gruinart Reserve in 1984. Later came more on the Mull of Oa and more again, adjacent to that block, in 2005.

10. THE MULL OF OA, MERLIN AND SEA EAGLE

The Mull of Oa in the far south, with its 426 foot (131m) high cliffs, is one of the most scenic parts of the island. We deferred visiting it until last in the hope of an improvement in the weather. Unfortunately that was the day the clocks changed from BST to GMT, causing us to fritter away the first hour of daylight, which saw the only fitful sunshine.

The weather had indeed set fair, with a dappled mackerel sky, but the mackerel shoaled too closely, leaving almost no clear blue between the strips of cotton wool clouds and none that coincided with the direction of the sun's rays.

Two roads run south along the western edge of the Dalradian rock outcrop, which is coated with peat except where the tough white quartzite protrudes as the bones of the mountains. These rise to 490 feet in Beinn Bheigeir. The main coastal road of our outward journey was built to give work to starving peasants in the bad old days. The original narrower one of our return further inland lay along the opposite flank of Duich Moss

A sturdy Fjord horse peered at us over a wall, this one of the few horses seen and of a type seldom found outside Scandinavia, with its sleek chestnut coat and yellow mane. Later we came across groups of children using their Sunday morning in a bout of pony trekking.

Threadbare reed beds, although so impoverished, displaced the brown moorland of the hinterland along parts of the roadside. They differed fundamentally from the dense reedbeds of kindlier climes which ornithologists are extending countrywide to provide cover for bitterns, bearded tits, water rails and reed warblers. Blowing sand around the airport and Machrie Golf Course had transformed the brown land to green with its welcome input of minerals.

A short stop by the beach at Kintra yielded some fine flowering sea radish, bearing a good crop of the diagnostic articulating fruits among robust compound pinnate leaves. This shared the strandline with the ubiquitous sea mayweed.

After ordering soup and sandwiches at a Port Ellen hotel for later, we followed the little road out to Oa proper for our morning walk. Just beyond the solar powered Carraig Fhada Lighthouse, we saw a sign board to the Singing Sands – the sort that I had explored on Eigg many years before perhaps, but time did not allow for everything.

From the chambered cairn at Cragabus we made for the carpark at the end of the road – the point for viewing the Upper and Lower Killeyan RSPB reserves. Hundreds of yards of new post and wire fence, the barbed wire topping tufted with Highland cattle hair in parts, had recently replaced the old concrete posts standing at crazy angles outside. This delimited the RSPB land, allowing the grazing regime to be controlled.

19. Sea Radish

This reserve, originally in Upper Killeyan, had come to occupy some 4,700 acres of the Kinnabus Estate by the 1980s. Quite recently another block of land had been added to bring the acreage up to around 5,000.

Farming had been favourable to bird life, with round the year grazing keeping the sward sufficiently low for feeding choughs and twites but not too low for nesting curlew, lapwing and redshank. Skylarks and linnets favoured this sort of terrain, which might easily disappear within five to ten years with a change of land management.

RSPB ownership would ensure continuity, keep stone dykes in trim and indicate footpaths to attract bird watchers and help the island economy. After weeks of heavy rain the footpaths left much to be desired but the ground had been stabilised at the metal 'kissing gates' that led us through the boundaries encountered. This was not goose country, at least not at this season.

Ornithological highlights to look out for were two of the island's six pairs of golden eagles, hen harriers, merlins, choughs and twites. Golden eagles had been lying low during the bad weather, but Peter thought some might come out seeking a thermal with this let-up of gale and rain. Sadly this was not to be and we saw none all the week. On the Oa they nest on the cliffs but elsewhere on the island they build on quite low mounds or even in trees. Our guide had ringed the young from one of the more accessible nests.

Nor did we see any harriers but a merlin, not much bigger than a thrush, put up a flock of twites and linnets as we set off on foot. It was there again on our return, shooting low over the sward in pursuit of a pipit-like small brown bird.

The finches were cashing in on a plot of sunflowers planted specially for them. Wind

20. Merlin

battered and scarcely half a metre high, these plants presented an identification puzzle. They resembled dilapidated nodding thistles but the gizz was wrong. Then an RSPB warden happened along and put us right.

Two whooper swans sailed into view, emitting trumpet calls as they flew but their unmistakable signature tune was the rhythmic whooshing of the mighty wings that had brought them in from Northern Europe. On our return some hours later there was another, bigger flock of passerines. These were mostly redwings, complemented by thrushes, starlings and the two finches.

Choughs, already encountered at Machir, were also important here, revelling in updraughts from the cliffs. The island is said to hold more than ten per cent of the entire Scottish population, the species being widely spread on a world basis but in small scattered groups. Up to sixty birds have been watched in a single roost here, feeding right up to nightfall in the short days of winter.

Peter pointed out a fairly fresh cow pat that had been given the once over by a chough. There were marks of the probing beak across the surface and a nicely sculptured black and white bird dropping – a message to the next comer- "No luck. I've had this one."

Some of the prey in the form of adult dung flies were very much in evidence. No doubt all but one of any settled flies would escape the first lunge, but there were eggs, larvae and pupae for the taking under the soft exterior. Little pits in the turf showed where the choughs had been probing for other prey, sullying the hooked tips of those elegant red bills. Plenty more rich pickings of kelp flies and the like were available among the severed wracks of the driftlines.

Only our leader, who had not arrived by air with minimum luggage, was equipped with gumboots. For some of the rest of us our foot gear soon filled with water on those soggy grass paths dipping in and out of shallow quagmires. After the first wetting this ceased to matter and our momentum kept us warm.

The original rushy moorland, with its coarse sedges and deer-grass, had been tamed to fertile grazing land, on which languished the last few flowers of summer. Here and there blue spheres of devil's bit scabious pushed up beside dishevelled pink ragged robins, or a lacy tuft of meadowsweet was surrounded by the yellow specks of tormentil.

Well suited to this tilted landscape was a herd of Highland cattle – a lordly coal black bull with a ginger harem, which had overcome his melanistic genes to produce a bevy of tufty ginger calves. They ceased their automatic munching and gazed at us with interest. Distractions on their lonely slope were few and far between.

Those magnificent horns, splaying sideways in the bull and curling upwards in the

21. *Black Highland Bull*

31

cows, was the attribute most disliked by those whose mission in life was to tend them. Because of their breadth and the bulk of what followed, it was almost impossible to squeeze the animals into a normal cattle crush for purposes of administering drenches and inocculations or dealing with warble fly or whatever. Their gentle temperament was at odds with their fierce appearance but the meekest of cattle, used to limitless open spaces, are likely to fling their heads around when being shooed into something as threateningly small as a crush.

The final short rise brought us to the stout stone column known as the American Memorial on Oa's most south-westerly point. It commemorates the two hundred and sixty six sailors and soldiers who lost their lives when the two troop ships, the "Tuscania" and the "Otranto" were sunk here in 1918. Islay is not far from the main Liverpool to Clyde shipping lanes and has its quota of wrecks, like many another western isle.

We settled on the pale boulders clustered about its base for a breather and a group photo, but only for a few minutes before an excited cry alerted us. Circling around, low over our heads, was a young white-tailed sea eagle wearing a yellow wing tag. It sailed leisurely past, no higher than the top of the monument. We could scarcely have had a better view.

Finally it drifted away on a weak thermal to the heights in the east. We hoped it might startle the resident golden eagles into flight after so many days of enforced inactivity, but there was no such luck.

Youngsters do not have the white tail of the adults and the wings are broader and more massive than those of the golden eagle. Taking three or four years to mature, the moulting of their wing feathers differs from that of most birds. In those the wing primaries are lost progressively from the angle amidships out to the tip and then back to the body. With the sea eagles slower moult, they may lose feathers in uneven tufts, giving a ragged appearance.

22. White-tailed Sea Eagle

This information was from our leader, who thought this marked bird must have flown in from the population recently introduced on Mull. He would inform the Mull ornithologists of the sighting. Hopefully this prospecting youngster might decide to settle here when the time came for it to breed.

11. OA'S WILD GOATS, SEAL BAY AND KIDALTON CROSS

From our point of vantage beside the sturdy monument we had fine views along the deeply dissected coast to the north and the loftier cliffs rebutting the ocean swells to the east. These primal rock faces spoke eloquently of the global tensions that had raised mountains, carved valleys and twisted coastlines in the shaping of this archipelago.

We set off along the south coast, viewing the steep but intricate slopes of Port an Eas. Razorbills nested somewhere along these cliffs, but were not, of course, in residence at present. Both mountain goats and sheep grazed the tousled plant life of face and brink and had been fenced off from the more orthodox grazing land above.

It was a while before we spotted the goats as we followed around lobes of cliff descending to the craggy black reefs below. Some were white, some black, some a bit of each and all were well upholstered against the elements. Billies were furnished with splaying, back swept horns, nannies with only enough armoury to protect themselves. All wore beards.

"One of the few places where wild goats are welcome as an ecological tool instead of a menace to the status quo." quoth Peter.

Goats, unlike the sheep, stayed together as a herd. Between them they were keeping the vegetation out of reach of the cattle in trim. Instead of scrambling away in terror, they ambled a little higher to watch us pass. Perhaps they knew they were welcome participant's in the RSPB's aspirations for a balanced landscape. At least they were not shot at, as no doubt they had been in the past. (Their initial presence on most islands, world wide, was due to introductions to provide fresh meat for passing mariners.) They were a fine sight with their scimitar horns outlined against the pale glimmer of the sea – empathising with the primitive wildness of their habitat.

On the face of a jagged crag we spotted an adventurous sheep silhouetted against the sky on a lonely ledge, as though not to be outdone by its more adventurous companions. The expert was not too worried, saying they were usually very canny about finding their way out of seemingly impossible places.

The chief danger was when they grazed their way along an ever narrowing ledge until it got so meagre that they were unable to turn their great woolly bulk around. Some might then leap off onto a lower ledge from which there was no return. Peter was not the only one who had risked life and limb "just to rescue some stupid sheep."

23. Twites

Quite near the cliff edge, where falling salt spray must be significant, despite their height, was a modest sprinkling of fungi. Waxcaps were most in evidence again, some deep crimson on top with peach coloured gills, others primrose yellow and paler throughout. Larger orange Agarics, with bulging, fibrous stipes rubbed shoulders with smaller fry, including the much abused, so called magic mushrooms.

Our return circuit yielded several sightings of buzzards but no eagles. A flock of passerines, including twites, was using the pleasant garden of an isolated farmhouse passed as we approached the carpark. Twites are a poor substitute for eagles but have their charms, not least their rarity except in a few special places. Here, with yellow bills, white wing flashes and twangy calls, they would be exploiting the garden seeds, leaving softer fodder, plant or animal, to the redwings and their kin. We left them to it, rolling back past the Lurabus village ruins – a reminder of the clearances, when outlying populations were moved into the neat whitewashed houses that typified all the main settlements on the island.

After our Port Ellen lunch we set off up the east coast as far as the road allowed. En route were the original Maltings, a large concern that formerly malted barley for all the island distilleries, although its own no longer functioned. We passed three of the distilleries it had served, first the Laphroaig opposite the rugged, low island of Texa, then the Lagavulin and the Ardberg, all making their fortunes from the tea-coloured water that drained their acid hinterland.

Near the last one stands the sixteenth century Dunyvaig Castle, seat of one of the ClanDonalds. Built right into the dark headland and of the same material, it seemed to have grown from the rock itself.

The next bay was the favourite basking haunt of common seals, snub nosed and altogether more feminine looking than the Roman nosed, more doglike grey Atlantics. Some were hauled out on low rocks, others drifting idly on the inshore waters. So faithful are they to this site that the bay is known as Loch ant-Salein, or Seal Bay.

We detoured towards the sea again near Ardmore Point to view the famous ninth century Gaelic Kidalton Cross. A bluestone cross on a bluestone base, it stood outside the ruins of Kidalton Chapel. Book in hand, Peter deciphered the intricate but worn carving on the various faces, including the presumably vandalised headless lions. It is said to have been carved by a sculptor from the religious settlement of Iona. Surely so handsome a relic should not have been left exposed to all the winds that blow, like this? It actually did blow down more than a century ago, when a man and a woman were found to have been buried beneath it.

The chapel alongside remained in use for centuries, its walls attributed to the fourteenth or fifteenth centuries. There was no roof, so the prone, mansized, sixteenth and seventeenth century high relief grave slabs within were as vulnerable to the weather as the cross without.

Walls were shaggy with maidenhair spleenwort, polypody and hart's tongue ferns, while tiny blue flowers of thyme-leaved speedwell struggled through the long grass. A peripheral wall and a notice on the gate "Please Close" kept grazing animals at bay, so the sward was neither munched nor muddied. Another walled cross stands on a mound across the track.

A few more miles and we were past Claggain Bay with its standing stone and McArthur's Head Lighthouse reared up a few hundred yards on. While Peter scanned the heavens for eagles and the sea for dolphins, we strolled back down the road to the sweep of raised beach fringed by the present day, slightly curved pebble bank. Parts of the higher level accumulation were as bereft of plants still, as was the lower, more mobile one.

Backing this and bordering a turbulent whisky-brown stream racing seaward between rock walls, was stunted woodland. Some was little more than hazel scrub mixed with crumple-leaved eared sallow, wearing its persistent paired stipules like cuff links at each leaf base. Birches, now quite leafless, unlike most of the woodland trees at the end of this unusually mild October, sent tight clusters of gnarled fingers above the canopy – clenched fists raised against the flying spray.

Port Ellen is where the car ferry from Kennacraig on the mainland docks on the island. We came to a halt as we returned, the road blocked by the blue and white bulk of the "Islay Sea Safari" tourist boat, presumably ashore for repairs. Its hull was firmly jammed against a sturdy stone gatepost, with heavy machinary trying to haul it off the highway. It proved less easy to move than the usual road blocks of ambling livestock.

On the lesser road north over Laggain Bridge we saw a number of deer. These were fallow deer, intermediate in habitat preferences between the larger red deer of the hills and the smaller roe deer of the farmlands. One handsome stag with a broad spread of palmate antlers was resting in a wooded hollow below the road. He remained unperturbed as we stopped to admire him. Fallow were introduced more recently than the other two and were less upset by human presence

24. *Fallow Deer*

Away to our right as we approached Bridgend was a series of iron age forts constructed along the edge of a steep scarp, We detoured to look at one at Duneose Bridge. The scarp face acted as a defence in itself, as sea cliffs do in so many others of this period. Defences on the more sloping sides were stepped down in three wide terraces.

We saw several hares but only a couple of rabbits. These, although so common where sand accumulates over peat or rock, seemed sparse to absent where burrowing was more difficult and the provender on offer less appetising.

Darkness fell an hour earlier than hitherto and we made a long stop to watch the thousands of geese gathering on an offshore sand bar before venturing into their final roost. The long drawn out Vs of skein after skein, came winnowing in against the darkening sky. A magic sight. Was this their initial landfall after the long ocean trek; birds built for air and water but grateful to set foot on land for a breather and long awaited snack? Rain was falling by now, this bothering them not at all. We lingered, entranced, as new mobs flew in over the backing trees, all talking at once, like excited children on a picnic.

12. DIVERS AND OTHERS AT THE ISLAND HUB

Various indoor pursuits were available to keep us occupied when the rain was particularly persistent, but each day got off to a good start with a spell of bird watching from the cosy interior of the minibus.

One day we started with a homely touch, out of synch with our usual exotic finds. This was a blue tit at a feeder in a garden bright with the late flowers of Hebe, Escallonia, Hydrangea and Fuchsia, white as well as red. While Peter was ordering our lunch we were entertained by a brown rat scavenging the largesse fallen from the rich little man's table. No doubt it would have relished the tit as well, like

25. *Black Guillemot in winter plumage*

the grey squirrels which fulfill this role of

35

scavenger on the mainland. (We saw none of those on Islay.) The interloper's hideaway was in the thick garden hedge of Fuchsia.

Our next stop along the Loch Indaal shore yielded two treasures far removed from squirrel territory – a black guillemot and a black-throated diver – these even before reaching Bruichladdich. The first was in winter plumage. Instead of the all-over black with white wing patch, as usually seen, it was all-over white with black wing primaries and tail and some faint grey barring and stippling running over the back, up the nape to the crown.

The black-throated diver was producing a melancholy mewing that was but a shadow of the urgent, eerie wail of the breeding season. It seemed to be in process of changing from the spectacularly barred and mottled black and white of summer to the drab black backed, white fronted garb of winter. Gone was the diagnostic black throat with its bordering stripes, engulfed now by white feathers on throat and face. In this it resembles the great northern diver, distin- guished only by its heavier build and bill and lacking the white patch each side of the tail retained by the black throated. Only one great northern was seen all the week.

26. *Black and Red-throated Divers in winter plumage*

At Bruichladdich we got closer on foot during a lull in the rain, but had to retreat from the gale into the lee of the harbour wall. The attraction here was a possie of red-throated divers, arrived from Northern Europe or Iceland – close inshore and eminently watchable. The obliquely skyward pointing head was more marked than in the others, giving a distinctive outline.

These, too, had lost the red throat and dapper livery of summer, resembling the other two except for the arcs of white spots on the dark back. One, loafing among the little boats in the lee of the pier, would rise occasionally onto its tail, flapping its wings and showing off the silvery neck and breast The odd shag, cormorant and guillemot patrolled the sea beyond and we clocked up no less than five herons engaged in solitary vigils at the edge of the tide.

The broad green pastureland of the raised beach inland of the road to Uiskentuie and Black Rock yielded oyster catchers, gulls and a flock of wind blown curlews probing in a rain water pool. We lingered long enough to appreciate the different lengths of those curvaceous curlew bills, longer in the females than the males.

A flock of starlings joined in the search for drowned soil dwellers along with a few pied wagtails, but defected to the haw-laden thorn bushes on the face of the older raised beach rising steeply from the pasture's inland flank. This appeared clifflike, but where a road cut through at right angles it was seen to consist of beach pebbles in a sandy matrix.

It is believed that sea level was fifty feet higher in relation to the land when humans first came to the Highlands and Islands and kitchen middens have been found around the fifty foot level on Islay, where the raised beaches are as well developed as anywhere.

Nearer to Bridgend, at the centre of an SSSI (Site of Special Scientific Interest) earmarked for waterfowl watching, a stretch of grassy marshland intervenes between road and sea. The yellow Irises that had brightened the edge of the layby in June, were now a tangled mass of broken stems. A vast flock of wigeon was surging slowly across, divided by a colourful line of shelducks. The swans here were mutes, not the now more familiar whoopers. How topsy turvy can bird counts get on this remarkable island! This was a spot that could be relied on to produce vast numbers of foraging geese at any time of day – a few grey lags with the predominant barnacles on this occasion.

Further along towards the open water, the sea became too choppy to distinguish birds among the froth and bubble of the little wavelets. Water that had been leaden grey, reflecting the sombre hue of pot bellied nimbus hanging ominously above, had become a dirty beige colour from the burden of displaced sand churned up from the sea bed.

13. WHISKY GALORE

Mention the name of Islay to the average southerner and those who have heard of it at all have usually done so because of the whisky it produces. Only wildlife folk think of it in terms of the goose flesh that we had converged to witness. Sadly, the powerful bitterness of the famous brew, when sipped, can induce goose flesh of another kind. I enjoyed the wartime film "Whisky Galore" made at the Ealing studios within a mile of my home as much as the next, but my Sassenach tastes have survived all subsequent visits to Bonnie Scotland.

Even back in 1984, Islay was contributing to the national budget the equivalent of £7,000 for every one of the 4,000 men, women and children on the island's two hundred and thirty five square miles. The whisky is prized by those with strong palates because of the local water and the water is the way it is because of the Dalradian slates and the peat over and through which this flows.

The word 'whisky' is a translation or corruption of the Gaelic epithet for 'the water of life'. This is conjured up in eight distilleries on Islay, each crowned by one or more pagoda shaped turrets, which are not just a badge of office but are functional. They were erected above the stills to let the smoke out and keep the heat in. Not quite so essential in modern times, they have been retained as a traditional badge of intent. A parallel can be drawn with the traditional shape of the Kentish oast houses producing that other popular alcoholic beverage, beer.

Our insight into the process was at the Bowmore Distillery, the oldest on the island and, indeed, in the whole of Scotland. Moreover, it claims to be the 'greenest' distillery in Europe. It lies at the edge of the tide, the waters of Loch Indaal lapping against the whitewashed wall of the narrow garden alongside.

That morning produced a series of scuds of rain hurtling down at an angle of forty five degrees with the ferocity of hail. We escaped the worst of one by racing for the Bowmore Visitor Centre. The next caught us en route for the Bowmore Distillery's Reception Centre, where we dripped among the bottles, glassware and tartans while awaiting our tour of the 'works'.

In only a handful of distilleries in Scotland can the ancient craft of malting the barley be seen. This is one of them. It is the primary stage of the whole procedure, dependent on plant enzymes locked up in those uncomplicated looking golden grains.

These were massed, ankle deep, on two spacious malting floors, moistened when laid out and again after a couple of days, when germination had started. Aeration was achieved in the traditional way by walking back and forth through the mass pushing a hand rake furnished with three triangular tines, which stirred the mulch and pushed it into ridges. During germination the inert, stored starch is converted into soluble sugars.

The aroma emanating from the peat fired kilns in which the mass is dried, imparts a special flavour, which varies between distilleries and between the brews from each, which are said to number as many as forty. The annual consumption of the home produced peat amounts to around eight hundred tons.

Wispy little roots and shoots rubbed from the germinated grains are collected and sold for poultry food, this being less bulky provender for less bulky consumers than the cattle which receive the bulk of the spent grain after its infusion in hot water. This is predominantly starchy, after removal of much of the sugar and protein.

It can be fed moist as a wet mash, like silage or the 'cheese' of apple pulp left after squeezing out the juice for cider and spread on the fields by Hereford orchardists for Hereford cattle. Or it can be powdered and made into cattle cake or nutlets equivalent to the cotton cake and coconut cake that I fed to my milking cows during the war. Another similar waste fed to uncomplaining cattle in modern times is crushed oil seed rape seeds after removal of the oil.

The heat from the Bowmore kilns is not wasted either. It is used to heat the water in a public swimming pool next door. Until this energy saving innovation was thought up anyone wanting to learn to swim had only the cold sea to practise in.

The sugary liquid is cooled and fermented with yeast in great black vats made of Oregon pine, tall trees fashioned into tall vats which stretch through the ceiling into an upper chamber where we could gaze in over the rim and watch the working of the invisibly small fungi. These cannot break down starch but consume the sugar, using oxygen in aerobic respiration, to bud off multitudinous chains of new cells all beavering away together.

When the oxygen is used up anaerobic respiration or fermentation takes over, breaking the carbohydrates down further to alcohol. This is the wort or wash, bubbling quite gently in the first vat into which we peered but as a veritable maelstrom in another, the boiling froth emitting grunts and belches, matching the best produced from MacBeth's witchs' cauldrons.

All fungi occupy themselves quietly digesting or breaking down organic matter, but the manifestation of the power inherent in those inoccuous looking single celled organisms must be among the most impressive.

The alcoholic brew produced is vapourised twice by double passage through huge copper pot stills, whose shape has scarcely altered over three hundred and fifty years. It is the pure part of the second distillation that is collected and matured. Only the customs and excise men have the key to the sealed cabinet in which alcohol levels are measured when the vapourised and re-liquefied product finally emerges from the great bulbous based, shining copper stills.

The resulting brew is kept in barrels for a minimum of about three years, a maximum of about twenty and an average of eight. Alcohol level drops as it matures but those in the know maintain that flavour increases – certainly the price does.

Islay's malt whiskies have been famous since the Middle Ages, when the MacDonalds, Lords of the Isles, ruled their empire here. No-one knows how many illicit stills there may have been in the cliffs around the island shores.

Our tour ended in one of the dusty warehouses wherein lie the casks of spirits – one of the oldest kept in trust for Her Majesty, Queen Elizabeth. Largely because of all this, one guide book is able to claim – "While so many of the Hebridean Islands seem to be slipping away into a gentle Celtic reverie, Islay, the southern-most of them, is positively vibrant."

Bowmore, geographically in the island centre, is its administrative capital. Another building of note here is the circular Church of Scotland, one of only two of its kind, its white walls bulging conspicuously onto the highway. It was built thus in 1767, twelve years before the distillery, to prevent the devil from finding a corner to hide in. I would have thought he would prefer a distillery to a church. Less opposition?

14. GREBES, SAWBILLS AND LONG-TAILED DUCK

Each morning's drive north from the Port Charlotte Hotel yielded something new. Sometimes our bird viewing started before we entered the vehicle, as with the little possies of purple sandpipers and others foraging over black rocks under the flickering white wings of mew gulls outside the hotel.

27. Long-tailed Drake

There were more at Bruichladdich, with up to nine turnstones, whose evocative trilling calls were impinged upon by the winnowing of whooper swan wings. A handsome pintail duck had sought the company of a sizable flock of scaup, while not far off was a much rarer long-tailed duck. This striking bird, with marlin spike tail prong, was boldly patterned in black and white. Breeding in North Scandinavia and Iceland, these might stay to winter here or pass on south as far as Portugal and Sardinia. This specimen dived out of sight at intervals. The nearby pintail duck, with similar marlin spike tail feathers, is a surface feeder, remaining more predictably in the field of the telescope.

There was a fine gathering of red-breasted mergansers on one occasion, mostly females in winter plumage. Those other sawbills, the goosanders, have been appearing on our Welsh rivers in recent winters, and it was good to see their more oceanic counterparts. Singly or in little flocks, the reddish throat of summer was now barred and separated in the drake from the dark by a white band.

Their thin necks, triangular heads and slender beaks gave them a grebe like aura as they dived for fish, resurfacing to lie low in the water, the anticipated plimsoll line well submerged. They, too, breed in Scandinavia and the European taiga, as well as Iceland and occasionally in Scotland.

We did, indeed, see grebes, but not our familiar great cresteds. A single little grebe turned up at one spot, but the gem was the Slavonian grebe – sadly not so gemlike in winter as in summer – when I had last seen some on a mountain lochan above Loch Ness in the Great Glen. This one had shed the diagnostic rufous red of summer. While the truncated stern was typical grebe, the low slung body was reminiscent of diver or sawbill.

28.
Slavonian Grebe

Eider ducks and drakes numbered as many as fifty on one occasion, forty and thirty on others. Popping constantly beneath the surface, they may have been diving for their favourite mussels, to leave the neatly cleaned out shells on the beaches.

Our biggest flock of scaup was estimated at about a hundred, of tufted duck thirty and of shovellers twenty. Ducks, in other words, offered no competition, number wise, to the countless thousands of geese streaming in from Greenland – after likely stop offs in Iceland and the Faroes on their way. There are other barnacle geese, breeding in sites other than Greenland and flighting to quite different parts of Great Britain and Ireland for the winter. Whole communities, not just families, stay together on these mammoth treks.

Waders, apart from the familiar curlew, lapwing and oyster catcher, digging in the sand for cockles, were more solitary, unlike the usually super abundant knot and dunlin of our estuaries. Redshanks once numbered ten, turnstones up to fifteen and twenty.

Islay House Square on the outskirts of Bridgend had seen better days. A long drive opened out into a spacious courtyard surrounded by somewhat neglected buildings. One was crowned by a stone tower, another held a large pigeon cote, while the big flock of pigeons that this housed wheeled around, from rooftop to rooftop. Beyond was the ornate house with its crowded pinnacle-like turrets – a once grand mansion, employing a staff of a hundred or so islanders in its heyday. It was backed by tall woodland, the tree trunks lichen caked and crumbly and the leaf mould sprinkled with toadstools. Across the drive beyond a solid range of out buildings was the old walled garden, mostly empty of crops and on a surprising, unterraced slope, but with a valiant attempt at renovation under one wall. Green fields descended seawards and a buzzard hung in the vacant sky, while a blackbird scattered the fallen leaves in search of grubs, each lunge accompanied by bobbing body and flicking tail.

Some of the buildings were being reinstated as boutiques, gift and craft shops and the Islay Fine Ales Micro Brewery. We gathered out of the rain under the raised roof of the back of the minibus for our mid morning thermos coffee and chocolate biscuits, instead of partaking of the ale.

Moving away along a back drive, we came to the little freshwater Loch

Skerrols. A pretty place this, surrounded by mixed deciduous woodland with a shrub layer of Rhododendron and gorse, bracken and foxglove. Elegantly tall pines showed the orange red of the upper branches that labelled them as native Scots pines, their flaking bark not flaking fast enough to prevent lichen growth on their surface. Despite the imminent onset of November, beech was the only tree here showing autumn colouration. A few Iris tufts grew in the shallows against firm banks.

Unruffled waters of the little lochan mirrored the pale sky but were not entirely empty. There were two mute swans, two golden-eye ducks and a flock of tufted duck on the far side. Peter had seen otters here – in this land where sea-going otters seem loath to repair to fresh waters.

From Loch Skerrols we proceeded to the Museum of Island Life, on the last day of its summer opening. It contained artefacts from the stone age to the twentieth century, but some of us oldies felt very much at home among domestic appliances that the younger generation probably regarded as twee, but which are still serving useful functions in our daily lives. Not so, however, for the farm equipment.

There was, for instance, a big, vertical bladed hay knife of the type I used to saw consolidated slabs of hay from well settled hay ricks to feed my shire horse and calves. Also a wooden shoulder yolk for carrying heavy buckets of steaming milk to the dairy for filtering and cooling; curve-tined dung forks, oat crushers, mangold slicers and other artefacts that took me back to the early 1940s, when farming practices differed little from those of the Middle Ages.

15. TRADITIONAL WEAVING MILL ON DIPPER STREAM

Another indoor activity available in the Bridgend area was a visit to a tradition-ally run woollen mill fabricating tweeds and tartans for the Scots and English alike. The lively little river that had turned the water wheel in past years was home to nesting dippers. As bird watchers, our first priority was to try and spot them. With flood warnings out on the adjacent mainland, the normally modest waterway was at its most tumultuous.

29. Dipper

We lined up along the parapet of the little stone bridge which spanned it, watching the current douching the circular leaves of winter heliotrope and curling up through marginal ferns and St. John's wort. Rain dripped from overarching sallows and gathered in little cascades to augment the main flow. No wonder the Polypody ferns grew so luxuriantly on the alder trunks and branches.

But we scanned the turbulence in vain for dippers – semi aquatic creatures which, of all the passerines, were the least likely to retreat from a mere downpour. Investigating the New Zealand Olearia daisy bushes, Berberis and Rhododen-drons in the woodland bordering the yard, we came upon the old leat that had brought water from upstream to power the mill. It ran at a higher level than the carpark and picnic tables with their pots of red and pink flowered Fuchsias. The penstock controlling the flow was topped by a gadget resembling a car steering wheel, to adjust the relative positions of the mossy planks below.

Gorden Covell, owner and master weaver, was hoping to return to water power to run the looms. Little but this source of energy had changed over the years. The stone walls were laced with flowering ivy-leaved toadflax and maidenhair spleenwort and topped with the traditional black slates, like so many of the island buildings.

Those were local, from Dalradian slates of Nether Lorn to the north, but they were less durable than the purple tinted ones imported from the great slate mines in the mountains of North Wales – as those were to so many other parts of Britain. Builders renovating a historic house on Islay to its original state, pointed this out to the powers that be and were allowed to break with tradition and use the Welsh to promote longevity.

As far as the mill was concerned, the planning authorities stipulating the preserving of historic authenticity were exerting more influence on development than the "Health and Safety Section" of the Nanny State that would have erected safety barriers between the big clanking machines and the parties of visitors.

Only weaving was done here, the spinning and dyeing of the finely spun woollen threads forming woof and warp being imported from elsewhere. The colourful patterns were designed on the spot, the spools of yarn threaded on wires leading to the looms with mind boggling intricacy. Interweaving of woof and warp were demonstrated on a tartan designed for a society's ceremonial occasion. Samples of newly thought up patterns were sent off to Chenille and fashion houses in Paris for them to pick which might look best on their cat walks or board walks (and not the sort built over quagmires.) From the noisy bedlam of fluff and grease around the cumbersome machines came exquisite fabrics fit for a queen.

Gordon Covell has, indeed, supplied the royal household with tweeds and tartans for many years. He took great delight in recounting, ostensibly to his friend, Peter, a recent visit made by the queen, Prince Charles and others of the royal family to the mill. (Thank goodness they are able to make a few private calls without all the razmataz of pomp and ceremony of their public lives.).

Twice he had gone to call his wife with "Here's a visitor to see you" and twice the answer from upstairs was "I can't come. I'm too busy." Hopefully she was extricated from her housework in time. Gordon's reported comment to the queen "You realise, your majesty, that I'll have to get counselling after this shock." Photographs of Prince Charles, resplendent in an Islay tartan kilt taken on the premises, showed that this was not the first royal visit. We browsed among tweed jackets, deer stalker hats, kilts, scarves, vegetable soap, candles and much else before leaving.

16. INLAND GROUSE MOOR AND LOCH FINLAGGAN

Various journeys took us across expanses of bog where domestic peat cutting had taken place in the past. A few unkempt stacks of peat remained, uncollected. Most people these days, in this affluent island had central heating and switches were easier to manipulate than peat cutting tools. Gone were the donkeys with panniers, as of old.

This, quoth Peter, was typical grouse country. We all piled out while he deployed a cryptic bit of apparatus that emulated their calls, in the hope of attracting a reply. He persisted, but the red grouse were as uncooperative as the dippers, remaining crouched among the heather that afforded them both food and cover.

We saw only buzzards, sitting dolefully on fence posts awaiting a body lifting thermal or being mobbed by hoodie crows. How too, could such far ranging birds as eagles manage to stay out of sight for so long, with all that spread of sky waiting to accommodate their mighty pinions? Hen harriers, as well, were an unfullfilled possibility here.

The botanically inclined wandered off where small bushes of rugose-leaved eared sallow bordered ditches of acid, peaty water. These harboured the two typical bog moss genera, Sphagnum and Polytrichum, cushioning shining winter leaves of lesser spearwort.

Huddled on the bank just above water level were some dewy crimson plants of round-leaved sundew, their traps innocent of incautious insects during the current downpours. Just as rain dilutes the sugary nectar attracting insects to flowers, so too must it mitigate against the stickiness of the sundew's insect catching tentacles – and dilute the strength of the digestive enzymes used to suck the vitality from any small animal unlucky enough to get caught.

30. *Round-leaved Sundew*

Meadowsweet and hard fern (*Blechnum spicant*) graced the ditch banks, the latter with fine plumes of fertile fronds rising from the centre of the vegetative rosettes.

Three quarters of the way along the road from Bridgend to the Jura Ferry a track leads off north and west to service two large coniferous plantations, each approximately a mile and a half in diameter. The first of these abuts onto Loch Finlaggan, itself considerably more than a mile long. Not too far away were the ruins of an old lead mine.

We set off to walk to Eilean Mor, an island in the head of the loch that was the eighth and ninth century headquarters of the Lords of the Isles. In those far off days the lordship extended right across Scotland and even embraced the Isle of Man. It is believed that early Celtic saints paddled across here from the not too distant north of Ireland in craft not much more substantial than a coracle or a curragh.

The hub of their activities was this small island in the head of the loch, while a crannog, or smaller, man-made island occurs near the south end. The headquarters includes the ruins of an old council chamber, a castle, a chapel and some horizontal, man-sized grave slabs, one with an image of the 'dear departed' carved on its prone surface.

Off through a modern, stock proof kissing gate, we followed a narrow path paved with dark local shingle, but not for long. It soon became melded into the marshy grassland, with its tapestry of late flowering buttercups and daisies, but again not for long.

Awhile later it was a soggy green strip threading through a brown bog of Molinia, rushes, sedges and the white tipped pennants of fruiting cotton grass. This last is esteemed by grazers because it gives 'early bite' for sheep and deer, starting growth in spring well before other moorland plants. The beige flowers resemble those of many another sedge and must be more palatable than the fruitlets which fluff out into the white counterpane that is spread across acres of drab countryside in autumn.

31. *Meadowsweet*

The inlet stream, burbling swiftly down from one of the conifer woods was safely below ground level, in a well demarcated channel, but the quagmires emptying into it were not. We were accordingly muddy by the time we reached the final lap, which started as a board walk and soon developed into a bridge over troubled waters. Our leader halted at the last little gate, with water half way up his gumboots, and excused us the rest.

The bridge continued, at increasing depth, through the reed swamp occupying the headwater marsh. It seemed the ruins were out of bounds today. A pristine flower head of meadowsweet laughed up at us from the beery fluid. No-one would be trampling on her today.

Instead, we were regaled with the saga of the glorious, bloodthirsty, rough, tough days in this centre of the known universe – a wilderness that could scarcely be more remote by today's standards. The old hierarchy involved Norsemen, Gaels and Celts from Scotland, Ireland and who knows where else.

With shank's pony almost the only alternative to sea travel, the ancients were well placed in the centre of their world. Today's port of embarkation to the mainland via Jura was not much more than three miles away if they set out on the long tramp to conquer new fields and the Norsemen were no novices at sea travel!

It is doubtful that they used carrier pigeons, but they must have had an excellent system of communication. How else would King Harold of Norway, in charge here, know that he should set out on the thousand mile journey south, to help King Harold of England at the Battle of Hastings? And all in vain, because of that Norman arrow! No doubt there was some cheery pillaging and killing to be enjoyed en route.

But all that is another story. It finished up with the MacDonalds having wrested power from the Vikings and remaining as rulers of this spreading kingdom for two hundred years before King James put a stop to their shennanigens. The clan still has an important presence here. Some of the offspring of those ancient MacDonalds, living frugally on what they could filch from an uncooperative landscape, are now contributing to the Western World's obesity problem. They could do with some of today's lean, surplus deer in those over fatty beefburgers, just as the warriors of old would doubtless have relished some of today's fatty beefburgers to power their bloodthirsty raids.

17. NIGHTFALL ON ISLAY

While our days began watching ducks, grebes and divers at the edge of the tide, so they ended watching geese and swans flocking to their roosts on the spreading sands beyond or the grassy marshes behind.

After hatching and rearing families in almost continuous daylight with little opportunity to rest, the geese had fled before the growing darkness, to share our shortest days. Families, clans and whole communities abandoning the Greenland Ice Cap had come to converge for sleep on Islay between four and five pm, as we sipped afternoon tea at the back of the minibus. As they shuffled down to sleep, we adjourned to preen, feed and, at the weekend, listen to traditional music.

There were many roosting sites, but the most public focal point was the grass marsh, part freshwater and part salt, occupying the largest bay on the extensive shore of Loch Indaal, between Black Rock in the west and Bowmore in the south.

The frontage is much the largest spread of tidal sand on Indaal, stretching out to sea for almost a mile at low water. Flowing out across its centre is the River Sorn, passing obliquely across the island, bringing water from Loch Finlaggen and Loch Ballygrant, past sundry weirs and Redhouse Mill to the final weir on the seaward side of Bridgend itself

The backdrop to their dormitory area includes some of the tallest sycamore woods on the island, clustered around Islay House. For us, when approaching from land, the trees blocked the view of the sea, but not for the geese, spilling the wind in a whirr of wings as they converged with a chorus of honks, at their greater elevation. When passing over the farmland their passage was made safer by yellow marker streamers flapping in the turbulence from telegraph lines crossing their flight paths.

Sometimes the last fitful rays of sunshine filtering through gaps in the hovering cumulus were rudely interrupted by rolls of black clouds shedding their contents. But that was as water on a duck's back.

Their companionable, excited chatter was a welcome change from the persistent moaning of a malignant wind. New arrivals from the unforgiving stretch of ocean between Greenland, Iceland, the Faroes and the Hebrides might almost be heard to chant the goosy equivalent of "Green grow the rushes ho. Food and rest at last."

Some would go no further, others might pass on south down the chain of islands, headlands and estuaries, to spread the load after taking on sufficient calories. But time enough for others as the winter progressed and the sward diminished to move on to pastures new.

We may wonder how they find their way, but their greater elevation gives them a flying start over those ancient MacDonalds, who found their way from West Scotland to South-east England, with no magnetic compasses in their all too human heads.

32. Barnacle Geese

Families of barnacle geese, which are much the most numerous here, travel together. The 27,000 barnacle geese which winter at Mersehead on the Solway Firth where I had watched them a few years before, had come from Iceland, as did the pink-footed and grey lag geese and the whooper swans. The white-fronted geese split up between Islay and the Solway's Ken Dee Marshes, the more southerly possibly stopping off on Islay to stoke up.

Wherever they were headed, the lines and Vs kept passing, like rows of machine stitching etched across the sky. The simultaneous rising of a thousand or so geese in panic was less orderly but equally impressive. The sheer numbers involved make these spectacles not easily forgotten.

Come spring they would be off again, flock after flock, surfing on the breaking wave of awakening chlorophyll, sparse though this may be on the unwelcoming permafrost at their arrival.

At the weekend, adjourning to the bar after dinner in the cosy warmth of the Port Charlotte Hotel, local music transported our thoughts from the feathered hosts out in the cold. On the Saturday evening a young couple entertained, against a backdrop of constant chatter and clinking of glasses, which seemed most off putting and bad mannered, but was apparently the accepted norm.

He played the bagpipes, with or without the mouthpiece, pumping away at the goatskin air supply, and she played the violin. She was garbed like a tramp in crumpled trews and skimpy top, but played like an angel.

On Sunday night the mood was quite different and loud enough to drown all irrelevant noise. Three elderly gents kept everyones' feet jiggling or fingers tapping with their fast and furious tunes and all pervading rhythms.

The 'chief', in a sleeveless red vest and with long silver locks, side whiskers and beard to match, but moustache of a darker hue, played a non-electrified guitar. He also sang, in Gaelic, with a power to match the speed, mopping up after each sally with a towel draped over his intrument stand.

One of the others pumped out the tunes on a squeeze box or concertina with great skill, the third switched from mandolin to banjo between items, which were decided on during tinkling, communal experimenting. Working garb was brightened with gold bracelets and rings and a silver necklet. This was the real Macoy, the flavour of the island and not the tuneless modern thumping pop which tourists usually get fobbed off with when hoping to experience the genuine national feel of these faraway places.

JURA

18. FEOLIN FERRY, SHELLY BEACH AND BUTTERWORT BOG

The island of Jura is almost thirty miles long from south-west to north-east and six to seven miles across at its widest. Occupying some 94,000 acres, it has been described as one of the wildest of the Hebridean islands – a wilderness of rock, moor and peat bog.

On clear days the famous Paps of Jura, which rise to 2,571 feet along its southern half, can be seen from Skye to the north, the Isle of Man to the south and tower blocks in Glasgow to the east. On the day of our visit they were not visible

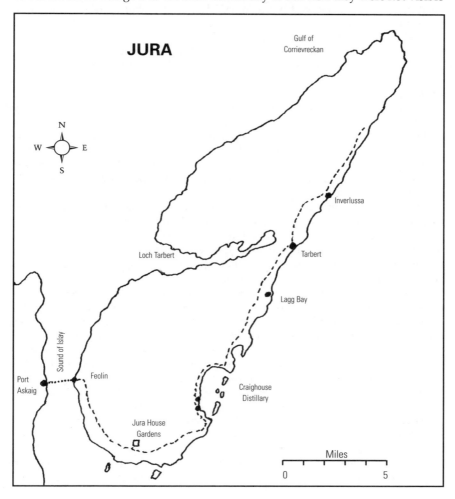

from our port of embarkation only three quarters of a mile away across the Sound of Islay. Nor did we see more than their immediate foothills when ashore.

They were sleeping beneath an impressive blanket of what cloud spotters refer to as *Stratus opacus nebulosus*. Stratus is flat, grey and featureless, with no beginning and no end. Opacus invokes claustrophobia in its complete hiding of the sun, entailing loss of orientation. Nebulosus signifies a formless, concrete-grey veil stretching to all horizons, like a scummy, stagnant lake.

Earlier in the week we had had glimpses of the three conical mountains, rounded like fulsome breasts, from across the sea, but they were revealing themselves very modestly during those late October days.

The car ferry crosses the Sound from Port Askaig on East Islay to Feolin on West Jura. After a brief wait beside a cliff draped with honeysuckle and ivy, it transported us smoothly on the brief sea crossing. Feolin is at the western end of Jura's one road, which is graced with the designation of A846. Where are all the others? Cliff and beach converge, cutting off vehicle access to the north. The A road, often single track with passing places, follows around the south coast and up the east, almost to the island's tip at the infamous Strait of Corrievreckan,

So far we had failed to see otters on Islay and country-wise locals maintained that these were more often sighted on the Jura coast, so these were our main target today. Feolin seemed as good a place to start as any. Binoculars were trained up and down the Sound, allowing time for brief exploration. The name Feolin is said to be derived from the word for shingle and there was a narrow strip of clean yellow beach here, the pebbles small, round and sprinkled with little shells to match.

Brightly hued blunt periwinkles (*Littorina littoralis*) were commonest, some orange, some yellow, a few gingery brown or humbug striped in brown and yellow. Here too were grey or purple top shells (*Gibbula cineraria & G. umbilicalis*), worn down to the silvery underlayer of mother of pearl by being tumbled among the stones. There were murmurs afoot that top shells were spreading north up the Scottish coast in response to global warming

Larger, more pointed shells had belonged to predatory dog whelks (*Buccinum undatum*). The wigwams of common limpet shells were unusually flat in this comparatively sheltered channel, this a feature of limpet shells, in which the powerful muscles which enable them to 'stick like limpets' do not have to strain so hard to maintain their hold as in rough seas, and pull the shell margins inwards as they grow. The more fragile test of an edible sea urchin (*Echinus esculentus*) was in pieces but beautifully patterned still.

Fresh water flowed almost indiscriminately down the cliff behind, but one of the more permanent runnels nurtured a mini peat bog rich in the anaemic leaf rosettes of insectivorous butterwort. These nestled in a soggy bed of Sphagnum moss and followed the base of the cliff, where the drainage waters lost their impetus and seeped along the back of the strand.

The incurled leaf margins had trapped little pools of water on the glandular surfaces developed to digest trapped insects. It is doubtful, however, if any would have settled with so much water about. If they had they were likely to have been washed off by rain.

There were, of course, no flowers at this season and it is possible that these rosettes, only three to five centimetres across, were those of the rare pale butterwort *(Pinguicula lusitanica)*, which persist through the winter. Those of the larger leaved common butterwort, which occurs in similar sites, disappear at the end of the growing season, the plants overwintering as rootless buds, sustained by moisture in the surounding Sphagnum.

Was the end of October summer or winter, in this anomalous year of 2006? The question might well be asked in such a mild year, starting and ending with storm force winds, rain squalls and even a tornado, yet designated as having produced the hottest British summer since records began, with temperatures soaring into the nineties Farenheit through much of July.

The butterwort bog nurtured delicate plants of trailing St. John's wort *(Hypericum humifusum)* and exploratory shoots of New Zealand willowherb. This invaded the mountains of Northern England, Scotland and Wales in the second half of the twentieth century, arriving as *Epilobium pedunculare* but now known as *Epilobium brunnescens.*

Stooping to conquer, its prostrate stems root at the nodes where the paired leaves are attached, enabling it to form mats infiltrating the Sphagnum or advancing across bare peat. From some of the often purple backed leaf pairs rose a slender stalk bearing the long seed capsule, scarcely any broader, that is typical of all the willow herbs. Some had split into four or five lobes to release the tiny seeds. The fluff of silvery hairs, light as swansdown, that should have helped their individual dispersal, clung limply to the fruit walls, awaiting a drying wind.

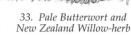

33. Pale Butterwort and New Zealand Willow-herb

Straw-coloured seed heads of bog asphodel *(Narthecium ossifragum)* speared up from the green mat. Formerly bearing shaggy orange-yellow flowers, these were now adorned with glistening raindrops similar to those hanging like pearl earings from our leader's ear lobes A rather damp song thrush and attendant dunnock were poking among rocks and nautical debris for food, and were still at it when we returned some six hours later.

19. WET WOODS AND LUSH LICHENS

A short detour off the main road at MacDougall's Bay brought us to an older hump-backed bridge over the last lap of the two pronged stream draining the western slope of Dubh Bheinn, southernmost of the Paps at 1,720 feet (530 m), as it raced down to the sea. This was dipper territory, but it seemed that all the wee creatures this dapper little bird might have been hunting had been swept out to sea.

Instead we heard the tale of another seen by our leader, Peter Roberts, on a former visit. That dipper had shot past and under the main road bridge at speed for fifty yards out to sea before turning back. Soon after it had set out again and headed off to Islay three quarters of a mile away. Was it assessing weather and waves before attempting the sea crossing? Swift as kingfishers when coursing along streams, these stubby little birds are well able to whirr away over large stretches of water between islands.

The soggy turf of the stream banks bore insidiously clogging clumps of dog's tooth lichen *(Peltigera canina)*, almost black above, with a mere tinge of green, the irregularly ridged underside white. Little fawn flanges of the fungal component of this symbiotic partnership folded upwards from the frond margins, like a broderie anglais edging.

Common among the undershrubs bordering the peaty road verges were eared sallows, as on Islay. Gnarled and knocked about by the wind, some of the ultimate twigs were knobbly with globose galls caused by gall gnats *(Rhabdophaga salicis)*. These were on living tissue, some with a foliage leaf still attached. Infection occurs when the twigs are young and each woody gall contains several packets of fly larvae.

We stopped shortly after, before the cliff steepened, forcing the road away from

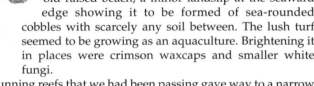

the coast. This was for another abortive otter watch combined with morning coffee. A little possie of black-faced sheep sheltered in the lee of a ruined cottage, while another was tucking into seaweed on the beach.

The terrace hosting the main group was an old raised beach, a minor landslip at the seaward edge showing it to be formed of sea-rounded cobbles with scarcely any soil between. The lush turf seemed to be growing as an aquaculture. Brightening it in places were crimson waxcaps and smaller white fungi.

34. *Willow Gnat Galls, Rhabdophaga salicis, on Eared Sallow*

Rugged seaward running reefs that we had been passing gave way to a narrow headland with a seal 'bottling' just offshore. The current storm beach curved out around the headland which was made up of the old one. With no otters, the only distraction was a small black boulder showing an anticlinal fold of a paler colour on its broken face.

A blue container ship taking a short cut around the south of Jura chugged past, with a kittiwake flying ahead and a pair of whooper swans overtaking. Gorse bushes climbing the moor grass hill inland had been munched down to lobed domes by deer or cattle, presumably when the tender young shoots first appeared in spring. It must be quite a sight when these neatly trimmed bushes are massed with coconut scented flowers among the crowded spines.

As though to own up as culprits, some red deer appeared among them, first a young stag accompanied by an elegant hind, and then a well grown stag with a full head of antlers moving up over the skyline. He joined the others, all three gazing at us with distrust. No doubt the rut had passed by the end of October and the whipper snapper presented no threat.

The landscape had become more wooded where we drew to a halt near the lodge of Jura House. Peter had been commissioned by the Islay weaver who produced the Balmoral tweed and the tartan for the film "Braveheart", to deliver a smart new pair of tartan trews to the gentleman occupying this little house in the woods. Anyone likely to be passing could act as carrier in this close knit community of twinned islands.

In the front garden was an ancient dogwood with deep red leaves and even quite small branches thickly clad with powdery, plated, lobed and branched lichens. Mingled with them on this very young growth, was epiphytic cypress-leaved feather moss *(Hypnum andoi)*, with wispy ginger capsules on horsehair like stalks.

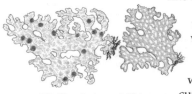

35. *Tree Lungwort Lichen*

We had time for a hurried exploration of the walled garden of Jura House, which lay a tidy walk away through tall woodland and was open to the public with an 'honesty box' near the lodge for contributions. Several paths wandered away from the fierce little stream cutting deeply into a narrow channel bordered by dripping ferns and herbs.

While the rest strode off along the main woodland track to the gardens, I was brought up short by the phenomenal growths of tree lungwort *(Lobaria pulmonaria)* coating the smooth trunks of the dominant trees to heights of many metres.

This must be one of the most prolific of lichens, romping up anything climbable in a profusion that could only be maintained in areas of high humidity. I recall seeing it before around tree bases on the neighbouring islands of Rhum and Colonsay to the north and west. It is now practically confined to ancient deciduous woodlands of north and west Britain, but is believed to have been more widespread in the past, though never common. Individual fronds might be as large as the palm of the hand but are attached at only one point.

Extensively lobed, they resembled in shape the carragheen of the lower shore but were firmer of texture, pale green above and orange brown beneath. Little globular pustules between the veins on the underside were matched by the mirror images of dimpled hollows on the upper. Scattered among these depressions were scarlet discs producing the spores of the fungal component, both here and on Rhum, although said to be produced sparsely or not at all.

When the lichen was more widespread some was collected and sold to cure lung disease. This was a case of 'sympathetic magic' based on the resemblance of the veined thallus to the intricacy of tubes within the lungs. In addition it emits a sweet smell and has been used in perfume manufacture. Also, surprisingly, in lieu of hops in beer making, but not, as were many lichens, as a dye for fabrics. Perhaps this widespread use in the past and not the atmospheric pollution that is so inimical to lichen growth in Britain as a whole, is responsible for its current rarity.

More familiar lichens crowded along smaller branches and twigs were mostly some of the finely branched old mans beard lichens (Usnea) and slabby, lobed

Parmelia. The first were employed in Scandinavia to produce an antibiotic and have been used in medicine, cosmetics (hair powder) and even as a source of glucose. Parmelia, a genus of many species, has been important in dyeing wool.

This woodland, its trees tall and stately by island standards, would not have been out of place in the Home Counties. Marginal trees bushed out, rebuffing the winds. Here was much more than the sycamore so popular on Islay, with beech, birch, ash and oak casting deep shade. Subtle hues were added by epiphytic ferns, as well as the lichens and mosses on trunks and branches, with red flecks of rowan and hawthorn berries glowing faintly in the gloomy interior. Spreading carpets of opposite-leaved golden saxifrage competed with moss mats where autumn leaves were drifting down and foxglove spires emerged from the underbrush.

Woodland trails converged on the big house, its curving drive lined with temperate plants emulating tropical ones as effectively as on the seafront at Torquay. Handsome stands of New Zealand cabbage trees partnered ebullient tufts of New Zealand flax among exotic looking shrubs. Sheep were pastured on the paddock sloping down from the garden to the sea, where the kindly Gulf Stream lapped among the pebbles, making it all possible.

There was great potential along the drive for shows of summer flowers, but the walled kitchen garden was away to one side, hidden among more trees, silent stones and whispering branches, deflecting winds that might dispel the aura of that mellow tide.

Until recently in poor shape, great efforts had been made to renovate the beds and coax plants into growth under poly tunnels, all neatly labelled. Such was the shelter provided by the ancient walls that a few red admiral butterflies were able to join the bumble bees and hover flies sipping nectar during a brief respite in the drizzling rain.

The seafront garden of the hotel where we later enjoyed our soup and sandwich lunch also boasted non hardy plants creating a false sense of tropicality. Cordyline was here again, as a backdrop to Gunnera with fat red flower spikes reaching up under the rough textured panoply of coarse 'rhubarb' leaves.

Twenty three eiders drifted languidly off the end of the little pier beyond the ruffled embroidery of wavelets along the shore. This was Craighouse, the island's main village, catering for visitors, with the only hotel, cafe, shop and garage – also a whisky distillery, built in 1810.

The more traditional crofting settlement of Kiels and the ancient graveyard of Kileannardil, named after St. Columbus's uncle, are just behind. Hamlets such as Ardfarnal and Knockrome were few and far between.

Most of the island's permanent population of some two hundred souls live on this sheltered southern end of the island, where Fuchsia, Rhododendron, Escallonia and many another shrub are garden favourites.

20. RED DEER COUNTRY AND THE GULF OF CORRIEVRECKAN

North from here we saw only a few scattered houses, whitewashed and spacious and usually among sheltering trees. The furthermost, Barnhill, overlooking Corrievreckan Strait in the north beyond the end of the A 846, was lived in for a

36. Escallonia
macrantha

time by George Orwell. Some of his best known novels, such as "Animal Farm" and "1984" were written here.

For the rest, the island interior has been described as one of the largest uninhabited areas in Britain, dangerous for inexperienced walkers, not only for the rugged terrain but for the liklihood of being shot in mistake for a deer during the stalking season from mid August to February.

These red deer are believed to have been running here since the ice retreated back to the North Pole where it belongs – some eight thousand years ago. Norsemen of the eighth and ninth centuries named the island for them as Dyr Oa or Dyr Ey. They are highly valued as pure native stock, living in isolation with no opportunity to interbreed with sika or fallow deer as have so many other populations.

Current figures for the deer in 2006 were sixty thousand, these outnumbering the two hundred human inhabitants by three hundred to one. Their numbers have always had to be controlled and the various estates still do so with periodic shooting parties.

The animals roam widely, keeping largely to the hills but leaving the bare, stony tops where grazing is sparse to the wild goats. Their tracks are well worn, as they tend to follow the easiest routes over rough ground. In the summer they move higher to escape the flies, grazing the mountain grasses until these give out or become too exposed, when they move to lower ground for the winter. They suit their elevation to the optimum current temperature and may come lower during fierce summer storms.

Our sightings were divided between animals on the lower moorland or over the fences, sharing the greener herbage with farm livestock. The much discussed subject of reintroduction of the once native wolves to keep deer numbers in check came up. Some folk thought that Jura would be the ideal place for an experiment of this ilk. The natural food available to the wolves was excellent and limitation of deer numbers by natural predation would help to prevent these from eating themselves out of suitable provender if numbers were not kept in check. With three hundred deer to every human being, it was unlikely that the wolves would bother with people.

Fences to protect farm livestock from wolves would only have to be half the height of those erected to keep farm grazings from deer, so existing deer fences would suffice to protect the sheep. So far the great armies of migrant geese, for which fences prove no deterrent, are happy with the greener grass on the other side of Islay Sound, causing no problem on Jura entailing compensation being paid to farmers for loss of grazing.

In fact the soil developed from the predominant quartzite rock with its thick blanket of peat is pretty poor. As much is also high and exposed, livestock

37. Red Deer

farming has not developed as on the sister island and we saw more sheep than cattle on such grazings as there were. It seems likely that Jura will remain primarily a 'deer forest', with the goats, perhaps, leading the wolves a pretty dance on the high tops.

The bedrock, deposited as sand in a shallow sea over five hundred and seventy million years ago, has suffered inevitable change by compression, folding and uplifting over the millennia. The Paps, which dominate the southern half, contain unusually few lines of weakness and have resisted erosion much more successfully than the surrounding land. Geologists rate the difference as 1,000 feet (330 m), which qualifies them as genuine mountains, even if measured from the surrounding land rather than mean sea level. Inevitably they were smoothed by moving ice and contain glacial features such as monumental corries and frost shattered rock piles,

Sea sculpted caves and arches were brought progressively above the lowering sea level as the land heaved a sigh of relief and started a gentle rise as the weight of its burden of ice lifted. The resulting raised beaches, for which all the islands hereabouts are famous, are up to 120 feet (40 m) above current sea level. This upper shoreline that we followed seemed frozen in time from the era of the first human inhabitants. Will global warming start to reverse this trend, as thawing ice begins to drown today's beaches?

The major part of our route around this ancient landscape coincided with an old drover's road used to get Islay cattle to the mainland markets. The herds crossed Islay Sound where we had and were driven around the south end and up the east. Where the A 846 turned inland the drove road continued straight on to a point where the animals were driven onto boats for a second sea passage.

Further north, where Loch Tarbert almost cuts the island in two, folk from Colonsay used to take a short cut by boat along the length of that loch and across the narrow neck of land to the sea again at Tarbert to reach the Kielmore Peninsula on the mainland. A standing stone and ruined chapel are reminders of those distant times.

We went "right on to the end of the road" as the great Harry Lauder would have put it, seeing what we could of the rolling brown moor under the rolling grey mist and trying to imagine the might of the Paps above. That was where the eider ducks nested, in the virtual absence of ground predators and where introduced ring-necked pheasants were doing likewise. Either might provide a welcome snack for a wolf.

Five of those handsome game birds lined up on the crash barrier beside the

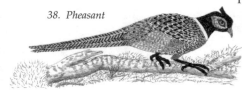

38. Pheasant

road stolidly maintained position as we passed within a foot or so. Four were still there on our return, unabashed by other traffic passing in the interim. Closeby was a "Road Narrows" sign. though it could scarcely get any narrower between the widely spaced, pole marked passing places. Nevertheless it was, part having slipped over the edge to be bolstered up with ballast.

At one point a fully antlered stag came careering down the hill and across the road, clearing the two bordering fences in graceful leaps – a fine sight that the fog could not mask, as it had masked the usually visible inner end of Loch Tarbert.

The road did not go as far as the much feared Gulf of Corrievreckan, site of one of the world's most dangerous whirlpools – classed as un-navigable by the Admiralty. Beyond lay the uninhabited island of Scarba, a barren mass of dark slate streaked with white bands of quartzite, rising to 1,500 feet and partially decorated with a crimson tracery of iron oxide, as though a fishing net had been flung across the grey.

The extensive lines of raised beaches along its western shore form two almost perpendicular escarpments dropping from 150 feet to 25 feet and to sea level, the cliff bases sculpted into stacks, pinnacles and caves by the waves. Although no-one lives on Scarba nowadays, there is one habitable residence in Kilmory Lodge. For the rest it is left to the deer and sheep.

Corrievreckan is at its most dangerous when a westerly gale coincides with a flood tide. A 1982 publication says of the outcome of this union: "The narrow channel is transformed into a whirling white maelstrom of merciless ferocity, at the vortex of which huge water spouts can be heard for more than twenty miles inland."

The unevenness of the channel floor sets the current on its lethal errand. In the channel, which is known to be 150 fathoms (900 feet) deep in places, a rock pinnacle 900 feet out from the shore pokes up within 15 fathoms of the surface. Fast moving water at flood and ebb tides strike the pinnacle, setting up a continuous whirling pool, stilled only for about an hour at slack water.

Its speed is eight knots, almost that of the average fishing boat sailing in calm water, so little progress could be made against it, even if the craft stayed on top. Many boats have been sucked down over the years, these selected, 'tis said. by the Cailleach witch, who has dominioin over the channel. What we would call white horses were regarded as her flocks and herds. Her wiles are enhanced by singing mermaids luring mariners to their doom in the great vortex – and featuring in old Gaelic tales and songs.

The Scarba side gets the worst of the turbulence when the tide is running in from the Atlantic, but the backwash on the Jura side is said to be quite spectacular. Did George Orwell derive inspiration for his more outlandish writings from the ancient lore as he sat pondering on his local shore?

Our return drive provided sightings of seal, deer, heron and buzzard, but no otters and no golden eagles, nor even the resident choughs. We spent a while in the unmanned Interpretive Centre just short of the ferry terminal, to learn something of what we had missed.

It seemed there were stoats here, a race taking on the white pelt of ermine on the snowy Paps in winter. Garments trimmed with fur of the deceased feature the black tail tip, which is retained throughout – rather scuppering the stoat's winter camouflage in life but enhancing the beneficiary after its death.

Sadly alien American mink are here too. Surely this remote outpost should have been far enough from the misguided 'do gooders' who had released them to desecrate so many habitats on the mainland to have escaped this scourge? Rats, mice, voles and shrews were also present.

We strolled the last few hundred yards to the ferry, admiring the fresh green of the floating bog pondweed and submerged sprouts of water starwort in the brisk roadside brook. A few flowering tufts of ragged Robin defied the elements. This was a good place to be if you were a water plant.

21. TAILPIECE; AN OTTER AT LAST

There was still an hour of daylight left when we got back to Islay, so Peter drove us north along the coast to see if we could get a view of those

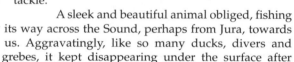
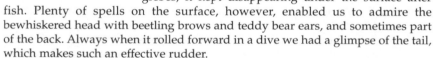

elusive Paps across the Sound. The north-east corner of Islay is as roadless as that of Jura, but we followed to its end. This was Bunnahabhain, the site of a northern distillery and a slipway used for small boats. Otters were still our main target and the two telescopes were set up on their tripods in readiness, pointing away from the whisky vats and fishing tackle.

A sleek and beautiful animal obliged, fishing its way across the Sound, perhaps from Jura, towards

39. Ragged Robin

us. Aggravatingly, like so many ducks, divers and grebes, it kept disappearing under the surface after fish. Plenty of spells on the surface, however, enabled us to admire the bewhiskered head with beetling brows and teddy bear ears, and sometimes part of the back. Always when it rolled forward in a dive we had a glimpse of the tail, which makes such an effective rudder.

It was heading for the shore, away from the busyness of the pier and slipway, but we were not to see it on land. It glided behind the reef on which two gulls had stood sentinel throughout, to bring its catch to land in private. Only the heron that had been fishing by other means, perhaps for its favourite butterfish, remained on our side of the rocky rampart.

We had achieved our goal, although not on the expected island. Two of our party who had a sea view from their hotel bedroom did a double take, seeing two otters together from their window before breakfast on our last day on Islay.

Before we left Bunnahabain some weak rays of the dying sun finally broke through the murk and lighted up at least the southern hump of Jura's backbone. It is said that the Paps hinder the rain-bearing clouds from the Atlantic on their way to the Scottish mainland, relieving them of much of their burden of moisture. We had a gut feeling that this could be very true!

II
Colonsay and Oronsay

COLONSAY

1. QUALITY AND DIVERSITY OF LANDSCAPE

Frank Fraser Darling in his 1947 classic New Naturalist volume *Natural History in the Highlands and Islands* states: "The islands of Colonsay and Oronsay west of Jura are excellent examples of islands which have the best of almost all worlds." And again, in summary: "Colonsay and Oronsay might well be looked on as an epitome of the West Highland world in its full range and consequences of Atlantic exposure and sheltered mildness." How true!

While possessing bleak heather moors and chilly, infertile lochs, Colonsay can also boast mature woodland in the island centre and fertile fields yielding generous crops of hay and silage. The cliffs, mostly low and rolling, rise in the west to support a clamorous population of sea birds, and there are dunes and sandy pastures, salt marshes and pebble beaches. Colonsay's greatest claim to fame, however, is her raised beaches, some as much as 120 feet above sea level and regarded as pre-glacial in origin.

The two islands are separated by an extensive spread of sea-washed sand and become one for about three hours on every tidal cycle. Together they reach about ten miles from north to south and between two to four miles wide, tapering at both ends.

They lie approximately twelve miles due west of the less welcoming heights of Jura at latitude 56 degrees north. The mainland is twenty five miles away beyond the Paps of that forbidding outcrop and Mull is fifteen miles to the north. Canada is the next land to the west apart from the lonely rock of the Du Hirteach Lighthouse. Along with their dozen or so islets in the south and west the two islands have been referred to in official literature as among the most remote islands of Argyllshire.

So delectable a site, with almost as much sunshine as Tiree, the record holder for Scotland, and considerably less rain, has for long been regarded as a desirable residence. Remains of Stone Age man and his imported flint tools have been found in uplifted sea caves to the north and south of Kiloran Bay, where they lay undisturbed for nigh on six thousand years. There are some twenty Pictish forts, some half dozen sites with standing stones and – a more recent relic – a Viking war lord with his horse and his long boat beneath the Kiloran sands.

The McPhies, who held Colonsay in historic times, instituted no forced evictions, so this is one of the few islands where crofters did not have to leave to

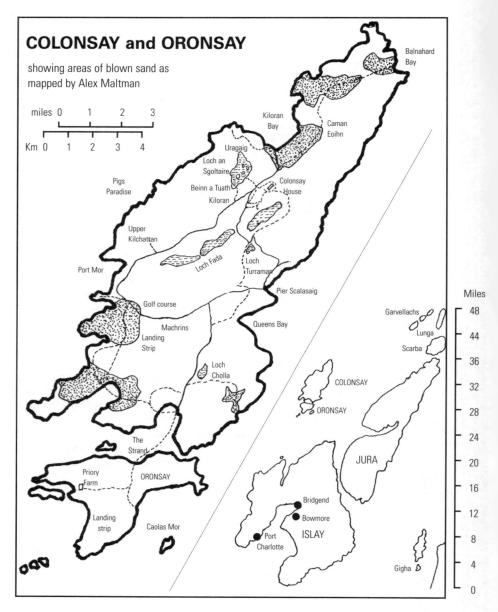

COLONSAY and ORONSAY

showing areas of blown sand as
mapped by Alex Maltman

miles 0   1   2   3

Km 0   1   2   3   4

Balnahard
Bay

Kiloran
Bay

Caman
Eoihn

Uragaig

Loch an
Sgoltaire

Pigs
Paradise

Beinn a Tuath

Colonsay
House

Kiloran

Upper
Kilchattan

Port Mor

Loch Fada

Loch
Turraman

Pier Scalasaig

Golf course

Machrins

Landing
Strip

Queens Bay

Loch
Cholla

The
Strand

Priory
Farm

ORONSAY

Landing
strip

Caolas Mor

Garvellachs

Lunga

Scarba

COLONSAY

ORONSAY

JURA

Bridgend

Bowmore

Port
Charlotte

ISLAY

Gigha

Miles

48

44

36

32

28

24

20

16

12

8

4

0

make way for sheep. Subsequent lairds, ancestors of the recent owner, Lord
Strathcona, created, over four generations, the wooded gardens around Colonsay
House, the nucelus of which was built in 1722, probably with stones from the

now defunct and undocumented Kiloran Abbey. Commonly referred to as subtropical, these gardens by no means aspire to such heights on the temperature scale, but do manage to sustain non frost-hardy shrubs and trees, with a strong flavour of the Antipodes in the Australian gums and wattles and the New Zealand cabbage trees.

2. THE ROCKS

(Material in this section is condensed from an investigation carried out by Dr. Alex Maltman -for the use of which I am much indebted.)

Geologists are still uncertain as to the age of the rocks which are, collectively with those on the Rhinns of Islay, known as "The Colonsay Group". This is because they are completely devoid of fossils and do not lend themselves to radiometric methods of dating. They are generally thought to be of Torridonian age – the same as the red sandstone of Handa Island in the north – deposited some nine hundred million years ago on the basal Lewissian Gneiss, which crops out at Balnahard Beach in north-eastern Colonsay. The possibility remains, however, that they may be Moinian or Dalradian, and as young (comparatively speaking) as six hundred million years.

40. *Wrinkle Fold in slaty cleavage, Oronsay*

Most are from marine sediments, which solidified after long burial to become sandstones and mudstones. Subsequently folded and faulted, some of them underwent a change or metamorphism, which resulted in the tendency to cleave into thin parallel layers or slates. Molten rock, forced into cracks at depth, became today's dykes. Other intrusions of molten material form igneous masses around the island harbour at Scalasaig in the east and Kiloran Bay in the north-west.

These rocks were eventually uplifted and the covering layers eroded away to reveal them at the surface. The slates weather readily under the influence of wind and rain and, along with the faulted zones, form the fertile lowlands. The slightly metamorphosed sandstones are harder and stand out as hills, rising to 470 feet in the north, 456 feet in the west and 321 feet in the south. Subsequent glacial action during the Ice Ages , with fluctuations of sea level as water froze over the land or melted and ran off into the oceans, produced cliff line sea caves and raised beaches extending well in from today's shoreline.

Lewissian Gneiss, the metamorphosed bedrock, which forms most of the Outer Hebrides, is the oldest of all Scotland's rocks. The little exposure of this at Balnahard Bay was covered first by pebble-strewn sand, which became compressed into puddingstone or Conglomerate visible on the lower slopes of Breac Bhuidhe at Colonsay's northern tip.

The igneous rocks of the intruded slabs or dykes are of two kinds. The southern ones are tough, fine grained black Basalt, the northern ones of crumbly dark green Lamprophyre, occasionally with some flaky Biotite. The igneous intrusion at Scalasaig Harbour is Diorite, coloured by dark green Augite crystals. The igneous intrusion at Kiloran Bay is Syenite with dark green Horneblende and salmon pink Feldspar, a mineral which also turns up in the quartz veins so common in the slates.

The dykes were squeezed into position at different times. First were some of the Lamprophyre ones, associated with the great Caledonian Orogeny which affected so much of northern Britain some four hundred and eighty million years ago – the time of origin of the Scalasaig and Kiloran igneous masses. Mica rich dykes at Riasg Buidhe and Kilchattan are of Carboniferous age (two hundred and seventy million years ago). The Basalt dykes are much younger, intruded in Tertiary times seventy million years ago. Limestone occurs only as a few narrow bands around Scalasaig and Kiloran.

The several glaciations of recent times occurred between two million and ten thousand years back, and the island is thought to have assumed its present form some five thousand years ago – soon after the known arrival on the scene of *Homo sapiens*. Strange pebbles to be found on the beaches were brought from elsewhere by ice or water.

3. SOIL FERTILITY AND LAND USE

In agricultural terms Colonsay and Oronsay lie between the unproductive soil derived from the ancient Lewisian Gneiss of the Outer Hedrides and the fertile loams from Orkney's Devonian flagstones. The sandstone hills, further denuded of fertility by soil run-off in the fierce Atlantic climate, support only the impoverished heather of the former. The slaty lowlands, further replenished by topsoil from the hills, conform more to the latter.

These have the modest agricultural potential of the so-called Slate Islands of Seil and Luing to the north-east, growing fewer of the arable crops that are such an important part of the Orkney scene, but producing good forage for immediate consumption or storage. Where uncultivated, the land relapses into (or remains as) rough grass heath rather than peaty moorland.

The Colonsay House woodlands are dependent on their sheltered situation and the endeavours of man rather than rock type, lying partly on sandstone with Feldspar, partly on slate and partly on raised beach deposits. That sandstone is quite adequate for the growth of trees is proved by the siting of the two remaining fragments of the original Caledonian forest, both on the sandstone slopes of the north-east coast.

The spread of Boulder Clay along the central fault occupied by the three partite Loch Fada, introduces an extra element of fertility in this central lowland and infiltrates northwards through the Colonsay estate towards Kiloran.

Sheep and cattle graze throughout the island, though sparsely on the heather hills, which are more the domain of the wild goats – at least in summer, when the milder conditions allow them to beat a retreat from the influx of visitors. They congregate at Balnahard in the north and Oronsay in the south; shaggy black hill dwellers with long, menacing horns.

The stock is said to be derived from ships of the defeated Spanish Armada wrecked offshore in 1588, and apparently better able to swim ashore than many of their captors. The same origin is attributed to the small ponies which are endemic to nearby Rhum. Legend or truth? Goat ancestors were kept in the hold to replenish the galley stores as required, rather than for stocking the islands as fresh supplies for future mariners. The Spaniards would have hoped for no such potential future needs!

4. WOODLANDS

Perhaps it is because the island was never given over entirely to sheep, that some of the original Caledonian forest has persisted. The trees are gnarled and twisted, but no more so than those of Wistman's Wood in the kindlier latitude of

Dartmoor. Woodland remnants are, as so often, on the poorest soils that have never been in demand for agriculture. They hug the eastern slopes but, even here, twelve miles of sea separate them from the potential shelter of Jura Their native components include oak, birch, aspen, rowan, willow, hazel and holly.

41. Colonsay House and Cattle

Best known of the woodlands at present are the plantings in the estate grounds, but establishment of these was not easy. As in the Forestry Commission's experimental plots of conifers on Hoy in the Orkneys, the trees that stayed alive showed little growth in the first ten years and moved only slowly thereafter. J de V Loder, writing in 1935, says that in many places they had to be planted over and over again, in spite of the five feet high stone dykes that protected them from wind and grazing.

Alders and sea buckthorn were planted to take the brunt of the gales while alders and poplars were put in sites too wet for most others apart from willows. The poplars failed to survive, most blowing over and this problem persists. Big twinned sycamores fallen near the sawmill in 1986, showed but a thin layer of soil enmeshed among the upended and completely superficial spread of roots, from which eight foot high disc no root seemed to have penetrated the vacated puddle on the stony, waterlogged soil, with its inevitable oxygen deficiency. (Poplars, although America's so popular riverside 'cottonwoods', prefer better aerated running water.)

Wind resistant sycamores, introduced to many Scottish islands, are still vulnerable. Saplings planted by Kevin Byrne, the hotelier, on a north facing bank at Scalasaig in 1985, all succumbed to the elements, in spite of the protection of plastic sheaths.

Plantings are mixed, native and alien, coniferous and deciduous. Pine, fir and spruce mingle with horse chestnut, Turkey oak and broad-leaved lime, while downy birch often dominates marginal situations. Beech, well north of its native range in Britain, has proved as wind-worthy as in the south. Native oak, ash and wych elm form a canopy above exotic Escallonia, Camellia, Azalea, Embothrium, Magnolia, bamboo and palms.

With the trees have come woodland understorey plants, some residual, some introduced, some blatantly alien. The visitor in May and June will find whole areas suffused with pink, where seemingly endless carpets of pink purslane (*Montia sibirica*) spread beneath the trees, giving way only in the deepest shade where *Rhododendron ponticum* takes over. The first is from North America and is virtually unknown in the wild in southern Britain. The second is from the Mediterranean. Both are highly invasive in these cool, damp habitats.

Prevalent atmospheric humidity is demonstrated by the abundance of lichens growing as epiphytes on trees. Even the usually all-exclusive Rhododendron, bears shaggy growths of old man's beard lichen along bare limbs. Most special, as on Jura and the Small Isles, is the tree lungwort, spreading up and down the trunks and branches of many different tree species, from water holding crotches. This essentially north-western lichen can get established on much younger and more isolated trees in these habitats instead of almost exclusively on big old trees in ancient woodland, as elsewhere.

Epiphytism is rife, with all the usual tree dwelling mosses such as Hypnum and Eurhynchium enwrapping moist bark, where Ulota forms little cushions. Polypody ferns romp along trunks and walls, honeysuckle and ivy droop in festoons from the treetops, deluding the susceptible into that 'sub-tropical feeling'.

Some limey element in the soil must be responsible for the lusty shrubs of spurge laurel (*Daphne laureola*) and ground cover of ramsons or wild garlic (*Allium ursinum*). Here too are early purple, common spotted and twayblade orchids, wood sanicle, bugle and devil's bit scabious, primroses, bluebells and red campion. Broad buckler and male ferns are as prolific as anywhere in the rainy west, with woodland loosestrife, wood sorrel and herb Robert.

42. Spurge Laurel

Wet areas hold kingcups or marsh marigolds, buttercups and yellow monkey flowers (*Mimulus guttatus*), which is a well established American alien. Delicate bog pimpernel succeeds the early flowering golden saxifrage in organic rich seepages. Many others help to supply the bees living in the hives by the track leading eastward to the nearer of the two primaeval forest plots. Specially attractive are the Welsh poppies (*Meconopsis cambrica*).

The trees themselves supply a more obvious harvest. Timber in all stages of preparation was lying round the working sawmill, with its cradle suspended over a creosote bath, for dunking fence posts before submitting them to the insidiously percolating moisture of the retentive boulder clay.

On our exploration in late June, chaffinches were busy shelling the early maturing winged seeds of the wych elm. Willow warblers occupied the grey sallow which co-habitated with the much more widespread eared sallows in woodland glades. The thin tseeping of goldcrests issued from thickets of dark spruce branches and wrens foraged among the deep pink flowers of spider-haunted Escallonia bushes.

The melancholy cooing of immigrant collared doves supplied a background for little bursts of song from robin and blackbird. A spotted flycatcher helped to vacuum up the midges and a greenfinch rustled through the bamboos. We saw none of the usually to be expected tits and heard no cuckoos, a species which was common throughout the Outer Hebrides at the time.

A rare landhopper, *Arcitalitrus dorreni,* related to the Talitrus sandhoppers of the shore, had recently been discovered here by P.G.Moore and J.J.Spicer. It lives normally in woodland leaf litter but has spread into the mulch below scrub, bracken and grassland. Few have been found under conifers and none on heather moor, although some animals are content to gnaw holes in paper sacks in more domestic settings.

Arcitalitrus is one of the few species which prefers the fallen leaves of the alien sycamore to the harder ones of the native oak and beech. Those they reduce to skeletons, leaving only a tracery of veins, so they play an important part in the recycling of nutrients in woodland soils. The species hails from Australia and New Zealand, from where it was accidentally introduced into Ireland and the Dorien Smith Gardens of Trescoe Abbey on the Scillies. There, predictably, it favours the litter under the Australian Dicksonia tree ferns.

No doubt it was introduced to the Colonsay Gardens in the same way – perhaps a hundred years ago, when the main plantings were made. Moore and Spicer reckoned that its natural spread from the gardens must have been at the rate of about twenty five metres a year.

At home in the tree fern forests of South East Australia, it prefers a humid woodland climate, with or without trees, avoiding the too wet and too dry. It also seems to avoid places that are occupied by ants but not the mites, which live upon it as ecto-parasites.

Colonsay, so far, was the highest latitude in which it had been found either north or south of the Equator – another pointer to the unexpected mildness of latitude 56 north with its stream of warming water from the Caribbean.

5. THE THREE PARTITE LOCH FADA

Scotland's Great Glen leading from Inverness to Oban, occupies a geological fault which continues south-west through the Firth of Lorne and along the north-west shore of Colonsay where it is identifiable about 5 km out from Port Mor. Here a considerable bay has formed at the end of a subsidiary fault cutting obliquely through the island and occupied by a trio of lochs, like a smaller version of Lochs Ness, Lochy and Linnhe. These three are lumped together as Loch Fada. They hold no depths suitable for a Nessie monster and shallow to a reedswamp where the road from Scalasaig to Kiloran crosses on a man-made causeway over the wetlands.

This fault zone runs back from Port Mor at an acute angle to the other, across the eroded slates of Kilchattan at the south-west end of the Loch Fada chain. For most of its length it cuts into the harder sandstones which form cliffs to the south east of the loch. The valley floor slopes more gently on the north west side and accommodates the loop road from Kilchattan to Kiloran.

Fertility is most apparent in the north eastern third of the loch towards the Kiloran Estate, where it is bounded by farmland, benefitting, perhaps, from fertiliser run-off, and dips into the woodland. Standing on the causeway separating this from the middle section, the view east is one of choking reeds and water lilies, the view west is of cotton grass and bogbean spearing out of darker, peatier water. The westerly third leading to the standing stones of Lower Kilchattan was not visited.

Where the track to Colonsay House abuts onto the eastern section, the spinney of downy birch fronting the moorland grades into soggy alderwood fronting the lake. These alders have the gnarled look of trees which have had to struggle to survive, their bases splayed and contorted like swamp cypresses in the Everglades. Among the wealth of common ferns flooring the alder carr stately golden-green fronds of royal fern *(Osmunda regalis)* push through the kingcups, encroaching on the reeds to lakeward and the Rhododendrons to landward.

Further along the lake beyond the shelter of the trees fine spreads of insectivorous 'common' butterwort were covered with Viola like flowers in early summer. Lousewort was here, as almost everywhere else, and hard fern *(Blechnum spicant)* in well drained crevices.

43. *Water Milfoil*

The stony shore below, haunt of sandpipers, extends to the burgeoning reedswamp and epitomises the barren acidity of the virgin loch so different from the apparent fertility at the other end. Not only are the pebbly shallows home to shoreweed *(Littorella uniflora)*, but to possibly even more of the tip-tilted leaf rosettes of water Lobelia *(Lobelia dortmanna)*. Pinkish stems topped by flowers of palest blue, protruded a few inches from the surface by June, their length depending on current water depth, to bring the flowers into the air.

Beyond, in the silt free but peat stained water, are deeply dissected red-brown fronds of alternate-flowered water milfoil, the smaller of the two commoner species and one of acid waters. Tucked between wet stones higher up were similar hued shoots of water purslane and abbreviated purple-leaved forms of water mint, with lesser spearwort, water forget-me-not and bulbous rush.

Left exposed by withdrawal of the water is a particularly attractive form of the liverwort *(Pellia neesiana)*. The cells of its fleshy crisped thallus seem crystalline under the hand lens and June fronds bore dark red, sperm producing antheridial mounds along their centre and young sporangia emerging from cylindrical sheaths beneath which the eggs had been fertilised.

A cause of puzzlement in June was a littoral fringe of what appeared to be tall stamen-decked rush stems, like giant mat grass florets. Closer investigation showed the 'stamens' to be the white vacated skins of many thousands of mayfly nymphs, tiny but perfect, with three splaying tail prongs.

Fragile though these were, they had endured intact since the lake waters were at a higher level and the aquatic nymphs had crawled out for the grey-winged duns to wriggle free for a brief aerial sojourn before the final metamorphosis to the second winged phase. This last is also lamentably brief in these so well named Ephemeroptera.

Their untold numbers emphasise the importance of even such tiny morsels for insect eating birds, not only those such as swallows and martins that sift them from the air, but those that prey on their more protracted aquatic phase. And birds there were in plenty.

With the common sandpipers communicating in piercing whistles were pied wagtails prodding the stony beaches for stranded titbits. Out on the lake were colourful teal and mallard and sundry quackings emerging from others hidden in the reedbeds. A little grebe dived repeatedly, probably after fish, but its kind are not averse to beakfuls of water flea or Daphnia soup. Haunting cries of lapwings formed a background for the harsher utterances of lesser black-backed gulls on some stony islands and the monotonous scratchy songs of sedge warblers in the littoral scrub.

The herons eluded us. They are of special interest on Colonsay in being ground nesters instead of tree nesters and not by virtue of necessity, as on the treeless Outer Hebrides. As many as twenty were seen together in September 1984, when there were nineteen occupied nests but a gale in 1982 had proved too much for some and ten of that year's nests were destroyed. Obviously it was better for them not to set their sights too high.

The loch surface showed the usual bronze patches of broad-leaved pondweed. Less usual was the spread of white water lilies extending back along canals between the reed culms. Shorelines showed a gradation from beak or bottle sedge (*Carex rostrata*) to the less usual true bulrush or clubrush (*Scirpus (Schoenoplectus) lacustris*), its spongy, air-filled stems topped by brown inflorescences. This grew taller than the common reeds, which had still not produced the purple plumes of summer by June.

6. LOCH TURRAMAN, THE NEW LOCH

Loch Fada is the most eutrophic (fertile) of the lochs, Loch Turraman, the New Loch, west of Bonaveh was less so, more by virtue of its newness since dam construction than from its elevation. The sparsity of the Boulder Clay lodged in the Loch Fada fault might also detract from its nutrient status. Loch an Sgoltaire on the higher ground to the north is less fertile again, qualifying as a true, oligotrophic mountain loch.

Most eutrophic of all are the field and woodland edge pools with their wealth of yellow Iris and purple loosestrife, meadowsweet and hogweed, hemlock water dropwort and Angelica, which combine, in time, to convert them to marshes.

The headwater marsh of Loch Turraman had not, as yet, been colonised by the viable, fluff-borne reed seeds and resembled a northern quagmire. Below the northern dam was a remnant of wet alderwood which had probably extended back up the valley before the dam was built. The alders hosted nesting chaffinches, carrying caterpillars to their young, and the sallows and brambles resounded to the thin songs of willow warblers. The spillover followed the old stream course down to empty into Loch Fada.

Marginal rushes showed no mayfly exoskeletons, but were alive with the slender blue, black and buff forms of damselflies, too newly emerged to have attained the full colour of adulthood and not yet mating.

As always, the debris accumulated on the lee shore gave clues to the vegetation of hidden depths. Commonest were the delicate matted shoots of the aquatic form of bulbous rush *(Juncus bulbosus var. fluitans)*. Crisply translucent leaves of curled pondweed *(Potamogeton crispus)* were of the same bronze shade as the more solid floating leaves of the commoner bog pondweed *(Potamogeton polygonifolius)*. Tall aerated tufts of shoreweed had floated up from deeper water, showing their quite different form from the squat rosettes of the beaches.

Draped across the surface were pale aerated ribbon leaves of floating bur-reed *(Sparganium angustifolium)*, with narrower but similarly disposed ones of the common flote grass. Both pushed green flower heads above the surface. The burs on the former were the only parts linking this soft leaved aquatic with the sturdy and more familiar branched bur reed.

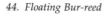

Floating club rush *(Scirpus (Eleogiton) fluitans)* shared the shallows in places with the bulbous rush, both with hair like leaves but the former with simpler flower spikes and pale green instead of the tawny shade of the other.

There were stands of spike rush *(Eleocharis palustris)* and smaller but more ornamental ones of bog bean in the peat stained water, with the odd clump of the more cosmopolitan greater water plantain. Bluish, five partite leaves of marsh cinquefoil encroached through the shallows, with forget-me-nots, kingcups and lesser spearwort.

44. *Floating Bur-reed*

The fringe of jointed and soft rushes was interrupted by yellow flags and budding meadowsweet, with the odd splash of pink provided by ragged Robin. Water level was high and some of the water mint was submerged. The soggy sward behind was carpeted with the button leaves of marsh pennywort in which grew star sedge *(Carex echinata)* and the common black sedge. The backdrop was brambly grass heath with white flowered marsh thistles and more of the ubiquitous eared sallow.

7. LOCH AN SGOLTAIRE

Loch an Sgoltaire north west of Kiloran is the most northerly, the higherst and the largest of the island lakes. It is studded with rocky islets and home to a thriving population of brown trout, the occasional two and a half pounder taking a fisherman's fly.

Enlarged over the years, it is dammed at both ends and falls away steeply below the northern dam to the cliffs of Urugaig. The original southern dam connecting a rocky knoll to either shore had recently been superceded by another to bring the level a metre or so higher, chilly waters in the newly submerged section lapping against dead, twiggy heather. Water is no longer required to power the water mill on the outlet stream – now a noble ruin tucked into a patch of woodland. It is burgeoning tourism which increases the need for conservation of the generous rainfall.

In times of drought several old stone piers protrude above water level. These were used for the retting of flax during the more self sufficient days of the last century when this crop was grown on the island. Laid out in bundles just below water level, the soft parts of the crop rotted away to facilitate extraction of the stem fibres. A drowned forest has also come to light – a relict of palmier days before the all pervading heather took over on these heights, although this may be no more than the relics of an old riparian strip of trees.

The climate potential for tree growth remains, most of the islets out of reach of wading cattle being bright with flowering rowan trees, these edged with the more sombre fruiting fluff of the sallows. Livestock, although sparse, account for the paucity of woody saplings on the mainland shore. Some of the non wooded islands are covered with bushy heather and bracken or bright with clumps of royal and broad buckler ferns.

A floating island was found to be composed almost entirely of the matted bases of royal fern, presumaly broken away from another island, as this palatable fern would not be expected to survive within the reach of livestock. Tangled roots and rhizomes will advance across the water surface in the manner of reedmace in the English broads and Sphagnum in the Welsh llyns.

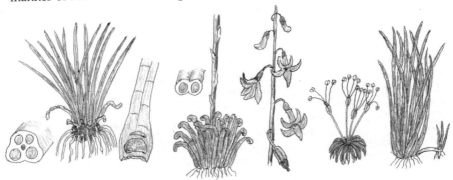

45. Quillwort, Water Lobelia and Shoreweed

67

Submerged ridges connecting adjacent islands become colonised by purple loosestrife and rushes.

Among dark, peat stained rhizomes washing ashore in little mounds of bubbly white foam were Lobelia and another special north western plant. This was quill-wort (Isoetes), superficially very similar to the shoreweed. In the rosettes of Lobelia the brittle leaves exuded a milky sap when broken and showed two air canals within. Quillwort leaves were cylindrical rather than flattened around four canals, longer, straighter and ending in sharp points.

Both types, like those of the underwater form of shoreweed, appeared succu-lent, but with contained air rather than water, Both are confined to impoverished, acid lakes, unlike shoreweed, whose dwarfed land form rosettes pressed close to the mud, thrive where cattle converge to drink or where gulls and water fowl come to preen and bathe.

Water Lobelia's leaves are short, slightly splaying, laterally flattened and with the tips bent sharply backwards in a little hook. The awl shaped leaves of quill-wort show a double row of septa demarcating the air sacs within, these visible through the delicate epidermis. These are the waterproof hatches that prevent the air compartments with their vital content of oxygen from flooding. Aerating tissue in shoreweed is in the form of a honeycomb. Difficult circumstances call for innovative responses!

Quillwort leaf bases bulge over an oval spore packet borne in their axils. These are not flowering plants like the other two but primitive fern allies, as are pillwort and the club rushes, surviving from ancient times in a few specialised habitats such as this.

Water Lobelia is an anomalous member of the harebell family. Its blue, two lipped flowers are born on stalks two feet or more long, to bring them above the water. Stem leaves are reduced to a few small white scales, the underwater photo-synthesis which remedies their inadequacy being possible only in waters as clear as these. Although sometimes stained like milkless tea, there are few suspended solids blocking light penetration.

Most special for us of the loch birds were red-throated divers, elegant on the water and magnificent in honking flight, but venturing only a few feet overland to nest. Three rose as we watched, circling repeatedly as they gained height before heading off south, possibly to feed in the shallows off the Strand where we saw some on another occasion.

Heron footprints appeared in fresh cow pats as well as mud beaches and a few tufted ducks idled around the islands, diving at intervals. Six Canada geese emerged from the undergrowth as we examined one of their feeding sites. These breed here. Few goose species winter here in large numbers, but big flocks of grey lag, pink footed and barnacle geese pass through at migration time – more, apparently, than before the RSPB opened the hospitality of Islay to them.

The recent invasion of Canada geese prefer to graze lush green grass. Their alimentary systems are not geared, like those of the red grouse, to chomping heather shoots. What could there possibly be for them here? In that rolling expanse of bushy brown heather the only green was alongside the paths or splaying tufts of wiry deer grass, which is eaten only by deer, which do not occur here to keep it in check. Perhaps both Canada geese and the whooper swans which winter here, reach down to pull up the softly non fibrous underwater rosettes.

Short grass, grazed or trodden beside the loch, was thickly strewn in selected sites with soft black dung sausages some 7 cm long and tipped at the hooked, 'walking stick' end with white uric acid- in the fashion of that of green woodpecker dung elsewhere. Their consistency, like that of self satisfied slugs, differed markedly from more fibrous remains left by overwintering geese. A similar comparison may be drawn between the leavings of cattle newly turned out to grass and their former offerings when feeding on hay and straw.

Killing of the heather by various means provided other green sites used by and maintained by geese, gulls and rabbits. With over use, these spots might disintegrate into bird slums. Common gulls nested by the loch and others came in to bathe and preen. They feed elsewhere, but favour the mounds for digesting, throwing up crop pellets and ejecting feces. Like those of kingfishers and owls, the crop pellets are rich in calcium carbonate. Not only little piles of fish bones were strewn around but also heaps of macerated blue-tinged mussel shells in a general mess of splashy white guano very different from the goose leavings.

Herons contributed little. Their alimentary systems, like those of buzzards, dissolve fish, frog and mammal bones, leaving only fur, feather and chitinous insect remains in the crop pellets to be recycled into the ecosystem.

Over the course of years, the combined phosphate, potash and nitrate brought into the system by the gulls, combined with the trampling of webbed feet, kills off the heather and opens the way for more palatable species. Among the ensuing grasses were green-ribbed sedge *(Carex binervis)* and field woodrush.

A goose loo, long past its vegetative peak, was a mass of crumbly black peat, sparsely clad with flowering pearlwort and water blinks, as in mounds in the skua colony of Stornoway on Lewis. Another, less worn, on an inshore islet, was of feather strewn grass and greater woodrush edged by meadowsweet. Run-off of excreta-charged drainage water nurtured soft shoreline growths of water pepper, often a species of trampled cattle drinking places.

Many of the greener mounds were shared by rabbits. These helped with the mowing and added their small quota of twice defecated dung pellets, with one of their characteristic plant followers, sheep's sorrel. These were social centres for the exchange of pheromones, as are more commonly used anthills.

46. *Gull Crop Pellets, fish bones and mussel shells*

8. UPLAND MOORS

The moorland leading up from the western shore of Loch an Sgoltaire to Beinn Bhreac is almost the highest on the island, but faces east and may be regarded as typical. The dominant ling forms deep, billowing masses leaving room for little else but dwarf eared sallow. Such growths are vulnerable to fire and the lower slopes between the water mill and the loch were a mosaic of burnt and unburnt patches. The succession after fire favoured tormentil as chief pioneer of the secondary succession. Bird's foot trefoil soon followed, both getting smothered as ling, fine-leaved heath and bracken recovered. Removal of vegetation without burning, as around the Strathclyde Water Department's Treatment Works, had given rise to an astonishing amount of lousewort exploiting the bare ground.

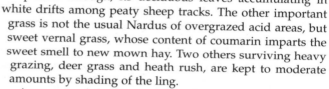

Purple moor grass pushes through, its deciduous leaves accumulating in white drifts among peaty sheep tracks. The other important grass is not the usual Nardus of overgrazed acid areas, but sweet vernal grass, whose content of coumarin imparts the sweet smell to new mown hay. Two others surviving heavy grazing, deer grass and heath rush, are kept to moderate amounts by shading of the ling.

A stony track leading up over the hill to the south was splashed with tiny orange-red discs of one of the cup fungi (*Melastiza chateri*), a small relative of the better known orange peel fungus, minutely fringed and stalkless.

47. Marsh Violet

The only flowers seen apart from tormentil and lousewort in the sparse grassy clearings were heath milkwort, heath speedwell, heath violet, marsh violet and a tiny purple flowered eyebright, probably *Euphrasia curta*, on a path. Boggy patches nurtured clumps of round-leaved sundew as well as butterwort, which is more widespread here.

Trickling water, often crowded with bog pondweed, may be bordered by depauperate gipsywort with the usual mint, spearwort and pennywort. Common yellow sedge (*Carex demissa*) and other sedges abound. Grass heaths on lower land are home to wild thyme and heath bedstraw, but the Sphagnum and Polytrichum moss of the uplands may persist.

There are valley bogs dominated by single headed and many headed cotton grass. One near the island centre. had recently been designated as an SSSI, chiefly on account of the rare moths which it harbours. Towards the farmhouses, where livestock pressure is greater, wet patches are likely to be dominated by yellow flags, their flowers crowded with small flies and smaller thrips in June. Disliked as food by all but horses, these flambuoyant growths escape grazing and crowd out most others apart from rushes and meadowsweet.

No peat deep enough to be used as a source of fuel is known – this deficiency adding significance to the endeavours of the generation that created the viable woodlands and saw mill.

The slopes of Beinn Bhreac and Beinn a Tuath yielded few birds on the occasion of our visit apart from the inevitable wheatears, some feeding young. One of the nesting pair of golden eagles was abroad, however, soaring majestically in the blue patches between rain showers. It was thrilling to watch it exploiting the air currents. So often these noble raptors lie low when there are folk about.

9. CLIFF FLORA

Sea cliffs in the vicinity of Pig's Paradise on the north west coast and eastwards to Uragaig are some of the highest on Colonsay and support the best sea bird colonies. They fall away in two tiers from one of the island's most elevated points, each tier involving a more or less vertical drop of well over a hundred feet with a considerable strip of moorland between.

Strata dip back inland, presenting their edges to Atlantic weathering to produce a fine series of bluffs, sometimes banded in different shades of grey, often contorted, with fine wrinkle folds zig-zagging across the exposures. Even well back from the sea these support sea spleenwort ferns as well as maidenhair and black spleenworts.

The double cliff seems sufficiently steep to be avoided by sheep and maintains a shrubby covering. An easy way down is taken by the valley of the main drainage stream, which cuts through the seaward facing brow above Loch an Sgoltaire. A flowery primrose path leads round the flank of the eastern hill for those not relishing the scramble down by the ferny watercourse that tumbles precipitately shorewards in parts. There is no shortage of hand holds on the lightly grazed thickets of ling, rowan and sallow.

Black crowberry invades the flora as the sea is approached. Towards the lower cliff line woody species are replaced by herbs. Then come blue swards of spring squills and pink ones of thrift. The two maritime plantains are present, along with ribwort, but seemed not to dominate, as so often in similar sites elsewhere.

48. *Black Crowberry*

The lower cliff is a splendid sight in early summer with a mixture of woodland and maritime plants alternating with sandstone faces and talus slopes. It is always a surprise to find primroses, first harbingers of spring from February on in the South, flowering on into July in the North. With the brighter gold of buttercups, they clothe the upper slopes, passing down into the more muted tones of red campion and bluebell and these to the more salt-worthy sea campion and bird's foot trefoil on drier outcrops.

The preponderence of woodland plants in these non wooded sites in the North suggests that the sea winds must be charged with moisture, or else the rainfall is sufficient to mitigate drying out. Lower temperatures would reduce evaporation.

Most spectacular is the roseroot *(Rhodiola (Sedum) rosea)*. Its succulence implies palatabilty, in contrast to some of the related stonecrops with acrid sap, and plants are confined to inaccessible crags and crevices. This beautiful and usually rare species is as common on these ancient rocks as in grikes between the clints of limestone pavement on the Burren and the Irish Arans.

The main stream spreads into a quagmire dominated by bog asphodel and butterwort where its bounding descent is checked on reaching the middle terrace. Marsh arrow grass borders pools brimming with bog pondweed. There are northern marsh orchids and early purple orchids here as well as the prevalent heath spotted orchids of the moors.

10. SEA BIRD CLIFFS

Otters are said to frequent the shore at Pig's Paradise, but we looked in vain for their spraints. Athletic as they are on land, it is doubtful if they ascend far up the tumbling stream. There are no mammalian predators – foxes, stoats or weasels – nor deer, grey squirrels or snakes on the island.

Birds abound, a hundred and fifty species having been recorded. Razorbills outnumber guillemots in sections of the cliffs visible from above, the latter seen only on slabs in the intertidal zone. The estimated number of the two together on Colonsay and Oronsay was around 15,000 to 20,000 pairs. Breeding tysties numbered around 50 pairs and we watched about thirty idling offshore with several hundred off duty razorbills, while more of the last thronged the small ledges. We saw no puffins and there were apparently few to see.

Fulmar petrels were nesting throughout, often on the upper cliff faces leaving the lower sites for herring gulls. Fulmars usually trouble little with nesting material and had been known recently to use old nests of both raven and hooded crows. Kittiwakes were much in evidence and a hundred or so used an island in Kiloran Bay further north as a daytime roost. They totalled some 3,000 pairs.

Herring gulls were commonest of the less pelagic gulls, lesser black backs the next and greater black backs are known to breed at eight different locations, common gulls at four. Inland sites carry two or three colonies of black-headed gulls. Recent counts for arctic terns suggested 225 to 250 pairs.

We think of gulls as creatures of the day rather than the night, but the summer nights were so brief here that they seemed to be abroad at any hour. The night time sorties, however. were carried out in eerie silence. in contrast to the honking activities of the daytime.

At 3.00 am on 26th June, in almost complete darkness, a few white forms flitted like barn owls past the Scalasaig Hotel on Colonsay. Gradually these alighted and more floated in, winnowing silently over the lawn until fifteen had settled, to quarter the sward systematically. They were evenly spaced, at more than their usual 'individual distance' as exemplified by those that cadge rides on ship's rails. Discipline was exemplary in these small hours, with none of the unmannerly squabbling that accompanies daytime feeding.

The flock acted as when after swarming ants, but it was too early for the ants' mating flight – and also for the cranefly hordes to be at their egg laying. They were probably hauling out earthworms, brought to the surface by the prevalent drizzle. Increasing light showed that three of the birds had darker backs but that all were the same size, showing them to be herring and lesser black-backed gulls rather than the more habitually grass feeding common gulls.

They left at 3.30 am as silently as they had come, slipping off into the gloom as the first oyster catcher began a tentative piping. Another quarter of an hour and a song thrush started heralding the dawn chorus, repeating himself to make sure that everyone heard. A lot later a blackbird materialised to tear the *Cydonia japonica* flowers to pieces, not for the insects that they contained, but to gulp down pieces of petal, probably for their sweet juices.

No shearwaters nest on Colonsay, but we had seen big numbers at sea as we approached the island from Oban for a 10.30 pm landing. The "Columba" nosed towards each swaying raft of several hundred birds, causing them to take flight, shearing low over the water in the manner that has given them their name. None were sighted until we emerged into the open sea south of Mull. These must have been birds from the thriving colony on Rhum. Small groups of storm petrels are said to breed along the west coast of Colonsay, visible above ground only at night.

Jackdaws were commonplace on the Pig's Paradise cliffs and choughs occurred on both sides of Kiloran Bay, one pair on the headland beyond Uragaig, another near the islet of Eilean Meall to the north-east. Blue rock doves, genetically untainted by racing pigeon blood, were also part of the cliff avifauna and have been seen as many as a hundred at a time when the post nuptial flocks gather.

The bird cliffs dip to beach level at Port nam Fliuchan to the east, where a steep strand of almost spherical grey pebbles harboured a few pairs of common gulls. Half grown youngsters trotted without hindrance over the obstacles and sought refuge among rocks to either side.

49. *Eider Duck and Ducklings*

It is in deep bays such as this and that at Port Sgibinis, that eider ducks bring their newly fledged young to learn the art of foraging in the absence of disruptive waves. Even so, the ducklings had to work harder than their dams to reach the same food source. When the ducks upended to probe the sea bed the ducklings had to dive, and this they did quite ineptly, with much splashy kicking of small webbed feet in empty air.

Even the least could be deflected ashore and change the mind of the whole flock, which seemed to have no appointed leader. They come to land at intervals, spending more time on wrack covered rocks than on wet sand – for the better foraging under the fronds. The small size of the families suggested a high mortality among the ducklings.

11. BEACH SUCCESSION AND URAGAIG FARM

The sea beach at Port nam Fliuchan east of Pig's Paradise grades imperceptibly into the series of raised beaches which connect the rock mass beyond to the main island. It is a jigsaw of closed turf and open pebbles at the top and is frequented by ruminating cattle as well as a nervous scattering of oyster catchers. The bay is at the narrow end of a wedge of consolidated pebbles, which rises and broadens eastwards to afford profitable farmland. Most zones are soil covered, sources of input being the cliff slopes to north and south and, possibly, the Kiloran sands to the east. The presumed isolation of the northern rock mass before the connecting beaches formed may have influenced the Pictish builders in their choice of the headland for the siting of their forts of Dun Uragaig and Dun Tealflaig.

A normal beach succession can be traced with increasing distance from the sea, first to grassland and then to arable land. Spear-leaved orache and cleavers or goose grass grew along the driftline of stranded wrack and tangle, passing back to an almost pure mat of silverweed with a few field thistles and curled dock plants.

These pebble pioneers graded into a sward of bent, fescue and Yorkshire fog, with ribwort and greater plantain, creeping buttercup and thistles. It was here at Uragaig that the rare Irish lady's tresses orchid (*Spiranthes romanzoffiana*) was discovered in 1930.

Bare pebble expanses were sometimes threaded with the creeping runners of large etiolated silverweed plants pushing up from deep down – a growth form quite different from the lower mats. Overturning of pebbles was not a major deterrent to plant colonisation here if their upper sides had been exposed to the light for long enough to have developed a covering of dark, crustose lichens. These disintegrate if deprived of light, adding their small quota to the buried humus. The persistence of bare pebble banks on even the hundred year old raised beaches, however, shows what a slow process this can be.

50. Irish Lady Tresses Orchid

Once the mat phase is reached the turf is consolidated by clovers and bird's foot trefoil, chlorotic pearlwort and mouse ear chickweed, field daisies, yarrow and common meadow grass. Only buck's horn plantain and scurvy grass hint at the maritime origin. Trickling streams and niches where driftwood collects increase diversity.

Despite the stony substrate, this is one of the few areas where we saw arable land. Most of the fields were of bare soil but one showed a spring sown cereal crop and another had already had a silage crop taken.

The one of paramount interest in pointing to the hazards of farming such terrain was where superfluous pebbles had been raked into parallel lines, parodying hay swathes. A tractor towing a small open trailer crept slowly along each row while a man forked the stones into the trailer – leaving quite a few behind. This was back breaking work. We hoped the two men changed places occasionally.

The loads of stones scraped from among the seedling corn were used to fill potholes in the track leading away over a shoulder to connect with the island's loop road. In times past the island had supported as many as a thousand souls, with every possible tract of land brought under the spade or plough. The ribbed contours of abandoned lazy beds were still to be seen in places, some of them so inhospitable to higher plant life as to have become blanketed by yellow Sphagnum moss.

There were still free range hens and yarded orphan lambs about, as then. Kiloran Farm boasted at least one fine ginger Tamworth pig, whose bacon was afforded added flavour with the dregs from the hotel's beer kegs. The farm sheepdog tied to the fence with binder twine while his master toiled at the pebbles, submitted good naturedly to being untangled by strangers. The house cat wove faithfully between his mistress's feet as she weeded her cottage garden.

The shoulder of land crossed by the track probably formed an effective barrier to sand blowing in from the Kiloran machair system which is, in any case, to leeward. This raises the vexed question as to where the pebble infill originated, and why it settled so haphazardly to leave some tracts bare and some buried.

The exuberance of growth on this rock barrier indicates that exposure is not another inhibiting factor. Steep birch woodland below the track was bright with tall flowering rowan and Rhododendron. Beneath were early purple orchids, bluebells, red campion, primroses and buttercups, as on open cliffs.

Pignut, red clover, germander speedwell and yellow rattle characterised the lowlands beyond and coloured the roadside sward all the way to Kiloran Woods, with an exuberance more like that of a Devon lane than a Hebridean island. Most of the foxgloves had been left behind on the slates with the Rhododendrons, as the infiltrating shell sands neutralised the inherent soil acidity.

12. KILORAN AND BALNAHARD RAISED BEACHES

On the other side of Kiloran bay, under the towering Carnan Eoin, the island's highest point at 470 feet, are more raised beaches, ascending in a series of tiers. These are probably the most obvious on the island, some still of bare pebbles, some vegetated but maintaining their sharp edged terrace structure.

The Balnahard Farm track, after traversing the back of the machair, climbs sharply through the northern col between the sandstone of Carnan Mor and the caves inhabited by early man in the slates to seaward. Paired strips of ribbed concrete overlay the sand and gravel on the steepest section, but the passage of vehicles in bad weather must be fraught with difficulties. A cleft on the inland side contained a quite well grown native aspen and some wind shorn hawthorns. A lot of pungently scented sweet gale or bog myrtle *(Myrica gale)* dots the adjacent moorland.

51. Bog Myrtle   Descending in more gentle curves, the rocky panorama opens out onto a different world. The heather clad bluffs and cotton grass hollows give way abruptly to shelf after shelf of green grass or silver stones, extending back round the corner to the right into green fields of sown perennial ryegrass, cocksfoot and clover with a sprinkling of buttercups and daisies.

All resounded to the repetitive calling of corncrakes. These birds, so rare now on a national basis, were down to three or four breeding pairs here. They are well named *Crex crex*, because this sound is usually the only sign of their presence. One senses that the scientific pundits who named them, so often bogged down in latin or Greek epithets, had tongue in cheek when this so onomatopoeic name was coined. Twenty three jackdaws cawed back from the opposite slope.

Tucked in behind the old beaches was a great natural basin hemmed in by high hills on three sides and comprising the bulk of the farm fields. Viewed from the elevated track, this flat well watered area, liberally strewn with rushes, had fairly obviously been entrapped from a former sea inlet. The barrier of pebbles now separating it from Port Sgibinis south of Eilean Meall is formidable, that from Port an Obain to the north less so, and possibly representing a later connection with the sea on this part of the north west coast. The broad headland between these two bays to seaward of the raised beach system is a replica of that to seaward of the Uragaig raised beaches and both were the chosen home of choughs.

The hills are set further back across the island at Balnahard. Lowland behind the innermost tallest, and presumably oldest beach ridge, must once have formed a lagoon, silting gradually with marine sediments as the growing storm beach eliminated wave scour. Salinity would be lost as the sea withdrew to form first a brackish and then a freshwater lake, leading on to today's rushy hollow. Instead of a mere infilling behind the suspected former island as at Urugaig, this seems to have been more of a tombola, a spit with the sea infiltrating behind before closure of the entrance. No trace of blown sand was apparent among the pebbles, which were banked against parent rock to north and south.

An interesting profile had been exposed during the digging of a silo pit . Uppermost was a depth of about half a metre of large sea-rounded pebbles underlain by a similar depth of small pebbles, grading downwards into gravel, shingle and sand, in which an opportunist rabbit had found it convenient to burrow. The transition between the zones was quite sharp, representing different wave strengths at the times of deposition.

The silo was floored with concrete and lined with heavy timber, looking like old railway sleepers in lieu of the Rousay flagstones commonly used on Orkney. The inner, airtight lining of black polythene had been folded over the silage , held down by old tyres pending the arrival of the next consignment.

Underlying gritty sand, both here and where road stone had been excavated, was pink with angular fragments of quartz and silica and none of the shell flakes characteristic of the machair sands. Nor did the bays to north and south show any of the yellow shell sand which blows inland at Kiloran. There it was silty and grey, pebble strewn in parts and not subject to wind blow.

Pebbles banked against the bedrock along the south side of the basin are aligned at right angles to the main series of raised beaches and must have been fringing beaches round an old shoreline before the growing shingle spits deflected the natural accretion. Sea rounded pebbles do not lend themselves to wall building as readily as do angular rocks and as fertility increased field boundaries were constructed of post and wire.

A stream seeping from the base of a pebble clifflet was heavily charged with ferric iron and spread over the current beach in a sludge of iron bacteria and orange iron hydroxide. Sea mayweed on the pebbles merged into a more mature community of thirty two species including bulbous buttercups, which need an input of minerals, and change to common meadow buttercups with distance from the sea. Yellow trefoil and white clovers took over as ground cover from the more coastal silverweed in maturing potential farmland. Elsewhere the generous spillage of field daisies dwindled with dwindling sand and the whole graded into grass heath.

Where unclad pebbles intruded between strips of mature sward dandelions , hawkbits and plantains with long, anchoring taproots did best in holding on to the mobile substrate, with sparse mats of biting stonecrop, thyme and eyebright. Sheep and cattle found a certain amount of bite here, slaking their thirsts in clear waters decorated with lady's smock and marsh bedstraw. The mystery remains. Why do some areas persist as bare pebbles so much longer than others?

A row of what appears to be half excavated stone circles 3 – 4 metres across occurs near the crest of one of the older beaches. Their rims of piled stones afforded shelter for livestock and are partially engulfed in nettles and bracken. They may have been old

52. *Wheatears*

shielings, possibly used as sheep fanks, or pits from which road stone had been taken, but their alignment and spacing pointed to something more significant archeologically.

The farm rubbish tip nearby must be one of the most attractive to be found anywhere. Fringed by cushions of sea pinks and drapes of creeping willow, the brink is overshadowed by slopes strewn with primroses, bluebells, campion and old iron under bracken and sorrel. Snowy white fulmars nested among the debris, wheatears chinked from discarded farm machinary and skylarks trilled jubilantly over a scene where almost every prospect pleased. Municipal dustmen do not function so far from the madding crowd and indestructible bric-a-brac can be made use of by the island's innovative animal life, including invertebrates seeking comfortable quarters.

Had the prehistoric inhabitants of the nearby caves in the vicinity of Columba's Well not left their kitchen middens behind, we should know less of their way of life. This midden could give archeologists of the future tremendous fun. Another relic on the shore hereabouts was the carcase of a stranded whale, subjected to the elements for forty years but still largely intact.

The farm buildings, as so often when land is at a premium, clung to the lower slopes of the old cliff line behind the alluvial basin. At the end of the big barn was the round house, typical of Colonsay farms, where cart horses revolved around a central pivot threshing the corn. The process was simpler here than in Orkney, where cogs connected with a rotating horizontal axis passing through into the barn to drive a threshing drum. Here the corn was simply trampled from the husks by the great hooves, for subsequent winnowing in the wind.

The water table was still inconveniently high in the entrapped basin and ditches had been dug deep to drain off the excess. Moorland mud crowfoot (*Ranunculus omiophyllus*) shared them with broad-leaved pondweed and marsh yellow cress. The mud crowfoot was formerly used as one of the main ingredients of poultices, the soft plants pounded between stones. Other members of the buttercup family are rich in alkaloids and have found various uses in medicine through the ages.

An extract from lesser spearwort had been used locally as a substitute for rennet in cheese making. The not too distantly related white water lilies of Loch Fada became the source of a black dye for colouring wool and yarn, the pigment obtained by cutting up the massive rhizomes from beneath the mud and boiling them.

Marsh horsetail encroached onto the ditches with Iris, meadowsweet and marsh foxtail grass. Foxglove and yellow sedge pointed to developing acidity, but superphosphate bags stacked by the silo suggested that the better quality pastures were getting a little extra help.

13. MORE ABOUT RAISED BEACHES

The raised beaches west of Scalasaig were seen only in passing, but were readily recognisable for what they were. They consisted of separate terraces banked against the 412 feet high Beinn nan Caorach, whose slope formed the old sea coast when they were being laid down. Parts of even the older, upper ones were still almost wholly unvegetated. The lower ones through which the road has been cut, were flat topped and sharp edged, grassed and carrying livestock.

These may have fared better than the upper ones because of the proximity of the machair sand around the back of Tobar Fuar in the case of the Kilchattan beaches and of Port Mor for those further north. Even if the flakes of shell sand have disappeared from the soil profile, their calcium carbonate content must have leached to lower levels to help the general well being of the whole. The presence of the Dun Meodbonach fort, the standing stones of Lower Kilchattan and the ruined chapel between the two, prove a long history of occupation.

Two conflicting forces were at work in the shaping of the coast after ice ages. Sea level rose all over the world as the melted ice was added, but it fell, or appeared to fall, as the land began to ease back into position after its compression from the former weight of ice. Northern lands, which had been most heavily burdened, show the greatest compensatory rise and in Scotland the land rose faster than the sea, and is still rising in relation to Southern England. This isostatic change becomes slight south of a line from the Humber to the Mersey.

The old 'driftlines in stone' were deposited during the quiescent periods of uneasy status quo, which allowed time for wave-borne pebbles to accumulate before the sea withdrew to leave them high and dry. The presence of the higher, pre-glacial, beaches is not quite so easily explained. Why did the grinding passage of subsequent ice not scrape them away, as it did so much else? Or were they west of the advancing ice edge?

J.A.Steers in the "New Naturalist" classic *The Sea Coast*, 1962, states:- "In northern Scotland there are beaches up to a hundred feet above present sea level. These are all probably late or post glacial and represent local isostatic movements. The pre glacial beaches at about 120 feet in the Treshnish Isles, Mull, Islay and Colonsay are still a puzzle."

J.B.Whittow, writing in 1977, maintains that certain rock platforms at the foot of sea cliffs were ice-scraped and had glacial till deposited on them before the beach pebbles began to accumulate, thus proving the intervention of a glacial period between the cutting of the platform and the stacking of the pebbles. Some think that late glacial seas were already piling pebbles on these ice-free platforms of the west coasts of the islands while the east coasts were still locked in the grip of the continental ice sheet.

14. DUNES AND MACHAIR

The sandy pasture known as machair is less well developed in the Inner Hebrides than in the Outer but here, as there, almost all is along the west coast, except for the little at Balranald in the north. At Ardskenish in Colonsay's south-west, sand extends inland from the head of the bay containing the extensive Traigh nam Barc Beach and continues westwards across a headland to join the coast again at Squidel an Leanna.

Due west of Scalasaig, between the raised beaches of Machrins and Kilchattan, is more sandy pasture. This accommodates the island's air strip and the hundred year old golf course, whose short velvety turf is claimed to be self sustaining, even in the absence of grazing sheep, needing neither mowing nor watering.

Wind exposure alone is regarded as responsible for the even texture. Extreme wind exposure on most grassland, however, gives rise to the phenomenon of 'waved heath', where the grass is whisked up into peaks and troughs, which induce turbulence at the ground surface and would be very difficult to roll a golf ball across! True, a plank or other windbreak will allow grass to grow long in its shelter, but this may be partly due to the shading factor and the deflection of animal grazing and human treading. Whichever, it is is good news for the groundsmen that it is so.

The Kiloran Bay machair terminates above the beach in a steep, eroding sand face and has various blow-outs further inland, unconnected by wind funnels to the expanse of sand that uncovers at low tide. Sandhills are low and uneven, not aligned in ridges, and the rolling, ice smoothed rock surface is not far below in places – as can be seen where the major stream cuts down to bedrock near its mouth.

Floristically it is uninteresting, less diverse and less colourful the those of the Uists and other Outer Isles. Dwarf field daisies, which are well able to push up above a complete covering of sand, were the only flowers at all abundant during our midsummer visit. A pointer to the rate of build up can be seen in the partially rotted bracken rhizomes up to a metre below current sand level – much deeper than they would have had need to descend in life. Some such were devoid of bracken at the time, in others the fronds were sparse or dwarf.

There was, however, little evidence that sand was still building up, the pioneering marram grass being seldom as robust as it becomes when pushing up through new increments of this and we saw neither tall dunes nor new foredunes advancing across the beach. Typical plants were soldierly lines of sand sedge shoots sprouting from long, straight underground rhizomes and that most typical of sand dune mosses *(Tortula ruraliformis)*. Drop a morsel of liquid onto a dried up mat of this and each little leaf rosette uncoils and spreads as by magic, assuming a fresh green colour in an instant.

Thyme, eyebright, milkwort, pearlwort and fairy flax, none much taller than the moss, were among the few managing to flower. Others which might well have done with a slight alleviation of grazing were yellow lady's bedstraw, harebell, dovesfoot cranesbill, common storksbill, dog violet and yarrow.

Stream water flowed fast and clear beneath vertical sand cliffs over a bed of pebbles. Blanket weed occurred where it had cut down to bedrock. Once free of the land, the water spread in a broad swathe across the beach, attracting hosts of gulls to drink, bathe and preen as the tide and its salty taint ebbed away.

53. Doves-foot Cranesbill

Three spined sticklebacks were present among the underwater beetles, while Gyrinus whirligig beetles pirouetted over the surface film among more sober minded Vellea water crickets.

On the hindmost dune the water crowfoot was the inland *Ranunculus aquatilis* agg. with big flowers and large dissected leaves. Towards the frontal dunes, in shallower water used by livestock, it was the brackish water *Ranunculus baudotii v. marina*, with smaller flowers and more abbreviated tufts of leaves. Neither produced circular floating leaves.

Fools watercress was the chief water plant in the upper reaches with the common water moss *Fontinalis antipyretica*, which tolerates a certain degree of brackishness when growing in association with the common green Enteromorpha weed of the shore. Two species of water starwort and Canadian pondweed mingled with true watercress, while broad-leaved Potamogeton pondweed occurred throughout, lapping about the culms of upstanding reed canary grass.

ORONSAY

15. THE STRAND BETWEEN COLONSAY AND ORONSAY. SALTMARSH

The sea enters the Strand between the two islands along two channels in the west and one in the east overshadowed by the beetling brow of Hangman's Rock. That prominent feature is formed by a bed of harder sandstone jutting from the slaty seaward flank of Beinn Eibhe, which rises to 321 feet. The basalt dyke passed on this same eastern side near where the Strand road terminates at high water mark, crops out again to the east alongside the expanse of tidal sand. The road across is only marginally above high tide mark and occupies an old raised beach surface.

Surprisingly the eastern saltings are more colourful in midsummer than is the machair. Levelling out at mid tide, they suit the growth of thrift, the great spread of pink flowers here not paler than those on the cliffs, as they so

54. Sea Milkwort or Black Saltwort

often are on saltmarshes. The usual downshore zone of salt lovers was replaced here by shifting, rippled sand, too mobile to be colonised.

The sward is closely grazed by sheep and rabbits, whose dung pellets form sinuous driftlines. Close investigation showed that much beside the thrift was flowering, but the flowers were sunk deep in the sward, out of harm's way and almost invisible except, hopefully, to the pollinating insects. Such were scurvy grass, sea milkwort and sea plantain which straggled between pebbles strayed from the raised beach.

The thrift zone terminates seaward in a rounded bank about a foot high, neither fading into the sands nor being cut back by the sea. Woolly yellow-green tangles of the alga *Rhizoclonium implexum* are intertwined and the whole becomes littered with drifted wracks and the vacated shells of limpets and mussels from the bordering rocks.

So much fresh water seeps out of the slates and beach deposits to landward, that the middle zone of the marsh is dominated by an essentially brackish species, the mud rush *(Juncus gerardi)*. Its wiry leaves are characteristically ginger tipped and are a darker green than the accompanying red fescue grass. It favours slight depressions around pans, pools and creeks, often with sea arrow grass *(Triglochin maritima)*. Grazing inhibits flowering of the fescue. The few shoots that manage to do so splay out over the pool surfaces to maintain the minimal height adopted by the rest.

Freshwater pools higher up are home to yellow Iris, Eleocharis spike rush and soft rush, in spite of inundation by the highest tides – as shown by the drifted seaweed and crab carapaces – yet still the whirligig beetles were pursuing their little lives in the fast lane. Silverweed came next, then grasses and clovers and finally bog cotton and cross-leaved heath.

Brackish shore pools on the south-west coast were found by Murdoch McNeill in 1910 to contain stonewort (Chara), a normally freshwater alga, tassel pondweed (Ruppia) of more brackish sites, and Tolypella, another, much rarer, member of the stonewort family of algae.

16. THE STRAND BETWEEN THE TIDES

For several hours each side of low spring tides Oronsay is accessible from Colonsay afoot, across a mile of sand which never dries out completely. This mile, connecting the truncated ends of the lane to either side, is almost the longest possible crossing, but it is the shallowest. Channels to either side of the islet set in the western entrance need a boat, as does that through which the tide enters from the east at Poll Gorm.

This deep eastern pool was the location of an oyster farm, the chief indications of which, as we splashed across through the chilly falling tide, being a series of orange buoys. It was intriguing to see how they were reared, but we all fought shy of the squidgy 'oysters on the hoof' that appeared on the morrow's menu, preferring the venison.

Another product here was the squat lobster *(Munida rugosa)*, red and blue striped and with long questing arms. Most squat lobsters live in deeper waters and the animals more likely to find their way into shoreline crab pots were aesop or king prawns (*Pandanus montagui*), which are served up as langoustine.

People have always lived here, partly from the sea. Conger eels were a favourite of Neolithic man on Oronosay and their remains have been found in ancient middens. They probably hunted them inshore. Modern fishermen seek them from low water down to about 680 metres, where those sinuous predators hid among rocks by day but rose to the surface at dusk in pursuit of fish and squid.

The crossing of the Strand. unlike the more heavily used one to Lindisfarne in Northumberland, is not surfaced and has no guide posts, but a rocky reef stands in as an 'escape tower' near the half way point. One steers for this headland, then for the barely discernible white mark painted on the cliff opposite. Too much deviation may land the traveller in something approaching quicksand, these soft patches occurring where freshwater springs surface from the depths. Midsummer it might be but the water was bitterly cold and we made the knobbly crossing earlier than we need have done on the falling tide. Only the two overseas members of the party, having heard much of the British weather pattern, were furnished with gum boots. Stretches long abandoned by the tide, remained as a mosaic of puddles, but the chief hazard was the layer of empty cockle shells embedded edgeways on, to cause maximum discomfort to the frozen soles in transit.

Vehicles made the crossing, as there was still an inhabited farmstead on Oronsay, and we were passed on our return paddle by a little red Royal Mail van with four passengers in the back. The sands are more easily negotiated than the rough terrain round about – even the saltmarsh, with its stabilising thrift, being dissected by creeks, so that any road would need to be surfaced. Perhaps by now it is. A subsidiary track curved westward over the flats from the Colonsay road to return to the same shore and ascend to the Garvard Standing Stones. This track was marked by small boulders, the sand alongside being somewhat treacherous.

The Strand flats were tinged a pale grey with organic matter but were black with anaerobically produced sulphides just below. They supported an apparently endless population of lugworms. Each worm inhabits a vertically aligned U shaped burrow, marked at the intake by a sizable dimple in the sand and at the hind end by a worm cast. To shoreward these were small. Out in the middle the discarded 'excreta' (from which the edible organic matter had been removed) were twice as wide and often radiated straight from the burrow instead of coiling into a neat pile like an earthworm cast.

The bivalves of the sand were replaced by an accumulation of periwinkle shells along the further shore, which is rocky with no saltmarsh. Islets visited on the way back provided a diversity of marine life, with shrimp pools, edible sea urchins, grey top shells, known locally as 'silver Tommies', isolated limpets, gregarious mussels, acorn barnacles and a host of others. Lobsters could be found among the rocks.

Moon jellyfish, characterised by the four purple arcs of the gonads, had become stranded and there was a good variety of

55. *Moon Jellyfish*

82

seaweeds. Some of the big oarweeds supported exquisite little blue-rayed limpets (*Patina pellucida*), which lose the translucent blue rays as they mature. Some of the bigger weeds brought in by the tides had acted as sails for quite large rocks. Bootlace weed, with thongs many metres long, had swirled in from the depths to coil around spongy green branches of Codium.

Two Arctic terns were defending nest territory on an islet off Oronsay against a gull, which they evidently supposed was loitering with intent. This ducked each time it was dive bombed, the head hunched safely down between the shoulder blades. The jabbing beak was a defiant but abortive gesture, always too late to be effective. It was not long before it was sent about its business.

Two oyster catchers defended their home plot, one of the pair returning doggedly to perch on a handy post after each disturbance by a member of our party, which had become widely dispersed picking the most favoured route back. Other 'pied pipers' more provident, concentrated on the vast, underused food potential of the long shoreline.

56. Shelducks

A rhythmic sound, between that of winnowing swan and goose wings, heralded the passage overhead of three red-throated divers, flying west with necks outstretched, headed for the oyster farm, which was apparently one of their favourite foraging sites. Great northern divers, common in winter, were away in the North between June and October.

Later a red-breasted merganser headed across in the same direction. This species breeds around Oronsay and along the west coast of Colonsay. Shelduck, most handsome of all, were also about, disappearing only for a short spell in autumn when they went away to moult. Ringed plover bred here and were said to build up to a considerable flock in winter.

17. ORONSAY, NORTH COAST

Oronsay is mostly low lying, its highest hill, Beinn Oronsay, being in the northwest, where it frowns down from a height of 304 feet on the priory ruins and farm to its immediate south. The island occupies about 2,000 acres, hilly in the north, pastoral and bordered by dunes in the south. It was virtually treeless with the exception of a few scrubby willows and elders.

Eilean nan Ron at its extreme southern tip is surrounded by reefs which provide a breeding ground for grey Atlantic seals. These can be seen off the island shores at any time of the year, along with sandbank frequenting common seals.

The rough pastureland was grazed by cattle, showing traces of Hereford, Shorthorn and Highland stocks, the rougher hill grazings by sheep. No 'improved' grass or arable land was seen from the road to the priory (the only part visited because of restrictions imposed by the tide).

Most of the underlying rock is mudstone or sandstone. Only at the point of crossing does it differ. Here the eastern strand cuts into an east to west outcrop of coarser sandstone which occupies the north-west corner of Oronsay and curves on to reappear in south-west Colonsay. This produces an interesting shoreline of little caves and columns, with compressed folds cut through sectionally and coloured as though the Creator had doodled across the surface with a half dry brush dipped in sienna and ultramarine. Well protected from both the Atlantic and the Firth of Lorne, the cliffs supported a riot of seaweed. Long fleshy fronds of shelter-loving egg wrack extended well out and had been macerated along a broad swathe by farm vehicles hugging the base of the cliffs – an unusual hazard for intertidal plants.

Shelter from offshore tern islets minimised the splash zone so there was little thrift above the littoral belt of channel wrack, the vegetation passing quickly up to land plants. White crustose Lecanora lichens clothed the cliff foot tumble of boulders with black inksplash ones but there was no orange lichen band. Nor was the shaggy, spray loving Ramalina able to colonise in such profusion as on more exposed sites.

With so little spray, the sandstone bore no maritime flora and it was bird's-foot trefoil which occupied low crevices. Rocky shelves leading back from the beach collected and retained soil slipped from the heathery slopes above to nurture bracken. Underneath were bluebells and sweet vernal grass, punctuated by little eared sallows.

In soil too shallow for the brake, and thus avoiding its shade, was a more muted blue carpet of spring squill. Mat grass and tormentil shared sheep-grazed knolls. The backs of some of the smaller bays were walled off to deter livestock from wandering out over the almost limitless beach where they might be caught by the tide, although cattle had free access where the track struck inland. These bayheads were bright with yellow Iris and creeping buttercup, in lieu of the often seen kingcups, these bordered by foxgloves and rowan saplings.

The ascent from the sands over finer textured mudstone was achieved through a quagmire of bog cotton and moor grass. Heath spotted orchids thrust up from the brown ooze in places, these in all shades from white to deep magenta. Only here did we see the fringed flowers of ragged robin. Lousewort was particularly ebullient among milkwort, heath bedstraw and hard fern.

18. THE PRIORY PRECINCTS

Lowland bog, upland heath and central loch occupy the rising ground, which commands fine views to the string of islands running parallel to the south-east coast beyond Caolas Mor – the northernmost with its own raised beach sited at the northern tip.

The ground was drier here, offering tumps of purple moor grass and tufted hair grass to the sure-footed – also patches of bracken, which avoids waterlogging and is a good guide to comfortable walking in such terrain. There was fluff-puffing creeping willow, down-drifting marsh thistle and vermilion spreads of the two sorrels, later to be dotted with the blue balls of devil's bit scabious. Mountain everlasting mingled with thyme, English stonecrop and heath speedwell on dry tumps obligingly disposed to afford comfortable viewing.

Rank, tussocky sedge moor, subject to seasonal flooding dipped towards a sizable pool where the track swept around to the west. The bog pondweed sward fringed by Eleocharis spike rush formed a focal point for the small population of waders and water fowl.

Plants in drainage ditches are cyclic, depending on how recently they have been cleared and some of the earliest colonists are invertebrates – either midge larvae or worms – which build close-set mud tubes on the channel floor, like the stubs of a desecrated water nymph forest. That these are an important food source for birds was shown by the many footprints and beak incisions. Bronze Carabid beetles, as big as the familiar violet ground beetle, scuttled over the banks, despite the rain, and there were plenty of other prey items.

Twenty eight plant species were spotted in the ditches, including two specialities, both of the primrose family. These were brookweed, which tolerates a certain saltiness, and pink bog pimpernel – a frequenter of coastal dunes as well as hill bogs. Red rattle or marsh lousewort was another of interest.

Floating clubrush, commoner in lakes, appeared in the older successions with the floating form of bulbous rush, jointed and sharp-flowered rushes, water starwort and mud crowfoot. Water blinks, water purslane and bog stitchwort, belonged to the earlier, open phases: marsh bedstraw, water forget-me-not and lesser spearwort to later ones. A transitional belt of 'non peat' plants had colonised soil excavated from holes now occupied by rainbow-hued water, coloured by minerals seeped from the parent clay.

57. *Marsh Bedstraw*

Priory and farm are side by side at the head of the long western inlet of Port na Luinge. This area had suffered the presence of man for a long time – ever since St. Columba was said to have landed on Oronsay on his way from Ireland to Iona in the sixth century – this the most important event in the history of the island. Masonry below the small cross on the east side of the priory dates from then, the rest from the fourteenth century. (St. Columba is credited with having emulated St. Patrick here by banishing all snakes, as he did on arrival at Iona.)

A tall Celtic cross rises in the graveyard. This and the cloister alongside rank among Scotland's finest ancient ecclesiastical buildings. Thirty splendid tombstones with intricate carving, gathered into the prior's house date from the fifteenth and sixteenth centuries. In stark contrast to this ancient tranquility was the occasional activity on Oronsay's airstrip occupying the smooth greensward nearby.

The priory walls had been cleared recently of their plant life by some non-botanical well wisher, but had subsequently recovered some of their former interest. The chief colonist, unexpectedly, was sea campion, flowering both inside and out, a few plants affected by purple anther smut fungus (*Ustilago violacea*). The greatest rarity was lesser meadow rue, not living up to its epithet of minus and possibly strayed from the sands to westward.

Surprising, as a meadow plant, was ox-eye daisy. More to be expected were wall speedwell, yellow stonecrop, very likely dependent on the limey mortar, sea spleenwort and the draped ivy. Maidenhair spleenwort, wall rue and polypody ferns provided an elevated grazing ground for the big garden snails which marched among them on their stomachs, enjoying the deluging rain.

The priory lawns, inside and out, had not been mown recently and were spangled with tall field daisies as well as raindrops. The more domesticated sown sward of hay grasses was rich in clovers, red, white and yellow. Opportunist annuals such as scarlet pimpernel and hairy bitter cress reflected the proximity of the farmyard, composites with wind-borne, parachuted seeds, had strayed further afield. Elegant interlopers were lesser celandine and lacy pignut.

Powder fine sands, as white as they come, soaring larks in full song and black and white ringed plovers trotting over the beaches during a lull in the rain, made this lonely outpost one of the most evocative of the twinned islands. The little waders stay on through the summer to breed and it was suspected that a few members of the golden plover flock which wintered here might also remain through the summer, but nesting had yet to be proved.

19. ORONSAY BIRDS

Heavy rain is not conducive to good bird spotting but half a dozen lapwings were wailing and wheeling around the half way pool and wild duck erupted sporadically from the rank vegetation alongside. McNeill, writing in 1910, stated that these were joined by pintails in winter, but these had now dwindled to rare migrant status. The winter flocks of barnacle and grey lag geese to which he refers, still come, several hundred of the former, fewer of the latter, but large flocks of both on passage.

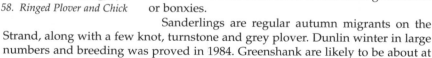

White-fronted and pink-footed geese also pass by en masse, but do not linger. Brent geese, which formerly wintered, are seldom seen at any time. Small numbers of gadwall visit Oronsay in winter, when more mallard come in to join the residents. Common scoter and wigeon are occasionally seen offshore. Cormorants sat around on the reefs. Many years before Arctic skuas had bred on Oronsay, now they merely visited in summer – a little more often than did the great skuas or bonxies.

58. *Ringed Plover and Chick*

Sanderlings are regular autumn migrants on the Strand, along with a few knot, turnstone and grey plover. Dunlin winter in large numbers and breeding was proved in 1984. Greenshank are likely to be about at any time except midsummer.

Families of wheatears called from the rain sodden hills and skylarks sang at Heaven's gate, despite the downpour. A twite indulged repeatedly in its distinctive song flight from the telegraph line linking the lonely farm to the outside world. It produced a series of harsh 'tweeps' as it ascended, then a smoother more fluid sequence on the descending flight, when the deeply forked tail was much in evidence. There were the inevitable meadow pipits and pied wagtails but most of the bird life was probably lying low.

The name Oronsay (local spelling Oransay) is derived from the old Norse and means "Ebb Tide Island". As ebb tide is the very time when it is not an island, "Full Tide Island" might have been more appropriate.

The lowest springs fall in the middle of the day, only the lowest but not very low neaps are conveniently at the beginning and end of the daylight hours, to enable a visit to be prolonged from one tidal cycle to the next. Many parts of the island are thus seldom visited and wildlife can pursue its activities almost unaware of the human presence. On Colonsay, visitor pressure was beginning to pose a problem in parts, so great are its attractions for the discerning tourist.

Oronsay's wildlife may, indeed, be freer from human interference now than it was at the dawn of the human era, when itinerant groups of *Homo sapiens* sought out this inaccessible retreat to escape the attentions of warring neighbours. Remote, sea girt Oronsay, with its wealth of getatable beaches for foraging, would have proved a lucky discovery, with edible wildlife, plants as well as birds and sea mammals, an added incentive to settlement.

Mesolithic remains from some of Scotland's oldest inhabitants have been found in the dunes backing its spacious beaches. The people then in residence, some eight thousand years ago, are known to us as Strand-loopers, Azilian folk who lived by hunting and fishing along the shore. Their sandhill middens of bones and mussel shells included skeletal remains of the now long extinct great auk, that was finally anihilated by hungry sailors long after the strandloopers' time.

People lived in that same early period on the site of Oban, in seashore caves now lifted forty feet above the tides, along with the beach – the post glacial raised beach that now accommodates Oban's Victorian Esplanade!

III

The Slate Islands of Nether Lorn. Seil, Easdale and Luing

1. LANDSCAPE

This complex of islands lies off the west coast of Scotland some ten to twelve miles south of Oban and is separated from the much larger island of Mull to the north-west by the Firth of Lorn, which merges with Loch Linnhe leading into the Great Glen.

Seil (pronounced Seal) is linked to the mainland by road in the north and to the island of Luing by car ferry in the south. The smaller Easdale Island to the west is linked to Seil by a small ferry boat and the even smaller island of Ellan-beich by a spit of waste slate discarded from past quarrying. Other islands in this complex which were not visited are Shuna, Scarba, Lunga and the Garvel-lachs.

The region of Nether Lorn in the South-west Highlands embraces mainland and islands, a jigsaw of land and sea, mountain ridges and wave-washed reefs, freshwater lochs and salty sounds. It borders the lower (southern) shore of the Firth of Lorn, the 'Nether' used as in the Low Countries of the Netherlands.

There are eight slate islands, but part of three of these are excluded on geolog-ical grounds and even those where the country rock is a genuine slate, are shot through by dykes of foreign material. Islands almost entirely of slate are Luing, Torsa, Shuna, Bellnahua and Easdale. All but the southern end of Seil qualify – as do the eastern parts of Lunga and Scarba. Jura and Islay away to the south belong to another world in procreational terms.

The islands, spilling like giant teardrops across the map south of Oban, that celebrated "Gateway to the Isles", are aligned parallel to the Great Glen fault, which divides around Colonsay further out to sea. Some are too insignificant size-wise to be included on many maps, but might, like tiny Bellnahua, have supported an many as 150 people in the industrial heyday of slate production.

Slate provided the only major industry in this part of Scotland and commanded a trade ranking almost as high as the great slate workings of Corries and Llechwydd in North Wales. If not quarried away, the slaty rocks wear down into a fair quality agricultural soil and some of the islands are famous for their beef cattle, Luing having developed a breed of its own.

The rocks are Pre-cambrian, the oldest of all, and have been metamorphosed or fundamentally changed under conditions of pressure and heat. They are classi-fied as Dalradian Metamorphic Graphite, Schist and Slate. All are permeated by

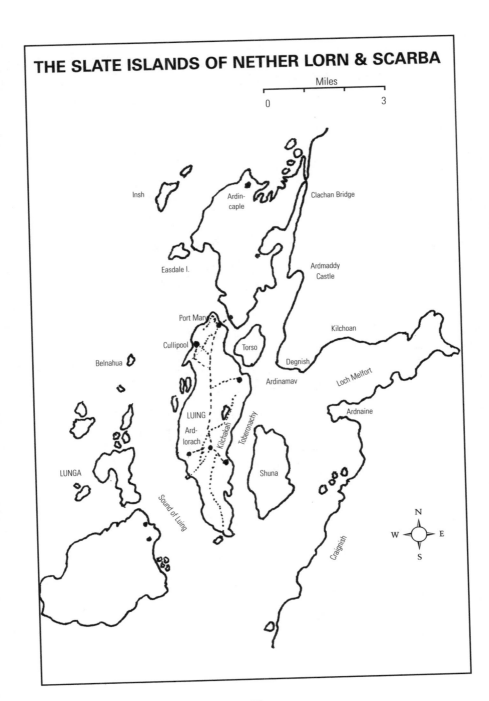

THE SLATE ISLANDS OF NETHER LORN & SCARBA

Miles

0   3

Insh

Ardin-caple

Clachan Bridge

Easdale I.

Ardmaddy Castle

Port Mary

Cullipool

Torso

Kilchoan

Belnahua

Degnish

Ardinamav

Loch Melfort

LUING

Ard-lorach

Kilchiakah

Toberonachy

Ardnaine

LUNGA

Shuna

Sound of Luing

Craignish

N
W   E
S

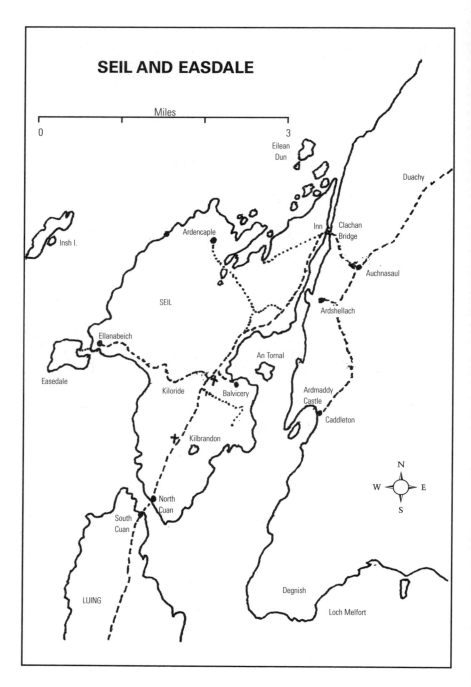

SEIL AND EASDALE

Miles

0   3

Eilean Dun

Duachy

Insh I.

Ardencaple

Inn   Clachan Bridge

Auchnasaul

SEIL

Ardshellach

Ellanabeich

An Tornal

Easedale

Kiloride   Balvicery

Ardmaddy Castle

Caddleton

Kilbrandon

N
W   E
S

North Cuan

South Cuan

Degnish

LUING

Loch Melfort

intrusive dykes of Basalt, Dolerite, Camptonite etc. in a parallel series running from south-east to north-west.

The southern part of Seil is of unmetamorphosed igneous rock, equally old, an Epidiorite and Horneblende Schist in the Dalradian and Moine Series of the Precambrian – and comparable with that of Shetland.

The more westerly islands, the Garvellachs, Western Scarba and Lunga and the northern and western outliers of Luing, resemble the mass of Jura in consisting of Boulder Bed and Conglomerate. These are still Dalradian Metamorphics and Scarba is similarly penetrated by the south-east to north-west dykes – which intrude again into the Torridonian Sandstones and Grits of Colonsay and Oronsay to the west.

Slates in the wider usuage of the term are metamorphic rocks derived from clays and shales altered at depth, by heat and compression, to a harder, more crystalline form. They are fine grained, indurated and can be split into fine layers suitable for roofing tiles.

In the narrower, now generally accepted sense, true slates are from clays splitting along close lines of cleavage which are often at right angles to the bedding plane. Rocks cleaving along the strata or bedding planes to produce slabs suitable for roofing are strictly shales.

The argillaceous (clay) sediments of true slates were subjected after deposition to intense pressure – sideways on to the lie of the strata – this causing the tiny flaky clay particles to orientate flatways on to the constricting force, altering their normal interlocking properties, and enabling the blocks to split easily along the multiplicity of flat faces. Nether Lorn slates are famous for the dendritic, anastimosing patterning of the cleavage faces and for the presence of fool's gold or iron pyrites.

There is always a tremendous amount of wastage with slate production – a mixture of the inability of the rock to cleave and ineptitude of the cleaver, but to watch a good worker prising the solid slabs into thin parallel layers is to witness something little short of a miracle.

Nether Lorn has dumped its slate waste into the sea to form new beaches and reefs, sometimes connecting islet to islet: North Wales has piled its slate waste into forbidding black mountains and has regimented some of the thicker slabs endways on to form barriers which are hybrids between fences and walls.

Dykes disrupt the smooth progress of quarrying operations in Nether Lorn, but they ensure that parts of the old surface of these small plots of land remain on site, affected only by natural

59. *Igneous Dyke on Seil Island, Nether Lorn*

91

weathering. The tertiary north-west dyke swarm of Mull, which crosses the older Devonian north-east dyke swarm of Etive in Argyll hereabouts, is quoted as one of the finest examples of these centred swarms of dykes anywhere.

The North Wales slates also have bands of paler granites passing through them, these in the news in September 2006 when it was announced that this granite was to be quarried for the walls of the imposing new visitor centre planned for the summit of Snowdon, Wales's highest mountain.

2. SEIL ISLAND

The islet studded Sound of Seil narrows at its northern end where it is crossed by an arched stone bridge having a span of 70 feet and a height of 40 feet. This is Clachan, the Bridge over the Atlantic. Its claim to this title arises from the sound being open at both ends and not merely an estuary or sea loch. (Certainly many offshore islands are connected, but by causeways rather than old fashioned stone bridges – otherwise many of the Hebridean and Orkney connections might qualify.)

The strait is fully marine and crowded with brown seaweeds which float to the surface as the tide floods. Another claim to marine status comes from a whale stranding when a female of unrecorded species ran aground under the bridge. Nowadays attempts would have been made to tow the unfortunate back into Balvicar Bay to the south. Then, in 1831, the locals fell upon the unexpected harvest of whale meat and blubber and made short work of her.

Built in 1792, this bridge looks like a smaller copy of the famous William Edwards Bridge, a single span of 140 feet with similar central hump, built over the River Rhondda at Pontypridd in South Wales in 1755 thirty seven years earlier and hailed as a masterpiece of its kind. Both bridges, ambitious projects for their time, fell down after the first building, the cure in Wales being to reduce the weight by leaving three large circular holes in each end buttress. A single smaller circular hole was left in each end of the lesser Clachan Bridge but their aim was partially defeated by building a wall across inside.

Nevertheless, Clachan has stood for more than two centuries. The builder, John Stevenson of Oban, was bankrupted by the repeat operation and folklore records that he was awarded a rent free farm as compensation. According to most "all Britain" texts, Clachan Bridge was built by Telford, but the locals should know. Perhaps too much is attributed to that great man, who supplied the brain rather than the brawn. We viewed it at its best, both weatherwise and for its floral decoration. It was midsummer day in 1986, the hottest day of the year and almost windless.

After leaving the Riverside Hotel opposite the cathedral in Inverness that morning, we had travelled down by the great Caledonian Canal to Fort William, where we made a speedy transfer to another "Highland City Link" going to Oban. After an abbreviated stop at the Rowan Tree Hotel we gathered at the bridge to stretch our legs.

60. *Fairy Foxglove*

The upper south facing wall was bright with fairy foxgloves *(Erinus alpinus)*, A splendid purple fringe of flowers under the parapet had spilled down to dot the face, as with wine-red Aubretia, and very unlike other members of its namesake foxglove family. None had colonised the more shaded inner walls where grew the three homely spleenwort ferns, the black, the maidenhair and wall rue, and there was little on the north side.

The incoming evening tide raced briskly through beneath – from right to left as we approached from the mainland. It raised first the kelps, then the wracks and finally flooded shorewards over the smaller channelled wrack, thrift cushions and scurvy grass. There is no splash zone to extend the briny influence upshore, but narrow strips of saltmarsh had developed alongside.

Nurtured partly by the surging sea below and partly by the seeping springs above, this was brackish in character. The small brown mud rush shared dominance with red fescue grass and the sward was permeated by pink-flowered sea milkwort and pierced by spikes of sea arrow grass *(Triglochin maritima)* bearing female flowers.

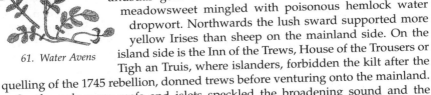

61. *Water Avens*

Above the salty zone among sharp-flowered rush was the unusual gem of water avens *(Geum rivale)*. Aromatic meadowsweet mingled with poisonous hemlock water dropwort. Northwards the lush sward supported more yellow Irises than sheep on the mainland side. On the island side is the Inn of the Trews, House of the Trousers or Tigh an Truis, where islanders, forbidden the kilt after the quelling of the 1745 rebellion, donned trews before venturing onto the mainland.

Southwards more reefs and islets speckled the broadening sound and the country rose in a rumple of dimpled hills, part grass, part bracken. This was a land of livestock husbandry and silage crops, soft and friendly in the midsummer sun but probably very different for most of the year.

Seil presents a fine indented coast of steep cliffs and stony bays to the Sound of Insh, which is a side channel of the Firth of Lorn and separated from it by the green wedge of Insh Island which beckoned from across the blue water. Rising grim and barren beyond the divided channel is the remote, roadless Buie Peninsula of South-east Mull, sometimes called Laggan (hollow), with the heights of Ben Buie beyond.

Mull and Skye are the two big volcanic centres hereabouts and the whole of the tangled hillscape has been shaped by the Caledonian disturbances. The geology was beyond us but we could not fail to recognise the magnificent upstanding dykes, thrust edgeways on and parallel sided through the country rock and eroded free as the damaged matrix fell away from either side. Dark red rocks surfaced at beach level and again on Insh. Most were grey, some slaty, some more massive.

The dykes were clad in a modified flora, the product of felling and grazing but of rare permanence in contrast to the successional phases on the tumble of slate waste at their foot. Sheep were present, but not too many, and the sward was scarcely wind-shorn. Tall oat grass bordered the cliff brink with eared sallow, wood sage and mayweed. Cliff seepages bulged with hogweed, Angelica and meadowsweet, while kidney vetch and bird's-foot trefoil permeated the sward.

Two delectable items on the inaccessible faces were roseroot *(Rhodiola rosea)* and lesser meadow rue *(Thalictrum minus).* The usual woodland

62. *Lesser Meadow Rue*

element of bluebells and red campion mingled with the thrift and sea campion.

These graded back to acid grassland with heath spotted orchids, tormentil, lousewort, heath and lady's bedstraw, heath and germander speedwell. Bilberry and ling clothed the shallow soil of the little eminences which protruded every-where, with wild thyme, harebells (the bluebells of Scotland) and more sea campion. Grasses came in many guises, tufted hair and wavy hair, sweet vernal and crested dogstail, as well as the bents and fescues, purple moor and Nardus mat grass.

Valley bogs might be filled with either of the two cotton grasses, with deer sedge *(Trichophorum caespitosum),* heath rush *(Juncus squarrosus)* and insectivorous common butterwort – by no means 'common' for visitors from the South. Streams held pioneering stonewort (Chara) speckled with orange fruiting bodies or oogonia, and the uncommon marsh St. Johns wort *(Hypericum elodes)* among the more widespread kingcups, lady's smock (now cuckoo flower) and flote grass. Eighty nine species were listed here as we enjoyed watching the small heath and small white butterflies which had ventured out into the June sunshine to join bees and drone flies supping from the flowers of bugle and mouse-ear hawkweed in an aromatic bed of wild mint.

The elevated moorland drops steeply into the village of Ellanbeich, the sward enriched with wild and barren strawberries, pignut and yarrow, celandines and primroses. A spread of Cotoneaster clothed the slope and the foot of the hill behind the Easedale Inn is wooded. Here are sycamore, ash, larch and fir, black-thorn, hawthorn, hazel and Fuchsia with an understorey of foxglove, greater stitchwort, bush vetch and woodland loosestrife.

Shags and gulls were the only sea birds spotted, the main denizens of the cliffs being hooded crows. Wheatear families were on the wing with whinchats and meadow pipits on the open hills, blackbird, song thrush, dunnock and robin on the lower wooded slopes and we found the sad corpse of a wren in the garden of the inn.

Ellanbeich village at the foot of this rolling upland on Seil Island is a corrup-tion of Eilean a' Beithick, the Island of Birches, and island it was until so much slate waste got dumped in the sea between that it became part of Seil. Easdale Inn where we stayed, is on Seil proper. The village of single storey, lime-washed quarrymen's cottages, post office and shop just down the road is on the satellite island.

Mostly the connecting beaches remain as unadulterated slate, some of them enclosing mirror calm lagoons. Along a few sections slates were packed in vast netting bags to enable them to cohere sufficiently to hold back the sea. Others had been built over and were acquiring a layer of soil as the dark slabs fragment and shatter.

Gardens have been coaxed into being and filled with dame's violet or sweet rocket *(Hesperis matronalis)*, roses and rhubarb. A lady was digging her potato patch, a task consisting mainly of the removal of unacceptably large chunks of quarry waste.

This midsummer day was the calmest of the year so far. The sea, even outside the slate barriers, lay glassy smooth and the sun sank belatedly in a blaze of orange behind Mull, a long way north of west, like a distant forest fire. At half an hour short of midnight it was still possible to take rose-tinted sunset photos, with the slates, dolerites and basalts etched against the flesh coloured backdrop like ogre's teeth.

Trustingly the locals had arranged a midsummer night's barbecue, toasting beefburgers over driftwood fires on the beach to music. Even the voracious midges had the good taste to keep a low profile this close to the sea, centreing their activities among the yellow Irises to landward.

We were too full to join the feast. Our evening meal had started with the local brand of squat lobsters. At home in Wales these would have been *Galathea strigosa*, but the two forward arms looked suspiciously menacing, the ultimate claw longer than the rest of the paired appendages that decorated the dish.

63. *Long-clawed Squat Lobster*

Someone slipped away for the marine handbook and we found that we were enjoying the related *Munida rugosa*. This tasty starter was followed by enormous salmon steaks from the local waters.

The last hysterical blackbirds went finally to roost after their long midsummer day and the chaffinches ceased their monotonous cheeping. Pied wagtails slipped quietly away, common gulls desisted from their overturning of stranded seaweed in search of kelp flies and and a shag winged off into the gloom like a flying broomstick. The midsummer moon rose in the east, fat and full and at least twice its legitimate size as viewed obliquely through the highland atmosphere.

Loose slates clattered underfoot as we walked along the beaches, where neither mayweed nor pineappleweed nor anything else had yet managed to gain a hold. The dainty hooves of the sheep rattled almost as loudly as the ewes led their lambs out onto the flat sun warmed surfaces to bed them down for the night. Before settling they pawed and scraped at the ground, like a cat or dog kneading its bedding, this the instinctive preparation for sleep that carves out the familiar eroding earthy 'sheep lairs' on the mountain slopes and cliffs.

We retired eventually from a world of uncanny stillness, scoffing mildly at the weatherman's prediction of thunder storms, and slept until all hell broke loose at 3.0 am. There was no rain but the noise of thunder was colossal as newly spawned waves pounded the black beaches as though an army of a hundred knights was clattering across on mighty war horses. No swell could have risen fast enough to make such a racket on a normal beach. I wondered how this slaty seascape sounded during winter storms, when the slates were aquaplaning all over and crashing home on the storm beach crests.

Not that the present gale was inconsiderable. The big sycamore outside the window was swaying and creaking dangerously and laundry had been snatched from the line and rehung along the woodland edge where it could not take off to sea. At 4.0 am the New Zealand cabbage tree *(Cordyline australis)* was still bowing groundwards under the influence of the forces ranged against it.

The world was awake by then, robin and blackbird joining with the storm cock in a defiant dawn chorus. By 5.0 am it was all over, with just the occasional gust to vindicate the weather man in the eyes of those who had slept through it all. By 7.0 am the sun was blazing again from a cloudless sky and continued to do so during the ensuing day.

3. EASDALE ISLAND

Easdale village spreads off Seil Island onto the lesser island of Easdale, the two parts linked by passenger ferry. We sounded the klaxon on the Ellanbeich jetty to summon the little open boat from the other side to take us across. Our route skirted the tumbledown wooden pier on the ex island of now non-existent birches and pushed up channel between artificial breakwaters to the little wharf opposite. Easedale quarrymen used their surplus stone to make harbour walls as the average crofter used his to make field walls – an obvious diversion of super-fluous waste to serve a useful purpose.

The original inner harbour wall, recently excavated from beneath the accumu-lated dumps, was of hard, igneous whinstone from the island's central dyke, which stands up from the denuded base of what used to be like the handle of a grid iron. Sea bed material was dumped along with quarry spoil as the jetties were kept clear and the whole was shuffled by longshore currents so that the harbour entrance has to be dredged out every five years or so.

All the Easdale inhabitants were deeply involved in the rise and fall of the slate industry, which rose to world fame before the more easily obtained asbestos 'slates' captured the market.

As early as 1626 Easdale slates were used to roof Iona Abbey and Castle Stalker in Appin. The peak of productivity was in the nineteenth century, when the Easdale quarries turned out nine million slates annually, exporting these to many parts of the world. This vast quantity of material was transported first by man power and wheelbarrows; then by horse power and tramways (the horses imported initially to work the gin pumps). Then small steam pugs took over from the horses and winches while cranes and inclined planes were installed to lighten the burden and increase production.

Nemesis struck on 23rd November, 1881, in the form of one of the biggest storms ever to hit the west coast of Scotland, and coinciding with high spring tides. Storm waves swept over both islands, flooding the quarries which had, by then, been worked down to as much as 180 feet below sea level, and had been kept open only by pumping. Two hundred and forty men lost their livlihood on that fateful night. Attempts were mde to salvage some of the shallower pits but the industry never fully recovered.

By 1911 commercial quarrying had ceased. Men went south to industries nearer Glasgow and the village fell into decay – which is another way of saying that the natural environment was given a respite from the ravages of mankind and a chance to recover some of its former glory. A new generation had now moved in to renovate the little white cottages as summer homes and the hard won soil of the little gardens was bright with flowers – Welsh poppies, pansies, columbines and even young rowan trees.

Easdale Island is but 500 yards wide and 650 yards long, yet it supported a population of over 450 souls in 116 cottages in 1839. For fuel the people used peat, imported from Seil and Luing. Not only could there have been no timber and little peat on the ravaged island at that time but precious little soil. Most cottages had potato patches, for which the soil had often to be imported with the peat.

64. *Ponies grazing on slate waste*

Today there is residual native soil on the broader end of the unquarriable central dyke and a new soil of accumulated sediments in the village. Most of the island surface, however, was still a litter of slate debris, with hard pressed vegetation subsisting on humus and dust sifting gradually down between the layers.

With all those slates about, it is hard to credit that most of the cottages are recorded as having been roofed with imported thatch. Today's renovated homes are roofed with synthetic tiles (as are most new Welsh cottages within striking distance of the vast slate quarries) The stacks of roofing slates on Easdale are mere museum pieces.

In the island's heyday boats were built by McQueens of Easdale and salmon were fished. As visitors we were still greeted by draped salmon nets and fishing buoys, as well as regiments of roofing slates and larger slabs suitable for flogging as tombstones. Their patterned surface was not quite as immune to adherent lichen growth as were the smoother ones of North Wales.

When quarrying above as well as below sea level the rock was dynamited out in the usual way. Quarrymen working at sea level, like feeding waders, had to gear their activity to the tidal cycle. Oak wedges were hammered into cracks in the intertidal zone during the ebb. These absorbed water from the incoming tide, swelled and opened up cracks for the layers to be levered apart. Such is the power of plants in disrupting rocks, alive or dead.

When burrowing down to 150 feet and more, sea defences of natural rock were left in situ, but not always enough. An attempt to dynamite some of the stone battered walls to construct a marina on what was by now a conservation area was halted and divers were exploring the hidden blue-green quarry depths to assess their potential.

Walls of the flooded quarries formed from cleavage faces are more or less vertical, those above water supporting only thrift, sea campion and scurvy grass. Sloping bedding planes showed massed kidney vetch, bush vetch and feral dame's violet, in all shades from mauve to white. The first covered vast areas of spoil as well, a prostrate, radiating form full of blossom but scarcely rising from the surface and rooted in no visible soil.

Early plant colonists on the wilderness of slate chippings are English stonecrop and wild thyme, bird'foot trefoil and blue milkwort, white and yellow clovers. Limited areas in the north had progressed to tiny buttercup fields, where free range horses were feeding and waxing fat. Obviously the breakdown of slates yields something above average by Highland standards in the way of soil.

It is neither excessively acid nor alkaline. Lime lovers – yellow pea wild carrot, feral columbine, mouse-ear hawkweed and knapweed – throve alongside acid lovers – tormentil, ling, fine-leaved heath and foxglove – in a parody of that biological anomaly, a limestone heath. There are primroses and violets, harebells, devil's bit scabious, woodsage and speedwells. A scrub of bramble, briar and blackthorn had developed in the shelter of the great dyke and rampageous montbretia and Fuchsia were more than holding their own. An interesting parasitic broomrape was spotted.

65. *Harebells*

4. EASDALE ISLAND'S GREAT DYKE, FLORA AND FAUNA

The massive grey stone dyke runs right across the island from the village and is the only part left which is appreciably above sea level. Quarried faces extend from top to bottom, suggesting that originally it must have conformed to the general level before the rest was stripped away. The trig point at its western end stands 124 feet above sea level.

Only a few feet wide at the village end, this molten intrusion broadens in the northwest to a sloping paddock, augmented by a bubbly brown rock seemingly petrified straight from a witch's cauldron – possibly vesicular basalt – and by adherent patches of poor quality, unquarried slate. We saw the nigger brown suspected basalt also on Seil, alongside the road to Ellanbeich and aligned in such a way as to suggest that it is part of the same dyke.

The upstanding wall is a natural rock garden rising sheer from the plain. Could this be where the Scots got the idea of calling an elongated bank a dyke while the less well informed English used the term for the ditch alongside? To simulate the English sort of dyke the geological dyke would have to be softer than the country rock instead of harder and get eroded out as a gully.

New plant communities, as seen on the island's denuded, virtually peneplained base, are typically more diverse than long established ones. That of the dyke, however, lacks little in comparison with the platform surrounding it. Its flora is long term, that to either side is successional.

Wild thyme is characteristic, some of the purple flower trusses replaced by woolly balls which are the plants' response to egg laying by the gall forming mite, *Eriophyes thomasii*. Scorpion grass and pearlwort occupy dry patches, grading out to common tare, while ivy drapes many of the steep faces.

Further from the village the 'wall' bulges to form the 'hill', ascended by a pathway and commanding extensive views. The horses evidently did not come here and the sloping summit meadow was white with elegantly fine-leaved and untrampled pignut in June, in a matrix of long grass and clover, with giant woodrush occupying the northern brow. Red campion, hedge parsley and bluebells mingled with sorrel and sea campion on the flanks in a red, white and blue explosion of colour. Brush strokes of different hues dominated the sward as each species came into its own.

Water seeping from the base nurtured a little marsh crowded with cat's valerian and meadowsweet, with Angelica and hogweed, yellow flag and giant fescue, and male and lady ferns. Water starwort reached for the surface of a small, clear pool.

Far below the village was green and white with field daisies in June and a clump of white dead nettle burgeoned in one of only about half a dozen sites this far north-west of its distribution centre in South-east England. Grasses, usually well to the fore in new successions, included bents, fescues, ryegrass, cocksfoot, tall oat, Yorkshire fog, sweet vernal, crested dogstail, tufted and wavy hair grasses, common and tall meadow grasses with field and many-headed woodrushes. The knee deep sward shone and rippled like wavelets on a calm sea

Only at the end furthest from the village is the island's centrepiece readily scalable. At the time of the 1881 disaster the villagers are said to have joined arms and tried to force their way across to take sanctuary there, but were beaten back by the waves to the buildings. Knowing how they had scooped God's earth from beneath their feet, it must, indeed, have seemed like judgement day.

And still we meddle dangerously with our environment, imagining that our superior knowledge can cure the devastation of past misuse, It is easy for us in this affluent age to think thus, when we believe that we no longer have to look to the land to afford us a living. How wrong can one get? The mantle of floral colour thrown across Easdale's dereliction by a forgiving Mother Nature makes such ill omened thoughts seem irrelevant.

This island complex lies directly opposite Mull, which is one of the main centres of past volcanic action hereabouts. The other is Skye – huge lava flows having emanated from both. Some dark red rock layers occur at beach level in the west and on Insh Island offshore, as also on Treshnish.

66. Otter

It was on the deceptively gentle sea off Easdale's western shore that we saw the otter, cleaving the glassy calm to leave a long rippling wake across the bottle green water. It was swimming like a dog, head well above the surface and back visible along its entire length. This was one of the island's natural treasures. We failed to find any of the semi precious stones said to exist on the beaches and old slate workings.

The grey Atlantic seal lolling in the vicinity had a quite different rolling gait. The sleek silvered body, fat and shining, seemed to lack direction, diving, spinning, surfacing and porpoising, seemingly for the sheer joy of movement, whereas the otter looked set on reaching a pre-determined destination. But otters play too, like all intelligent mammals when the necessary work of the day is done.

Adolescent common gull chicks, brown and fluffy, pottered on the slate waste beside one of the flooded northern quarries, taking occasional tumbles on the rough terrain, but righting their featherweight bodies unharmed. A parent bird, dark-eyed and yellow-legged, in contrast to the vulgar, screeching herring gulls, sat on the wall 'chipping'at us, apparently used to passers by and quite unphased. More were scattered along tiny ledges of the rock face behind, but we saw no nests there.

Young gulls are nidifugous, wandering from the nest as day old chicks, and would fall straight into the water from such sites, which are more suited to kittiwakes, whose young have learned through aeons of time to sit tight until they have full powers of flight. Most gull chicks will waterlog if they get into the sea too soon, but these day old mites are highly buoyant and could paddle happily ashore before sinking too low, taking no more harm than those others that nest by quiet, inland waters, the black-headed gulls.

67. Stonechat

We saw oyster catchers on the southern reefs and an eider duck paddling along the shore, but the true sea-going pelagics were few. A song thrush's anvil on the path was littered with the broken shells of pink Cepaea hedge snails and a stonechat chinked from a quarry brink. Pied wagtails poked among the slate chippings and a cock twite was spotted as we surveyed the scene from the trig point.

This is not a bird which we southerners are familiar with. It reminded us most of a linnet, but, instead of the crimson head and breast there was a pink flush on the rump. The back was heavily spotted with black instead of being the smooth cinnamon of the springtime cock linnet, and the head, too, was speckled instead of grey.

Most surprising in this denuded landscape were the woodland birds, A very grubby great tit settled among the brambles for a belated preen and general tidy up. A whitethroat, with fat green caterpillar dangling from its beak, stayed patiently in a bush, waiting for us to go away before she revealed where she was delivering the goods. Blackbirds and dunnocks, garden and woodland birds by habit, seemed quite at home in this more open landscape.

The unaccustomed calm had brought out clouds of insects. Craneflies were everywhere and the many pea flowers were buzzing with bees. Creatures with larger wing areas were in no danger of being blown out to sea and peacock and red admiral butterflies were on the wing and basking on the sun-warmed slates. The peacocks would be the tail end of the over-wintering population, soon to disappear, with the new generation emerging from the chrysalids in late July or early August. The red admirals might have come winging in from the continent and up the length of Britain at any time during the past six weeks or so.

Painted ladies, also migrants from further south, were spiralling up over the 140 feet high triangulation cairn in mating chases preparatory to producing a British brood. The new immigrants, necessarily strong fliers, are well known for this habit of making straight for a high vantage point to indulge in courtship rituals prior to egg laying.

Thistles and nettles below might nourish their offspring, recycling energy from the slate leftovers through unassuming caterpillars and transforming it into magnificent little flying machines capable of making such journeys over Scotland, England, France and the Mediterranean to Africa. as their parents had. We have a long way to go to catch up!

John Gay's little ditty plays down the wonder of this metamorphosis and staying power on the wing very unfairly in his doggerel verse:

"As in the sunshine of the morn, a butterfly but newly born, sat proudly prinking.
And what's a butterfly? At best – he's just a caterpillar drest."

5. LUING ISLAND, FROM QUARRYING TO FISHING

The vehicle ferry to Luing Island crosses the 200 yards of Cuan Sound from North Cuan on the southern tip of Seil Island to South Cuan on the northern tip of Luing. Vehicles drive onto the tubby floating platform obliquely, to be swung around in midstream, where treacherous tide rips commonly reach a speed of eight knots. Sneaking off it cornerwise at South Cuan, our passage was soon blocked by the sewage lorry emptying cesspits, an orange clad attendant marching behind with the end of the broad unsavoury pipe tucked under his arm like a pet pekinese.

Returning at the end of the day this same lorry just beat us to the ferry on which, as sole occupant, it was shuttled to and fro with the long pipe trailing overboard – either blowing or sucking? We cringed at the thought of the grisly contents being emptied into the translucent waters of the sound. Perhaps the tanks were being swilled out after emptying elsewhere. So much nutrient should not be dissipated at sea anyway when a hungry land is crying out for phosphates and nitrates.

In fact the cry is not so loud here as it sometimes is on the Outer Isles or Inner Mainland. The slates of the country rock weather to a quite amenable soil, which bears grass and bracken. Nowhere did we see it deteriorating to acid moorland, although valley bogs were often wisped with the silky heads of cotton-grass.

Slate taking at Port St. Mary a little west of where we landed, had ceased to be commercially viable in the 1930s and was finally abandoned in 1974. At

Cullipool, our first port of call down the west coast, the big quarrying enterprise had lasted until 1965. A tall cut face of black rock frowned down upon the white-washed village, which is now the home of lobster men and clam fishers, served by a little post office cum general store. Gardens were furnished with Escallonia and Fuchsia, lupins and dame's violet, against a backdrop of the humble privet.

Here, as at Ellanbeich, sheep clattered over double ranked, slaty beaches and kept the maritime sward of the fishermen's boat park in apple pie order. Long fleeces blowing in the wind, they were busy recycling the prevalent red fescue and mud rush which surrounded the brackish pools into tender meat and coarse wool.

Islets and reefs were scattered offshore, as after an explosion, these breaking the force of the sea and minimising the splash zone so that few true halophytes appeared in the turf. Those like scurvy grass which did are as happy with brackish conditions as with salt and go adventuring alongside inland roads treated with salt in frosty weather. Permeating the sward were silverweed and white clover, carnation sedge and jointed rush.

Oyster catchers and gulls foraged along the shoreline. Flocks of starlings, to be augmented later as the broods matured but already large, swarmed over the turf and poked along the driftline. Wheatears had joined them on the saltings, pied wagtails on the beach. A song thrush watched from a fence rail and two stonechats clinked from a telegraph wire. Just up the road the forminadble shape of a buzzard was hunched atop a post. We disturbed its soliloquy by rattling over a cattle grid and it flapped lethargically off to perch again as soon as opportunity offered.

Luing, once home to six hundred families sustained by crofting and quarrying, probably supported no more than a hundred and twenty souls at the time – living off their fellow creatures on land and sea. The fishing was based at Cullipool. We approached a group unravelling ropes where the spirits of the deep had been having fun entangling them with each other and the crab pots. Encrusting wigwams of acorn barnacles (Semibalanus) and calcareous homes of tube worms (Pomatoceros) had lost no time in taking over the new, if somewhat impermanent substrate, suggesting that pots were usually re-set as soon as emptied to ensure growth to their present state.

68. Scallop and Scurvy Grass

The lobstermen puffed luxuriantly at cigars as they sorted out the tangle and talked of hard times.

"No lobsters to speak of at all last year."

"Overfishing?"

"Who knows? Bad weather all summer."

They had gone over to 'clams' instead. I suspected they were referring to scallops as there were plenty of shells of giant scallops *(Pecten maximus)* lying around but none of the various clam species. We viewed the rusty iron rakes and chains which they towed behind their small boats to scrape these creatures from the sea bed into a coarse net.

"Damage to the bottom living communties?"

"Not us. The big boats."

"They only fish occasionally, you fish all the year."

"They blame us. We blame them."

We left on good terms, thanks to their tolerance of interfering strangers. It seems there is cause for blame, but can a man deprived of his lobster fishing by bad weather or whatever, be expected to sit and twiddle his thumbs all year? We broached the subject of the squat lobsters which we had enjoyed. These they despised.

"Poor man's prawns! Bi-product of scampi fishing. Just fall into the prawn kreels. Get a pound a pound for the scampi tails, but need three pounds of squats for one pound of tails. Now real prawns!"

They quoted an astronomical sum for the big ones down to something quite substantial for the smaller fry.

Some fine specimens of violet tinted edible sea urchins (*Echinus esculentus*) were scattered over the turf, these too, presumably bi-products of the fishery. I have never known an Englishman (or a Scotsman) who ate these rather sloshy, salty creatures as folk of so many other nationalities do. A fact which scarcely surprises me after trying them on the Maori island of Motiti. Evidently the man who dubbed them 'esculentus' regarded them as agreeable tucker.

These urchins, whose shells or tests appear occasionally as lamp shades, have a wide latitudinal range, from Northern Spain to Northern Norway, where life is made possible by the ameliorating waters of the North Atlantic drift. The urchins' salinity tolerance is also wide, from the thirty five parts per

69. *Edible Sea Urchins*

thousand of the open Atlantic to as little three to five parts per thousand in some of the Norwegian fiords and, indeed, in some of the brackish sea lochs of the North Uists. They can be found at extreme low water mark along the West Scottish coasts, but are more a part of the skin divers' realm off South Wales.

6. LUING CATTLE COUNTRY

Luing Island is a little over five miles long and two broad. It consists fundamentally of two parallel ridges running north to south, with the island road threading the series of cotton grass swamps in the valley between. One long stretch, Glen Dubh Leitir, the Glen of the Dark Slopes, is reputedly haunted, chief of the evil spirits a malevolent demon who chases travellers by night.

The soil derived from the slate is black, impermeable and clayey, with the wet bits apparently more acid than the dry. Drainage is complicated, the land forming a dimpled mosaic of ups and downs, ideal for far flung skirmishes of 'cowboys and Injuns' as opposed to urban 'Cops and Robbers'.

Pasture grasses, ryegrass, cocksfoot, Yorkshire fog and meadow grass, probably occupy as much territory as moorland grasses, while rushes are rife, indicating flushing by slowly moving underground water rather than a stagnant water table. Knolls were covered with bluebells and pignut, ditches filled with yellow flags and lined with red campion., all suggestive of a soft woodland climate.

The idea that the whole might once have been wooded is vindicated by the frequent spinneys of ash, oak, rowan, birch and sycamore. Square conifer plantations shed a piney aroma over the land and the broad-leaved trees were doing well. The tendency to acidity was shown by the presence of foxgloves, tormentil and heath bedstraw, but more specific lime haters made a poor showing.

Our impression as we travelled south was of poor, hummocky grazing in the north, occupied mainly by sheep and of rather better quality grassland in the south used mainly by cattle. In between, to the west of Tobernochy, the southern village, a broad. fertile lowland sweeps inland from the west coast, a tract fairly obviously gained from the sea and probably enriched by marine sediments.

Here the fields were devoted to high quality grass production for winter feed. Big machines plied back and forth, cutting and gathering a silage crop that was being stacked in an enormous barn at Kilchattan Farm. A tractor was rolling up over the yielding mass in the barn to near the lofty roof, consolidating and bulldozing it into the furthest corners, a more effective storage method than the usual, polythene-lined outdoor silos.

Local birds knew the potential of these sown leys. Vast flocks of rooks and gulls followed the mowing machine, feasting on the disrupted invertebrate life that was possibly boosted by the induced fertility, and continued to feed over the yellowed aftermath from which the crop had been removed. We saw no rookeries, but rooks are said to nest as readily in pines as in the traditional elms, and there were pines at the edge of the local spruce plantations as well as broad-leaved spinneys available to them.

The gulls were mostly common and herring gulls, with a few black-headeds. The grassland generally looked suitable for wintering wild geese. Did they come here, we wondered, or were they all funnelled off to the new Islay Bird Reserves?

The dark red Luing beef cattle are famous and were registered as a breed in their own right twenty years before. They are derived from red shorthorn and hardy Highland breeds, showing more characters of the former but the curly pates and a little of the sandy shagginess of the latter. Sufficiently hardy to spend the whole year outside they are "Excellent doers. Stay out all winter and calve on the hill." The Cullipool postmistress proudly claimed that they had been exported all over the world – or at least to Australia, New Zealand and Canada.

There is nothing unusual about breeding the hardy Highland strain into beef shorthorns, Herefords or Poll Angus stock. It is done all over the Outer Hebrides, where crofters no longer enjoy sharing their houses with the cattle in winter, but Luing had gone one better to develop a widely recognised breed.

Far to the North, on Orkney, the cattle are wintered indoors, but this is lowland style farming with Charolet and Simontal bulls, pampered on yard feeding for six months of the year and on the lushest of lowland grass for the summer. This grass has even more hours of daylight in which to photosynthesise than it has here on Luing, over two hundred miles further south. Luing grass, theoretically, has correspondingly more hours to photosynthesise in winter, but low temperatures and high winds probably prevent it from doing so, and the stock must be sustained with previously harvested forage.

Leslie Thomas (1968) in his "Some Lovely Islands", tells of the redoubtable spinster, Irene MacClachlan, who rowed 'the wee boat' from her cottage on North-east Luing every day through the winter to the Torsay Island grazings across half a mile of water to feed her livestock. The beasts were driven over the intertidal sands of the tidal island at low water of equinoctual springs and the fodder was stored on the spot, ready to be apportioned out. The fact that she was unable to swim worried her not at all. Perhaps, as one of the Australian crewmen remarked on my Antarctic visit, it was a case of "If you fall into the drink here you'll die of cold before you drown!"

Torsay is a particularly fertile island, which once sustained more than a dozen thriving crofts. Early man evidently found it equally desirable, a big cairn of stones existing on the lesser tidal island of Sgur Carnach, marking the remains of an ancient lake dwelling. The sixteenth century Castle of the Dogs on Torsay itself was the hunting lodge of the MacDonalds, lords of the Isles.

When we drove westwards from Kilchattan to picnic by the derelict pier in Blackmill Bay south of Ardlarach, we passed a yard full of almost vulgarly fat beasts, presided over by a lordly red bull. Out on the windswept turf, by the roofless, windowless fishermen's cottages, our lunch companions were sheep. These, like most on the island, were hardy Scottish Blackfaces, which also brave the winter out of doors, unlike the softer Cheviot:Sussex cross of the Orkneys.

Driving through the island centre, past the many sheep-shaped humpback hills, we came across a flock of a different sort. The sheep were primitive, but not as much so as Soays: small, mostly dark brown, some black only a few white and some blotched, like Jacob's sheep but without the doubled horns. We wondered if they might be Shetlands, the sort of sheep whose wool is rooed (pulled) rather than shorn and used to make the many tinted patterned Fair Isle jumpers.

The flimsy terraces scarring the flanks of these hills are the result of rotary soil slip, the shelves so formed made more pronounced by their use as sheep tracks. The poached cattle country of the South is served by no road. Two miles before the southern tip, beside the ruined chapel of Kilchattan, the island road turns west to Ardlarach and east to Tobernochy, a mere track serving the ranching country of Aird Luing. A fine display of polypody and spleenwort ferns decked the laneside walls, with wall speedwell, but some of the banks below were a sorry sight after treatment with herbicides.

A soil profile several feet deep alongside the south going track was of yielding black clay, its texture greatly improved by the fragile flakes of incorporated slate. These fragments produce wildlife habitats as well as facilitating drainage and Carabid beetles, woodlice and other soil fauna live in the trapped air pockets. Water lingers in the profile before seeping into the ditch below, nurturing a partial fringe of greater woodrush, which grades upwards through soft rush into the poached pasture characteristic of most, once the proximal sown leys are left behind.

Long term winter trampling around feeding troughs had produced a jumble of hummocks which had become grassed over, like anthills, in summer. Water logging produced swards of marsh foxtail with broad-leaved dock but few moorland plants.

Meadow Poa dominated much of the rolling hill country west of the track, along with bracken and thistles. Moorland associates were heath spotted orchids, lousewort and tormentil, pastureland ones clovers, common sorrel and mouse-ear chickweed, with pignut as a woodland relic. Oval sedge and star sedge, lady's smock and water mint huddled between little thickets of gorse and broom and there were glades of broad buckler, male and hard ferns with foxglove, marsh thistle and much else.

70. *Pignut*

On the southern tip we lolled on a sward of buttercups and daisies lulled by the rhythmic munching sound of the red host round about. The timeless scene was suddenly interrupted by the hysterical cries of a cow who had suddenly realised she had mislaid her calf. She raced distractedly this way and that, bellowing. He, fat with her entire yield of milk, detached himself languidly from a group of friends and joined her, with exasperating unconcern and a mere ritualised nudging at her udder.

On the southern horizon beyond Scarba lay Jura, the island of deer, where red deer played havoc with the farmlands and outnumbered the human population by thirty to one. The crofters who suffered their depredations were domiciled along the east coast where the soft slates weather to a fertile soil and are protected from sea swells by the natural breakwaters of Epidiorite sills. The rest of the island is of an unyielding Dalradian quartzite, the weather resistant rock that has withstood the ravages of time to form the Paps of Jura.

Close below us the sea had detached the tidal island of Rubh Aird Luing. Looming large to the east was the island of Shuna, with its dense broad-leaved woodland and factor's house, its fertile grassland and less than fertile bog where three Bronze Age swords had been found, placed ceremonially upright in the peat.

Between Shuna and Luing are more ancient remains and with them the more modern but now abandoned ridges and furrows of old lazy beds. Just inland is a coastal lowland of yellow flags and rushes, rising to the track and a cattle pen with troughs for winter feeding. Alongside is a ruined house bearing the caption "Built by Captain John Campbell, 1876" over its mouldering door. More ancient remains on the rumple of mounds behind take the form of circular grassed stone banks, some concentric, and evidently from a considerable pre-historic settlement.

7. BELLNAHUA ISLAND AND THE GARVELLACHS

Bellnahua Island we did not visit, but its ill fated story dominated our wanderings on other islands – a sad précis of the decease of the slate industry on them all. From the heights above Ellanbeich we had viewed it away to the south, with the jagged outline of the Garvellachs rising ominously beyond. The Easedale Museum made much of its history and the role of the other islands in supplying it with peat for fuel and water for the tea kettles. When on Luing we had stood on the shore at Cullipool gazing south-west over the low white lighthouse of Fladda Island to its black deserted bulk lying to the north of Lunga.

Occupying only a square half mile, this scrap of land supported 150 people at the height of its industrial prosperity. The men, working diligently on their small patch, quarried away the entire area, saving only the part on which they had built their houses. The shell survived into the early twentieth century before it was finally abandoned. Derelict homesteads, occupied only by gulls, stand now on what is described as "The Great Gaping Void of the Beul na h'Uamh". Named for the "Mouth of the Cave', the island itself now a cave.

There are conflicting stories regarding life as it was lived during the slate boom. Already Bellnahua had passed into the realms of legend. Some say that no springs of natural water occurred on the island, others refer to an artesian well which failed during droughts. Whichever is true, barrels of drinking water were brought in by boat from Lunga and Eilean Dubh and one fateful consignment brought typhoid, which ran riot through the crowded population. Some have it that this virulent killer wiped out sufficient inhabitants for the rest to move out. Others say that quarrying split the island in two and the workings were irretrievably flooded.

The machinary remains, corroded with rust, the buildings stand roofless and the people have gone – reminders of the transience of man in this tumultuous, timeless seascape.

The Garvellachs, Holy Isles of the Sea. together with the Skelligs off South-west Ireland, hold the oldest ecclesiastical buildings surviving in the British Isles – dry stone edifices linked with St. Columba and St. Brendon of the early Celtic church.

J.B.Whitlow (1977) in "Geology and Scenery in Scotland" comments: "It is a sobering thought that it was on such isolated oceanic rocks as the Garvellachs and the Skelligs that christianity managed to survive on the Celtic Fringe when all was turmoil elsewhere in Dark Age Europe, but the islands have been uninhabited for centuries and only the ruins bear mute testimony to the golden age of the Celtic Church. Their holy stones are now surrounded by a carpet of beautiful flowers, including scarlet pimpernel, blue pansies, yellow flag Irises and primroses, all of which flourish on the dark alkaline soils of the limestone." On Skellig Michael, which I climbed in 1995, the flowers below the monastic beehive huts on the summit were sea campion, dotted with meditating puffins.

We viewed the Garvellachs from various angles but never better than from the sunlit heights above Ellanbeich on Seil. Etched sharply against the crystal clear air were the steep scarp face looking out to the Firth of Lorne and the Atlantic and the gentle dip slope facing back to Luing.

The rocks are Pre-Cambrian, like the rest hereabouts, but are of Quartzose Tillites with the bands of easily weathered limestone to which Whitlow attributes the riot of flowers. His scarlet pimpernels are interesting, being normally plants of open wasteland or post conflagration sites, but arrival of disseminules is the key factor in places as isolated as this. Having once arrived, the inclement elements are likely to keep sufficient niches open for the seed to find room to germinate.

IV
The 'Small Isles' off Mallaig' Muck, Eigg and Rhum

MUCK

1. INTRODUCTION TO THE ISLAND OF MUCK, AND GETTING THERE

Muck is the smallest of the inhabited islands in this group, which lies north of Mull and south of Skye. Eigg is the next largest with Canna between this and Muck. Away to the south-west are Coll and Tiree west of Mull, with Colonsay, Jura and Islay further off to the south

Around two by three miles in extent and occupying 14 hectares, Muck rises to 457 feet at Ben Arein. The small sheltered anchorage is at Port Mor in the south, while a second settlement of Gallinaich lies on the opposite shore. The island's only road links the two. Its somewhat unfortunate name is derived from the Gaelic word for swine, making it "The Island of Pigs or Porpoises".

Outliers accessible on foot at extreme low tide are Horse Island and Lamb Island. There is no lighthouse with keepers able to offer radio communication when necessary. Until 1956, when the first telephone was installed, the only communication with the mainland in rough weather was by smoke signals!

I had followed the route to these small Isles, from Fort William to Mallaig, on a camping holiday in 1935 when I was barely into my teens. Hailing from the non stone wall country of South-east England, I was mightily impressed. Through many more years of touring, this stretch remained as the family's "finest road in the British Isles".

By car then and by rail now, fifty two years later, we had traversed some of Scotland's finest scenery on that jaunt – a fitting introduction to the lovliness of the isles beyond. From Fort William both road and rail skirted the northern shore of Loch Eil, passing the much photographed Glenfinnan Monument to Bonnie Prince Charlie at the head of Loch Shiel.

On past the smaller Loch Eilt, along the north by the tortuous little road or

THE SMALL ISLES

Canna
N
Rhum
W ─ E
S
Muck
Miles
Eigg
Ardnamurchan
Skye
0   10   20

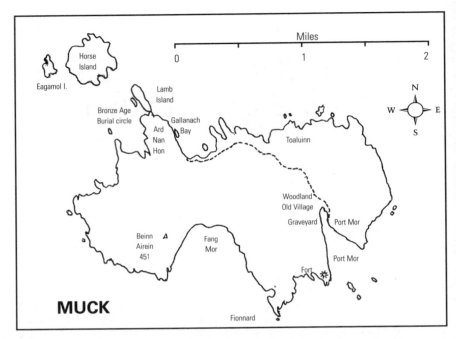

MUCK

the south by rail, we passed the heads of Loch Ailort and Loch nan Ceall – names that have re-echoed in my mind ever since those impressionable days, like chimes of fairy bells from a more primitively beautiful kingdom.

From Arisaig the rail journey by-passed the coastal section, rejoining where the tide-washed sands of Morar dipped inland to meet the firmer shores of the fresh-water loch by the same name. That surreal landscape had lost none of its inborn, wind-sculpted beauty in the intervening half century.

Olfactory memories are said to conjure up more nostalgia than visual ones and there was no mistaking the powerful pong of kippers – or was it bloaters – wafting from the curing sheds of the herring shoals that still supplied the busy little fishing port of Mallaig.

Our 'Small Isles' party savoured its domestic ambience to the full as we assembled on the busy quay to await our sailing. All too soon it was swapped for the unappetising stench of diesel as we boarded the "Loch Mor", which looked awfully small compared with the car ferry to Skye moored nearby.

We headed out into the Sound of Sleat, bound for Muck, but there were complications ahead. The "Loch Mor", the only vessel voyaging in the appropriate direction, was carrying passengers for four islands, but was not putting into port on at least two of these.

Skirting the south-eastern corner of Eigg, we hoved to for transhipment on the high seas to a boat which appeared from behind an offshore rock. "Loch Mor" had been likened to a tug boat with seats and a strong tendency to roll in a cross swell, but the sea was in benevolent mood today. The two boats did not rise and fall in perfect unison when they lay alongside, but the transfer was achieved with few problems. We chugged inshore and disembarked across the deck of the "Shearwater" in preparation for the next hop, from Eigg to Muck.

We had not long to wait before the little open boat "Wave" appeared with the reassuring, weather-beaten figure of Lawrence McEwen at the tiller. As we clambered aboard a hungry black cloud swallowed up the sun and the heavens opened. The wetting was intensified by douchings from the cold Atlantic that sent the more nimble burrowing under the tarpaulin thrown over stores and luggage amidships.

"It willna be verra wet." It wasna – for those under cover – but they missed the bonus of the basking seals and loitering eider drakes as we purred into Muck Harbour forty minutes later. This was an all purpose vessel.

71. *Eider Drakes*

"A wee boat, built to carry people, livestock and cargo and not doing any of these terribly well." It had been built by Lawrence's naval father, who had bought the island of Muck in 1922.

We had got off lightly. It is worth putting on record the entertaining account of the party which had pioneered this wildlife holiday the previous May, sent to me in advance as a warning from its leader, Sandy Mitchell.

"Our journey to Muck was athwart a vigorous south-westerly that bucked and swung us in some style until we hoved to in the lee of a large lump of rock opposite and concealing the Eigg pier. We waited as the nearby cliffs rose and fell in front of our eyes until out from behind the landward end of the rock a small red boat appeared, then disappeared and reappeared and so progressed towards us dipping out of sight in the troughs and reappearing on the peaks. I watched my little flock. Glances were exchanged. Only the matter of fact behaviour of the crews of both boats soothed our troubled breasts. It arrived, the Eigg boat, amid cheery shouts from wind-pink faces and soon the two boats were heaving against each other like two poorly matched dancers while stores and spares and our stuff flew unceremoniously from one ship to the other. Then it was our turn.

"A high wooden platform with steps that Captain Hook might have favoured, led up from the deck of the Eigg boat to more or less of a height with our superior gangway. One by one we were led to the gangplank and siezed, an arm apiece, by two stalworts of Caledonian MacBrayne who waited until the two vessels lurched up (or down) more or less synchronously – at which point with an urgent shout of "now" they shot one of us over the shuddering space into the clamp of two of the Eigg men and down into the pile of people and boxes of cauliflowers with their ears hanging out and bleeding packages of butcher's meat and drums of diesel and carton upon carton of cans of beer. There were Eiggers and well as Muckers to be shifted, so the whole process took some time.

"We then huddled among our chattels under a dark bit of covered deck, with the smell of sheep and vegetable and diesel and tarpaulin and our own wettish selves…

"Some of the party huddled under the covers like emigrants, others stayed in the open, hanging onto the mast and got buckets of sea down their necks from time to time. I was pulling rank and chatting with the captain in the cockpit. From there, the wind-torn seas and skies were thrilling and the boat lay low and safe among the waves, as it butted its way onwards. Storm clouds round the horizon blew rainbows from their muzzles."

Lawrence's brother Ewen, who was to host our stay, met us at Port Mor with a tractor and the means of transporting domestic stores and visitor's luggage in an angle iron basket.

The tide had ebbed well clear of the lower jetty and the two littlest members were carried pick-a-back across the mud, clasped by the legendary large hands of Lawrence. The rest of us teetered shorewards over seaweedy boulders and trekked around the bay to log fire warmth and the first class cuisine of Port Mor House built largely by Ewen's own hands.

This was to be our sanctuary during our stay. A house in Scandinavian style with floors of oak blocks, the furniture was mostly made by hand on the island and both lounge and dining room commanded splendid views to the rugged Ardamurchan Peninsula in all its moods.

Like so many islanders, the McEwen brothers and their father before them were as self sufficient as any man can be in this demanding age. A geologist by profession, Ewen was also an organic gardener and a competent cook, baking our daily bread, as well as oatcakes and scones. He also worked the Home Farm of Gallanach which supplied us with succulent lamb, milk, butter and eggs. The whole island was farmed as a single unit, absorbing all the former small holdings.

2. AROUND THE BAY TO THE ISLAND SUMMIT

The 18th May 1987 dawned with a blaze of sunshine but paled to a chilly grey by lunchtime, then blossomed to brilliance again – fickle as Highland weather so often is. An energetic day was spent exploring the ins and outs of Muck's southern promontaries , the heights of Ben Airen, mixed woodlands and upland and lowland lochans.

Scrambling up the crag beside Port Mor we enjoyed a plan view of the house and garden with its new lawn, colourful Polyanthus, Saxifrage and golden Alyssum, alongside cloche-protected fruits and vegetables. Eider drakes puffed and preened below cliffs draped with a hedgerow selection of hawthorn, briar, ivy and honeysuckle, but the top was closely grazed. The colour here was from the small and lowly scattered among red and yellow catkins sprouting from the two sexes of creeping willow, which formed a loose, knee-high thicket.

Most notable of these for us was the bitter vetchling or mountain pea (*Lathyrus montana*), with two to three pairs of leaflets and no tendrils, the flowers changing from pink to blue as they matured. This is an uncommon plant of mountains, mostly in the North and West. Mountain everlasting or cat's

72. *Bitter Vetchling*

112

foot (*Antennaria dioica*), was another, even more closely tied to the mountainous North and West.

Whole valleys were carpeted with celandines, their glossy petals losing little of their glow when the sun slipped behind a cloud. Inland bluffs were adorned with primroses and violets, coastal ones with thrift and scurvy grass.

From the Bronze Age fortified eminence west of the bay we watched arctic terns cavorting elegantly over the waves and oyster catchers probing for titbits at the water's edge. We kept an eye open for mergansers, but saw only the exuberantly coloured shelducks bobbing over the wavelets, birds which we associate with the Severn Estuary mudflats rather than these exciting rockscapes.

Some shags had hoisted angular wings to dry after a bout of fishing, ignoring the pied wagtails and rock pipits which pottered round about. Wheatears bobbed and scuttled over the short grass and a skylark rose ever higher, pouring out thanks that he was not being buffeted off course by the wind.

The way to Fionnard, the island's southernmost tip, was across consecutive ridges and valleys, the former a series of parallel Dolerite sills running across the general grain of the country. Geological sills, like those under windows, tend to be horizontal, as opposed to the more or less vertical walls of dykes. Snuggled against those were the ruins of ancient cottages, high and dry above the valleys between, which were often marshy.

Some were dominated by reed canary grass, some by yellow Iris and some by purple moor grass. Colonies of kingcups or marsh marigolds stood out like beacons, a foil to the gentle mauve of cuckoo flower or lady's smock. Later on in summer meadowsweet would froth out into an aromatic haze, bubbly like whipped cream, with less flambuoyant square-stemmed St. John's wort rising from a mosaic pavement of marsh pennywort leaves. The floral gem here was marsh cinquefoil (*Potentilla palustris*), with its rusty red and purple flowers and silvered palmate leaves.

Land bordering Camas Mor, the Big Bay, is partly composed of a massive Gabbro dyke, this mineral, along with Basalt and Dolerite, being among the more basic, non acid, types of igneous rock. It exceeds 40 m high in places, dipping to a low ridge in the north-west.

Sea birds were scattered along the tall face, which fell sheer to the sea, the crisp air aflutter with their vibrant black and white wings. They seemed very much at home in their

73. *Marsh Cinquefoil*

bustling environment, but did not live trouble-free lives on this seemingly impregnable precipice. On our way down we had seen both guillemot and shag eggs dropped by marauding gulls or crows and still sticky with the yolk that would now go to nourish the robber's chicks rather than those of the legitimate owners.

Fulmar petrels were much the commonest nesters, decoratively disposed on the weathered faces among sea pinks and sea campion. Guillemots were more localised, but more densely aggregated – mini penguins huddled together by the score. Razorbills and puffins were in smaller numbers, seven of the former popping out one by one from a hole just immediately below our feet, to pause and stare at us with interest rather than fear before taking off to make way for the next to emerge. Kittiwakes were vocalising in flight, but not at their nests. Herring gulls shared the cliff face with fulmars and the southern bluff with greater black-backs.

Fibrous cylinders of dung littering the maritime turf, showed where winter flocks of grey lag geese had been recycling the wind dried maritime turf. Here were clifftop pools, whose dark beery fluid held straggly water starwort and marsh pennywort.

Botanical treasures of the gabbro faces included shining drifts of black spleen-wort ferns, depauperate spreads of dwarf Juniper and polished Scots lovage leaves clustered around the stem bases of last year's dead umbels. Black bog rush huddled with primrose and violet along along the cliff base, while golden rod, wild carrot and mats of thyme trailed over the black walls. Wild garlic and kidney vetch pointed to the calcareous nature of the dyke.

The find of the day, however, was the pyramidal bugle (*Ajuga pyramidalis*) on the summit of Ben Airien. One of Britain's rarest plants, this softly downy version of the common woodland bugle is found only in the north and west of Scotland with an outlier in the English Lake District.

Spread through the intertidal zone at Camas Mor were limey shales of the great estuarine group of Middle Jurassic age- forming a smooth wave-cut platform, shot through at

74. *Pyramidal Bugle*

right angles by a series of narrow dykes which continued out to sea as parallel reefs. These more calcareous rocks were packed with fossil oysters.

Above were the famous raised beaches, silvery pebbles nestled among sheep-mown grass at the lowest, twenty five foot, level, fully grassed ridges at the fifty foot level and the oldest running into a farm field at a hundred feet – all on a more muted scale than those of Islay and Colonsay. Persisting over the millennia, they tell a story of higher sea levels as the land adjusted to the loss of its burden of ice.

In the long woodland occupying the seaward side of the northern continuation of the gabbro intrusion, we saw a fledgeling blackbird fall from a tree and a similarly truncated young song thrush coughed up a crop pellet at the third try and wiped its beak fastidiously on a twig. There were robins and chaffinches here and wrens creeping in and out of crevices in the dry stone walls.

Many tree types were represented – from Mediterranean cypress and Australian Eucalypt to Swedish whitebeam and Japanese flowering cherry. White-tailed bumble bees blundered through the gean flowers, scattering loose petals, while others pollinated the flowering currants.

The whole was carpeted with non-flowering, sheep-chomped bluebells. Primroses and celandines covered less ground but were faring better and there was a full cover of lacy white pignut to come. Other woodland ground floras investigated were grassier, with knapweed, sweet vernal grass and creeping willow. Herons were flushed several times in the open, but their treetop nests were not spotted.

The series of lochans in the ridge and furrow system evinced considerable variety, although all were dominated by splendid stands of the beautifully fringed pink and white flowers of bogbean (*Menyanthes trifoliata*). Some of the softer shores were ringed with yellow flags. Valley lochans contained water horsetail, marsh cinquefoil, and black sedge: upland ones were partially choked with floating Scirpus (*Eleogiton fluitans*) and rooted bottle sedge and bordered with bog pondweed. Whirligig beetles scudded merrily over their surface.

75. Bogbean

A buzzard was flushed from a bare hilltop to go soaring off into the blue. The once familiar notes of a cuckoo echoed through the vibrant atmosphere and fifteen hooded crows were lined up like vultures along the skyline during our tea break. The final descent to Port Mor house, among churring starlings, was via the hill cemetery where graves are clustered around the Bronze Age fort, their covering grass kept neat by the beasts of the field.

3. BEACHCOMBING AROUND THE SHORES OF MUCK

Another day of peerless sunshine we spent following the coast. The wind persisted, little changed since leaving its Arctic spawning ground, but the southeastern cliffs provided a fine windbreak where we were able to shed layers of clothing and forget the latitude.

The little saltmarsh at the head of Port Mor was based on dark peat with sea milkwort flowers peeping from the sheep-chomped turf of thrift and fescue.This peat was laminated, the narrow layers showing in the vertical erosion faces fronting the beach pebbles, these formed as today's waves nibbled away at the successive layers of alluvium deposited by other waves of long ago.

A few solitary bees were investigating the bald stretches – for possible underground nest sites, having evidently survived the cold wet winter better than Ewen's hive bees had. Khaki Campbells quacked and dabbled on the tidal flats, some laying eggs in the garden hedge, but few managing to keep their ducklings safe from marauding gulls and hoodie crows.

The substrate here was blackish sand, produced from the weathering of the soft, dark, Basalt cliffs and so fine as to be washed away except in sheltered inlets such as this, so the island has few sandy beaches apart from the impressive spread at Gallanach. Those white sands of the north, viewed under hand lenses, contained a lot of shell fragments and white silica grains from harder, more resistant rocks.

Crossing the shoulder of farmland to the east, we had good views of the patterning of walls in the old village above the cemetery. Then we dropped to sea level to investigate a spectacular band of red rock along the base of the cliff.

This bed, only four to six inches wide, was noticed in several places around the shores of Muck and on the cliffs of Horse Island. One of a series of layers of tropical laterite soil it had had time to build up on an old lava bed before being overwhelmed by the next flow. It reminded us of a more modern organic soil layer overwhelmed by blowing sand in a dune profile. Above was the angular

Basalt, pocked with little round holes, gas bubbles, perhaps. Below was a purple-red agglomerate, seemingly spewed from a volcanic concrete mixer and frequently interbedded with sheets of columnar Dolerite – as are beds of volcanic tuff.

Both major rock types supported a good growth of acorn barnacles, but few of these had managed to get a grip on the smooth red Laterite between. Where the rocks reached above tide level, it was the knobbly agglomerate that supported the unusually prolific growths of Britain's most truly maritime moss, *Grimmia maritima*, though lichens were at home on both. The agglomerate was obviouly the harder and protruded seawards as a wave-cut platform two to three yards wide.

Some oyster catchers had nested on an accumulation of shells and pebbles in the bayhead and four of the birds were standing quietly off duty while the sun warmed their eggs. This was a desirable spot to linger out of the wind and, with no pilfering gulls around, we had few qualms about sharing their sunny corner for a short spell. Eiders idled offshore, while four rock pipits and two pied wagtails were busy among rocks inhabited by sea slaters, craneflies and kelp flies. Intertidal pools were full of squiggling life and unusual algae, particularly brown Scytosiphon on rocks crusted with pink Lithophyllum. Green algae found safe lodging on the backs of algal-eating limpets, which had the good manners not to graze over each others shells.

Narrow gullies eroded out between intrusive dykes were packed with wave-borne oarweeds, easy pickings for kelp gatherers when this was the mainstay of the island economy. Walls built parallel to the backing cliffs and giving the appearance of small raised beaches, had been constructed for the drying of the seaweeds in places and the remains of kelp kilns were discernible in the old village.

The burning of 'sea tangle' to produce exportable ash, was in full swing here when Boswell and Johnson visited in 1773. The alkaline ash obtained from the burning of the brown oarweeds was in great demand for glass, soap and gunpowder making and was a remunerative industry until about 1820. The rise and fall of the Small Isles kelp production is discussed in the ensuing section on Eigg.

The Muck population of 280 engaged in it had neglected the farming and fishing that had sustained them before. Without capital to restart, many are recorded as having emigrated to Nova Scotia and Cape Breton. In 1826 the then laird, McLean, cleared the land and ran it as a single unit for livestock from 1830.

First came beef cattle, then sheep, then dairy cattle and crops. The McEwen brothers have reared Cheviots, their fine wool selling for clothing, and Scottish blackfaces, producing much coarser wool used for carpets and mattress stuffing. Variety was added with the more decorative Jacob's sheep. Currently root crops, oats and silage were grown to feed the animals, the sale of lamb and the cattle providing the main income. One of the assets for the growing industry of tourism was the wide sweep of sand in Gallinach Bay, although the more prevalent rocky shores held a special charm for lowlanders.

116

4. HORSE ISLAND AND LAMB ISLAND OFF MUCK

If there is such a thing as the perfect day, the one on which we visited Muck's two north-western outliers was it. The sun beamed encouragingly from a peerless blue sky although the chilly north wind persisted.

Lamb Island consists of 2.7 hectares of gently sloping rock terrace dipping north from low cliffs in the south. With careful planning it is possible to follow the pebble isthmus to Lamb island, traverse its long axis and scoot across a quarter of a mile or so of seaweedy rocks to Horse Island. At low spring tide this allows about two hours on Horse before return but we had missed low springs.

Ewen nobly volunteered to row us across in two dinghy loads and return for us later in the day. This involved him in a bicycle ride along the length of Muck's only road, to the further shore of Gallanaich Bay to launch Lawrence's dinghy and row along a mile of shore to pick us up on the point of Lamb for the crossing. He moored the dinghy on Lamb to return afoot and awheel and repeat the process in reverse later in the day.

As a result we managed a much longer spell on this delightful 52 acre (21 hectare) island that had loomed so enticingly on our starboard bow as we voyaged back from Rhum earlier in the week. Low cliffs reared behind the raised beach by the causeway to Lamb Island, the land rising gradually to fall away in sheer cliffs along the north side, these interrupted by several steep gullies or geos. Lava flows, as on the main island of Muck, appear as terraces.

76. *Gray lag Goose*

Our most interesting find was the nest of a grey lag goose, because the first of these had not been recorded breeding on the Muck group (on Horse Island) until 1981 and on Muck itself in 1984, with numbers increasing only to three or four nests by 1986. We discovered it as we stumbled back in haste over the central bog for our rendezvous with the boat. There was a splash and a whoop as a party member slid off a Molinia stool into the mud and a goose flapped out in consternation to reveal three warm, slightly soiled white eggs in a great strawey nest. There had been four geese flying around during our stay and fourteen non breeding birds had been seen on Horse Island earlier.

The geese fed mainly on the lush green of the south-western gullery on grass and bluebell leaves – which ultimately produced large piles of soft black dung pellets, very different from the pale fibrous remains left by the over-wintering flocks subsisting on more wiry herbage.

The numbers of geese overwintering on the island had been increasing since the 1960s. their presence as grazers a growing problem for the farming enterprise. Not only the grazing paddocks, but cereal and vegetable crops, contributed forage for the geese. In the previous July (1986) grey lags had resorted to Horse Island to moult and moved to Muck itself to graze in August. This flock, of up to a hundred birds, outnumbered the breeding population on the whole of the Small Isles group, their origin unknown in the absence of any ringing programme.

Up to fifty eight barnacle geese were moving in at this time to feed on Lamb island and roost on Horse Island between December and April. Brent geese appeared only as small groups on passage, feeding up for about a week in autumn before moving on. Greenland whitefronts over-wintered, feeding on the hills and roosting on the bogs in modest numbers of around forty birds.

The lushness on Horse Island was a combination of no grazing by farm livestock and a generous input of guano from a substantial colony of great black-backed gulls, which had increased from the odd pair in 1963 to thirty or so, distributed mainly between here and Eagamol Island just offshore. Of particular interest plantwise was the dense stand of Scots lovage spread through the colony. This was a low shining green in May but the whole must be a forest of three foot high flowering umbels in August. Many of the old dry stems were now incorporated in the bulky nests, most of which contained their full clutch of three eggs.

Herring gulls shared this sea level colony, but their number around the cliffs were insignificant compared with those of the ever present fulmar petrels, which had increased to over four hundred pairs since the first colonists arrived in the 1930s. They leave by mid September and are not around in winter. Kittiwakes, also, had increased encouragingly since 1963 and were divided mainly between the lofty northern cliffs of Horse Island and the south-east of the satellite island of Eagamol. Lunch was eaten on the shore opposite the latter, with binoculars trained between bites on these and their auk companions. They mingled indiscriminately with the guillemots on steep faces, but were below most of the razorbills. Up to three hundred can be seen offshore in September but very few in winter. We lunched to the resonant accompaniment of crooning seals in unseen caves.

While some fulmars were still scraping away at the red soil to form level niches in which to bring up their families, the numerous shags were well advanced with their nesting, crests raised, feathers shining and a belligerent glint in their bottle green eyes. Around seventy five pairs were breeding, returning to their cliff sites as early as February. The winter population hovers around a hundred. Both Eagamol and the precipitous north coast of Horse, yielded good numbers of guillemots and razorbills, the odd displaced egg visible from above, green-tinged and tapered. There were a few black guillemots or tysties off the south shore and a dozen puffins off the north, but we saw neither of these on land.

77. *Black Guillemot in summer plumage*

Encounters with incubating eider ducks were many. Laying was only just starting and none had more than five eggs. The birds were insufficiently broody as yet to be sitting as tightly as they would later on. All saw us first and took off, leaving us to cover their pale, conspicuous eggs with eiderdown to shield them from predatory eyes. One had to be rescued from a wire mesh fence along the brink of a hundred and sixty foot high precipice, beside which she had laid her three eggs. We wondered if she had worked out how she would get her ducklings down that hundred and sixty feet.

118

She had certainly worked out how to slip successfully through the wire mesh after being gently replaced on her nest. Some fifty families make their way to the shallow offshore waters at fledging time in July, but mortality is high. Adults are around offshore all winter.

A more everyday touch was afforded by the swallows skimming the cliffs – perhaps for flies bred in the guano impregnated soil below. A snipe was flushed from one of the central quagmires that occupied valleys between the upstanding parallel dykes. These crossed the island as ridges, protruding as headlands to the north-west and south-east. Vegetation generally was of waved heath on the exposed headlands, the swooping, strawey grass crests leaning to leeward. Creeping willow and burnet rose grew along the eastern cliffs, but heather was negligible except at the southern ends of the dykes. Bluebells and lovage were widespread, even on the western heights.

We hadn't noticed the wind rising and it was a choppy passage back – impossible in the opposite direction, loaded and without the following wind, according to our intrepid oarsman. He dropped us among the wracks on Lamb and beat his way back empty for the second load. We now had a couple of hours to explore Lamb Island.

The gradual dip of the terrain towards the north-west from the low cliffs facing towards Muck reflects the general dip of the superimposed layers of basalt lavas. The north shore yielded sixteen occupied nests of common gulls, the amount of grassy building material used being midway between that of the bulky herring gull nests and the negligible amounts used by the arctic terns. The air was full of these elegantly proportioned, urgently screeching birds, which nested somewhat later and were still undergoing the rowdy business of staking out their respective claims.

A lapwing's nest was found, still with eggs. Most were earlier. A redshank strolled languidly along the tideline and ringed plovers had laid their eggs on brief scatters of shells drawn together on the pebbly beach, in lieu of something more comfortable. The shattered shells of small spider crabs and large edible sea urchins, their Aristotle lanterns still intact, showed where gulls had been dropping their booty on the rocks to make the contents more accessible. Their expectorated crop pellets included crushed mussel shells and shore crab carapaces as well as calcareous urchin spines.

More substantial, although well on the way to disintegration was a hefty, stranded log, riddled by shipworms or Teredo borers. Such perforated driftwood washes up not uncommonly on these western shores, the timber useless for construction work and only marginally acceptable for fuel, the infestation, however, not as disastrous as when the animals invade the timbers of working boats, pier piles or bridge stanchions.

The causative organism is a bivalve mollusc, the paired shells only a centimetre long and forked at the tip, the fleshy body wormlike and up to twenty times as long. A calcareous lining is deposited over the tunnel walls as the shellfish works its way forward. Some food is obtained from the substrate, but most enters at the tube mouth, through siphons protected by a pair of pallets.

Burrowing was across the grain of the wood in this instance, but can be either way. A driftwood log with a few larger tunnels entering at the cut end had probably been bored by a terrestrial animal before taking to the sea.

Lamb is low-lying, much of it clothed in thrift and fescue, its brackish pools with a mixture of salt marsh or mud rush and freshwater bog pondweed and water starwort. Higher parts bore grass heath. The tide had dropped and we got off the landward end more easily than we had got on, to an intertidal platform. There was time to linger on the sands of Gallinach, beachcombing, among semicircular driftlines of bright orange and yellow blunt periwinkle shells. Backing the shell sand beaches was true machair with a wealth of lime-loving flowers.

We detoured to visit the stone circle of the McEwen graveyard sited, like that of the opposite side of the island, on an old Bronze Age burial mound, before heading back towards the farm, a delicious meal of home-killed pork and home grown vegetables, including the island staple of potatoes.

EIGG ISLAND

5. INTRODUCTION TO THE ISLAND OF EIGG

It was with reluctance that we finally dragged ourselves away from the friendly little island of Muck, that had treated us to so much sunshine. In fact we were moving to somewhere even richer in unusual geological and botanical phenomena.

We lingered to examine a photogenic cluster of *Bovista plumbea* puffballs ornamenting a sward starred with celandines, violets and speedwell. Then somebody found a neat little nest of fine grasses made by a Muck field mouse – a unique Hebridean subspecies that lives also on Eigg. The small shop by the Muck quay was bursting with home made cakes and crafts and claimed our attention until departure.

"Shearwater II" lay between the slippery weed of our arrival and the inner jetty. Boarding involved climbing an aluminium builder's ladder to drop in over the gunwhale. The indefatigable Ewen waved us "Goodbye" from his precarious perch on a window sill, where he was doing some outside painting. This was in between dealing with the massive pile of laundry and making rhubarb jam from the garden. There seemed nothing between house building and flower arranging that this versatile man would not tackle – when not out helping to man the boats.

Second largest of the islands that constitute the Parish of the Small Isles, Eigg measures five miles by three and occupies 7,500 acres. The dramatic mountain ridge of the Sgurr that dominates the scene, at 1,289 feet, is not the only exciting geological manifestation of its turbulent, volcano-dominated past. Here, too, we were to see alpine flowers not present on Muck and view the two majestic pairs of resident golden eagles.

This Atlantic Isle lies seven miles out from Arisaig and twelve miles from Mallaig. The boat crossing from the first occupies an hour, from the second

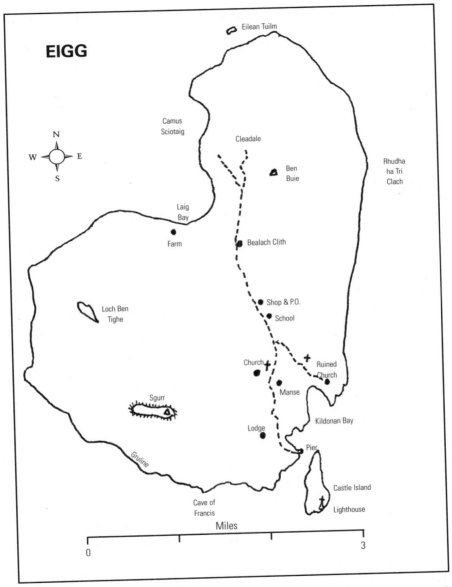

EIGG

Eilean Tuilm

Camus Sciotaig

Cleadale

Ben Buie

Rhudha ha Tri Clach

Laig Bay

Farm

Bealach Clith

Loch Ben Tighe

Shop & P.O.

School

Church

Ruined Church

Manse

Sgurr

Kildonan Bay

Lodge

Gruline

Pier

Castle Island

Cave of Francis

Lighthouse

Miles

0   3

anything up to five hours depending on the route taken by the steamer around the island cluster. Our voyage in "Shearwater II" from Muck was rather less, but sufficient to afford some fine views of flesh and blood shearwaters shearing the waves with a speed and elegance that few other birds can achieve.

Our craft ran through a much more disorderly mob of gulls exploiting a shoal of sprats. At Castle Island off Eigg we came close in under the herring gull colony with its border of screaming terns and spotted a grey lag goose on the beach. Later, on a visit from the warden of the Scottish Wildlife Trust Nature reserve on Eigg, we learned that a mere six pairs of terns were nesting here among a rabble of 350 pairs of gulls and were yet managing to get their chicks off successfully. The gulls were seemingly acting as watchdogs rather than predators, mobbing any individuals moving in on the terns. The grey lag geese nested here. In the past geese had been bred and released for shooting, but there had been more than ten wild living generations of birds since then so they were now regarded as a genuine part of the natural fauna.

78. Arctic Tern

Peter Wells, our host at the Kildonan Peninsula Hotel, a converted eighteenth century farmhouse, met us at the Galmisdale pier in South-east Eigg. He drove us north around the bay to Kildonan through wooded gardens resplendent with fan palms and Australian flame trees alongside more familiar Rhododendrons and drifts of bluebells – the finest this year that he could remember. The woodland had a soft southern look, with none of the moist, elfin forest impression given by that on Rhum.

A substantial tea and excellent dinner left time for us to absorb the sunshine and atmosphere between the towering cliffs with their resident buzzards at the head of Kildonan Bay on the one hand and the monument to St. Donan at its mouth on the other

Our first tentative exploration revealed two well camouflaged oyster catchers' nests and a little flock of diligently probing curlews. A pair of flipperty gibbet pied wagtails sported by the water mill and nesting swallows zoomed in and out of the farm barn. The warden, John Chester, caught us up and advised on how to avoid disturbing the two pairs of golden eagles that were nesting in absurdly accessible places, also how to find and recognise some of the other birds.

6. PAST EXPLOITATION OF SEAWEEDS FOR KELP

Boswell and Johnson visited Eigg as well as Muck in their travels and were overtaken here by a storm. They seemed more concerned with the popish nature of the people than the kelp industry, but recorded that the blacksmith resident on Eigg also served the needs of the folk on Muck. A quote from the journal of their Hebridean travels edited by R.W.Chapman (1924) goes as follows:

"The Romish religion is professed only in Eigg and Canna, two small islands into which the Reformation never made its way." And later: "Eigg is the principal island of a parish in which, though he has no congreration, the Protestant minister resides." That sounds like a cushy job!

Traditionally the ash produced by burning the giant oarweeds or tangle, was used in the making of glass and soap and extraction of iodine, but a subsidiary product was gunpowder. The need for this commodity during the Napoleonic wars gave the industry a boost. More was needed just when supplies from Europe and elsewhere were difficult to come by.

Lairds, spying a remunerative market, brought in more crofters to service the trade. On Eigg each newcomer was given a small plot of land for subsistence and was allowed to pay his rent in kelp, while the boss pocketed the lolly.

The end of the Napoleonic wars at Waterloo in 1815, not only reduced the need for gunpowder but reduced exports as the old European markets reopened. It also coincided with the discovery of mineral deposits of potash in Germany. Market prices dropped from twenty five to three pounds a ton and the trade languished.

Eigg, grossly over-populated, could no longer sustain the crofters and their families and there was yet another exodus of displaced peasants overseas while the lairds, many of whom were absentee landlords, hoarded the spoils.

The high grade ash coming in from Europe when the markets re-opened, was known as barilla or barrilla. This name also applies to some of the terrestrial seashore plants from which it was obtained, as well as from the brown algae. Such species were *Salsola kali, Salsola soda* and *Halogeton soda.*

The first of these is our familiar but lowly prickly saltwort, which is widespread along the tops of sandy beaches just above high water mark, but not in commercially viable amounts. Sodium and potassium, the two components needed by the industry, were extracted from the sea by both categories of plants. High osmotic pressure in the cell sap of the land plants enabled these to absorb them from saline ground water. The brown seaweeds won hands down as suppliers in Western Britain until industrial chemists got busy and plants of any sort became redundant as an intermediate stage.

Their use was by no means confined to Europe. The plant known as barilla in Australia is a grey-leaved saltbush *(Atriplex cinerea),* of the same genus as our oraches. Some of its Australian relatives were also used, these mostly herbaceous and shrubby samphire glasswort *(Salicornia or Sarcocornia species* and *Arthrocnemum arbusculum)* seaberry saltbush *(Rhagodia candolleana).* All are larger than our British Chenodpods apart from the biggest specimens of Norfolk's shrubby seablite *(Suaeda fruticosa).*

I had been involved with these Australian halophytes during my work with the muttonbird industry in the late 1950s and early 1960s. (The edible mutton birds are mainly short-tailed shearwaters in Australia and sooty shearwaters in New Zealand.) All the plants are rich in sodium and potassium and the word barilla is used there for the derived ash as well as the plants.

Australian ash, mostly from the Tasmanian islands, was sent to Hobart for processing and, as early as 1826, this local industry had supplanted imports from the UK, contributing to the demise of Hebridean and Irish enterprises. Eventually, however, the barilla stocks, which took several years to regrow after cutting, were insufficient to sustain the process. The change to chemically produced soda and alkali brought the extraction of plant minerals to a halt on both sides of the world.

When hard pressed, particularly between 1804 and 1810, Australian workers had boiled their raw product and eaten it as 'Botany Bay greens' instead of melting it into perfumed beef suet or mutton fat to make scented soap. Chenopods from our East Anglian saltmarshes, glassworts and others, are still eaten by quirky gourmets for their salty savour. Like the folk of our Atlantic fringe, the Tasmanians also ate seaweeds.

Favourite food species in Scotland were dulse and tang, the red *Palmaria palmata* and the brown *Alaria esculenta*. In Ireland carragheen was the favourite, the red *Chondrus crispus* and *Gigartina stellata*. In Wales it was, and is, the delicate red laver (*Porphyra umbilicalis*), which is still sold in Swansea market as laverbread to accompany the breakfast bacon.

79. *Dulse and Laver*

Sea rods, the hard stalks of the big oarweeds which do not rot down for use as fertiliser as the flattened blades do, were being exported from the Scottish and Irish islands at least to the end of the twentieth century. Big stacks waiting to be shipped out to the factories have been a common sight on quays from Orkney to the Aran Islands off County Clare for many years.

This is not the end of the story of seaweed utilisation, but the big new products are alginates. These are mineral rich colloidal gels obtained largely from the big brown weeds and used in a bewildering array of unexpected products. Red algae also have a place in commerce and every bacteriology student is familiar with agar gel from Gracilaria and other species used to provide the growing medium for cultures of bacteria and fungi in petri dishes.

Working among the Tasmanian islands again in 1991, I was fascinated to come upon a large scale kelp gathering operation on King Island in the Western Bass Strait. This was a new kelp industry, started in 1975 – the proceeds to be exported to Scotland where collection had fallen off irretrievably.

The brown oarweeds used, mostly *Durvillea potatorum*, are bigger than our Laminarians. They were being brought in by islanders on trucks, trailers and utilities to be processed on this particular beach for shipment to Scotland by Kelco/AIL International Ltd. of London and Webster Ltd. of Hobart.

Fronds were hung in rows by meat hooks from a network of iron poles four metres high – like oversized versions of the fish drying racks seen in countries of little rainfall. After two weeks of drying, they had corkscrewed into rubbery spirals, before having the residual moisture driven off in a wood burning oven until it was brittle enough for milling.

Granules in bags weighing one and a half tons apiece were to be transferred in standard steel containers to that land on the other side of the world where it had all begun and whose multiple shorelines are still surrounded by swaying beds of oarweeds.

The journey was not a little complicated. By truck to the deep water port of Grassy on King Island for sea passage to Melbourne, where the containers were loaded onto the OCL Fleet bound for Tilbury Docks in London. Then came a rail journey to Glasgow and finally by truck to Girvan or Barcaldine on the Scottish coast.

Transferred to hoppers, this product of Bass Strait was now the sole property of Kelco/AIL, the world's largest producer of "Over 380 types of alginate for more than a thousand uses around the world. "In one form or another, we think that you eat, drink, wear or in some manner enjoy the products of our King Island bull kelp every day."

To name some of the uses. We have alginates as thickeners in sauces and syrups and gels in blancmanges and table jellies, cosmetic creams and lotions. Stabilisers in the foam of detergents and shampoos, improving adhesion of water for fire fighting and in root dips for crop and garden plants by increasing moisture retention: Control of penetration into paper and fabric of rubber, synthetic lattices and some adhesives, assisting the ease with which these are washed from textile and printing pastes.

Alginate colloids prevent the formation of ice crystals in ice cream and hinder dripping in water ices, as well as adding body to tooth paste, imitation cream and fruit drinks. Handymen use them unknowingly in emulsion paints, ceramic glazes, creamed rubber latex, sizing paper and textiles, grouting tiles, dental impressions, pharmaceuticals, calcium alginate yarns, hardening gelatine in photography, sugar processing, flocculating impurities in water treatment and even in sausage skins. This list is getting tedious. No wonder few of us have time to read the list of contents on supermarket packages.

There must be a lesson here somewhere. When the world's oil eventually runs out, as it surely will, and our pampered society can no longer satisfy its multiple needs from the furthest corners of our planet, the harvesting of home grown seaweed may stage a comeback. By then, with no powered wheeled transport, we may be feeding ourselves from our own small cabbage patches and clothing ourselves with that now spurned but once revered commodity of "pure wool", for so long ousted by synthetics.

Fortunately Shetland sheep and other Highland livestock can consume our algal riches direct, as do crabs and fish. All power to those historians who are trying to keep alive the ancient crafts which made life so much more bearable when we were more dependent on our own efforts for life's little comforts. We may need them again yet. (For the background to barilla and alginates see Gillham, 2000, "Island hopping in Tasmania's Roaring Forties" from page 317 and 488.) Such philosophising in a book of this sort, however, is out of place – it is time to return to the delectable sights and sounds of Eigg.

7. FROM CLEADALE HEIGHTS TO LAIG BAY

Wind-spiced sunshine stayed with us through yet another day, which was dominated by the cloud-free outline of Rhum, a full four miles away to the north but seemingly much nearer in the dust-free air. Packed into Peter's land rover, we made an early rendezvous with the warden about half way to the north of the island.

John Chester was primarily an ornithologist and sought confirmation of a plant which he thought might be rare. It was. We crept one at a time under a thick scrub of hazel and eared sallow to view a fine clump of pyramidal bugle among tall heather and bracken. It made us feel not a little smug, although our own first sighting had been but a few days before on Muck.

More impressive for us was the long-winged outline of a short-eared owl coursing back and forth, perhaps in search of those special Hebridean mice. This, like the simultaneously calling cuckoo, had been a not unusual experience during our youth but neither were often encountered in England and Wales nowadays.

The harsh croak of a pheasant struck a more familiar note. This was one of the descendents of birds reared for shooting in earlier days. They were said to be as tame as hens, but that went in lesser degree for some of the more rustic songsters in this island haven where conservation now ranked higher than extracting profit from the land, as in harder times. Willow warbler, whitethroat and wren were in full voice in the 'bugle glen'.

People of the Bronze and Iron Ages lived on Eigg, growing crops and tending flocks and herds. The island remained populated during the times of the Picts and then the Celts, who arrived from Ireland. The Norsemen came and went – or integrated.

A survey of 1771 had recorded 459 Gaelic speaking people living on the island, mostly in the crofting townships of Cleadale (or Cliffdale), Kildonnan, Grulin and Galmisdale. Potatoes were grown on lazy beds, oats to make porridge and oatcakes and cattle reared for milk, butter and cheese. Crofters reared sheep for wool and meat and some owned goats or draft horses. This healthy but samish diet was alleviated with generous helpings of shearwater chicks, harvested when plump and ready to go to sea, as in the mutton bird industries "Down Under". By taking the progeny after the 'geese which laid the golden eggs' had left for their winter at sea, no inroads were made into the total number of birds likely to live for forty years and more. In thirty five years of breeding each pair has only to produce two living replacements to keep the population steady.

As well as the widespread consumption of carragheen, which was by no means restricted to Ireland, the Eigg folk apparently found sustenance in the above-ground runners of silverweed. They also exploited the rabbits, introduced by Clanranald as a source of food but now something of a menace, although their numbers were checked at intervals by Myxomatosis. (Muck had so far escaped the rabbit problem). And then, of course, there were fish and other marine creatures to be exploited.

No large mammals such as deer were present to supply protein and hides. Otters were seldom spotted but rats were all too numerous, though feeding mainly around the seashore, at least in summer. Of the small mammals short-tailed voles were the commonest, the special field mice and pygmy shrews less so. The mice arrived with the Vikings, their DNA linking them still with their Norwegian forbears.

Boom and bust occurred in the 1800s when the island people outgrew the ability of the island to support them. Crops failed, prices crashed and many left for America. Cottages fell into ruin, but as we moved on to the north the landscape showed signs of the general comeback of subsidised crofting to what had threatened to become a dying community. Currently, in the mid nineteen eighties, fifteen hundred lambs were being exported annually and the inhabitants were pretty self sufficient in dairy products, with the crofters' small holdings averaging around fourteen acres.

They worked mainly here in the north, centred around Cleadale, while the present owners farmed 2,000 acres in the south as a single unit. The sheep were predominantly crossbred blackface and Cheviot, while with the hybrid cattle were some of the local Luing breed from the Slate Islands of Nether Lorn. There was better yet to come, when the islanders became responsible for their own destiny as corporate owners in the nineteen nineties.

Most of the boulder clay that might have added soil fertility was scraped away by the ice, but some remained around Kildonan Bay in the south-east. Subsequent addition of wind-blown sand there has produced a fine, loamy tilth, but this needs generous applications of superphosphate.

Most of the island consists of basalt lava flows of tertiary age – from volcanic outpourings on Rhum or in Ardnamurchan, The step-like features that we were traversing were individual lava flows with more slowly cooled and hence harder cores than margins. The cores withstood erosion to form escarpments, the softer material above and below weathering more easily into gentler slopes. We encountered more of the thin red layers of tropical laterite in between successive flows that we had seen on Muck.

The tall cliff, a thousand feet high and two miles long set well back from the coast at Cleadale in the north-east was formed by accumulated basalt sloughing away from the flank of Ben Buie due to collapse of the more easily eroded sediments below.

The broad shelf of land separating the Cleadale heights from the sea and terminating in lower cliffs behind the beach, consisted of sandy and shaly limestones of Jurassic age. This lower platform runs all around the north coast and round the east to Kildonan It formed a green apron where a hundred and fifty crofters gained a living in 1841, when the entire population was five hundred and forty six. After the clearances and voluntary emigration, lands where loads of hay had been harvested to feed the livestock in winter reverted to heather moor.

8. BIRDS AND PLANTS AROUND CLEADALE

At the north end of the main island road we scaled the Dolerite cliff behind Cleadale. A large population of shearwaters burrowed in the seaward skirt of this ridge, but were sleeping the day away in their burrows or gliding effortlessly over the sea. It is only when out in a boat that it is possible to appreciate their numbers, unless venturing forth with a powerful torch at night.

Shearwater numbers were declining on Eigg at this time but the colony on Rhum was thriving, and birds had recently been found nesting in burrows at Camus Mor on Muck. The only other candidates as full pelagic birds were the fulmars, a small group of black guillemots on Castle Island outside the landing bay and a few cliff nesting kittiwakes.

Because of its larger size and greater diversity of habitats, including well established woodland, there were twenty eight more bird species breeding on Eigg than on Muck in the mid eighties. These were mainly woodland birds, also finches and buntings on the stubbles, long-eared and short-eared owls, red-throated divers, red-breasted mergansers and dippers on the lochs and streams. Here we were in golden eagle territory, the nest site visible on the cliff beyond the shearwater rookery, but the owners eluded us.

81. Opposite-leaved Saxifrage

We set off, seeking out the high spots for alpine plants. The deep purple flowers of the opposite-leaved Saxifrage break bud in March and April and were over now, but we have the opportunity of seeing these in the Brecon Beacons in Wales, nearer home, where the species grows almost at its southern geographical limit.

Much rarer were the unassuming, creamy white flowers of artic sandwort (*Arenaria norvegica*). This tiny tufted perennial is as unassuming as it is rare, its white flowers borne at ground level on the partially bare scree. It is an arctic species, not an arctic alpine, native to Norway, Sweden, Finland and Iceland. Our Floras say of its British distribution "A rare and local plant of rocky places in West Sutherland, Shetland and Rhum." It may have been a new record for Eigg, but we came across it again on top of the Sgurr.

More eye catching were the low domes of pink moss campion (*Silene acaulis*), which can be viewed in local profusion on the island of Mull. As the specific epithet implies, the plants are practically stemless. Scarce away from Northern Scotland, they appear in the English Lake District, Northern Ireland and as far south as the mountains of North Wales. Mostly on ledges and screes, they descend right to sea level in the far North.

Of similar growth form in Eigg was the mossy Saxifrage (*Saxifraga hypnoides*), its spiky, crowded leaves resembling moss cushions, as do those of moss campion. This extends further south – again to the Brecon Beacons in South Wales. Its Irish counterpart, recently promoted from varietal status, to *Saxifraga rosacea*, is a major beautifier of the natural rock gardens on the the limestone pavement of the Aran Islands.

Others more upstanding on the heights of Eigg were roseroot and globe flower (*Sedum roseum* and *Trollius europaeus*). Essentially northerners, both extend as far as South Wales and both are very handsome, the one like an overgrown stonecrop, the other like an overgrown buttercup. Roseroot occupies dry rock crevices. Globe flower prefers wet places, tolerating the spray from waterfalls, but having the golden

82. Tutsan

petals incurved to exclude water from the flowers' vital parts. More humble relatives with them on the Cleadale heights were drifts of wood Anemones, purple tinted when the petals closed together in fading light. Wet patches were starred with the convoluted mauve flowers of insectivorous butterwort (*Pinguicula vulgaris*). Seldom does this flower so profusely, but the leaves with their inrolled margins for restraining insects on their slippery surface for digestion by enzymes from the covering glands are always fascinating. It occurred in the boggy areas not far from where crofters had dug peat for their hearths.

From the mud crowfoot and red rattle of a rushy field where lapwings nested, we moved across grassy cliff shelves bright with early purple orchids among the usual plethora of primroses, bluebells and celandines. Some of these narrow terraces separated vertical walls of limestone above and below, like a brief replica of the terracing on the Burren's older Carboniferous limestone. At sea level we found plentiful growths of roseroot and sea spleenwort ferns occuping crevices and woodland flowers spilling down from the moist limestone and sandstone glens.

9. THE SINGING SANDS

The white beach and sapphire shallows of the Singing Sands (Camas Sciotaig) were gained via the wide limestone amphitheatre dipping back into the Jurassic cliffs, which were themselves but a shadow of the mighty volcanic cliffs of Cleadale behind.

The 'singing' comes from the rubbing together of translucent quartz grains underfoot. These, said to be spherical, are actually angular when viewed under a hand lens, although equal sized and isodiametric. The sands give voice only when dry and when the feet are dragged. Tradition has it that the agonised screeching sounds were the voices of drowned sailors trying to communicate with the walker.

Around the corner the dark sands trapped on the wave cut platform were of black shingle and white shell flakes and the dykes ran parallel to the cliffs instead of straight out across the beach at right angles. In Laig or Surf Bay the sands were white again but non-vocal.

Dividing the first beach is a limsestone arch that has been likened to the super-structure of a Gothic cathedral. Here were steep sided rifts in the limestone and displaced rock slabs, sometimes held away from the cliff face by rock spheres like inflated boat fenders. Waterfalls came tumbling down from the high Cleadale cliffs behind, to burrow their way through the lower, more soluble limestone to seaward. They reappeared as springs where they escaped from underground and found their way across the beach between the long, low dykes. One had cut a subsidiary gully starting twenty feet deep and only three across within a vertical erosion face.

The Laig beach is backed by a single marram-topped sand ridge rising from the beach fringe of succulent sea sandwort (*Honkenya peploides*), but there are no dunes or machair, the boggy land behind being apparently clay. A hundred years ago there was a lagoon here behind the dune ridge, into which the kelp collecting boats were floated at high tide. Possibly before that there had been a boat building enterprise, as the unused stem or keel of a Viking ship has been found. All has now been sanded up, presumably helped by the general post Ice Age rise of the land above sea level associated with the raised beaches.

The Jurassic limestone, a Valtose sandstone formation, perhaps because of debris or acid drainage from the backing cliffs, confounded the botanical rules relating to lime tolerance. Dry place plants included burnet rose and kidney vetch that we often find on shell sand beaches, alongside heather and tormentil which characterise the local moors. Lime loving broad-leaved garlic and tutsan throve in seepages and by a bubbling torrent where a statuesque heron was poised on the watch for prey. Are there frogs here? Toads are, these tolerating more salt in their watery medium than do frogs. There are also palmate newts and common lizards, but no snakes.

83. Globe Flower

Drapes of *Marchantia polymorpha* liverwort plastering sheer faces, like the translucent, undulant fronds of *Mnium undulatum* and other mosses, were nurtured by the silvered spray. Black bog rush and white bog cotton crowded the peaty slobs where digging had occurred.

84. Cuckoos

A cuckoo alighted just above us, tail cocked and wings drooped, assessing, perhaps the location of the nearest pipit's nest able to host her next egg. Juvenile terns, lacking the tail streamers of their elders, dived rather ineffectually off the seaward end of the dykes, while sandpipers and ringed plovers foraged over the intervening sand. In the presence of so many plant and animal riches, however, it was the geology which intrigued us most.

10. LIMESTONE BALLS; THE CARBONATE CONCRETIONS

This was an argillaceous limestone, deposited in short-lived lagoons, the fossil fauna indicating brackish conditions of low salinity when these sea floor deposits were settling out, perhaps estuarine, perhaps sea-flooded deltaic lagoons.

A quite magical sculpturing of the wave-cut beach platform had produced an intricate maze of solution hollows up to a foot deep, the curved limestone ridges between solid enough to walk on. Where the backing cliff was undercut, waves curling up the recessed face had produced a miniature version of the open honeycomb on the horizontal surface facing downwards.

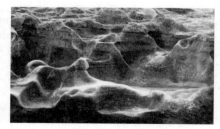

85. Sea-eroded Argillaceous Limestone

86. Hollows left by erosion of nodules, showing horizontal layering of matrix

87 & 88. Dark Limestone Nodules in situ on vertical faces

Quite the most fascinating, however, were the balls and domes of rock, sometimes darker than the pale matrix but of matching texture. They were single, paired or piled, sometimes a large one surrounded by a flock of satellites, and were anything from a few inches to a few feet across. Most were neatly spherical but flattened horizontally like a not too well filled but outsize hamburger.

They were formed in situ, in the rock itself, this shown by some which bulged from vertical cliff faces, firmly held, at least until the centre of equilibrium was passed. Far more appeared on the beach like a drift of stranded mines or monster jellyfish. These were not stranded but were firmly cemented to the rock platform beneath where they had evolved.

One cut vertically into two halves by a rift in the cliff showed narrow parallel plates or septa, protruding slightly as the matrix between wore away. Nodules broken across horizontally exhibited concentric circles of deposition, suggesting radial growth from the centre, layer by layer, as seen in tufa pebbles from limey streams, which are covered by successive films of green or blue-green algae. As more limey particles are thrown out of solution by the water and deposited on those growing pebbles, the surface algae are deprived of light and die. The process is constantly repeated, as in a rotund version of a stalactite or stalagmite.

If this was true, they would resemble the larger stromatolites in the intertidal zone of Shark Bay in Western Australia which I have had the privilege of walking over. It was many years before this tentative stromatolite theory was found to be invalid, the nodules having formed within the rock in the absence of the light needed to sustain algae. Nevertheless, a subsequent investigator refers to "Distinctive beds of stromatolitic algal limestone, which occurs widely in this horizon of the Inner hebrides."

Embedded in Eigg's Middle Jurassic beds laid down under water, the nodules appeared to us, with little geological knowledge, like fossil mounds of blue-green algae formed prior to the solidifying of the fine estuarine mud which had come to embrace them, but not so tightly as to prevent them from eroding out as entities many millennia later.

Peter thought they had their origin in vulcanism, which suggests volcanic bombs, as seen on Hawaii, but bombs being thrown from the vent of a volcano would not show concentric layering, as by long term deposition. With no reference books and no Ewen to advise us on matters geological, we had to leave the matter open to question. None of the geological tomes or dictionaries which I consulted subsequently so much as mention stromatolites, and they are not a form of plant life that would appeal to many botanical writers. For us they had to remain as 'calcareous concretions' or 'calcium carbonate concretions', origin unknown.

Twenty years later I showed my photographs to two geological colleagues, who diligently sought out the answers in modern literature. The balls had, indeed, built up little by little concentrically around some undefined nucleus and were referred to officially as 'carbonate concretions' or the odd term 'doggers'.

Wilkinson (1992) wrote of them: "The concretions probably formed at depths of several hundred metres around temperatures of 31 to 34 degrees Celsius, when meteoric pore waters dissolved carbonate from shells. The concretions started to grow about fifteen millennia after burial of the host sediments and the metre sized examples may have taken several million years to form. Particularly fine examples of concretions occur in the Valtos Sandstone formations around the north end of Eigg, from Laig to Kildonnan."

So far so good. At least in our ignorance we had plumped on a suitable and later accepted name, but were no wiser as to how and why they had been stimulated to form at all after many millennia of existence as undifferentiated rock. There were plenty of ancient shells available to supply the necessary lime.

Particularly plentiful were shells of oysters *(Praeexogera hebridica)* , also Ammonites. Further sources of lime had been located by Hugh Miller when he found pelvic bones and ribs of sea roving Pleisoaurs in the north of the island. No-one has yet suggested what triggered the movement, so the aggregation of this inanimate material remains a mystery.

It seems the system awoke, bored after fifteen millennia of inactivity and opted for selective migration routes. "Let's get moving, let's have a ball." Our planet would be less intriguing if we knew all the answers!.

No matter, the larger balls made comfortable seats and we settled down to lunch, our attention diverted to entomological matters. We were entertained throughout by the burnet moth caterpillars attempting hari kari by dropping off vegetated parts of the cliff to the plantless boulders or beach platform below. Most of them were fully grown and ready to pupate.

One, less than half size and darker because of the closer spotting, came racing along a sun-warmed dyke edge at breakneck speed as we ate. Halted by a pile of apple peel, it curled gratefully up in the moist atmosphere, to be taken back to its mislaid food plant (bird's-foot trefoil) half an hour later.

This tiny youthful creature had hot-footed it over thirty yards of bare, dry rock from the nearest land vegetation and forty two yards from the nearest food plant – into which it chewed feverishly on return! A collection of larger caterpillars was gathered up from the intertidal zone and taken upshore to a patch of bramble where there were plenty of dead stems to climb for pupation. Could this be Eigg's rare transparent burnet moth *(Zygaena purpuralis)*, we wondered, a rare species but recently seen in profusion on the Burren limestone in Ireland?

89. *Transparent Burnet Moths and Caterpillars*

The 'teniquoit rings' scattered over the beach, and used as such by some islanders, were actually the floats from trammel nets used to catch surface fish such as herring, the nets anything from half a mile to three miles long.

11. THE GREAT PITCHSTONE RIDGE OF THE SGURR

The day we were granted to visit the mighty Sgurr was another of peerless blue and gold – despite the fact that Eigg's greater elevation intercepts an average

133

annual rainfall a deal greater than Muck's, only two to three miles away: sixty and forty eight inches respectively. How lucky could we get?

The Sgurr is a great whale-back of black pitchstone spewed from the entrails of a volcano some sixty million year ago. That was when the Atlantic was opening up, to separate what we choose to call the New World from the

90. *The great Pitchstone Ridge of the Sgurr*

Old. Dinosaurs were roaming the earth when the liquid rock started to solidify into this, the largest mass of pitchstone in Great Britain and Ireland' snaking along the length of Eigg for more than a mile.

This acidic lava flowed along a valley eroded into an earlier lava flow that had been floored by woodland, as shown by fossil trees entombed beneath and later dubbed *Pinites eiggensis*. During cooling and solidifying, the newly added rock crystallised out into more or less vertical, roughly hexagonal basalt columns, narrower than the pink basalt ones of the Grulin slopes below, these some six and ten inches across respectively. Always impressive, these columns are not so neatly aligned as are the famous ones framing Fingal's Cave on Staffa.

Being harder than the valley that it came to occupy, the pitchstone monolith outlasted its surroundings. Those eroded away to leave it standing proud, a landmark for mariners on the surrounding waters. Conversely, it affords magnif-icent views from its height of 1,285 feet (393m). It provides an effective windbreak and shelters some of the island's best farmlands and ancient woods, also the big house and the harbour.

It was quite a hike to the top, where we were walking on the ends of the columns, which huddled together in parts like close set, giant cobblestones. Almost devoid of vegetation, it was only gradually that heather infiltrated, with increasing distance from the crest. The rest seemed too potholey even for sheep and was home to dwarf juniper, which we encountered otherwise only on steep sea cliffs. Arctic Sandwort was the most special, along with a few clumps of pyramidal bugle and a little succulent roseroot tucked away in crevices.

One of the golden eagle eyries was quite low down here, just beyond the Gruline, but the raptors did not show themselves for us. There was, however, a pair of red throated divers nesting on one of the remote mountain lochans. They flew in over the watchers' heads and launched into their mating display, an impressive sight in full

91. *Red-throated Diver in summer plumage*

134

breeding plumage, the grey head a foil to the bright red throat. With legs set so far back for swimming, these loons are fairly helpless on land and must, perforce, nest close to the water's edge.

It was possible to examine the pitchstone at close quarters without scaling the heights, or even approaching the base, as a mighty chunk had broken free and toppled into deep heather below. This, Clack Horsdale, dwarfed the black house by which it had fallen.

Pete Wells had restored one of the many ruined black houses hereabouts, one from which the tenants had been evicted and shipped to Barbadoes. He gave us a conducted tour of one on a remarkably sheltered, hummocky site, with splendid views of Muck nearly three miles away, even from below the great ridge.

Some of the substantial seventeenth century cornerstones that had supported the heather thatch, still stood firm. They were rounded, like the ends of stone houses on the French Camargue, which are subjected to the full force of mistral winds. This was said to produce warmth-giving friction instead of draughty turbulence from the all too prevalent Highland winds. Internal walls separated the living quarters from the cattle, which provided warmth from their body heat as well as dried dung and much needed calories in the form of meat and milk. The four foot central hole in the roof for the escape of smoke had to be imagined.

This land, part grass and part heather dissected by sheep tracks, was the haunt of wheatears, skylarks and hooded crows It provided good grazing for the black-face X Cheviot sheep, whose rather coarse wool was being used for tweeds, carpets and mattress stuffing. Those with downland blood needed the softer habitats of the fertile basalts which they shared with the cattle – those a mix of black, blue-grey, Hereford and Highland breeds.

Bracken is disliked less by farmers than it once was, since its role in protecting the grass beneath its fronds was recognised. The tracery of its airy leaves is never dense enough under these conditions to choke the understorey of grass. The season of cover is brief and fronds are likely to get blown away when they wither at the end of summer. Sheep thrive on this hidden asset, gaining shelter as well as grass drawn up to tender heights in its enhanced shade. Cattle, apparently, are not attracted by it, but we heard no mention of bracken poisoning.

12. SOUTHERN CAVES, SHORES AND WOODS

Across undulating, often soggy pasture, we descended the Gruline cliffs west of Castle Island and worked our way along the black shoreline rocks, cave viewing, armed with rather inadequate torches. Vegetation of the first cave, a big one, demonstrated the relative shade tolerance of surrounding plants.

Too far above sea level to show the velvety red growths of Rhodochorton seen in some, it was blue-green algae which graded outwards here to greens, then to scurvy grass, with circular leaves orientated at right angles to the incident light. Next came sea mayweed and celandines, below walls matted with Marchantia liverwort and tufted with sea spleenwort ferns. Lastly there was lovage, creeping buttercup and coltsfoot among grass and moss. A well watered shelf held primroses and valerian, as well as the remains of a lamb fallen from above.

The next cave, eroded along a fault at the back of the boulder beach where we lunched, was less impressive but more famous – or infamous. This was Francis Cave, scene of the great massacre of 1577, The small bottleneck ten feet within the entrance enabled the invading MacLeods of Dunvegan to murder three hundred and ninety five people, almost the entire population of Eigg, hidden within, by the simple expedient of lighting a fire in the entrance and asphyxiating them. The inner refuge is 22 X 13 feet and 17 feet high,

Eleven years later MacLean of Duart again wiped out the island population. Life is pleasanter now that the mainstream of Highland animosity in the surrounding sea lanes has ceased. Marchantia and sea spleenwort have returned to the blackened walls, while juniper, kidney vetch and bird's foot trefoil are once again burgeoning on the cliffs alongside.

Further west, beyond a shining, bifurcated black dyke resembling coal or obsidian, is the impressive Cathedral Cave, heralding in a series of smaller caverns. The first, 25 feet long, 20 feet wide and 20 feet high, was used for illicit Catholic services after the 1745 rising and for Free Church services after the disruption of 1843. The sea enters further here and fresh water trickles are few, so hemp agrimony was the only addition to our list of cave dwellers.

In extreme and unaccustomed heat, we found our way up the cliff and wound our way seawards for tea and delectably sticky home-made chocolate fudge shortcake. Next we followed the seaward edge of lush woodland full of spring flowers, to grovel on the famous cowrie beach and to find almost every kind of shell apart from the coveted cowries. These small ribbed treasures, we learned later, appear in jars on residents' mantelpieces, representing the owner's lifetime collection. They are not for casual visitors!

Failing to locate the final mile of cliff face path around Kildonnan Bay, this lap proved hard work. Some climbed from the daisy starred machair playing field and went along the brink of the columnar basalt cliff, from whence they could look down onto nesting buzzards. The rest of us clambered over boulders of awkward shapes and sizes, straying sometimes knee deep among the flowering bluebells and ramsons of the partially scrub-grown hinterland with its hidden, bottomless holes and sometimes stepping through the rising tide.

We paused en route to sing to the seals. It worked. They came nearer to gaze at the lumbering land lubbers and demonstrate how much easier it would be to go by sea. There were twenty six here in all. At low water we might have crossed the sands, but not now. Nevertheless, we still had sufficient resources left to explore the old water mill, used as a corn mill and a distillery, with working parts still more or less intact, and incorporated into the holiday accommodation into which it had been converted. And so to another of Pete's delicious meals.

On another gem of a day, our last and not the sort to be leaving so exquisite an island, we woke at 4.15 am to a mackerel sky flushed rose pink over the north-eastern hills. This was just six hours and ninety degrees after Pete had called us outside at 10.15 pm to view the splendid pink sunset in the north-west and the flashing of the automatic light on the point of Castle Island.

Common gulls were probing systematically in the half light for the night's worms. The tiny tents of four canoeists caught the horizontal rays by St. Donnan's statue. Their owners had skulled past us the previous day on a mirror calm sea, and we had found the smoking remains of their lunch fire on an otherwise deserted beach.

We left Kildonnan House at 9.0 am for the "Loch Mor", but it was extreme low tide and she was delayed due to problems of ferrying people and chattels on other shores. The reprieve was put to good use, combing the rocks where a hoodie crop pellet of millipedes and woodlice remains were found. We also explored the old harbour where ancient clan chiefs used to meet.

Between the new and old harbours was yesterday's fine sweep of woodland, its ferny floor carpeted with bluebells and broad-leaved garlic, with smaller drifts of water avens, kingcups and wood Anemones. Wild gooseberries, currants and blackberries would supply the island's jam makers later on. Strangely there were no bilberries or blaeberries, a usual mainstay of dwellers on heath and moorland. Others that failed to contribute to the conserves, cranberries, crowberries, cowberries, bearberries and cloudberries, hard to come by anywhere but here in the North, were also rare or absent. Grassy knolls were awash with early purple orchids and polypody ferns among primroses and violets. Pebble beaches beyond were massed with silverweed, the sands with daisies and hawkbit.

92. Kingcups or Marsh Marigolds

We saw our first Eigg shelduck in the Old Harbour. Two fishing boats jostled for position at the pier, alongside exposed beds of tang (Alaria), while the kelp beds swayed and stretched, as wafted by the gentle swell. Eventually the working boats gave way to the red island ferry. We boarded, along with the eight kiddies from the island school on their Saturday spree.

The hauled out seals took no notice, this was all part of their routine. Better to carry on basking while the sunshine lasted. Terns were busy along the edge of the Castle Island gullery, as before, but today we circled around the outside of the island, past the roosting knoll of several score shags and, later, their nesting colony near the lighthouse. We idled well out from the land, feeling small and vulnerable as the "Loch Mor" came bearing down on us, but the seamen achieved the perfect rendezvous and we headed east into the sun.

The 12.20 train from Mallaig was delayed half an hour to receive the boat passengers and we munched on Pete's home made bread and raisin cake as we sped through the sunlit countryside to Fort William.

We came down to earth with a bump when spewed out at Glasgow into a milling throng of youths, policemen and tracker dogs. England had been playing Scotland (Nil nil, so no cause for retribution) and both railway stations were on the news next day for the fracasse witnessed there. On Eigg just four strangers had comprised a crowd. How we envied the Eiggers, Muckers and Rhumuns their idyllic summer world!

137

13. FULFILMENT

During the latter part of the twentieth century Eigg suffered a succession of short term. often absent, owners, who failed to make the island pay and allowed the infrastructure to deteriorate. By 1996 the current owner was leaving after only eighteen months. The islanders had had enough.

When their home came on the open market yet again, they joined with the Highland Council and the Scottish Wildlife Trust to form a unique partnership, "The Isle of Eigg Heritage Trust", and set about raising the eight hundred thousand pounds by public appeal, to run the property on their own terms.

Our friend, John Chesters of 1986, was still the Scottish Trust's much valued resident ranger and he played a key role in the changeover. The islanders were very much in favour of conserving and enhancing their island's remarkable wildlife assets and their wildlife champion reported that he "had never experienced less conflict with residents and farmers. The people love and respect their wildlife."

By 1997 the appeal had raised over a million pounds and the sixty three strong community celebrated with a party on the 14th April. The uncertainty of security of tenure operating since the 1980s was over. Inward investment was available to support low intensity farming, tackle the spread of bracken, expand the broadleaved woodlands and restructure the plantations.

Flower rich meadows were to be promoted by controlling mowing times and grazing regimes, in the hope of bringing back the corncrakes among other assets. Squelching mires and moors were to be nurtured for their intrinsic value, visitor access enhanced and information on the locality made available.

Crumbling infrastructure and reduction of maintenance work in woods and fields leading to an attrition of wildlife became things of the past as jobs were created in road making, erecting and repairing buildings, dry stone walling and forestry, all involving training in new disciplines and a sense of achievment.

One major undertaking was to reduce the rampant Rhododendron which had run amok in the broad-leaved woodland planted in the late nineteenth century around the colonial style lodge. The considerable conifer woods established in the late 1980s were in urgent need of thinning and management. Part would be thinned, part grown on as timber and part felled to revitalise the original moorland. Plots were fenced off from sheep to allow natural regeneration of scrub. The population came to top seventy, with eight children in the island school.

An article appearing in a national Wildlife Trusts' Magazine of 2002, reporting progress cited Eigg as an example of what might be achieved in other parts of Scotland. As stated:- "Eigg had symbolised the most polarised system of land ownership in Europe, whereby a small number of people owned a huge proportion of the land", and some as absentee landlords. "A feudal hangover in a modern state." But not any longer.

The people now have a feeling of community, with three hill farms, twelve crofts and opportunities for guest house, cafe, shop, field centre and other tourist amenities. Former residents were coming back and everyone had at least a part time job.

There is likely to be no shortage of potential visitors with those lovely sandy beaches, fine scenery and fascinating geology. With the others in the Small Isles Parish, Eigg is classified as a national scenic area flanked by a site of European importance for marine wildlife. Heather moors, bluebell woods of ash and hazel, golden eagles, buzzards, seals and otters. Was it mere coincidence that John was granted sightings of such rarities as rose finch and red-breasted flycatcher on the same morning, soon after success had been celebrated?

RHUM ISLAND

14. VITAL STATISTICS OF RHUM

Rhum, largest in the "Small Isles Parish", lies to the west and slightly north of Muck and Eigg at latitude 57 degrees north. Shaped like a four sided diamond, it is almost as broad as it is long, at about eight miles across, and occupies 26,400 acres. This makes it about the same size as Jersey, whose kindlier latitude

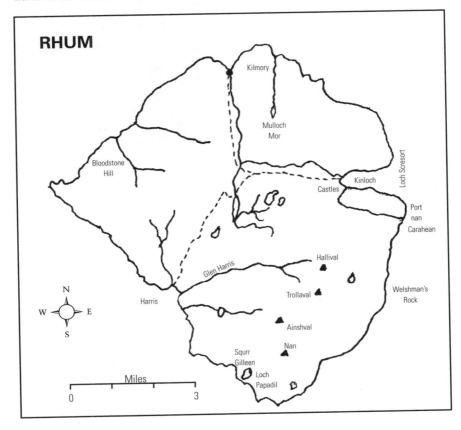

supports a much larger population and thriving tourism. But tomato growing would be singularly out of place on Rhum.

Pre Cambrian Torridonian sandstone strata are exposed on the lower ground of the north and west. The south-eastern mountain block has been thrust up through this ancient base and is showing a greater development of ultra basic rocks than is found anywhere else in Britain. Granite, Granophyre, Felsite and other incorporated minerals include Allivate, named after Hallival, neighbour of Askival, the island's highest mountain at 2,659 feet.

The three peaks rising as close to the sea as they do appear more lofty than they otherwise might. They intercept rain clouds, making Rhum one of the wettest parts of the British Isles, with rainfall on the tops of up to a hundred inches a year. We had the good fortune to be visiting during fine interludes.

There has been intense volcanic action locally and Rhum is notable as the centre of Tertiary Plutonic igneous activity hereabouts.

Population wise the island seems to have escaped the ancient monkish phase which characterises post Iron Age settlement on so many islands around our coasts, there being few written records of habitation before the seventeenth and eighteenth centuries. Quite rapidly then the population built up to three hundred souls, rising to four hundred and forty by the early 1820s. This was more than the island could support and there was a mass exodus to North America in 1826.

93. *Tall Trees near the Rhum Landing*

The laird brought in people from Skye to tend his sheep and the population crept up to a hundred and thirty four by 1831, dwindling to fifty three sixty years later. When the Bullough family, owners of the famous castle, moved in at the beginning of the 1900s, they needed staff and builders and the population shot up to a hundred and sixteen.

Severe losses occurred during the first world war and more during the 1930's slump. The modern era started in 1958 when the Nature Conservancy Council took over. All residents then were incomers. The scientific staff numbered around thirty six and were supplemented seasonally by volunteer field workers. When their contracts ceased they left the island, which was run as a research establishment. The indigenous crofting population was no more and the grazing regime was monitored as part of the long term ecological projects being undertaken.

As well as conducting research to find answers to land use problems, which were of all too common occurrence throughout Scotland, the Conservancy, now renamed the Scottish Naturalists' Council, was also running the island as a centre for training field biologists, conservationists, land managers, game keepers and reserve wardens.

The remarkable outpost of Victorian England that greets the visitor landing at Kinloch, was built by Sir George Bullough in the early part of the Twentieth century from the local red Arran sandstone.

It was chiefly famed for its lavish collection of period furniture and fantastic baths, also the mechanical organ or giant music box, which simulates a forty piece orchestra in the great ballroom, one of few such pieces now in existence.

The castle was geared to the showing off of wealth and fashion – staff being given bonuses to work in kilts. It was second in Scotland only to Glasgow in acquiring electricity, this bringing central heating. When it changed hands in the 1950s, Lady Bullough presented some furniture, tapestries and porcelain to the Scottish National Museum. The rest came to the Nature Conservancy with the building and was available for viewing by visitors.

The conservation world was delighted to have acquired such a pristine open air laboratory where long term experiments on land management could be protected from interference by the non involved. Visitors were welcomed if interested in the projects but needed special permission to enter areas not set aside for general public exploration and picnicking. There was no overnight accommodation for those not directly involved.

Most of the indigenous forest had been destroyed long before by over grazing or burning and the island was now predominantly grass or heather moor with sedgy mires, reedy marshes and a few small upland lochans.

94. *Stone Bramble*

The high tops fall within the category of arctic alpine fell field and nurtured rare flowers such as alpine pennycress (*Thlaspi alpestre*) and Norwegian sandwort (*Arenaria norvegica*). Other floral delights which, not being mountaineers we failed to see, are stone bramble, mountain avens, Scottish asphodel, moss campion, purple and snow saxifrages and mossy cyphel (*Cherleria sedoides*). The evocatively scented bog myrtle is unexpectedly rare.

15. OCEAN CRUISING

I first came to Rhum as a passenger on MS "Devonia" in mid July 1966. The liner had been chartered for the official field expedition following the fourteenth International Ornithological Conference held in Oxford and Cambridge.

We sailed from Glasgow and back into Edinburgh after a circuit of the Scottish Islands, including far flung St. Kilda, and north around Muckle Flugga, the furthermost point of Shetland.

"Devonia" weighed anchor at Greenock to the strains of "A life on the ocean wave" from our loud speakers and an answering skirl of bagpipes from the ship in the next berth. The sun beamed down on the Isle of Bute, separated by the Kyles of Bute to either side, and on the rugged fells of Arran as we moved majestically down the Clyde and out to sea.

95. Mountain Avens

We circled around Ailsa Craig under a shrieking mob of the resident gannets and were able to pick out kittiwakes, fulmars and guillemots, bluebells, primroses and the red campion which is such a feature of sea bird colonies in the north.

Few landings are made here now, but it was formerly a granite quarry. Ailsa Craig is the source of the meticulously polished curling stones that get persuaded and cajoled over smooth icescapes. These were much in the news forty years later when curling was embraced as a bona fide Olympic Games sport.

Only two hundred of the nine hundred ornithologists assembled from all over the world were from America, but these were more vocal than most and the ship seemed full of them as we rounded the Mull of Kintyre. There were four with us in the Magellan Dormitory, where four Swedes, three Germans and six from the UK made our number up to seventeen.

Rhum was bathed in sunlight as we approached on our second morning, the mountains clearly etched against a sky of peerless blue. The view, we were told, was this good because of the all pervading, chilly north-westerly airstream. "Warm air from the south brings mist and drizzle."

A few largish boats had come out from Mallaig to help "Devonia's" lifeboats ferry the nine hundred of us ashore – no small upheaval for the forty residents who strode these lonely moorlands in splendid isolation for much of their working lives. Needless to say, we were not expected to swarm freely over those pristine acres, but assembled in front of the glowing red castle walls at the head of Loch Scresort to be apportioned out appropriately.

We had four options. The most energetic set out to scale Hallival and Askival to the south. Those only slightly less capable took to one of the island's two roads to walk to Kilmory in the north. Most split into groups to follow one of the two nature trails – inland up Kinloch Glen or along the southern shore of Loch Scresort. There were gentler options: a snooze on the intensely green grass of the castle lawn or exploration of the castle itself. We opted for the southern walk – a pleasant mixture of lowland woods and sheltered shore terminating at the mouth of the sea loch. There we were among the ruins of the fishing village of Port na Caranean, where Nature was claiming back its own.

The little community, founded in 1827, during the Highland Clearances from the crofting lands, lasted only sixteen years – to 1843 -when the people may have emigrated, like those before them, mostly to Canada. During that period Rhum became first a great sheep walk and then a private shooting estate, change starting when Bullough bought the island in 1887. At the next change of ownership in 1957 it was declared a National Nature Reserve, its destiny from then on a shining example of what the conservation of our planet is all about.

16. MOUNTAIN SHEARWATERS

Deer are king here here, under the modern management regime, but birds are a major part of the fauna and of these the many thousand pairs of Manx shearwaters win hands down for sheer numbers. Their colony is claimed to be the largest in the British Isles – which is synonymous with the largest in the world as the only known outliers breed in the Faroes and off the coast of Iceland.

The much publicised twin islands of Skomer and Skokholm off the South West Wales claim to host "Half the world's population of Manx Shearwaters". This does not negate Rhum's claim because the Welsh population is shared between two major units.

The Welsh birds are better known, having afforded torchlight viewing to some thousands of visitors over the sixty years since the second world war, helping to pick up incoming birds and hand them to the ringers. These lucky people had overnight accommodation on the islands to which to repair after this unique wildlife experience. Ringing has ceased in modern times, but opportunity for viewing continues.

Secreted away in their mountain fastnesses, the Rhum birds will always remain more of a mystery, known to most of the few who get within hearing range as a distant cacophony of weird calls penetrating the darkness – tantalisingly unavailable except to the dedicated few.

Trollaval, most westerly of the three high peaks, is thought to have been named by Viking sailors, who believed that the shearwaters' outlandish cries emanated from the supernatural world.

Norsemen populated their remote, half frozen forests with those rather unattractive trolls. I favour the gentler picture of 'elfin forests' for these damp, north-westerly woods. To me they are welcoming sanctuaries, characterised by moss clad boulders, tree-climbing ferns and lichens draped from boughs and twigs. It was here, in the old forests by Loch Scresort that we sought ephemeral sightings of ethereal beings rather than on the harsher terrain of the peaks.

The Rhum shearwaters differ from most others in being mountain dwellers. In this they resemble some of New Zealand's sooty shearwaters and Australia's short-tailed shearwaters that I had been working among during the 1950s and 60s. (My function was to research the plant cover of their underground rookeries, be these in tall tussock grass, low scrub or high forest, burned, grazed or left to mature naturally.)

Less dominant pelagic birds around Rhum's cliffs were shags, puffins, razorbills, common and black guillemots, fulmar petrels and kittiwakes. Others were the four common shore gulls, golden eagle, merlin, peregrine, golden plover, snipe, red-throated diver on the lochans and red grouse on the moors. In more modern times white-tailed sea eagles have been reintroduced. Other flying fauna, midges and horse flies, were purported to be notorious, but we were bothered by neither.

96. *Young Golden Eagle*

The shearwater burrows are clustered in the south-eastern mountains, three of which rise above 2,500 feet. My friend Dr. Robert Falla, recently retired from his post as director of the Dominion Museum in Dunedin, New Zealand, was one of the active party who scaled the heights. Lean, sinewy and a sea-bird specialist, age was no hindrance to him. He was in his element as the Rhum warden guided the party round the partially hidden burrows, lifting out a few fluffy chicks for inspection.

Falla probably knew as much about shearwaters as anybody present, having sailed so often through the uncountable multitudes that throng the waters around South and Stewart Islands in his homeland. He was deeply involved in maintaining these healthy numbers to support the thriving Maori mutton bird industry without depleting the numbers of these notoriously long-lived birds. (Forty and fifty year olds have been recorded among ringed individuals of the breeding population.)

Joining me for lunch to chat about mutual acquaintances he waxed enthusiastic about the 'tube-noses' that are represented by so many different species in those southern seas. His instincts led him to suspect that Rhum's mountain shearwaters might be a separate race from the normal coastal nesters, just as there may be more than two kinds of stormy petrels in Britain.

He quoted *Puffinus huttonii*, mountain nesting shearwaters of New Zealand, for long recognised as a separate species, although their breeding site had only just been discovered. These birds encounter very harsh conditions when they return to their rookeries in the southern spring, having to scrabble through hard snow and frostbound soil to find their ancestral burrows. The ornithologists had only just been able to follow up as conditions ameliorated.

The Rhum mountain shearwaters may also have to dig through snow when they return to the island in February and March, locating their burrows precisely, despite the changed terrain. The Gulf Stream, however, ensures that their homeland is more welcoming than that of their counterparts in the Antipodes. Mostly they dig through green vegetation into deep peaty but well drained soil. Are there fewer areas of burrowable depth at lower elevations on Rhum in more orthodox sea cliff sites?

17. RED DEER RESEARCH

By the 1960s and still today, half a century later, Rhum is the main centre in Britain for the study of red deer. These are the only deer present but are not of a unique genetic strain like those of Jura. They were so persecuted during the eighteenth century that they became extinct, to be reintroduced during the mid nineteenth century. Numbers rapidly increased and the island was officially designated a deer forest, this not implying the presence of many forest trees.

The Nature Conservancy launched their long term study of deer biology on their arrival, studying birth, growth, maturation and death rates, reproductive physiology, movements and diet: also their internal and external parasites. Results, in conjunction with others found on the mainland, came to serve for deer conservation and control in other parts of Britain.

By the early ninety sixties herd size was held at about 1,690 animals: 718 stags. 725 hinds and 248 fawns in 1963. Work being carried out there forty years later was featured prominently on our television screens during the "Autumn Watch" series portrayed during 2006, when we were treated to intimate spectacles of the

I. Islay

Highland X Red Shorthorn is a popular Beef cross

A Beef Herd treks to shelter for the winter night

Historic Semi-circular Cattle Steading at Kilchiaran

Late Autumn Colour by a Moorland Loch

Portnahaven Harbour at the Southern tip of the Rhinns

Sand build-up against the Northern Rhinns, Machir Bay

II. Islay, Jura and Colonsay

The American Monument,
Mull of Oa, Islay

Tree Lungwort
(Lobaria pulmonaria), Jura

Some of the few Houses on Jura's lee side

Cordyline and Gunnera at
Craighouse, Jura

Clumped Common Butterwort, Colonsay

Individual Common
Butterwort

III. Colonsay

Fertile Boulder Clay Field near
Colonsay House

Pink Purslane in Woodland

Loch an Sgoltaire

Stone Bramble

Quillwort

Water Lobelia

Brackish Water Crowfoot

IV. Colonsay

Kiloran Bay, Raised Beaches of sand

Kiloran Bay, Raised Beaches of pebbles

Approaching Kiloran's Raised Beach Terraces from Urugaig

*Collecting Stones from arable field on
Raised Beach*

*Round House from the Days
of Horse Threshing*

V. Slate Islands

Atlantic Bridge, Clachan

Fairy Foxglove on Clachan bridge

Lagoons from Flooded Slate Quarries

Dame's Violet by Easdale Harbour

The Great Dyke on Easdale

A sample of Nether Lorn Slate

VI. Slate Islands and Muck

Flooded Slate Quarries

*Muck Harbour. View to the
Sgurr on Eigg*

Cemetery above Port Mor House, Muck

*Red Bands of Tropical Laterite or Volcanic Tuff between main black beds of
Basalt or Dolerite*

VII. Muck

Eider Duck's Nest with Eggs

Eider Duck pulls down over nest before leaving

Cheeping Eider Duckling, newly hatched

Oyster Catcher's Eggs, minimal nest on beach

Ringed Plover's Eggs, scanty grass nest on sand among Silverweed

Two-layered Mew Gull's nest

VIII. Muck and Eigg

 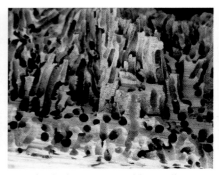

Driftwood bored by Teredo "Shipworms"

Multiple damage caused by Molluscan Teredo Borers

Giant Kelp (Durvillea potatorum) *from Australia's 'Roaring Forties' drying on King Island, North-West Tasmania for Export to Scotland's Kelp Industry*

Restored Black House at Gruline under the Sgurr of Eigg

Renovated Water Mill, Kildonan Bay

IX. Eigg

The Author and the Sgurr of Eigg in 1987

*Rift between Dykes
near the Singing
Sands*

Cave on South Eigg

*Laig or Surf Bay. Yellow Depression of Old Silted Boat
Harbour*

Artic Sandwort, Cleadale

Pyramidal Bugle

X. Eigg

Clustered Limestone Nodules eroding from Beach Platform

Erosion of Nodules showing layering

Two tier Nodule set in Beach Platform

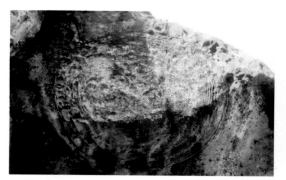

Vertically cut Nodule showing concentric plates

Burnet Moth Caterpillars on Beach Cobbles

XI. Rhum

Open Pinewood and Heather

Horse Chestnut and Bluebell Wood

Kinloch Castle

Sweet Cicely

Moss Campion

XII. Iona and Staffa

Iona Village, Abbey on right

Iona, Ruined Nunnery

"Visibility nil' on Iona Machair

*Swooping curves of
Staffa's Basalt Columns*

*Fulmars nesting on truncated grassed
ends of columns*

XIII. Staffa

Erosion of 'organ pipe' jointing in Basalt

Entrance to Fingal's Cave

Curvature of distorted Dolerite Columns

Junction of separate Lava Flows

XIV. Treshnish Islands

*Approaching the Dolerite Terraces of
Lunga Island*

*Cairns and Low Water Mooring on
Lunga Island*

*Two views of approachable Razorbill and
Guillemot Colonies on Lunga*

XV. Coll

The new Coll Pier

Arinagour Village. Hotel to right of Church

Irises between our Guest House and the Sea Loch

Corner of our Garden carved from the Moor

Arinagour Main Street and Chapel on the Hill

Sheep shelter from the sun by Village Street

XVI. Coll

Old Castle at Breachacha in the South-west

Breachacha Beach from the Castle.

Highland Bull near Ballyhaugh

Pop-eyed Ewe with Black Lambs

Dunes piled against mountain, Hogh Bay

Daisy Path through Hogh Bay Buttercups on piled sand

XVII. Coll

Bay near Struan in North-west Coll

Thrift among half buried Sea Milkwort

Roseroot at Ballyhaugh

Thatched Hay Store at Sorisdale in the North-east

Distant Black Sheep at junction of Dune and Mountain in the North-west

Grey Lag Goose Lake and Ballyhaugh Youth Training Centre

XVIII. Tiree

Wreck of the "Mary Rose" in Scarinish Old Harbour

Cystoseira tamariscifolia, *Vaul Beach*

Machair Ponies, North-east Tiree

Sheep Muster. Tiree Pier beyond

St. Columba's Mourning Dove in fourteenth century Churchyard

Leathesia difformis, *Vaul Beach*

'It's always greener on the other side"

XIX. Tiree

Belted Galloway Heifers by Loch Bhasapol

Flag Iris infected by Thrips

Battered Kingcups in Kirkapol Cattle Grid

Cornaigmore Old Mill, Loch Bhasapol

Hynish, Land Base for Skerryvore Lighthouse

Hynish Walled Garden

XX. Tiree

Pastoral Machair and bleak
Mountainside, Sandaig

Old Thatched Cottages and (right) the
Sandaig Guest House

Bird's foot Trefoil on Sandaig Machair

Lady's Bedstraw on
Traigh Baigh Machair

Yellow Rattle in Loch Bhasapol Haycrop

Tall Eyebright in Loch Bhasapol Haycrop

XXI. Shiants

*Ruined Croft by beach connecting
the two larger Islands*

Aspen Sapling in crevice

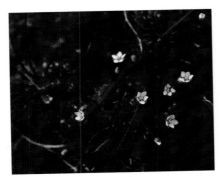

Awled Pearlwort

Tilted 'Organ Pipes' on Galtachean

Inland Cliff of massive Columns

Old Lazy Beds on Eilean an Tighe

XXII. Handa

Daytime Shelter at landing Bay

Bonxie Chick being Ringed

Light Phase Arctic Skua alights at Nest with three eggs

Duckboard Path leads over the top to Puffin Bay

Sphagnum and Bog Pondweed on Moorland Pool

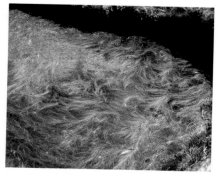

Aquatic form of Bulbous Rush fills Moorland Pool

XXIII. Handa

Dissection of Torridonian cliffs: Shags on wave-cut ledge

The Great Stack Sea-bird Citadel

Auk Ledges

Auks on the Great Stack, Razorbills to right.

Fulmars on vegetated faces

Sandy Bays on South-west Handa

XXIV. Handa

*Poll Ghlup Blowhole. Blue-green
Roseroot both sides*

*Sheep prefer Maritime Sward to the
brown Moor on left*

Sheep Lair scraped out among Thrift

*Rabbit Burrows penetrate
between Thrift tumps*

*Narrow Greensward between clifftop
Thrift and central Moor*

*Old Strip Cultivations. Eared Sallow
spreading since grazing ceased*

rutting behaviour and of the scores of shed antlers from known individuals ranged across the ceiling of one of the buildings. A tally was kept on numbers and genetic lines, individuals easily identified from a distance by virtue of their green or yellow 'cow collars'.

During our leisurely exploration in the sixties we managed to get within thirty feet of five stags which, according to the young man who we met later, frequently leapt the fence which was meant to protect the lusher coastal grass, and usually in groups of around this size. Many also came down to the beaches to feed at night,

The herd of wild Rhum ponies numbered about twenty. These are smaller than average, none exceeding fourteen hands, but were very strong and well able to withstand the harsh conditions. The story is that the herd arose from animals swimming ashore from wrecked ships of the Spanish Armada in 1588. They had certainly been here a long time, having been well established when Dr. Johnson toured the Hebrides in 1773. The animals wander at will, some having been successfully broken as work horses, serving particularly to carry deer carcases down from hill shoots.

Inevitably there is a herd of wild goats, as on most islands where hungry sailors of pre-refrigeration days were likely to be in need of fresh meat.

An example of the endemic long-tailed field mouse of the Small Islands was on show in a live trap near the landing for all to see. There were no records of voles, hares, moles, rabbits, squirrels or those essentially Highland animals, wild cats and pine martens. The island was formerly overrun by brown rats, five hundred of which were killed by one man in 1881. Otters and seals are as much at home as deer, but much less numerous.

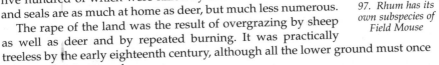

97. *Rhum has its own subspecies of Field Mouse*

The rape of the land was the result of overgrazing by sheep as well as deer and by repeated burning. It was practically treeless by the early eighteenth century, although all the lower ground must once have been tree covered.

It is said that after the crofting population had felled all the trees apart from a single ash, the laird had the option of arranging their passage to Canada or Newfoundland or letting them starve. The exiles had no hard feelings, admitting that he had done his best.

Half an acre of sycamore, ash and beech was planted behind the post office around 1840 and the Bulloughs installed eighty thousand trees in the early nineteen hundreds around Kinloch and their grandiose home. Some succumbed but many were alive and well sixty five years later. These trees and subsequent plantings, have brought back some of the lost woodland passerines, and not just far ranging individuals, but tiny species such as tree creeper and goldcrest.

We encountered blackbird, robin, wren and chaffinch in the coastal woodlands, pied wagtails on the castle lawns and skylarks and pipits on the rough grassland between the dwindling gorse and thorn bushes. Hooded crows foraged on coastal sandbanks with gulls and oyster catchers. A raven cronked in passing, causing some concern to the eider ducks shepherding their half grown families over the waters of Loch Scresort. A red throated diver and a merganser were spotted a little distance further from the shore. A few terns foraged along the water's edge where patient herons fished and shags spread their wings to dry. Only the mountaineers saw golden eagle and merlin.

So much faith did the Inverness-shire County Council have in the Conservancy's attempts to bring order back to the languishing landscape, that they built a new schoolhouse in 1962 and appointed an island school mistress to bring the fifteen children of the staff up to the eleven plus exam and their transfer to the big wide world – for more than just academic learning.

18. KINLOCH AND THE EXPANDING FORESTS

It was twenty one years later when I came again to Rhum, on a day trip from Muck in July 1986. We boarded our small craft with a local lad who had been sorting live periwinkles and packing them in transparent plastic sacks for export. The outermost individuals gripped the container with fleshy feet – not immovably, as limpets might have done – so that the packs resembled giant tapioca puddings, spawning bubbles, as though already in the cooking pans.

The rain eased, but we were headed into a biting north wind for two hours and got steadily more spray-spattered and chilled. Nevertheless, our pilot managed to steer us round the outside of the downpour which emanated from the girdle of purple cloud encompassing the "Far Cuillins" of Skye. This dropped to sea level, its perpendicular edge perilously close.

We glided smoothly into the jetty by the School House, which doubled up as the church. Currently this served only one pupil but there would be three the next year. The school teacher was the only paid resident not in the employ of the Conservancy.

The post office, further north, was the oldest inhabited building on the island. Before renovation in the 1970s, this had served as the kitchen for Kinloch House, home of the laird before the Edwardian Castle came into being. Hereabouts we were on the island's most venerable plot of woodland, planted a hundred and thirty six years before, around 1830 and somewhat the worse for wear.

Beneath the young green sprouts of beech, sycamore, horse chestnut and elm, we shouldered our way through Cotoneaster underbrush, enlivened by the yellow flower trusses of gorse and broom and the bursting bud tassels of Laburnum. Here, too, were banks of the invasive Rhododendrons, a seasonal asset for their flambuoyant flower display, set off to advantage now by the sea of bluebells lapping at their evergreen undercarriage.

The lively River Kinloch racing down the glen between ferny banks completed the rural idyll. A little further upstream was the farmhouse, which had outlived the former landscaped gardens, heated turtle pond and glasshouse for tender plants. These had fallen into neglect when the number of workers dwindled after the first world war. Lawns formerly terraced with imported soil, were currently being used as grazing paddocks, hay meadows or potato fields, but a lesser lawn and the shrubbery were still intact.

Reversing direction, we turned back across the head of Loch Scresort and came upon a lesser stream which had powered a turbine generating electricity. Not far off was an old lime kiln. Here we were moving beneath the eighty thousand trees planted on seventy two acres by the Bulloughs at the beginning of the century and echoing to the strains of bird song. We had already spotted the new tree nursery beyond a white gate near the old farm.

These different generations of trees formed the nucleus of the scientists' long term programme of reafforestation in their efforts to recreate the richly wooded island that it must once have been before crofters and sheep as well as deer had wrested a living from it. Their policy was not that of the Forestry Commission's coniferous monocultures, nor even the usual more modern preference for keeping to native species. They opted rather for variety, among which were long accepted introductions such as horse and sweet chestnuts – ostensibly to give shelter to indigenous species which might eventually prevail.

In order to assess how the expanding woodland cover was affecting the bird and other animal life, personnel were carrying out census work on eight selected plots varying in size from the seventy two acres of the Kinloch Wood and forty four acres of Kilmory Moor to the four and five acres of the Harris tree plot by the south-west coast and the Kilmory South plot.

Significant changes occurred in the bird life between planted and unplanted moorland, the number of individuals doubling, even in the first year. These were all moorland species, notably red grouse, snipe, meadow pipit and skylark. It seemed these were benefitting not only from the enhanced cover but from the increase of disturbed ground, exposing a greater variety of invertebrate life as deep furrows were ploughed across the moor prior to tree planting.

98. *Red Grouse*

As the saplings coalesced into scrub the first three bird species continued to increase but skylarks disappeared. Gradually in their place came an influx of newcomers. Typical of scrub were stonechat, whinchat, cuckoo and wren. True woodland birds moving in were song thrush, willow warbler, sedge warbler and whitethroat.

It was suggested that the smallness of some of the plots, giving a greater edge effect of shrubs burgeoning with the lateral light intensity might have boosted the results. To save the young trees from gnawing incisors the plots were fenced to keep out red deer, wild goats and Celtic ponies, so ground herbs would have waxed lusher until shaded out by the underbrush.

Eleven bird species were recorded in these young plantings as compared with six on the open moor and twenty in the old established Kinloch Wood with chaffinch and willow warbler the most abundant. I am indebted to L. A Batten of the Nature Conservancy for these figures published in August 1968. No doubt there have been sweeping changes in the forty years since. What we experienced in 1986 was very much an early interim stage.

19. THE WOODED SOUTHERN SHORE OF LOCH SCRESORT

Heading east along this sheltered north facing shore we were in the deep green shade of the Bullough's open floored, eighty five year old forest. This was a mixture of coniferous and deciduous trees, the first mainly the native Scots pine and European larch. As on Islay and some of the Welsh islands, the comparatively wind-worthy sycamore had been favoured among the broad-leaved species.

Holly, an important undershrub, is not too spiny to be nibbled when the young leaves appear in spring. Grazing animals had been excluded quite recently so spontaneous tree regeneration was only just beginning.

We spotted some of the victimised young hopefuls among recolonising saplings which had been beheaded in their youth. Deer are ruminants, like cattle, having no upper incisors but a hard pad against which the lower incisors work. (This type of dentition had made the hand feeding of calves from a bucket in my youth a pleasant rather than painful task.) The missing leading shoots were thus torn off rather than neatly sawn across as by a hare with a full set of dentures. With larger branches the deer's lower teeth had made a clean cut when they were pushing against the wood but left the final edge frayed.

Another sign of past deer presence was the damage to branches and twigs in the underbrush where stags had been scraping the velvet from their newly ossified antlers. Strips of bark were left hanging and branches broken, all a bit shabby now, some nine months after the event.

'Velvet" is a layer of skin abundantly supplied with blood vessels which break up when their work is done allowing the skin to slough away. This is normally eaten by the owner after shedding, as part of the recycling process that Nature is so much better at than we are.

In habitats as poor in nutrients as deer forests usually are, and acid rather than calcareous, it is remarkable that so much calcium carbonate can be spared to grow a new set of antlers every year. Deer may, in fact, scrunch some of the shed material back (as do mice) towards production of the next set of armoury – but not on Rhum, where shed antlers are diligently collected, labelled and stored for the records. Deer have been known to kill and eat shearwaters – bones and all.

99. Red Deer Antler

The main woody recruits now that the deer were excluded were birches because of the ease with which the tiny winged seeds in the brittle, disintegrating summer catkins are wafted from herbivore-free outliers beyond. Any who have shovelled up drifted birch seeds from kitchen floors and window sills will appreciate that these need only the slightest of gamin breezes to infiltrate places that real winds never reach.

We left the track at intervals to tread softly on the mossy woodland floor, where elegant drifts of flowering wood sorrel speckled with deep purple violets, flowed out from sheltering tree bases. Early flowering golden saxifrage swarmed across a different suite of mosses in damp patches of marsh pennywort. Wandering beside red campion, willow herb and speedwell snuggled against the crumbling walls of ruined cottages in the verdant gloom, we half expected to see those trolls. It was like an upland mist forest, with lesser plants romping over rocks and logs alike. Unusual here was a little clump of filmy fern tucked in a damp hollow.

Polypody ferns sent scaly rhizomes snaking along trunks and boughs while less determined epiphytic ferns, mosses and lichens were rife. King of the lichens was the tree lungwort, as on Jura, so much more grandiose than others of its ilk. Overlapping, pitted fronds embraced the trunk bases but did not climb to the phenomenal heights reached by those on Jura. encountered twenty years later.

100. Polypody Fern

I wondered if they had been curtailed in their ascent by deer scraping their antlers in readiness for the autumn rut. Certainly there were scuffings and scarrings of the bark in sites where those had been infiltrating before the fences went up. Nevertheless the uncommon little crimson discs of the sporing bodies were present. It was the intention to let deer back into the afforested areas when saplings had grown beyond the vulnerable stage of being mown down. Sea winds, that other scourge of tree growth on islands, were less of a problem in this particular locality than usual.

There were gaps in the seaward canopy where we could look out across the loch to spy the dipping beds of sedimentary Torridonian Sandstone on the opposite shore. Nearer, beyond the oyster beds, eider drakes were cruising the shallows on the lookout for titbits. Their less strikingly dressed mates were probably still busy with family matters up on the moor where most of them nest. It would be a long walk down with the family for them but the tree canopy would keep the wee ducklings safe from aerial marauders during at least part of the trek.

A prolonged, rather eerie call drew our attention to a red-throated diver settled low in the water. Red-breasted mergansers were also spotted popping in and out of view as they dived for fish. We watched in vain for the communal wing flapping by which these sometimes marshalled shoals of fish to facilitate their capture. These sea duck, rather incongruously, nest in the woods. Statuesque herons were dotted along the shore, but had apparently only just started to breed on Rhum. Did we or did we not see a peregrine falcon over a rocky stretch of coast? Chaffinches, and thrushes were in evidence but tits, so much a part of mainland woods, seemed confined to the older plantings. Nor had any woodpeckers arrived.

20. TREELESS MOOR AND COASTAL ROCK TUMPS

Away inland stretched a billowing moorland of purple moor grass and heather, including the two bell heathers, with two louseworts, heath milkwort, tormentil, bog asphodel and difficult to determine subspecies of eyebright. Flecks of colour were contributed by cuckoo flower, lesser skullcap, ragged Robin, bog pimpernel and forget-me-not.

149

We listed ten rushes, three wood rushes and six sedges as well as Eleocharis, Schoenus, Isolepis, Trichophorum and bog cotton. The most special find was that elegant little relative of the club mosses, *Selaginella selaginoides*. This habitat also yielded some viviparous fescue, the most unusual of the nineteen grass species recorded.

This was another, more austere world where most burnable peat had been dug out by former inhabitants and a few of the small plants eked out a living by becoming carnivores. Both the more usual butterworts were here, the common and the pale, but not *Pinguicula grandiflora*, which is the prerogative of South-west Eire.

All three of the sundews are recorded, the common round-leaved *Drosera rotundifolia* hybridising with both the others to give stickily armoured leaves of different shapes and sizes. The great sundew *Drosera anglica* grew in shallow water rather than the spongy mire. Oblong leaved *Drosera intermedia* we failed to find. Cotton grass, deer grass and rushes speared from the soggy expanses of different hued Sphagnum mosses.

This was the haunt of red grouse, secretive creatures, although by no means silent. The cuckoo calls wafting acrosss the heather where these lived are as rare a sound now as are those emanating from the grouse. Small heath orchids were replaced by early purple orchids as we regained the shelter of the trees. White helleborine orchids were a bonus, yellow flags a special pleasure.

We noticed an aura of decay as we progressed, not only with the little spleen-wort ferns on the tumbled, overgrown walls of past settlement – peoples' homes – and the grave of an unknown sailor, but in the frequent fallen and decaying trees. Some had been toppled by wind, others squeezed out by more vigorous, unthinned neighbours, but all provided potential living sites, for beetles, moth caterpillars and other small fry and a climbing frame for brambles and honey-suckle. Old man's beard and other lichens ran riot here.

Outliers of woody species occurred on rocky knolls rising from the beaches of dark Torridonian pebbles. Similarly weatherbeaten, these remained largely ungrazed and unburned. Birds feeding on rowan, honeysuckle, hawthorn, holly and elderberries here might expectorate or defecate the undigested seeds in the regenerating wildwood. Bramble needs little help to achieve such advances!

Winged and parachuted seeds of birch and sallows could get swirled up the beach and drifted into corners to germinate. Regeneration is more assured now that fences are in place. Finches could deal with the disseminules of alder, ash, larch and pine. Those of oak and hazel might prove more of a problem in the presumed absence of squirrels. Perhaps the wood pigeons might help here.

Primroses, celandines, bluebells and stately splaying plants of greater woodrush, with whiskery leaves had survived from former woodland on these untrashed outcrops, as if on nunataks above an enveloping ice sheet. Neat bilberry or blaeberry clumps are as at home in the intermittent shade of these scraps of woodland as on the open moor. Pushing up among them are foxglove spires and the neat symmetry of hard ferns with their central firework of sporing fronds, also species of old tufty grassland such as yellow rattle, sneezewort, and self heal, even ox-eye daisies

Ancient aspens found sanctuary here, their trembling foliage a favourite with browsers elsewhere. They have also been found to provide tender eating for the caterpillars of puss moths, poplar hawk moths and pebble prominents. Speckled wood butterflies, whose caterpillars feed on grass, are spreading from such outliers into the new woodlands as these come to provide sufficient shade, albeit with sunny clearings. The woolly bear caterpillares of fox and drinker moths were more a part of the moorland scene.

Some of the rockier knolls were sprinkled with the shattered shells of cockles and mussels, these dropped from a height by hooded crows to spill out the contents. Jackdaws, which have many wiles and are by no means stupid, were watching this performance, but seemed not yet to have acquired the skill for themselves. Waders probing among the muddied pebbles stabilised by sea milkwort, thrift, sea arrow-grass and saltmarsh grass, were the inevitable oyster catchers, with curlews and common sandpipers.

101. *Common Sandpiper*

Eiders and common and greater black backed gulls built their nests against crumbling cottage walls adorned with English stonecrop and rock spurrey in the ruined village of Port nan Caranean which lay at our furthest point. It had housed five crofting families from Skye who moved in from 1827, the year after most of the Rhum population had given up and sailed away to try again in Newfoundland.

Remnants of stock enclosures showed that the people farmed as well as fished, but they, too, gave up the unequal struggle and moved out after thirty four years. At no stage were there more than twenty seven souls there. Now swathes of bracken had swallowed up most of the foundations and little trees had been planted in 1984 – oak, ash, black cherry and hazel.

The uncertainty of life in these wilderness outposts was brought home to us a short time after our visit. Vice warden on Rhum in 1986 was Wilf Nelson, a friend of ours in South Wales, where he had held a similar posting on the Kenfig Burrows National Nature Reserve before moving here. His delightful young wife had laid on a tea party for our little group. Not long afterwards we learned that Wilf had fallen to his death while working on the cliffs. He had lived life to the full, but was cut off in his prime in the course of duty.

This sad news came later. We left Rhum in good spirits, the following wind making for much more comfortable travel than when butting into it on the way in. Elusive sunshine played hide and seek with the rain, treating us to views of some long lasting, low arched rainbows.

Both inward and outward journeys yielded sightings of guillemots, tysties, shags, fulmars and the odd puffin. Big flocks of shearwaters were gathering in rafts on the sea, working up the courage to fly into their mountain hideaways when the predatory gulls had retired for the night.

151

Terns dived about our homeward boat and we watched three large concourses of black-backed and herring gulls converging on a shoal of sprats. As many birds were in the air as on the water, with more flying in as they got wind of the bonanza on offer.

When we unkindly drove into the centre of one of the gatherings, several hundred gulls rose in a single cloud, screaming annoyance and revealing a dozen or so guillemots on the surface and formerly hidden in the fracasse of flapping feathers. These were less alarmed as they had the option of diving if we got too close. A concourse of fatly speckled, pale coated seals were out in force on the rocks to welcome us back to Muck.

V

Some Smaller Isles: Iona, Staffa and The Treshnish

IONA

1. IONA, A CHRISTIAN COMMUNITY FROM ANCIENT TIMES

Iona must be better known on a national scale as a religious community than Islay is for its whisky – both islands finding fame for their spirit, though these are manifested somewhat differently. Christianity, however, is not the first of the spiritual pursuits practised here.

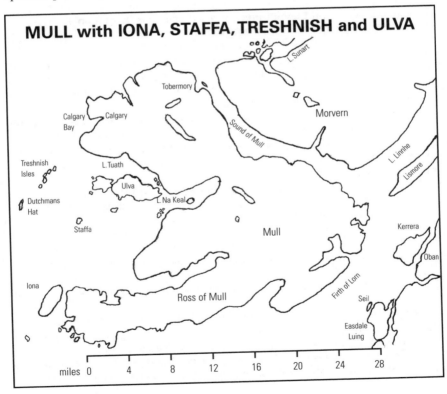

MULL with IONA, STAFFA, TRESHNISH and ULVA

153

Iona was a centre of druidic worship with an extant temple long before the coming of Christ and the later coming of St. Columba, following his escape from Ireland via Oronsay. By no means as remote from inhabited lands as many such retreats, it must possess a powerful aura of enchantment to have attracted mystics from earliest times and retained them until this age of questioning and disbelief.

Early converts sought sanctuary here from persecution, as well as to imbibe inspiration from the awesomely beautiful backdrop. Moderns, still inspired by the beauty, seek refuge from the hustle and bustle of the frenetic urban world that we have created to cope with our ever growing numbers. Man-made landscapes seldom aspire to the elemental beauty that Nature can evolve.

St. Columba, founder of Iona's great tradition, shared a name with the pigeons and doves that inhabited the land before he appeared on the scene. By then those would have been named by scholars from the classical world – Greek or Roman – with the epithet that they were to share with the great man.

Doves are traditionally regarded as gentle creatures, perhaps because of their soothing cooing and cuddling up together in pairs, but this is a long way from the whole truth. They are far more likely to scrap among themselves than are more powerfully equipped avifauna like birds of prey, which could inflict serious damage on their kin if they indulged in such tantrums. Evolution cannot allow that sort of goings on if the race is to survive.

St. Columba, thus named we presume for his gentleness, arrived here in AD 563 with twelve followers and is credited with being the first to bring christianity to Scotland. He is reputed to have referred to his new abode as "Iona of my heart" and settled here, as he had failed to do on Oronsay, where his shorter stay is commemorated by the now ruined priory.

Of the saint's original Iona monastery, built probably of wattle and daub, nothing now remains. After his death it was sacked several times by the Vikings. Its inmates were massacred, some of them on the beach which is still known as Traigh Ban nam Monach 'the White Strand of the Monks'. The founding saint is buried on the precincts.

Despite tribulations, the christian tradition lived on through the Dark Ages and Iona became a place of pilgrimage for outsiders. As Bardsey in North Wales is known as "The Island of Saints', with a thousand such said to be buried in its consecrated soil, so Iona, too, became a coveted site for burial.

Its St. Oran's Cemetery is credited with being the oldest burial ground in Scotland. No less than sixty two christian kings are reputedly buried there – forty eight from Scotland, eight from Norway, four from Ireland and two from France. Included in this auspicious company are Shakespeare's MacBeth and his victim, Duncan.

The present St. Mary's Abbey dates from the thirteenth or fifteenth century in different accounts – possibly both correct, as such buildings could take a hundred years to complete and were added to as the wherewithal became available.

It was extensively restored during the nineteen hundreds, this work involving a two foot deep excavation during renewal of the drainage system. At that depth treasure was unearthed – rather more than three hundred tenth century coins, some thick gold wire and a gold and silver brooch. Expert examination of these and comparison with similar hoards found elsewhere, led to the conclusion that this was a Viking hoard collected by raiders who were interrupted before being able to carry it all away. It is known that there was a Viking raid on Iona in 896 – a time when the coins were in current use.

The oldest building still standing is St. Oran's Chapel built by Queen Margaret in 1080. This name must be another link with Oronsay. Facing it is St. Martin's Cross, with its intricately carved east face, this outside the west door of the cathedral, priory or abbey as it is variously called. A Celtic monument, standing seventeen feet high, this is more than a thousand years old.

The twelfth century nunnery is now a noble ruin. Like Joseph, it wears a coat of many colours. One feels the builders must have had fun arranging the different coloured stones at their disposal. Pinks and purples are the brightest, offset by the various shades of grey. Crystalline granites contrast with fine grained sandstones and mudstones. Bottle green 'Iona marble', reminiscent of Cornwall's Serpentine, contrasts with sparkling white quartz. Rusty brown blends with steely grey. They are all there, neatly squared by the master mason's assistants and interleaved with slivvers of dark grey slate to bring each course of stones into line. Only the broad stone arches at ground level and narrower ones above are framed by uniformly pale grey stone, carved as bathstone and shaped to fit neatly together.

The Iona Community is still alive and well, attracting thousands of tourists, many drawn in to join the various services being conducted, regardless of their preconceived beliefs. The sense of timelessness engendered is accentuated on emergence into the timeless landscape of rock tumps and plant life, sun and sand. Climbing the 326 feet (101 m) high Calva Dun to gaze across to the Outer Hebrides over the broad sweep of sparkling white machair and shimmering blue sea, can fix the image in the mind for all time.

The current leader of the Community in this twenty first century speaks words of wisdom and comfort to the world at large as a regular contributor to the thought provoking "Thought for the Day" programme just before the 8.0 am news bulletin on the much listened to "Today" programme on BBC Radio 4.

2. IN TRANSIT TO IONA

Although it is possible to travel direct to Iona by steamer from Oban in Western Argyll, many of today's pilgrims take two shorter voyages in smaller boats, travelling across the substantial island of Mull to Fionnphort at the end of the sinuous south-western promontary of the Ross of Mull between the two.

My first visit in the mid 1950s was for purposes of researching the coastal vegetation of Mull and Iona – sea lochs of the former and sandy shores of the latter. Subsequently, in the late 1960s and the mid 1980s, I was here with parties of naturalists to absorb as much as we could of the beauty and intricacies of the varied landscape. On each occasion, being already on Mull, we sailed from Fionnphort.

In 1968 we travelled from Salen on the Sound of Mull, across the narrowest part of the island to follow the shore of Loch na Keal, past the islands of Eorsa and Inch Kenneth. In transit we spied mergansers and divers on the sheltered waters and watched four herons being rebuffed by a single, feisty tern whose fishing spree they had interrupted.

Six eider drakes and six cormorants were already in occupation with a flock of small brown waders and a possie of Atlantic seals. The road doubled back around the head of Loch Scridain and along its southern shore formed by the northern flank of the Ross. Pied wagtails of the beach gave way to pipits and wheatears towards the hills and to those now so rare yellowhammers along field boundaries.

102. *Pied Wagtails*

Topography changed as we progressed, the land lowering and the wind increasing, with rocky mounds descending gently to narrow strips of sea beach. Here were fewer trees, in a balder countryside more like Sutherland, with the occasional peat stack. A buzzard surveyed his kingdom from a telegraph pole and the alarm call of a deer wafted in through the open window of our vehicle.

As we approached Fionnphort we passed a cornfield ablaze with corn marigolds, of a warmer hue than today's acid yellow oil seed rape crops. Sadly these handsome, sunflower-like plants have disappeared from most of Britain's arable fields in the forty years since, under the onslaught of agri-chemicals.

The Fionnphort headland was a visual delight with its outcrops of crystalline coral pink Lewissian gneiss pushing up through the dark heather like icing on a chocolate cake. More, washed clean by the sea, emerged from pristine, tide scoured sands. Downshore it was laced with decoratively draped seaweeds. Upshore it graded into the particularly shiny green of a sward of black crowberry, which is so much glossier than the more widespread heather.

With sunshine picking out the mosaic of pink and white shapes in the granite and reflecting from the silvery backs of the few well named *Larus argentatus* gulls, it was indeed a pretty picture. The bones of the land are so near the surface in this sort of country that geology cannot be ignored by even the most dedicated flower lover or bird watcher.

Out across the pink tinged sands and reflective blue water lay Iona, a low peneplain dotted with a few white cottages around the grey outline of the priory, with a steep ended, flat topped hill rising from near the centre. In the immediate foreground a little flock of mallard drakes poked under the flopped wracks and idled among the swaying downshore oarweeds.

When we sailed from here again in mid May 1987 a fishing boat had just pulled in with a bumper catch of handsome green-striped mackerel, firmly held in the clutch of great blocks of ice. The ferry was substantial enough to take a vehicle across with the foot passengers, but, with so short a length of road on the island, that service was reserved for residents and freight. Day trippers were likely to fill the boat at this season. It was eider drakes hanging round the pier this time. They moved unconcernedly out of the way as the ferry eased a passage out to accomplish the shortest possible crossing – of just one mile.

3. IONA, UNYIELDING ROCK AND SHIFTING SAND

Iona is two and a half miles long, one to one and a half miles broad and covers seventy one acres. Although closer to the mainland than many of the Inner Hebrides, its ancient, dark pre-Cambrian rocks and sandy machair pastures have more in common with the Outer Hebrides. Lewissian and Torridonian in age, the bedrock is as ancient as any on the Earth's crust.

Most rock on the neighbouring island of Mull is of much later, Tertiary origin, forming square edged basalt terraces which have engulfed former surfaces.These basaltic lava flows of Mull are shared with Ulva. Gometra, Staffa, the Treshnish and other islands but not with Iona. As a result this island has a character of its own, different from the rest and having none of the famous basaltic columns seen so well on Staffa only six miles away.

Nor is any of Fionnphort's pink granite native to Iona, although formed closer in time of origin than the basalts. We encountered it there only as erratics, isolated pink boulders transported by the westward moving ice flow connecting Iona with the mainland of which they had been a part many years before.

As southerners, we were much more conscious of the geology here than at home, where most of the rocky bones of the land are decently buried. It is the smoother, more accommodating substrate that marks Iona off so sharply from nearby Staffa.

Iona, with its sandy pastures and machair spreading back from acres of silvery beach sand at low water, speaks of gentle mellowness. Staffa's towering vertical cliffs frown down on the ocean, rebuffing each wave with a single impact instead of letting it roll in along a more gentle gradient.

Staffa has no sandy beaches and the water looms ominously dark in the deep shadow cast by the iron-grey cliffs and the answering darkness of the rocky sea bed. Iona's sunlight filters through clear water to be reflected back from the white sandy bed in a translucent green glow that cannot be bettered by coral islands in the Tropics.

Fragments of land crop up round about, a hazard to unwary mariners and calling for warning lighthouses. A dangerous reef, The Torran Rocks, stretches seaward from the south-west point of Mull. The name comes from the Gaelic torunn, referring to the growling sound heard on Mull as swells break endlessly on and over the outcrops.

Their outermost end is marked by the Dubh Hirteach lightouse, built precariously on an islet 250 feet long and 35 feet high in 1872 – with help from none of today's mighty machines. The lantern gallery is 106 feet above the sea, but may yet be reached by waves licking up from ferocious surges around the base of the tower.

Like the ferocious tidal current through the Strait of Corrievrechan north of Jura, this marine phenomenon nurtures the tale of a West Highland witch overseeing the disasters and near disasters with relish. Readers of Robert Louis

103. Cattle on Iona Machair

Stevenson's "Kidnapped" may recall that the brig "Covenant" of Dysart in the story was wrecked on the Torran Rocks.

While the seashells of which the beach sands are composed are pulverised beyond recognition, the multi-coloured pebbles of the upper beaches hail from many sources. Rolled around by the tides, rock fragments are worn to balls and buttons of uniform hue or of a pink and white amalgam reminiscent of a fossilised brawn or German sausage. They make attractive trophies for would be shell collectors or beach combers.

My investigations in the 1950s showed that more than half of the sand samples taken from Iona's machair was composed of the shells of living organisms rather than of mineral fragments.

Calcium carbonate or limestone comprised up to eighty per cent of the air dried whole, equivalent figures for other shell sands being around sixty seven per cent and for mineral sands only twenty four per cent. This resulted in a higher pH of 8.3 to 8.4 in the sandy soils- and alkalinity sufficient to negate the potentially harmful acidity in soil arising from the country rock. Soil fertility was thus enhanced and more plants able to grow where sand had settled by whatever means.

Alkalinity speeds the decay of dead plant material so that undesirably acid peat builds up slowly or not at all. Initially new soils accumulating under the influence of wind err in the other direction, with too little moisture-holding humus. Given time, a more desirable middle way is achieved and fertile loams come into being.

A fertility gradient develops with increasing distance from the sea – from friable, non-retentive "white land" atop the beach, through an optimum mix of mineral and organic matter to the non-productive acid peat of ill-drained "black land". Crofters farming western land in the Outer hebrides often work strips at right angles to the shore so that all have a bit of each land category, from too dry and alkaline, through the more productive mixture to unproductive acid peat.

4. IONA PLANT LIFE

Forty plant species were found growing on the Iona sands, sufficient to provide a variety of colour, the season through. Brightest was the warm crimson of bloody cranesbill, sunniest the orange-flecked yellow of an unusually succulent form of bird's-foot trefoil. Some, like the aromatic thyme and acrid yellow stonecrop hugged the ground to conserve available moisture although these two are unpalatable to grazing animals. Others have a double reason for lying low. Among the tallest were reddish purple knapweed and bluish purple scabious.

Plants growing only where there is plenty of lime include fairy flax, wild carrot, common milkwort and a special dune form of lesser meadow rue (*Thalictrum minus* var *arenarium*). Neutrality of soil can be enhanced by sea salt as well as lime, the two being to some extent complementary so that each can compensate for low levels of the other.

Then there are seaside specialists which grow only where sea salt is sufficient to quell the growth of more vigorous competitors. These include the attractive pink mats of thrift and sea milkwort, sea arrow grass and sea plantain. Pioneers of loose and hence mobile sand can be short-lived annuals like prickly saltwort and orache (Salsola and Atriplex), exploiting short spells of calm summer weather before being blown or washed away, but not before leaving some seeds for their next appearance.

104. *Prickly Saltwort and Spear-leaved Orache*

Succulent mat formers such as sea sandwort (*Honkenya peploides*) have a high internal water content useful for combatting drying winds and the difficulty of absorbing water from salty soil. Osmotic pressure in the plant's tissues must be high enough to enable it to take in moisture from a weaker solution outside, hence the salty tang of those which need to do so where the soil is saltier than optimum.

Holding on to wind blown sand is achieved by those able to send stabilising roots deep into the substrate, notably the dune building marram grass, but also sand sedge with its long underground stems and yellow-flowered members of the daisy family with deep taproots such as dandelion and cat's-ear.

Build up of tide-borne or wind-borne seaweeds from the driftline helps with both water retention and stability, favouring carpets of silverweed, which send slender runners snaking over the soil surface and mouse-ear hawkweed with its hairier creeping stems.

Middle of the way plants contributing to the sandy pasture include the ubiquitous field daisies with clovers and other legumes able to improve the habitat for the rest by fixing atmospheric nitrogen about their roots. Other delights are harebells, the 'bluebells of Scotland', violets and swards of yellow-flowered lady's bedstraw. It behoves all to lie low, whether as rosettes or creepers, if they are to escape constant gnawing by the ever present rabbits – supplemented to a lesser or greater degree by farm livestock.

Generous increments of blown sand burying much of the sward make it less accessible to herbivores as well as stimulating upward growth to the light. Dune grasses such as the bents and fescues along with field daisies, are particularly adept at rising above such tribulation. Fine examples of this can be seen where farm implements lying fallow in field corners become firmly embedded in a closed turf a foot or more above original ground level at the time of dumping.

This, of course, can work both ways. Sand can move out as well as in. It is a wonderful burrowing medium for industrious rabbits and the wiser among these may favour the added stability afforded at roof level by the abandoned implement. Particularly wise rabbits will open out their burrows on the leeward side, but baby bunnies are not always wisely taught by their elders. An orifice facing into the prevailing wind can be the focus of a new blow out, leaving that neatly knitted daisy sward suspended in empty air.

5. IONAS ROOKERY, HAY HARVEST AND CATTLE

Our 1968 visit was in early August at the height of the holiday season, with ferry crossings at half hourly intervals. Even the odd vehicle was making the journey, but wheeled access was at one end only, so the boat swung briskly round on arrival to enable these to disembark backwards.

The tide was well down and the water calm. From time to time a breath of wind passed across it, brushing dark shadows over the surface, as over the softness of a rabbit's fur. We lingered awhile on the beach, fossicking among the oarweeds of the the lower littoral zone. Tips drooping with their own weight caused the fronds to elbow their way above the water, like a flotilla of brown-sailed dinghies rocking gently as wavelets passed among them.

Sunlight reflected from their mucilagenous surfaces in glints of many colours, like light passing through a prism. The frilly edged sugar weed (*Laminaria saccharina*), was a particularly attractive participant in this ethereal dance.

Beneath was a wealth of more delicate red algae, ones with insufficient substance to maintain their shape when unsupported by the water. The Victorian ladies who fashioned them into Christmas cards had to float them onto the paper after washing away the salt. Reds are generously imbued with mucilage and are self adhesive, holding fast when dry.

Sand in the little harbour was not such a dazzling white as on the ocean beaches, being seemingly mixed with finer silt particles unable to drop out of the choppier waters swirling along the outer shores. From the clarity of those it was evident that there was not much held in suspension there anyway.

Jagged reefs of dark grey rock reached out across the beach and some must have connected the tied island that we explored later with the main land block, as big kelps had found anchorage along the connecting sand bar.

A row of smart two-storey houses, one of them the Argyll Hotel, lay but a short stretch of lawn grass from the shore, whitewashed or of mellowed stone. All had dormer windows

105. *Rook and Sycamore*

protruding from their grey slate or red tiled roofs. Buxom Fuchsia bushes were ablaze with crimson blooms, some invaded by a pink-flowered version of hedge bindweed. This scrambled between the dangling red and purple lanterns, to add further colour with its generously large trumpet flowers.

A plot of tall sycamores near the manse came as a surprise, the fifty or sixty rooks which had set up home in them being even less expected, as rookeries are usually associated with spacious tracts of arable land.

Sycamores are much maligned by conservationists as aliens, although firmly established in Britain since the sixteenth century. They are, however, more windworthy than most of our native trees and have been the favoured choice of a number of island communities anxious to establish viable wind breaks.

Many of the crumbling ruins in the British countryside, where the wildwood has taken over will be enwrapped in the firm embrace of veteran sycamore or ash trees. Sinuous woody roots clasp the stones and clamp them to the mosaic of crevices. Both species shed myriad seeds producing swarms of saplings to sprout from other cracks and both produce noble trees to counteract the onslaught of blustery winds.

To attain rookery status approved by these often fastidious birds is, notwith-standing, quite an achievment. It says much for the fertility of the gneiss-sand mix, which also supported some arable crops – cereals, potatoes and probably other 'roots'.

Nesting was well advanced, if not over and almost the entire corvine flock took off to circle over the abbey, complaining in no uncertain terms at our intrusion.

They were not alone. We put up an even bigger mob of starlings working their way across the aftermath of a newly cut hayfield. The eighty to a hundred lapwings wheeling over the farmlands were commonplace then, forty years ago.

106. *Iona Haycocks in 1968*

Would that such sights were as frequent nowadays. Perhaps they still are – on Iona.

Haymaking, later here than in the south, was still in progress. In the absence of today's modern machines, hay cocks were scattered across the shorn culms of the after-math, which were already greening with the new influx of light and nourishing rain. Hay cocks on the windward side of the island had been protected from losing their topknots by mob caps fashioned from substantial rope, procured in all liklihood from a fisherman.

No caps were seen on the grass pyramids nearer the harbour, but the cut crop here had not yet been fully gathered, so these may have been destined for netting later on. The temporarily parked hay rake and swathe turner alongside the still drying swathes took me back to my own haymaking days of the early 1940s. I

161

saw neither tractor nor working horse, but the implements were fitted with shafts for a horse. Either may have been the motive power in that era, but certainly the neatly conical hay cocks had been raked together by hand, rather than spewed, ready tied , from a machine.

Out on the open machair pastures we met the animals that would be benefiting from these products of the husbandmen's labours come winter. The velvet smoothness of the turf from which they were trying to wrest a living now, in high summer, suggested that they could do with some of it already.

There were no sheep, whose close grazing seemed more appropriate to such a close sward. Cattle like to curl their long tongues around sizable bunches of fodder to pull into their mouth and munch at leisure. I have watched fascinated on Barra and other islands as cows plucked whole bunches of primroses at every out-thrusting of that mobile tongue, happy for the cow but devastated at the plundering of so much delicate beauty. Fortunately primroses are by no means rare on Barra.

The nurse cows were a mixture of breeds. There were shaggy, pale coated Highlanders with yellow calves, their lineage possibly involving a white Shorthorn bull. A Jersey cow, with the lustrous appealing eyes that characterise the breed, was suckling a black calf. Was the sire Galloway or Angus? At home it would likely have been a Welsh Black. Plain red dams may have had Shorthorn blood, but there are various possibilities here.

The neatly diminutive red and white Ayrshire with upturned horns reminded me of my favourite "Scotty" who I had hand milked through the war – her particular brand of milk, with small fat globules, making excellent cheese to supplement our meagre rations. My Jersey charges producing milk with a high butter fat content, had guaranteed us a little extra cream from the top of the churn – as no doubt here – while still leaving the three per cent required by law.

Highland cows are home bred. The Ayrshires' northern affinities come from Scandinavia, but so, too, do some of our Jerseys, despite their association with the far off southern island for which they were named after their introduction in the eighteenth century.

The thick fringe of hair reaching from the forehead almost to the muzzle of the Highlanders shielded their faces from wind and rain but must have rendered them almost blind. Unless blown aside all vision was blocked except directly downwards, so they could at least see what they were eating. Some set up an anxious lowing when the calf they were nursing wandered off. It was up to the calf, with unrestricted vision, to reassure its dam that all was well.

Some cows had given up the unequal struggle to ingest the closely shorn sward, whose chief attraction must have been the tender carpet of lady's bedstraw. These had lain down to ruminate. Having softened those pathetic wisps of vegetation by bacterial action in the first of their four stomachs, they coughed them up for further chewing or cudding. Satisfied with the result, the mulch was then sent on its way through the other three stomachs and what I have seen described as fifty metres of coiled intestine, to service the dung flies, burying beetles and eventually, perhaps, choughs.

Three pairs of choughs had been recorded on Iona in 1852, but by 1947 they were extinct. With the general increase along the West coast of Cornwall, Wales and Ireland in recent years, they may have returned by now to these short swards that they and their prey insects so favour. Even now, in 2007, choughs are apparently confined in Scotland to a few islands in the Inner Hebrides.

Some cattle were paddling out from the sand flats. Others were strolling along stony storm beaches, apparently untroubled by the cobbles. Yet more were picking at salty strands of seaweed to supplement their meagre diet.

Grazing areas might terminate in rock faces accommodating brackish Enteromorpha pools. Another was bounded by a vertical sand face where some twites were pecking away at the anaemic blue flowers of prickly bugloss (*Anchusa* formerly *Lycopsis arvensis*).

The whole area was strewn with rabbit droppings, which had not been passed through four stomachs as in the ruminants but had been

107. Bugloss and Sticky Storksbill

through the whole alimentary system twice, the soft pellets first ejected being re-ingested to squeeze out the last scrap of goodness.

Entrances to some of the many burrows showed an increase of sticky storksbill (*Erodium lebelii* formerly *E. glutinosum*). This was evidently a plant which these furry innocents left severely alone, probably because of the amount of sand adhering to the sticky hairs and likely to blunt those busily gnawing incisors before their time.

6. IONA TWO DECADES LATER

On stepping ashore from the turnabout ferry boat in May 1987, we renewed our acquaintance with the ancient complex of buildings. Here were Norman and Gothic doorways, ancilliary chapels which we had missed before, a mausoleum of the Dukes of Argyll and a wonderful collection of Highland grave sculpture dating from medieval times. The diligently carved eighth and ninth century Celtic crosses are regarded as the finest of their kind in Britain.

Once again we admired the motley collection of stones comprising the walls of the old nunnery, a veritable liquorice allsorts of colour intersected with the dark lines of slate. These walls were further adorned by verdant trails of ivy-leaved toadflax, the dainty snapdragon flowers curving back on maturity to find another home niche once the seeds of the next generation had been set.

As we moved on the rocks intrigued us, as always. Most were greenish black schists, but blocks of pink gneiss lay atop these in parts, these no doubt transported hither by a glacier from the sparkling granites of the Ross of Mull across the strait. Shiny white quartz was in ample supply along with humbug striped banded schists.

Lawns and gardens around the religious precincts were neatly tended and tourists were catered for with food shops, tea houses and book and novelty stores. We did not linger but set off northwards on an exploratory walk.

Sand cover was minimal on most of this leeward side. The only mature woodland was the rooks' sycamore plot by manse and kirk behind the village. Nesting was at its height and a chorus of provocative altercations came from the treetops. Any nest left unattended for long might well lose some of its substance to a neighbour, so they shouted rather than abandoning them.

This had an understorey of bracken with bluebells sprouting from inadequate seeming crevices in the slaty rock. A pleasantly aromatic component of the extensive bordering heather with its purple moor-grass, deer-grass and Sphagnum, was bog myrtle or sweet gale.

Much of the island was open and grassy, the stocking rate increasing with the increments of wind-transported sand. Certain parts squelched underfoot, suggesting impermeable bedrock not far below the surface. In other sections the sand was deep, this well shown near the northern tip where a big blowout had undermined a post and wire fence, leaving the once deeply buried points of the posts dangling in fresh air, girt about with a thin circlet of turf like a ragged gipsy skirt. Still held by the connecting wires, they projected like a row of sharpened upper dentures. A more surprising survival was an unvegetated sheep track following horizontally along a sand face lying at it its extreme 'angle of rest' and liable to be set in motion by any careless step. Those dainty hooves had not yet started a landslide.

The peoples' track on the level was stabilised with well trodden red fescue grass but the sward alongside was more herb than grass, with dovesfoot cranesbill, common hawkbit, daisies, ribwort and the little white cress, Danish scurvy grass. This was sheep country, the cattle now mainly higher up on the hillside. It was also the part most frequented by common linnets and those linnets of Scottish and East Anglian heaths, the twites.

Turnstones, resplendent in the rufous and black tortoiseshell plumage of the breeding season, picked their way through the flopped seaweeds in search of goodies with a few less well camouflaged oyster catchers. Four groups of ringed plovers, each of six to seven birds, were encountered, along with a few more sombrely dressed dunlins. Some of the cruising terns were large enough to be sandwich terns. Offshore flocks of eiders were of both sexes. Evidently the ducks had not yet settled into their eiderdown nurseries. There was so little cover for building a nest here that we wondered if they were domiciled on the Mull side of the mile wide strait, with Iona serving as their daytime larder.

There was just time for an ice cream on our return to the village and then a race for the ferry, which achieves a rapid turnaround and waits for no man.

STAFFA

7. STAFFA, THE DISCOVERY OF A GEOLOGICAL TREASURE

On the standard 1:100,000 2 cm to the mile map, Staffa is the size of a small pea. About three quarters of a mile long and a quarter of a mile wide, its fame in scientific, travel and musical circles far outweighs its size.

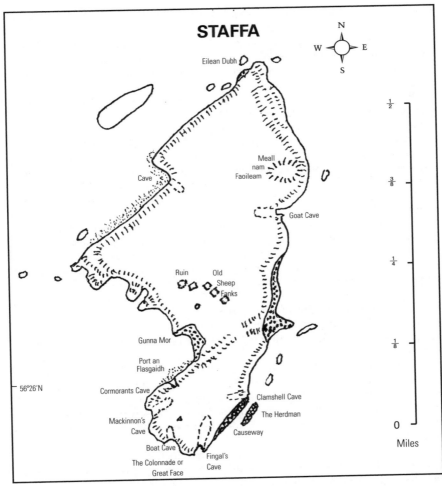

STAFFA

N
W ← → E
S

Eilean Dubh

Meall
nam
Faoileam

Cave

Goat Cave

Ruin   Old
Sheep
Fanks

Gunna Mor

Port an
Flasgaidh

56°26'N

Cormorants Cave

Clamshell Cave

The Herdman

Mackinnon's
Cave

Causeway

Boat Cave   Fingal's

The Colonnade or   Cave
Great Face

½

⅜

¼

⅛

0

Miles

There are puffins, yes, and fulmar petrels, wild orchids and primroses, but it is the spectacular rock formations that account for its notoriety in a region with more than its share of volcanic manifestations, reconstituted rock, sills and dykes.

It is small enough and low enough, with only one hill, 135 feet high at the steeper sided southern end, to have been overlooked by the world at large until well into the eighteenth century.

St. Columba would have been familiar with its angular outline as seen from Iona, and he may well have covered the few miles between in his flimsy coracle when venturing forth to spread the gospel among the heathen Scots. But his mind was probably pre-occupied with a different sort of miracle than the one manifested in these ancient rocks. Indeed, having come from Northern Ireland,

165

he may already have seen this sort of thing in the Giant's Causeway and regarded such rock formations as a matter of course.

As with all these islands, it would have been known to the seafaring Vikings and its name derived from Staph-Ey is Norse for the Island of Staves or Pillars. The Western Isles were under Norse rule for nearly four hundred years, from 890 to 1266.

Obviously Staffa was known to the inhabitants of neighbouring islands, who may have benefitted from its sea life or even its grazing land from earliest times. It lies but four miles from Ulva and eight miles from Mull, with the nearest occupied island of Gometra only four short miles to the north-east.

These neighbours, knowing little or nothing of the more mundane landscapes beyond, would not have regarded the Staffa formations as anything remarkable. Having been born among such columns, albeit of less imposing dimensions, they would assume that this is the way rocks are. It was left to strangers to notice their significance.

Pennant, the famous Highland traveller, was in these waters on 11th July, 1772, but bad weather prevented him from landing. It was an Englishman, or suspected Irishman, a Mr. Leach, who brought the news of the island to the wider world, through a chance meeting with a man who would be listened to with respect by the erudite members of Britain's Royal Society.

A few days after Leach's visit and only a month after Pennant's near miss, the first met up with a party of scientists headed for Iceland, both having been offered hospitality by the local laird on the Sound of Mull. This was on 13th August 1772, when the adventurers' vessel had sought refuge from inclement weather in Tobirmore (Tobermory).

Their leader was Sir Jospeh Banks, who had sailed with Captain Cook to more distant parts and was the most eminent botanist of his time, famed for the exotic collections brought back from the other hemisphere. Over refreshments, Leach described Staffa to Banks as resembling the Giant's Causeway, a site known to his listener by repute and one which he dearly hoped to visit at some time in his adventurous career.

He forthwith ordered his ship to wait for him in Tobermory and set off in the laird's little boat for an overnight excursion to Staffa, equipped with a tent, some helpers and rations for two days. It was dark when the party arrived to pitch camp. Next morning they woke to view columnar basalt at its best – give or take a few manifestations in Northern Ireland and North America. Bank's reactions were summed up in his later published comments.

"We were struck with a scene of magnificence that exceeded our

108. *Sweeping curves of Basalt Columns on Staffa*

expectation." "Compared with this what are cathedrals and palaces built by man?"

He wrote about his findings at length, as well as addressing the elite of the Royal Society in person. Six pages of his account were included in one of Pennant's several volumes of "A Tour in Scotland and Voyage to the Hebrides in 1772.", published in Chester in 1774-5 and dedicated to Sir Joseph Banks, who was elected as president of the Royal Society in 1778, retaining this honour through his knighthood and until his death in 1820.

Of his own near visit, Pennant wrote"

"Nearest lies Staffa, a new Giant's Causeway arising amid the waves, but the columns of double the height of that in Ireland, glossy and respendent from the beams of the eastern sun."

On a subsequent visit Joseph Banks scrambled to the almost inaccessible end of Fingal's Cave and carved his initials "J.B. 1772" into one of the columns, These were not discovered by the modern world in this obscure site until 1928.

Voyages to the sacred island of Iona had been quite commonplace for many years and, almost at once, from 1773, Staffa was likely to be included in the itinerary. Boswell and Johnson were among those visiting in October of that year.

As its fame spread, many other personalities with the means at their disposal went to view it. Visitors in subsequent years included Sir Walter Scott, Keats, Wordsworth, Tennyson and Jules Verne. All the above wrote about it, but it was probably Mendelsohn, with his epic "Fingals Cave" in the "Hebridean Overture" that exposed it to the ears of the arts world not necessarily interested in travel and geography.

The young Felix Mendelsohn visited during his 1829 tour of the Hebrides. The story goes that, despite sea sickness, the great musician was overawed by the aura of the place. He staggered straight to the piano on his return to try out the melodies that had been conceived in his mind as he tossed uneasily on the briny outside – only to be sternly reprimanded by his host for being so insensitive as to work on the sabbath!

The romantic movement of the first half of the nineteenth century was much in tune with Staffa's impressive grandeur, and Queen Victoria was among its distinguished visitors. She sailed on the 317 ton steamer "Fairy" on 19th August 1847, this the first screw steamer, as opposed to paddle, to carry royalty. Although Staffa has had regular summer steamer trips to Staffa since then, all were in paddle steamers until 1931, despite the frequent turbulence of the seas.

The island is still much visited, but is without permanent inhabitants – especially since coming into the ownership of the National Trust in 1986. For a few years before that the ownership had been disputed – one potential owner having been refused planning permission for a million pound development, involving a pier, a hotel and chalets! All that remained of man's footprints in 1986 were the clustered ruins of old black houses and sheep fanks near the well. The island's only other fresh water is in two small streams. Sheep continued to be pastured there.

8. STAFFA'S PLACE IN THE RUPTURE OF CONTINENTS

The regularity of the neatly regimented basalt columns, like the pipes of a giant organ, must have been at least slightly perplexing to the residents of those ancient black houses, who would have been more familiar with the gentler topograhy of Iona and the Ross of Mull. It was probably superstition of unknown forces within the heart of the island that eventually persuaded the farmer-fishermen who eked out a living here that there were more hospitable places to settle.

Their final departure is said to have been because of their unease at the rumbling reverberations, as from a canon, that shook the island every time the prevailing westerlies exerted their full force. The reports were due to a large stone being shifted around by the swell in what must have been a growing pothole in the cave known as Gunna Mor, the Big Gun Cave.

Local legend attributes the existence of Staffa to a giant named Torquil McLeod, who lived on Eigg. On a visit to the Giant's Causeway he decided to take a piece home. Wading back across the sea some scraps fell out as he approached Mull, to create some small islands. Then the sack burst with the weight and the remains splashed into the sea to form Staffa, the bearer too tired by then to salvage his prize.

Staffa was prone to the same volcanic outpourings that affected Mull, Islay, Treshnish and the Giant's Causeway in the Cretaceous period twelve to thirty million years ago, but it was on the last of these and on Staffa that the colonnades of basalt were manifested with such precision.

Between successive lava flows the newly arrived rock weathered to soil and bore vegetation. These organic layers interbedded with the flows, some compressed into coal seams, were of temperate plants, from the Miocene or middle Tertiary period. If from the Eocene or early Tertiary, as at first thought, they would have been of tropical species.

Plants are, in their turn, building up on the current surface, but not as trees this time, the livestock are seeing to that. At present another laval flow is not antici-pated, as the old volcano has expended its strength.

The lowest laval flows in the Mull complex, of which Staffa is an integral part, lie on a thin layer of early Cretaceous rock consisting of compressed desert sand, the individual grains rounded by the wind. These overlie Jurassic rocks, as on Eigg. Ensuing layers of compacted plant material show the climate to have been getting damper and changing gradually from warm to temperate. Their presence, continuous across the sea from Mull to Treshnish and Staffa, shows that this entire area was land at the time. The western parts became carved out as islands much later, but before the onset of the ice ages.

These, along with the Giant's Causeway, Ardnamurchan, Rhum and Skye to the south and the Faroes, Iceland and Greenland to the north, lie along the line of rupture where the so called "New World" broke its ties with the old and started drifting westwards.

It was not until the late 1950s that paleomagnetism studies proved the truth of the continental drift theory propounded by Wegener in 1912. Two hundred million years ago all the continents formed a single land mass and early geologists thought that the North and South Atlantic Oceans were sunken land bridges.

The drifting apart of the two sections of the old Earth's surface and replacement of the gap with new material from the great north to south Mid Atlantic Rift commenced between two hundred and a hundred and fifty million years ago. The movement started in the south and skewed slightly to the north-west, so that the gulf separating Britain and Scandinavia from Greenland and Canada was born more recently, eighty to seventy million years ago.

The general area is regarded by geologists as the remains of a vast volcano worn down to its very roots by millions of years of erosion. At its peak of activity the volcano's height was thought to be at least ten thousand feet.

9. STAFFA'S BASALT COLONNADES

Staffa's basalt resembles the gabbro of Eigg's great Sgurr and includes felspar, augite and olivene. Its chief characteristic is the smoothness of the rock – this due to the small size of the crystals of which it is composed.

Granites and other coarse-grained rocks were formed deep underground, where they remained hot for aeons of time, allowing the crystals to carry on growing in the molten material to impressive size. Liquid basalt was spewed out over the Earth's surface and was soon chilled by the atmosphere, allowing the rock to harden quickly before the crystals had time to grow beyond microscopic dimensions.

Ground down to a thin film and viewed under a microscope, it is seen to be composed of lozenge shaped crystals of green olivine, granular green augite and a dusting of iron oxide. Arrangement of the tiny crystals in rows, as well as the aligned gas cavities, which are globular at first but get drawn out with the movement of the matrix, show the direction of flow. Shaped like almonds these are known as amygdales, after the almond tree (Prunus amygdalus). The browning of weathered surfaces is due to the rusting of the iron oxide, as on the surface of a rusty nail.

The prismatic columns so beautifully evolved on Staffa are due to contraction of the rock as it cooled, the even shapes arising from even pressures round about. Walking across the truncated ends of the columns is similar to walking across the cracked clay of a dried up pond bed, where pieces of the jigsaw are much the same size but not necessarily the same shape.

The basaltic piles are often referred to as hexagonal, but this is the average, they may be anything from three to nine sided. The truncated ends form an attractive mosaic, particularly when the intervening crevices become colonised by small plants. Sometime these plants include thyme and stonecrop, plants likely to be selected by top notch horticulturalists for the crevices of their carefully constructed crazy stone paths or other garden features.

The long axes of the columns are perpendicular to the surface which is cooling fastest, so that on horizontally bedded deposits they will be vertical, at right angles to the underlying stratum. On Staffa this dips gradually at an angle of seven degrees to the north-east, so they are slightly tilted – although appearing vertical as we sailed in close beneath the Colonnade in our little boat.

Sheer cliffs are formed by breakage along these vertical joints, which are the obvious lines of weakness and separation, this sometimes affected by faulting. Lava flows move much too slowly when mobile to end so abruptly. Whole columns break free to leave the regular series of vertical or curved faces which are such a feature of Staffa. They are broken off successively lower where the waves are continually pounding at the cliff base, to give a neatly regular succession of steps surfaced by the severed cross sections.

Fingal's Cave shows three distinct basalt formations, the massive parallel columns ceasing abruptly above and below. The middle zone is of rather thinner, wavy columns induced by secondary pressure during faster cooling. The top zone of slag has no regular patterning, consisting of a jumbled mass of fragments whose sharp edges are gradually being smoothed off by wave action.

Underlying Staffa's lava is a narrow belt of red ash or conglomeritic tuff, like we saw on Muck and Eigg, this passing under other basaltic flows at the little offshore island known as the Herdsman or Am Buachaille. As on the other Small Islands, it appears just above sea level, as below the beautifully curved columns reaching back to form the receding cliff face in the south-east. It results from the eruption of rock fragments during time gaps between successive basalt flows.

10. BASKING SHARKS EN ROUTE TO STAFFA

My 1960s visit to this famous island was from the port of Oban in "Alfreda", an open decked cabin cruiser carrying twenty five people, It was a sultry day, but the air whisked into life as we got under way – not so briskly though to prevent us from remaining on deck. The cosy comfort of the cabin could not compete with the ever changing lure of the passing scene.

Rounding the northern tip of the offshore island of Kerera, we sailed the length of the Sound of Mull and out past Tobermory, capital of the island of that name, with its warning Rubha nan Gall lighthouse offshore. From Ardmore Point, Mull's northern extremity, we headed west along the deeply indented north coast.

Along the route were three cormorant colonies, the outlying birds posed like heraldic emblems and overlooked by sentinel great black-backed gulls. Fifty shags idling on the water proved more entertaining. Some reached up, duck-like, after each dive, for a bout of wing flapping to rid their feathers of excess water. A few gannets were about, the spread of their great wings balancing them against the press of the wind. One, right above the boat, peered down at us with the sinister binocular vision of those pale steely eyes set so close to the businesslike bill.

109. Basking Shark

The main excitement of this stretch, however, was the encounter with two basking sharks. Two triangles, the dorsal fin and the tip of the upper tail fluke, were so far apart that we thought at first we had twice as many. Only the whale shark exceeds these ungainly monsters in size among the world's fish. Our skipper cut the engine and we drifted in closer, to savour the bulk and texture and look for small hangers-on cadging a ride. The great blue-grey fish ignored us, cruising slowly past, their great maws wide open to scoop up enough plankton to sustain their mighty bulk. Tiny copepods are believed to be their main prey animals.

As shapeless as overgrown garden slugs, these mighty animals can reach as much as thirty six feet or eleven metres long and weigh over three tons. Youngsters are four to five feet long at birth, reaching almost twelve feet in two and a half years.

With so much dilute plankton soup having to be passed through the seiving mechanism to sustain this great bulk, the lateral gill slits through which the rejected water is discharged reach from well under the throat almost to the withers, if fish can be said to have withers.

Normally seen around our western coasts, from the Scillies to Scotland, only in ones and twos, shoals of a hundred or a hundred and fifty may sometimes gather to scoop up small fry out at sea. At the time of this sighting it was thought that the gill rakers were shed in winter to be replaced in spring, so that they must hibernate during this period, but this has since been disproved.

Instead they are known to dive much deeper during winter, further than any other vertebrate and certainly than any air-breathing whale or dolphin could. During 2002-3 data was obtained from satellite transmitters attached to individuals in home waters. The bearers were found to be constantly on the move, travelling between the Hebrides and Cornwall.

They do not hibernate in winter, as had been supposed for the past fifty years, but undertake extensive movements, up to three thousand four hundred kilometres horizontally and to more than eighty five metres vertically, with one individual diving regularly to between three hundred and a thousand metres. Plankton can be found in high concentrations at considerable depths in winter and it is thought that these deep plunges may have been prospecting dives aimed at locating such a food source.

Although we know little of their secret lives, we did know of their wasteful exploitation for shark liver oil, meat and shark fins during the past two hundred years. Fisheries data from Scotland, Iceland and Norway show that about 105,000 individual basking sharks were taken in the past fifty years. The liver alone, which accounts for nearly a quarter of the body weight, can yield as much as five hundred gallons (2,270 litres) of oil, used for oil lamps, candle making and much else. Many more got entangled in fishing nets and were found dead.

I recalled my first sighting, this also off the Scottish coast. I was land bound then and surprised at the way canoeists and folk in small sailing skiffs approached so close to creatures which could easily have overturned them with an untoward movement of the great torso, even though the gentle giant intended no harm. While there was ample room for a human in the great maw, this would have been an unwelcome intrusion into the fish's blameless life style.

Their inoffensiveness has encouraged too many of today's holiday makers to take liberties with them. In 2006 the Marine Conservation Society, which had been organising basking shark watches since 1987, was complaining about groups of power boats, jet skiers and photographers 'herding' groups of sharks by too close an approach.

Despite this harassing, 2006 proved the best year ever for basking shark numbers recorded in British waters, Perhaps the great ocean browsing fish treated human interference with disdain. Perhaps their frequency here was due to global warming. Undoubtedly the greater surveillance of coastal seas by the Wildlife Trusts' Basking Shark Project has added to sightings of these and other marine animals. Even the great flat, disc-shaped sunfish of warmer waters are now well established in the seas off Western Scotland, the small temperature rise boosting the long term effect of the friendly Gulf Stream. Knowing that so many are still around is good news. Seeing some so close forty years before was a bonus indeed.

11. STAFFA, UNSUCCESSFUL ATTEMPT TO GET ASHORE

We dragged ourselves away, moving on through Lock Cuan, which leads south to Dervaig with its standing stones and folk theatre where we had enjoyed a recent performance.

Guillemots, their nesting chores over now by the beginning of August, were part way through their post-nuptial moult from summer to winter plumage. This was a recuperation period for the parent birds, while the youngsters, which drop into the sea so prematurely, could get their bearings and their elders relax before moving off for their winter far out to sea. As we turned south past Calgary bay it was the rarer black guillemots which engaged our attention.

Kittiwakes were nesting along the lintel of a shallow cave and peeling off into the surrounding nothingness, with noisy chorusses of their unmistakable, urgent cries. A cluster of twenty great black-backs surveyed their world from a point of vantage – of haughty mien, like monarchs of all they surveyed. A lone fulmar sped past with the rigidly held wings which distinguish it so readily from the angle-winged gulls. Nearby was another shag colony with twenty five to thirty off duty birds whiling away time on the rocks below.

Soon we were on a level with the Treshnish Isles. To seaward of Gometra's old wave cut platform were three flocks of Manx shear-waters containing many hundreds of birds. Some were shearing the water and were close enough for us to distinguish the diagnostic beak of the 'tube-noses', more slender than those of the related fulmar petrels – our closest relative of the albatrosses of more southern waters.

Shoaling moon jellyfish (*Aurelia aurita*) with their four mauve arcs drifting round the boat were of no interest to these birds, which take smaller prey of easier dimensions. Earlier we had passed through a mass of shoaling compass jellyfish (*Chrysaora hyoscella*), with their ring of narrow isosceles triangles or brown Vs. The trailing mouth tentacles of these were generously frilled and nearly three times as long as the jellified bell was across.

110.
Compass Jellyfish

172

Our plan was to land on Staffa and look in on the Treshnish Group later, but this was not to be. We sailed on past that archipelago but made three unsuccessful attempts to get ashore after viewing Fingal's Cave and other rocky wonders of Staffa from the sea. The landing place near the cave was out of the question weather-wise, but our skipper thought we might make it further along.

Three times the youngest member of the crew jumped ashore, painter in hand, looking for an emergent pinnacle on which to make it fast, while two of us adjusted the sorbo rubber fenders to soften each scrape of the hull against crusty barnacles. The final verdict was "Too much swell. Might do her a damage."

We lay off for a while, watching the puffins fly in over our heads carrying quite large fish to what should be well grown chicks by now, Their burrows had been cleared among the tumble of soil and angular rocks quite close to sea level. Plants were out of reach of livestock here, with a line of low but vertical cliffs to landward and ferny tufts of flowering mayweed nodded conspiratorially to each other in the light breeze sneaking in round the curved basalt columns.

Drifting slowly along the shore we were rewarded with the spectacle of fine banks of primroses romping through the long grass. Then we were headed away, to the north and west for the Treshnish Islands where landings were easier and we got ashore there with no problems of scratched paintwork.

12. STAFFA, A CLOSER SCRUTINY OF THE SOUTHERN CAVES

On our next visit in mid May, 1987 we succeeded in getting ashore to clamber among the giant's playground of monster organ pipes. This time we sailed with Iain Morrison on "Puffin II" from Ulva Ferry on a peerless sunny spring morning. Our craft was a forty seven foot, partly covered passenger launch, her skipper resident at Dervaig on the Isle of Mull, from where we sailed. His advertising brochure included a cautionary rhyme:-

> "On some rare days when there are few
> We cannot go, but please don't sue.
> When ten or less are to be found
> Next trip you have you'll save a pound.
> Just please don't think "I'll go and look"
> The deal's not on unless you book."

The boat's prow turned first towards the angular outline of the Gribun Cliffs at the mouth of Loch na Keal, etched blackly against the eastern sun. Closer, to starboard, lay Ulva Island, softly wooded at first and glowing with the sunlit green of newly opened leaves, but becoming more austere to seaward, with fine, columnar basalt cliffs matching those by Loch na Keal. The striking volcanic plug rose beyond, reminders all of the island's volcanic past.

Sentinel gulls watched us closely with an eye to the main chance of what might spill overboard, but the grey seals lolled luxuriously, caring nothing for our passing. Auks and shags began to appear on the water almost as soon as we pulled away from the jetty.

Little Colonsay came to lie straight ahead and, way beyond it, Colonsay proper, with its hidden woods, dunes and raised beaches absorbed into the distant blur of impregnable rock. Coll and Tiree undulated across the western skyline, affording a modicum of shelter to these Atlantic facing bastions, but not so much as to tame them.

The zonation of shore organisms showed how high the spray might often be hurled. The gleaming orange belt of lichens extended right to the clifftop in parts, with a correspondingly broad band of black lichens reaching down to meet the tenacious off-white acorn barnacles reaching up from wave battered rocks where brown seaweeds were unable to maintain a hold.

As we headed towards the blocky outline of Staffa Inch Kenneth lay to the east, this a burial place of kings subsidiary to the main honeypot of Iona. On an almost glassy calm "Puffin II" pulled round to the south and nosed into Fingals, most famous of Staffa's caves. The iron safety rail or its successor along the broken eastern columns, used as a walkway, but not by us, twenty years before, was still in place, a great deal rustier from its many salty douchings.

The cave had been carved out by the waves after the island rose above sea level, following the long period of inundation when the hundred foot high raised beaches were being carved on lands to the east and south. Currently it was some two hundred and thirty feet long and sixty six feet high, with each tide entering right to the back, so that erosion must still be proceeding. The converging arch at the summit, like the knave of a cathedral, was dictated by the inward curvature of columns at this level.

At the foot of the vertical walls on this smiling summer day the water was so still that the sandy sea floor glowed through the translucent green water like the pale backing of an opal brooch. The mood changed abruptly where the shade of the black columns excluded the light.

We learned that the cave is named after the third century Irish hero Fion McCoul, who the Scots call Fingal and who is also associated with the Giant's Causeway. For the Scots he defended the Hebrides against Viking invaders.

We did not experience the harmonies that prevail when certain winds blow into the interior, causing it to be referred to as "The Singing Cave", with no reference to Mendelsohn.

Just around the corner our craft was dwarfed by the towering cliff of the Colonnade or Great Face, rivalled only in my limited experience by some of the mighty cliffs of the Shiants. Boat Cave opened out to the south, this accessible only by boat, as the name implies. More majestic and penetrating far inland was McKinnon's Cave, facing into the full force of the prevailing winds after we had turned the corner to head north.

The name of this is attributed to a bishop who was said to have drowned off Staffa after doing penance following an affair with a certain Matilda of Skye. He had lived for a while in another cave which bears his name on Mull – that said to be the largest cave in the Western Isles. Maybe he wasn't responsible, however, as many of the locals have born the name of McKinnon over the years between.

Neither McKinnon's nor Boat Cave are framed by majestic collumns like those that make Fingal's so special. Those two were hollowed out by the waves from the more vulnerable, easily eroded underlying tuffs. The bases of the vertical 'organ pipes' form their roofs and are held fast by mutual sideways pressure.

Some of the difference may depend on the tilt of the underlying strata, but their greater age was more crucial. McKinnon's is regarded as the oldest cave on Staffa, Clamshell Cave the youngest with Cormorant, Boat and Fingal's in between in decreasing age order.

The upper layer of more erodible tuff in McKinnon's is fifty feet higher than it is at Fingal's, sloping down with the gradient of the land beneath to sea level there. It was thus subjected to the power of disrupting waves much earlier than the others, which remained submerged for longer as the island rose above sea level.

From evidence on a raised beach near Oban, it is believed that the cutting out of Fingal's Cave began around the time that Bronze Age Man first walked these shores, some five thousand to six thousand years ago. Clamshell Cave is not only less vulnerable by being on the leeward, eastern shore, but is well protected by natural breakwaters.

The Geological Memoirs state all the Staffa Caves to be post glacial in origin, or not more than ten thousand years old. They go further, to suggest late post glacial – to allow time for Staffa to rise sufficiently after release from its load of ice to coincide with the level of wave break. The thickness of the Pleistocene ice sheet over Staffa was reckoned as about one thousand six hundred feet at maximum – more than enough to depress the stoutest section of the Earth's crust, with a long spell of gradual recovery.

111. Inland Gully on Staffa

More modern seas had taken a great bite out of the island north of McKinnon's Cave. The smaller Cormorant Cave lies on the south side of Port an Fhasgaidh Bay, opposite the Gunna Mor noise-maker on the north. A steep-sided rift had been cut into the plateau from the head of this bay, one which we were able to explore later.

It would have been good to circumnavigate the whole, but that was not to be. We retraced our passage round the island's narrower, more dissected south end to make our landing opposite the mouth of Clam Shell Cave, just north of the Herdsman. This cave was named for the resemblance of the curved columns to the commodious backing shells of flat-sided scallops, which are referred to locally as clams.

Stepping gently from the glossy sheet of green algae onto which we had jumped, we gazed our fill on the curvature of those columns, so solid, yet swooping so gracefully up the island's flanks to the tall cliff above Fingal's Cave where Joseph Banks' party had descended so long ago. A wooden stairway had been installed on this steeper route down, and replaced when it wore out, but had now been removed.

Our route back to the cave overland was along the so-called 'Causeway' of the wave-cut platform just above sea level, where we stepped from each truncated column top to the next as though engaged in a childish bout of hopscotch on urban paving stones. Waves swept over the rugged platform in rough weather.

Even on as calm a day as this, white-capped surges were pounding through a narrow channel opposite the Herdsman – that islet so-called for its fanciful shepherding of the island in its charge. The gully between is ten feet deep at mean tide and at high tide the Herdsman itself is divided into a northern and a southern tump.

Viewed from sea level its basalt columns leaned inwards from the north and south to expose their long axes. Over its summit we looked upon their truncated ends – as a receding pile of neatly arranged blocks, each stepped back above the last like the rock steps leading up the flank of some ancient South American pyramid.

13. STAFFA'S GREEN PLATEAU

After paying homage to the famous cave, we retraced our steps and climbed the steep path to the plateau. The naked rock became progressively hidden beneath a skin of maritime turf, this grading into closely cropped grass heath as we progressed. The sheep responsible for the cropping moved off as we made our way west to the more maritime sward above Boat Cave which lay invisible below – this the site of a fulmar colony.

Splendid views were obtained from here, the cliff falling steeply away from the island's highest point to our south and dipping and rising again along the west coast to our north. The great sweep of Port an Fhasgaidh, which continues inland as a deep rift with low bordering cliffs, is mirrored to a smaller extent by a similar gully on the eastern side.

The two are not exactly aligned, but it almost seemed that the island, at a time long hence, might become cleft in two here. Fresh water trickles above added their small but persistent erosive force to the pounding of the sea below.

This tendency may be offset by the gradual rising of the land in relation to sea level that has left those splendid elevated wave-cut platforms around the margins of the neighbouring Treshnish Islands. Global warming may complicate matters further. It is the contemplation of such far reaching phenomena, achieved too slowly for finite humans to witness, that makes us feel so small on this planet that we so abuse.

The sweet waters of the stream that may well have supplied past inhabitants with the elixir of life, spilled from the eastern rift over the shore to nurture a bright sheet of green Enteromorpha, displacing the brown seaweeds locally.

Trampling sheep kept the herbage short and puddled beside the water course, to produce a quagmire where purple moor grass and jointed rushes replaced the finer grasses. Celandines, first of the three kinds of buttercup to burst into bloom in spring, had been caught up here by lesser spearwort and creeping buttercup.

112. *Silverweed*

Silverweed leaves presaged later colour among insectivorous butterwort already covered with Viola-like flowers.

Marsh pennywort and water blinks had little to offer in the way of colour. Dwarfed creeping willow spread from the indeterminate stream bank across the clifftop turf, thriving as well on flying sea spray as on ground seepage. Scurvy grass was in its element here, growing in the bubbly spindrift among sea pinks and sea plantain.

Almost homogeneous across the top of the base-rich, brine-spattered rock further inland, was a smooth greensward with shaggier, straw-coloured patches of mat and moor grass in a matrix of bent and fescue. Smears of dark brown indicated where depauperate heather was fighting a losing battle with the more sheep-resistant grasses, and no woody plants aspired to greater heights than the tangled mounds of brambles. Dwarf juniper eked out a living on the eastern cliffs.

Much of the island had been ploughed up during the latter part of the eighteenth century, when a visitor had recorded seeing crops of potatoes, oats, barley and flax. At one time there were three red deer, these replaced by more manageable and more productive goats.

An 1800 record states that around fifteen cattle were landed on the island in autumn and taken off in spring. In the 1900s sheep were run here until the second world war when beef was in high demand to augment meagre rations and the foraging was turned over to cattle again. By the 1970s both sheep and cattle were brought in from Iona to utilise the grazing.

The National Trust had taken over the running of the island the year before our visit, on 26th April, 1986, after some controversy about ownership. Perhaps the grazing pressure would now be alleviated and the bird's-foot trefoil, then minimal and non-flowering, be allowed to bloom as profusely as it did below the eastern cliffs with primroses, sea pinks and sea campion.

At present there was well distributed cattle dung as well as sheep dung and the strawey cylinders left by a wintering population of migrant barnacle and grey lag geese. Yellow dung flies prefered the fermenting warmth contributed by the cattle for their mating and breeding.

The livestock were now left to their own devices, the crofters having given up permanent residence by the start of the 1900s – despite the fertility of soil now derived from the disintegrating fine-grained basalt.This would have been more highly prized when poor or non-existent roads on the mainland ensured that the main traffic hereabout used the sea lanes between islands. With the coming of road and rail links farmers responded to the inconvenience of life in isolation and left their livestock to enjoy, or suffer, an unfettered existence on their own.

Men's only ecological footprints by the 1980s were the crumbling stone ruins of black houses and sheep fanks where they mustered their flocks in the vicinity of the well near the island's south-western watershed.

Only forty four species of flowering plants were recorded on this visit. No doubt there were more and would be more again if the grazing level dropped.

Soil contains little or no peat here and western clifftop plants were sufficiently suppressed, by salt, nibbling and trampling, to be dominated by buck's-horn plantain. Daisies and celandines, field woodrush and carnation sedge were the chief associates of the tufty rushes in areas with a high water table.

Mountain everlasting, with its pink female heads and white male ones, was commoner away from the sea, with purple-flowered bitter vetch, heath orchids, heath violets and yarrow.

113. *Mountain Everlasting and Carnation Sedge*

Bluebells and sweet vernal grass occupied favoured corners, hogweed, hawkweed and cat's-ear the rougher patches, with tormentil strayed in from more acid sites. English stonecrop and pearlwort grew on the more rocky outcrops, sea mayweed and scurvy grass with primroses on inaccessible cliffs.

Staffa supports a small quota of summering sea-birds as well as the wintering geese which prefer the salted grasses to the more heathery sites. Fulmar petrels seemed the most numerous, decoratively disposed among thrift and campion on the mosaic of severed column tops. Their torpedo shapes skimmed low over our heads, curious about the then rare human visitors.

Each pair had taken possession of a truncated basalt column in the multiplicity of terracets on which to build its scanty nest, using only those softened by a modicum of plant life or completely covered by a thin skin of turf. Hexagons bare of plants were likely to remain bare of fulmars.

Twenty to thirty pairs of great black-backed gulls and herring gulls nested together in the west, but spread their influence through the island, leaving disintegrating crop pellets at favoured resting stations. These were composed of the crushed shells of blue mussels, orange periwinkles, white dog whelks and pink crab claws. The occasional bonxie or great skua was about, pirating the hard won fish of the others.

Cormorants have a cave named after them but may nest in any of the caves other than the low set Boat Cave, while resting shags were a common feature of offshore outcrops. Not for nothing does the angular outline of static shags against a bright sky put the watcher in mind of Pterodactyls. Fossils of shags closely resembling those of today have been discovered in rocks laid down sixty to sixty five million years ago, following the great upheaval that extinguished the Dinosaurs. Shags, as well as basalt columns, had their origin in the island's Cretaceous past, when the world's first birds and small mammals began to take over from the monster reptiles.

Guillemots and razorbills favoured the faces around McKinnon's Cave. Black guillemots do not venture far up the cliffs, frequenting rather the shoreline rocks and stacks. Puffins, as noticed in the 1960s, preferred the more easily penetrated tumbles of rock fragments at the foot of the eastern cliffs.

Eider drakes warbled their evocative notes from the waters of McKinnon's Cove while their partners incubated clutches of buff eggs in secret corners, and we saw a few oystercatchers. Apparently storm petrels nest here, although of these nocturnal residents we saw nothing. Wheatears and rock pipits were the only land birds spotted in June, but no doubt many others pass through on migration to harvest the autumn crop of grass spiders and insects, along with seeds from fruiting heads not nipped off by livestock.

Sea life was rich, low tide revealing great underwater forests of Laminarians and thongweed, with a red understorey of carragheen and dulse below and laver above, along with the animal life which these hide. Here were the usual sea anemones and whelks, limpets, edible sea urchins and crabs to help out with provender for hungry humans, while fishermen from other islands such as Gometra set their lobster creels around Staffa's precipitous bounds.

14. THE TRESHNISH ISLES; TOPOGRAPHY AND GEOLOGY

The Treshnish Isles are out on their own, scattered loosely across the flank of the Western Ocean. A straggle of islands, islets and skerries, rather more than six miles long, they are orientated from south-west to north-east. Staffa lies some five miles to the south-east and on a clear day the uninterrupted vista to the west embraces the distant, rhythmic outlines of the Uists and Barra in the Outer Hebrides.

Lunga, the middle one of the three main islands, is the largest, at one and a quarter miles (2 km). It is also the lowest, except for a rounded hill in the north rising to 337 feet (103m) Dutchman's Cap or Bac Mor lies nearly two miles to its south-west, Fladda rather less to the north-east.

Like Staffa, these islands are composed of basalt columns from the great lava flows spewing from Mull's now extinct volcano, but the columns are higgledy piggledy and nowhere as impressive as the neatly aligned ones of that special island. Amorphous basalt rises sheer from spreading, wave-lashed platforms beloved by seals and wading birds. Jointing of the rocks is at right angles and fractured fragments

114. Dutchman's Cap from Lunga, Treshnish

fall as sharp-edged blocks, their angularity soon softened by fringing seaweeds.

Flat-topped, the islands have been likened to a flotilla of off duty submarines with emergent conning towers, or partly loaded container ships. Horizontal terraces are stepped up towards the island centres like the tiers of giant wedding cakes. The level surfaces are due to peneplanation or marine erosion when the islands lay beneath the sea.

The Dutchman's Cap is the most striking when viewed from offshore, but the hat brim is multi-layered and far-spreading, resembling that of a Mexican sombrero rather than the soft peaked cap worn by the baggy-trousered Dutch-man pictured in my nursery books depicting the famous boy who put his finger in the dyke to prevent the land from flooding.

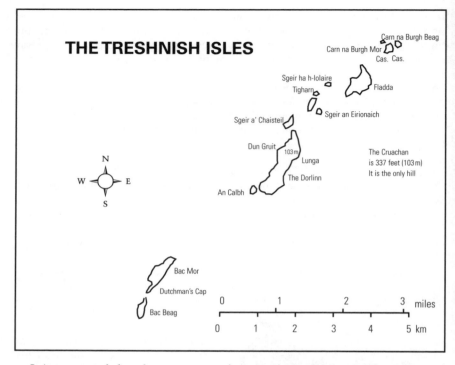

THE TRESHNISH ISLES

Carn na Burgh Beag

Carn na Burgh Mor

Cas. Cas.

Sgeir ha h-Iolaire

Tigharn

Fladda

Sgeir an Eirionaich

Sgeir a' Chaisteil

Dun Gruit

103 m

N

Lunga

The Cruachan
is 337 feet (103 m)
It is the only hill

W — E

The Dorlinn

S

An Calbh

Bac Mor

Dutchman's Cap

Bac Beag

| 0 | 1 | 2 | 3 | miles |

| 0 | 1 | 2 | 3 | 4 | 5 | km |

It is suggested that the name arose from confusion of the Gaelic spelling of Dutchman with Doideach, a famous Mull witch who features in various mythical tales. Interesting landscape features such as these were often ascribed in folk lore to witches or giants. The image of a witch's black hat outlined against the setting sun – at 284 feet above sea level – is not so outrageous, although lacking the crucial peaky point.

The final topography is largely dependent on pre glacial marine erosion. Changes in level of the ancient seas triggered the carving of the several brims before the ice moved in. The head piece consists of the part that stood above the waves throughout that time. Staffa is thought to have been entirely under water during this period of denudation.

A simplified version of the same is recognisable on some of the smaller islets such as Sgeir a'Chaisteil, which affords protection to the north-westerly landing place on Lunga. The 'conning towers' of Bac Mor and Lunga stand out like volcanic plugs.

The current surface of these islands does not go as far back as the dawn of time, as does the pink gneiss of Fionnphort. Like Staffa and Mull, the rocks from which they are hewn were laid down in the mid Tertiary era. Gargantuan forces presaged the eruption of the great volcano sited where the green hills of Mull are now softly clothed in ample grazing land and all enveloping peat bog.

Vulcanologists tell us that the initial explosion blew large chunks of rock into the air, followed by a long period when plant and animal life could move in and pursue its natural course. Then came less violent activity manifested by random outpourings of liquid basaltic lava. Probably about fifty feet deep, this river of molten rock moved especially westwards, to and beyond the present Treshnish Archipelago.

This solidified to rock, the surface of which disintegrated to soil, allowing vegetation back once more. And so it continued: all life extinguished again and again, but doggedly returning and taking over in some instances for long enough to allow the maturation of quite large trees.

Geologists think that the sequence of flows built up to a depth of ten thousand feet near the centre of activity but to only about two thousand feet this far west. A huge depth of rock layers subsequently disappeared, leaving only fragmented remains of those basalt flows spewed initially from the entrails of Mull.

Erosion was the main manipulative force when the virulence of the volcano finally subsided, this stripping off successive lava flows from the top down until only the lowest and oldest was left. Faults or tension clefts may have helped the separation of Staffa and Treshnish from Mull. As the land wore down, sub-aerial erosion was replaced by more dramatic marine erosion and the islands became separated from the mainland and from each other.

115. *Sea-bird Cliff on Lunga Island, Treshnish Group*

We regard the tangible remains as impresive. How much more impressive must that which has disappeared have been?

It was much later, in pre glacial times, when the present land surface saw the light of day over Scotland. Then the whole country, including today' islands, subsided to a hundred feet below their current level in relation to the surrounding ocean. That was when those raised beaches were carved that are now uplifted a hundred feet above today's nibbling tides.

Erosion continued after the ice had come and gone, sculpting the cliffs to the forms we see today and scouring out the caves. The solidifed lava proved harder than the neighbouring rocks and remained standing, as had the great Sgurr of Eigg, when those wore away.

15. TRESHNISH. LUNGA'S NORTHERN ROCK APRON

As we approached Lunga in 1968 the tide was receding and low seaweedy reefs emerged progressively from the shimmering water surface, one after another. Seven or eight of these low skerries are marked only by dotted lines on Bartholomew's map, but some are deemed important enough to have been named.

Many of these names begin with Sgeir, but this is not significant heightwise, because the name is applied to islets with grassed, peneplained summits, as well as those disappearing below the waves at high water – to become a very real danger to shipping, being unmarked by warning lights.

The bulk of these cryptic hazards lie between the handiest landing rocks in the north west of Lunga and the environs of Fladda, reaching out to the cluster of isles further north again – where the ancients had seen fit to build their defensive forts, leaving the more amenable islands for settlement and grazing.

Some of Lunga's islets rising minimally above high water had been taken over by gulls – an unusually high proportion of which were great black-backs. Summer was far enough advanced on this visit for coarse 'bird slum vegetation' to have taken over on the liberally 'whitewashed' rocks, with ragwort and Umbellifers in the ascendancy. These graded through straggling mayweed to thrift and fescue on the lip of the ocean, too close to wave splash to accommodate nests.

Gull families were well established then, in late July, with youngsters bobbing about on exploratory voyages on the still waters of the temporarily emergent creeks. Some were fully feathered in camouflage buff and white. Others bore remnants of their baby down, which did not ball up globules of water to roll off as their 'grown up' feathers would. These chicks were liable to get waterlogged if they ventured into more turbulent zones before their waterproofing was complete.

Those deeper waters beyond held drifts of shags, puffins, guillemots and tysties. Flocks of terns were fishing, held in suspended animation over the same spot, their rapidly vibrating wings keeping them headed into the light breeze, but their ground speed nil. Onshore was a flock of oystercatchers and we gained a fine cloe-up view of a sandpiper, but saw no eiders – birds that were plentiful here in 1987.

Gannets swept past, totally aloof, but we were investigated quite closely by several fulmars as we drifted by. The mass movements of these birds from their origins in the St. Kilda Group of islands in the early part of the twentieth century had brought the first breeders to the Treshnish Group in 1925-26. This was fifteen or sixteen years later than the first arrival on the Shiant Isles further north and nearer to the centre of the population explosion.

We think of fulmar petrels as essentially coastal, but they nest as much as six miles inland in Northumberland, well back from the famous Bamburgh Castle colony, and as much as twenty miles inland in Spitsbergen.

16. TRESHNISH. COASTAL GULLERY

It was nearly twenty years before I came again to the intriguing bedlam of this busy gullery. We chugged ashore through a host of puffins, duck-diving into the green depths as we approached or skittering away across the surface with inade-quately short wings but usefully spreading orange feet.

After avoiding sundry obstacles, we hopped out, ankle deep among flopped wracks. The weather was exemplary, sunshine glinting on a glassy sea so calm

116. Boat (centre right) among low reefs, Lunga

that Iain, our skipper, left his craft moored and came ashore with us. He carried a tape recorder, to add to his collection of sea-bird sounds.

Splashing our way to a low promontary, we found ourselves on a tidal island, with another paddle through cloying seaweed to reach the shore proper. That was deferred, however, while we lingered to savour the sounds and smells of the busy gullery, three months earlier than last time.

The whole promontary was painted orange by Xanthoria and Caloplaca lichens, which get a major boost from generous applications of bird guano and are geared by aeons of evolution to tolerate more blown and splashed sea salt than most.

117. Shags on Bac Beag, Lunga

Now, in early May, domestic chores were only just beginning. Nests under course of construction were often being fabricated of fresh green grass. Most were of seaweed, more easily come by locally, along with the trash of last years cow parsley and thistle stems. Any remnants of the previous year's nests that might have been utilised had been swept away by winter storms. Egg laying had started and some nests contained the full clutch of three, brown-blotched on a fawn background, and of good marketable size for human consumption if ever population numbers got out of hand.

Some birds had built on a stack among lush sea campion and thrift, these far enough from the main island shore to escape grazing. The whole was littered with crop pellets of macerated shells and dotted with brackish pools. The foulest of these were choked with guano-loving *Prasiola crispa,* a green alga able to toler-ate a more powerful soup of bird droppings than the cosmopolitan green sea lettuce and green strings or gutweed Enteromorphas.

More Prasiola was coating dank patches of soggy soil littered with fragments of Ensis razor shells brought in from distant sands by the gulls. It seemed that there was no let up of bird pressure here in the winter, the whole gullery being littered with disintegrating cylinders of fibrous goose dung. We learned later that thousands of barnacle geese from the far North wintered here. Did they share these quarters with the gulls, or did those move elsewhere when their families were reared? Maybe some of the lesser black-backs migrated south during the cold weather, but the other species are always with us.

The geese must use this area as a roost. It certainly supplied none of the lush grass on which they like to feed. Rather were there nettle and curled dock exploit-ing the powerful mineral leachates from the droppings, along with more short term recipients of the goodies, such as chickweed and water blinks *(Montia fontana)*.

Creeping thistle and burdock encroached among the dead stems of last year's ragwort, affording cover while that year's leaf rosettes were manufacturing the wherewithal to throw up another crop of yellow daisy heads. Rose tinted runners of silverweed swarmed across more open areas among grasses and sedges, English stonecrop, creeping buttercups and even lesser celandines, along with heath violets.

Thrift and sea campion had been pushed back to eke out the sparse goodies available in rock crevices, which they shared with *Grimmia maritima*, Britain's most maritime moss, and a patchwork of crustose lichens.

Where fresh water seeped from the backing pebble beach were the spear leaves of yellow Irises and spreading rosettes of unusually succulent bluebell leaves, very different from the elegantly ascending foliage of the woodland bluebells that characterise less spartan regimes.

Withdrawing to the main beach, we found more dock and silverweed sharing with bristly cleavers or goose grass and mayweed. Scurvy grass was in full flower, orache seedlings just pushing through, from seeds washed up to lodge in the organic dampness of the driftline.

118. *Northern Oyster Plant*

It was on expanses of beaches such as these, but less trampled, that the rare oyster plant *(Mertensia maritima)* was to be found on the island. This prostrate, mat forming perennial, is very much a northerner, growing only around the coast of Northern Ireland, North west Scotland and advancing briefly into England along the shores of the Lake District.

Its pale grey leaves, merging with the pale grey pebbles, are succulent and are said to taste of oysters. Perhaps this is why it is rare – and decreasing, but we did not taste. Like those of many of its viper's bugloss family, the clustered trumpet flowers are pink when they first open, but turn a forget-me-not blue as they mature. The tetrads of nutlets are flattened.

We did not encounter the oyster plant until later. Here the high spot for us southerners was the roseroot, tucked into crevices of the backing cliffs. Its leaves were also grey and succulent, but larger, the stems more upright. A feature of these northern islands, and of western ones off Eire, this is rare in England and Wales. Resembling the horticultural ice plant in many features, it is always a visual treat to find such lush beauty burgeoning from so frugal a local environment.

Behind us as we made our way up to the island plateau was a stone cairn, built on a rocky tump beside the gullery. Its purpose was to guide land bound mariners back to the anchorage in the event of a sea fret settling over the intricate terrain where each elongated shelf of rock looked very like the next.

17. TRESHNISH; HARP ROCK SEA-BIRD CITADEL

Lunga's marginal terrain harbours a clamorous colony of truly pelagic birds more special than the cosmopolitan shore-bound gulls. For these Lady Rankin, widow of the famous Nial Rankin, had conserved the island as a bird sanctuary. Guille-mots and razorbills jostled each other in noisy dispute in unusually level clifftop nooks around Harp Rock or Dun Cruit. Not for them the danger of their one precious egg being flipped off a narrow ledge as they took off. The worst that could happen here was that it might roll off into a neighbour's territory. It would be a foolhardy gull or crow that tried to pilfer goodies from among that spread-ing array of sharp, uptilted beaks.

Not all the auks were thus domiciled. We had seen others aligned along ledges of quite low cliffs as we passed in the boat. Such sites are the norm, these auks being more closely geared to the open ocean than gulls, and no more nimble on land than penguins. For us their overflow into these cosy, landward hollows was a bonus, enabling us to approach them on their own terms.

It says much for the lack of predation and disturbance on this delectable island that they should risk occupying such level territory. We moved in circumspectly towards the avian Piccadilly Circus, receiving scarcely a suspicious glance from marginal birds. Most were too busy squabbling with their neighbours to bother about the stealthy approach of aliens.

This site was also of interest topographically, being the entrance to the island's central hollow. The shoulders of land which the birds had chosen are behind rocky bluffs between which a narrow, vertical sided gully reaches inland, almost dividing the island into two.

This widens into a central hollow known as the Dorlin, twenty feet deep and sixty feet across. The sides are sheer, except at one point where a stepped slope provides access. Engrossed with the birds, it would have been easy to miss this feature. We did not learn until afterwards that there was a secret way out from the hollow, enabling an explorer to emerge from a dark tunnel further along the western cliff, from where it was possible to scramble back along its base below the sea facing bird ledges.

A few birds had taken up sites along the brinks of the gully, but the majority spilled back into the easier territory alongside. We watched two of the brink nesters sparring, pulling at each others bills. One swung its opponent off the edge and then tumbled down after it. Many stood neatly to attention, minding their own business and seemingly waiting for an egg to pop out to be incubated. Nevertheless, such crowded quarters inevitably generate clamour and excite-ment.

A thin, tightly meshed turf of thrift, plantain and grass had advanced towards the divided auk colony, but was shunned by the guillemots and razorbills. Not so the puffins, which were markedly fewer. Some of these dumpy little birds, which are more at home on land, with their useful orange feet more centrally placed, had moved in. After breaking through the skin of turf they must have found sizable gaps between the boulders below, suitable for accommodating their single white egg and the fluffy puffling that was to spend its early weeks there.

Most of the puffins encountered, however, were on grassy slopes where there was sufficient soil depth for them to dig burrows in the time honoured way. It seemed they had not yet laid, for a number were busy furnishing their quarters with dead grass. We sat alongside watching, as one after another came toddling down the slope with a bushy moustache of sun-dried hay and popped underground, after a quick look round to see that no-one was watching.

Shags were nesting along these clifftops, more conspicuously than the cryptic burrow dwellers and more cosmopolitan in their choice of nesting material. Their contemporaries in the Antipodes and Africa usually build their bulky nests of twiggy material, but that was in short supply here. So, too, was it uncomfortably far inland, as British shags, unlike our cormorants, are seldom found far in from the coast.

Their chosen material here was gathered from the shore and the gullery. There was thongweed and oarweed, dulse and fragments of driftwood or discarded fishing gear. One had incorporated some green fishing net to hold the rest together. We hoped the chicks would not get entangled, and unable to get away. The dead haulms of ragwort, dock and thistle had proved popular and one had added some fleshy roseroot. Grass, green or dry, was spurned in favour of more substantial material.

Shags, too, were in the early stages of their breeding cycle, with couples copulating eagerly in the expectation of things to come. We watched one disputing territory with a feisty razorbill, which had no nest, only a patch of ground to defend. As this was earth and not rock, it seemed rather more appropriate for the shag.

Both shearwaters and storm petrels nest on Lunga, presumably in burrows or rock crevices which serve the same purpose, but we saw nothing of these and would have been unable to tell a shearwater burrow from a puffin's anyway.

Locals maintained that storm petrels nested only on the smaller islands in these waters, often on their even smaller outliers. They would be more vulnerable to predation than the larger shearwaters – hence their nocturnal habits when ashore – and these 'walkers on the water' evidently liked to know that the ocean was not too far off when they were forced ashore to breed. This does not apply on the Welsh islands of Skokholm and Skomer, where the stormies nest all over, particularly in holes of the dry stone walls from past farming enterprises.

Perhaps predation of birds of this size is not confined to gulls, as we came across the plucking post of a peregrine falcon, marked by a pile of pale feathers. Buzzards, too, were soaring overhead. There were sometimes seven on the island, sustained by the plethora of rabbits, which could be numbered in thousands.

In the apparent absence of farm livestock (we saw none) the grass of the plateau sparkled with the exuberance of well watered Maytime green, despite the rabbits. Those, indeed, were helping to prevent the sward from getting coarse and tufty and maintaining it in the state beloved by the wintering barnacle geese, which cannot deal with the more fibrous forage accepted by some of the other migrant geese.

The sward also supplies plentiful invertebrate life to sustain flocks of starlings and lapwings probing diligently through the chill of winter. Fraser Darling reports hundreds of blackbirds and a good many thrushes here then. There were few now, but a skylark was carolling away overhead to remind the world that the busy breeding season of summer was under way.

18. TRESHNISH; OUTLIERS BEYOND FLADDA

Nestled in the shelter of Ben Cruachan, the only hill on Lunga, was a cluster of half a dozen ruined cottages. These had thick walls and rounded corners, like those we had seen on Eigg. It seems they had been deserted well over a century ago, the old shieling peopled now only by memories of a life shared with the bird hosts, those, no doubt, contributing to the crofters' summer menu.

Did they salt the birds down for the winter, I wondered, as the New Zealand Maoris and Australian Aboriginals have from time immemorial? With all those rabbits, a seasonal crop of gulls' eggs and a wealth of meandering creeks harbouring crabs, lobsters and much more, life might not always have been as hard as we sometimes envisage – with or without livestock. If they possessed the latter, the low shoreline would have eased the process of getting animals to and from the mainland.

We sat to admire the view of the Dutchman's Cap framed by the divided auk colony, but had to exert ourselves for the more extensive view from the 337 feet high Cruachan. This commanded not only the other small islands, but a fine panorama of Mull, including the shapely peak of Ben More. At 3,169 feet that is the highest elevation attained by the Tertiary Basalt in Scotland.

We made our way back to our little craft which bobbed gently on the ebbed tide, and pushed off to weave our way between the smaller isles around Fladda. The two largest were Sgeir a' Chaisteil and Sgeir an Eirionnaich, each a grey harmony of angular rock chunks and wave smoothed pebbles.

The waters were dotted with Atlantic seals, regarding us with interest, some dipping beneath the water to surface more closely for a better view. One of the islets bore a mass of gulls, settled among a feathery-leaved umbel resembling hemlock, although not identifiable from afar. Some of this material had been incorporated into more shag's nests.

Following the western shore of Fladda we crossed more open water to the two lesser and northernmost islands that had been lived on from earliest times and had been fortified by the local lords to protect the others that were big enough to provide a living.

These are Carn na Burgh Mor and Carn na Burgh Beag. On the first are the remains of a fort, built by Clan McDonald on the ruins of an earlier one, erected in the time of the Norse overlords. In 1354 the McDougalls ceded it to the then Lord of the Isles, who appointed his vassal, McLean of Duart, as its hereditary keeper.

Around 1380 John of Fordun had written: "Out at sea, at a distance of four miles from Mull, is Carnaborg, an exceeding strong castle." The Carn na Burgh forts were garrisoned as recently as the Jacobite risings of 1715. The one of Carn na Burgh Beag had crenellated walls and functioned as an army barracks.

We heard tell of an old monastic settlement as well as a military one. Later came the information that, during the religious persecution of Iona, the books and archives from there were sent here for safe keeping. The story goes that they were lost when Cromwell's forces besieged and captured the fort around 1561.

A tall cliff gully had been walled in with rocks, like the Culver Hole dovecote tucked into the cliffs of Gower in South Wales, but the entry (or exit) here was through an arrow slit at the top instead of the many small holes fashioned to persuade rock doves to enter and supply fresh meat for the troops or their overlords during winter. The name of Keyhole here was applied to a narrow sea arch in the side of the last of the islands to be manned.

Sidling between this island and the next, which boasted an orifice which was part arch and part cave, we were among seals again. Some rolled around in the water, their sleek black and olive green torsoes glinting in the sun, as they dived to emerge nearer the boat, or swirled away to describe arcs around their fellows.

Some had hauled out on the rocks, warming up, and had been so for long enough to have fluffed out into the pale, teddy bear phase. New arrivals rolled over to expose shining, mottled bellies to the warm rays. Superb aquarists that they are during most of their time, they obviously enjoy sunshine. As each wave surged higher over their perch they would lift bewhiskered heads petulently and raise both ends above the cold flood to resemble a balanced banana. Not until overtaken by a particularly vigorous surge which broke the magic of their dreamy spell, did they slide, moaning and complaining, into the unwelcoming fluid.

Iain told us that he had seen a hundred seals together about seventy five yards upshore on Lunga in January. This seemed late for breeding, which is said to be in October or November hereabouts. After the lumbering around ashore to feed the pups, they tend to break up into smaller groups through the summer.

We passed clusters of shags wing drying on outlying rocks and witnessed many eider drakes idling around the shores of the Carn na Burghs, their spouses probably ashore seeing to family matters. The tide was still fairly low and we looked among the seaweeds for otters, but in vain. "Ye dinna see otters out here," quoth Iain "Plenty on Mull."

He speeded up and headed for home, past that delectable large island, with enough splash coming over the bow to flavour tea drunk subsequently through salty lips.

VI

Coll and Tiree

COLL

1. TO COLL VIA TIREE

Seven months after my squally spell on Islay and Jura at the end of October 2006, I was off to others of these Islands of the Simmer Dim – in summer this time. Thanks to the organisational abilities of my companion, Gilian, the two of us set out from our South Wales village before 8.0 am on 7th June, 2007, and arrived fourteen hours later, by courtesy of British Rail, at Oban, the "Gateway to the Isles".

Maridon House, where we were to snatch a few hours' rest, was close above the harbour, but it took us a while to find, by devious means. An affable lady introduced us to the breakfast room and contents of the refrigerator for unaccompanied use in the wee small hours and pointed out the best way to the Caledonian MacBrayne's Ferry that was to take us to our destination.

"Ye tak the wee track, steep down under the trees, but mind the jaggy nettles". The wee track continued up the slope as "Pulpit Hill leading to Taggart's Brae." Yes. We were once again in Bonnie Scotland. Where else would one find a brae?

On a practice run we duly minded the jaggy nettles and reached the quay just as one of the CalMac liners was disembarking passengers from somewhere beyond the horizon. It seemed enormous after the small boats that had taken me around Staffa and the Treshnish Isles, twenty years before.

Our brief exploration of the fine new, glass-walled ferry terminal almost resulted in us being locked in, but we made our escape in the nick of time. Eleven pm and it was still daylight, the mellowed orange haze fading reluctantly from the sky. Little boats lay asleep at their moorings, rocked by nary a ripple on the glassy calm of the bay.

When I woke at 2.30 am daylight was already filtering back over the eastern horizon, as dawn snuffed out the stars. The eyeless "folly" on the hill behind gazed vacantly down, just as I remembered it from my first visit here as a child. Lights along the opposing water front were reflected as long yellow bars, like a line of giant fenceposts, the tall silhouettes of the buildings behind putting me in mind of Tobermory. Two hours more of restless inactivity and we were breaking our fast and hastening to obtain boat tickets "Not later than 5.30 am for a six o'clock departure".

We were sailing on "The Lord of the Isles", the bigger of the two boats employed on this route, with seating on two outer stern decks. It was the smaller "Clansman" that transferred us from Coll to Tiree the following week.

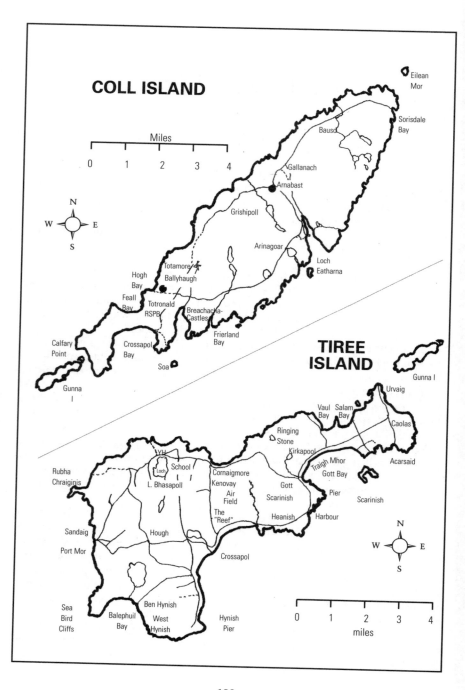

COLL ISLAND

Miles

0   1   2   3   4

N
W   E
S

Eilean
Mor

Bausd

Sorisdale
Bay

Gallanach
Arnabast

Grishipoll

Arinagoar

Loch
Eatharna

Totamore
Hogh
Bay
Ballyhaugh

Feall
Bay
Totronald
RSPB

Breachacha-
Castles

Frierland
Bay

Calfary
Point

Crossapol
Bay

Soa

Gunna
I

TIREE
ISLAND

Gunna I

Urvaig

Vaul   Salam
Bay   Bay

Caolas

Ringing
Stone

Kirkapool

Traigh Mhor
Gott Bay

Acarsaid

Rubha
Chraiginis

YH
School

L. Bhasapoll

Cornaigmore
Kenovay
Air
Field

Gott

Scarinish

Pier

Scarinish

Sandaig

Port Mor

Hough

The
"Reef"

Heanish

Harbour

N
W   E
S

Crossapol

Sea
Bird
Cliffs

Balephuil
Bay

Ben Hynish

West
Hynish

Hynish
Pier

0   1   2   3   4
miles

The only other passengers trekking up the gangway seemed to be a stag party of about twenty gents of mature years, seemingly escaping from their wives for a couple of days on Tiree. Most stayed below decks, engaged in jovial whetting of their whistles, ignoring the fabulous panoramas that materialised out of the evanescent mist as the sun rose higher.

A number of cars and a vast pantechnican had driven into the hold, but there were few other passengers, no children in the play pen nor ladies in the ship's shop. The harbour still slept, as viewed from the upper stern deck.

Not a squawk came from the sleeping gulls floating motionless on the somnolent sea. Only the town house sparrows and a lone song thrush were up and about their business ashore. It was, however, a sprucely pied black guillemot floating a few yards below my lofty perch that intrigued me most.

This was facing the vessel, obviously waiting for something to happen. That something materialised as the deck began to tremble under my feet and the throbbing of the great engines became more insistent. As soon as the propellors started turning, churning up a bubbling cauldron around the stern, the guillemot paddled rapidly towards us and dived into the melée.

It had obviously learned that this noisy motion displaced a wealth of small edible creatures from the somnolent life on the sea bed and made them available for an easy breakfast. The noise attracted another, hurrying to the feast, and the two dived together among the froth and bubble, no doubt steering well clear of the whirling instigators of the turmoil. A flock of terns had been woken by the cafuffle and were breaking their fast among the motionless yachts. Little turrets of silver spray rose at each shallow plunge. A stately mute swan paddled alongside a ship moored at another quay, dwarfed by the black hull, and a narrow V shaped wake trailed past, a seal's head at its apex.

The foreground basked in the light of a bright sun, shining benignly as if it had never considered doing otherwise, but narrow belts of mist, aftermath of the night, girdled the mountains of Mull and of Morvern across the low-lying island of Lismore. These began to disperse as we moved sedately past the monument, sea mark and cluster of small yachts off Kerrrera Island on the port side. Then came Duart Point with its ancient castle on Mull and we headed into the even less ruffled waters of the Sound of Mull.

Ardnamurchan to the north and Mull to the south rose in a jumble of mounds and peaks, girdled on their lower slopes by irregular blocks of conifers, the trees tall and pointed, like the snow-shedding ones of northern taiga forests. Heathery knolls graded up through grassy heath to a mosaic of bare, ice and tempest-smoothed rock.

Coll lay some fifty miles out from Oban and the big ferries took about two and a half hours for the crossing, depending on tide and weather, but our voyage via Tiree was to take four hours. Away to port two major embayments in the coast harboured Salen and Tobermory. What happy memories those names evoked. Soon we were bearing west into the more open waters of the Southern Minch with the narrowing mouths of Mull's Loch Mingary and Loch Cuan fading into the lingering mist.

This was shearwater territory, the birds flashing from black to white and white to black as they wheeled around in loose flocks. Little parties of razorbills, more sure of where they were bound, whirred low over the surface, a few lone shags even lower, but raising no splash from the dark mirror, so precise was their navigation.

119. *Shearwaters in flight*

Our wake of white foam feathered away on either flank, displacing the fishing terns by disrupting their vision of the fish shoals they sought. Light clouds that had tentatively gathered earlier, dissolved as a veritable scorcher evolved under a clear blue sky with a few errant cumulus clouds away to the north.

We sailed along the coast of Coll, gaining a rudimentary idea of the juxtaposition of peaty hills and sandy bays, before finally passing the little island of Gunna and drawing into Tiree pier. By this time Mull's smooth grey basalt had given way to obliquely banded, sparkling gneiss.

This hard, impervious, acid rock had been more apparent as we followed the less sand-laden cliffs of Coll. Lewissian gneiss is the oldest of all Britain's rocks, igneous in origin and showing none of the bedding planes of sedimentary rocks, although it was easy to imagine these when viewing the parallel veins of quartz and other minerals passing through them, particularly when folding has set these at disparate angles.

These rocks are matched by others in Greenland, the two sliding apart as the Atlantic opened up in the dawn of time between Britain and America. It is tempting to speculate that the barnacle, white-fronted and grey lag geese that breed on the Greenland gneiss and escape to the Coll and Tiree gneiss in winter had had to fly ever further to the more amenable climate as the continents drew apart. Nothing is ever quite that simple. The pre-Cambrian rocks had parted company long before birds evolved in the Cretaceous period, around the time that the more modern basalts of Mull were being spawned from the great volcano.

An expertise of lateral navigation brought "The Lord of the Isles" in, sideways-on, to the long, angled Tiree jetty. The pantechnican drove out of the ship's bowels, full of goodies for the islanders and another drove in taking the empties back. After much shunting ever closer to the hull, this was clamped to the lower deck by a seemingly inadequate canvas band. But there seemed no danger of it rolling out of place today.

We drew away and moved smoothly back past the sandy beaches of Tiree and the bleaker moorlands of Coll. Once there, we turned northwards past a cluster of little islands and the larger 'tied' headland of Eilean Ornsay into the mouth of Loch Eatharna. There we moored to the newest of three piers, just half a mile south of the island's only village of Arinagour, pronounced Arnagooer.

2. COLL. ARINAGOUR, A FRIENDLY VILLAGE HAVEN

We accepted a lift offered by a sun-tanned resident. She opened the capacious boot of her car to receive our luggage – a mountain of waterproofs, winter woollies and spare garments to wear while others dried. None were needed, as the sun continued to shine throughout our stay on both islands, causing islanders to worry about the potato crop which "needs the rain to plumpen them up."

She dropped us off at the first building about half a mile up the road. This was the Tigh na Mara Guest House, tucked between a rocky stretch of loch shore bordered by a glory of flowering Irises and a gently rising heathland, dark with heather. Eight bedrooms overlooked Loch Eatharna and commanded panoramas to distant Treshnish and Mull, while views from three sides of the comfortable lounge encompassed homelier terrain, in and beyond the neat walled garden.

The fact that we had enjoyed a second breakfast on board ship, embellished with Gaelic black pudding, did not deter us from setting off to and along the village street to the little shop at the far end in search of lunchtime victuals. There was much to waylay us en route.

Roadside walls, not rendered and white-washed like most houses, intrigued us with the range of crystalline rocks that had been used in their making. All were granitic, some with outsize crystals, and in various shades of grey, pink and buff. Parallel bands of quartz

120. Ariganour Wall on Coll

and other minerals crossed individual stones decoratively at conflicting angles. They were well mortared, with almost none of the usual plant life in crevices. The top layer consisted of sea-rounded, somewhat flattened boulders the size of rugby balls.

Local ladies and itinerant tourists chatted like old friends in the village shop, which was well stocked, although the bramleys and bananas looked tired after their sojourn in the hold. This was the only food shop and the ordering of goods, their value balanced against freight charges, must be a skilled job.

The ferry was heavily subsidised, as were the doctor and the nurse. We were assured that the island economy would grind to a halt if they were not. As in any village, the store was the hub of activity and an essential meeting place. The windows were covered with notices of forthcoming events, not displaying wares to tempt shoppers in. It was this or nothing.

No matter that one had arrived only that day: everybody was accepted as 'one of us'. Out on the open road, drivers 'saluted' as they passed and would stop to help if one looked lost. Such is the legacy of small communities, where numbers are not too overwhelming for people to care.

The post office and book shop was a short distance away up a side road. The front garden was tiny but fascinating and a handy bench outside enabled me to sit in the sun and absorb the unhurried atmosphere of the place. Multi-coloured pansies burgeoned in borders and boxes, while a flagpole flying the Scottish lion rose from a bed of blue Geraniums. Discretely placed were a miniature palm and a straight-sided ten gallon milk churn of the type much preferred by wartime land girls to the then standard fourteen gallon ones with sloping sides.

Two discarded, single share, horse-drawn ploughs painted red and black were spreadeagled on the lawn, which must have been difficult to mow. Dominating the whole was a big press painted to match, with screw down wheels and dangling weights. My thoughts flew to cider making, but this was no place for apple trees. Of course, this was a cheese press.

As in Islay, there had been a thriving cheese-making industry here when cows' milk was more highly valued than it seems to be today, but both had collapsed. With few exceptions, all milk drunk on the island now came with the MacBrayne boats from the mainland, notwithstanding that there were far more cows on the island than the current 201 human residents. Those cattle were beefers and the often bulging udders which we saw were for the benefit of suckler calves – which were produced the year round.

I got into conversation with a certain weather-beaten Angus, who wielded an oilcan and screw driver beside a cluster of push bikes by the garden gate. Formerly a policeman, now a hirer of bicycles to visitors – "Don't back peddle whatever you do" – he was also a north end farmer and he put me in the picture, so to speak, agriculturally.

In the cheese making days most of the farmers kept herds of black and white Ayrshire cows, which produced the right textured milk, with small fat globules. Women churned it by hand, the churn emitting loud warning clicks if they worked too fast and grinding to a halt if they dallied too long.

The cheese industry here was more durable than that on Islay, lasting nearly a hundred years from its beginning in the 1850s. About sixty tons of cheese was being made annually by 1900 and those best versed in its niceties could tell on which farm the cheese they were tasting had been produced. It was the islanders' proud boast that Coll cheese had been served up in London's Houses of Parliament.

New hygeine rules and red tape, coupled with the post war demand for the beef which had been in such short supply during the years of rationing, brought the cheese making to a virtual end. New breeds of cow were introduced, their fattening potential boosted by fast maturing bulls of continental breeds.

The old native sheep had been largely abandoned in favour of Cheviots, Leicesters and their various crosses, these too, producing larger carcases in less time. On his Red Rock or Fishing Gate Farm in North Coll, however, Angus had kept on the old breed – the black Hebridean sheep, whose rams were four horned.

121. *Hebridean Black Sheep*

These last had been referred to as the blessd sheep on the Uists and here, as the four horns might form a cross, or, as Angus more picturesquely put it, might cast the shadow of a cross on the ground when the sun was behind, converting the image from three dimensional to two dimensional. Others of the breed bear a sturdy pair of ribbed horns, backwardly curved and worthy of a mouflon or a billy goat.

Despite this armature, they are said to have a biddable nature and are easy to manage, the ewes making attentive mothers. Formerly a rare breed, like the other

194

four-horned Jacobs and Manx Loghtans, they had been bred up since 1969 to reasonable numbers and were being used as conservation tools, "nibbling without destroying", in conditions too harsh for the pampered lowland imports. Angus described them as "Fat little sheep, brought by the Norsemen and crossed with our native Soays, these, like that better known breed, originating on St. Kilda.

Their wool is coarse to the point of stringiness and may hang in long ringlets, Rastafarian style. Unlike Soays, they are shorn, the black wool being sent away for spinning and some, at least, returned for weaving. A specimen blanket, fixed to the inside of the post office door was uncompromisingly whiskery – not to be placed next to a thin nylon sheet to induce sleep, but no doubt admirably tough for a crofter's outer garments.

Angus told us where to locate his flock and gave us the Gaelic password for calling them down from their mountain fastness – which we promptly forgot. We did, indeed, locate them later on, but attempted no calling in our Sassenach ignorance. A subsequent acquaintance cast aspersions on the efficacy of any such attempt to entice them from their never ending lunch. Could the dour Scots enjoy pulling the legs of gullible tourists as much as do the fun-loving Irish?

On the rising ground above the shop were the hotel, the Kirk of Scotland and the free church. While dining one night in the first – on Argyll venison and exotic summer fruit cheesecake – we enjoyed views of the garden and the loch beyond.

The immediate foreground was enlivened by some house sparrows emulating South African sunbirds by feeding on the flower spikes of red hot pokers. Alighting on the stem, they would shuffle upwards to thrust unsuitably shaped bills into the

*122 House Sparrows
on Red-hot Pokers*

dangling flower trumpets, presumably to suck the nectar. What else? Closer examination showed no insect life that might have tempted them. The habit had caught on and we saw the same behaviour in gardens at the other end of the village.

After the meal we wandered around outside, admiring the floral display, from intensely blue Delphiniums to red and white button daisies. Dark Escallonias augmented the thick Fuchsia hedge alongside, while chunky alders separated the plot from the brackenny knoll above the loch. Two of these had been lopped off, chest high, to clear the view to the sea from a newly constructed elevated lookout. Throughout our tour we were accompanied by the resident tabby, who went along with the custom of welcoming strangers.

A robin hopped companionably among the alders, while a willow warbler trilled, appropriately, from the bordering bank of willows. These were osiers, rather than the commoner eared sallows occurring in the wild.

An article spotted in the current Coll Magazine related to experiments with tree planting on the island by "JLD". He regarded alder as the most successful tree here, remaining wind-firm in poor damp soil, along with osiers, whose long, whippy growth had to be cut back each year until the stem thickened sufficiently to hold firm against the gales. Shelter, supplied by either of these, was found necessary to protect aspen and white poplar from "savage winter winds, which can shred the bark of young shoots". It was hoped that the two poplars would sucker to produce thickets.

One species found to sucker freely, even in its first year was the pink flowered *Rosa rugosa* or musk rose, which "takes all the weather that Coll can throw at it". This fits well with its name in New England, USA, where it is known as the salt spray rose. A consignment of the plants ordered from Europe escaped when the ship bringing them was wrecked offshore. They floated into terra firma on their own and established a thriving colony on the dunes, with no help from horticulturalists. (I am indebted to JLD for use of the information from his informative article – and all the work that went before.)

He found that oak did better than firs where, as he afirms,"Life on Coll is tough for a tree." Strolling up the rough track to the church we passed a sizable oak that had got away, despite the hazards. At the other end of the size scale by the track was the charming little pink bog pimpernel.

Gil found thale cress *(Arabidopsis thaliana)* , common enough on the mainland but rare here. An unassuming little weed, this is to the plant genetiscist what Drosophila flies are to the animal genetiscist, having few chromosomes to complicate inheritance experiments.

Although it was Sunday night, the church was deserted and the door barred. We thought this must be to keep out the free range sheep but decided that it was more likely related to the renovation of the church tower that was currently under way.

The free church, built in 1884 a little further up the slope was in worse case. The congregation had dwindled and the windows had been boarded up to save them from wind damage. It was not completely abandoned: there was one service a year. That had been today. The mainland minister visiting to conduct it was one of our fellow guests at Tigh na Mara, along with the policeman, on temporary loan from Tiree.

3. COLL. VILLAGE WILDLIFE OFFSHORE

Arinagour was furnished with a low stone wharf where a stream emerged to ripple through the brackish marsh near the shop. This was virtually the head of Loch Eatharna at most states of the tide, although a steadily narrowing tidal gully extended north, half way across the island from this point, followed by the road from Arnabost. Looking down on the intricate community of brown seaweeds, I would dearly have liked to get down there and search for the tangled, balled-up relative of egg wrack, *Ascophyllum mackayii,* that I had encountered on sea lochs many years before. Remarkable, rare and found only in such sites in Scotland, this would have been something special, but it was not to be.

Further down the permanently submerged stretch, were the "Old" and "Middle" Piers, very different from the one built nearer the open Minch in the

1970s to accommodate the big liners. Prior to that ferries had anchored offshore, landing passengers in smaller boats while farm animals were swung off the ship into open boats with slings under their bellies, or swum ashore.

123. *Grey Herons*

I wandered out on the Middle, Municipal Pier with defunct telephone box and functional toilet at its base to get closer to the patient herons that foraged alongside. These had formerly nested on an ungrazed, and hence wooded, island in Loch Ghille-calium but, by the 1980s, the pines in Martin's Wood Plantation had grown sufficiently to provide more traditional treetop nesting sites. The population there swelled to twenty or twenty five pairs, with another two couples in the trees around the Lodge, making Coll's one of the largest heronries on the west Scottish coast.

The tide was falling and, in the absence of any sort of swell, the tall Laminarians had adopted an open forest formation of right angled fronds. The metre long stipes of each rose vertically and the ultimate, more pliable metres turned seaward at ninety degrees in parallel phalanxes, drawn out by the invisible pull of the ebbing tide.

Wafting gently between them was a hemispherical jellyfish, probably Pelagia. The central gonads were an amorphous pink with evanescent flowing skirts dangling amidships and a peripheral circle of transparent tentacles.

The sea bed was muddy here and decorated with a complete cover of lugworm burrow mouths and casts, but the water was so placid that it had raised no silt and appeared a clear bottle green. Little shoals of fingerling fish wove among the kelps. I wondered if these might grow into the fifteen spined sticklebacks said to inhabit tidal pools. The only sound was the intermittent cronking of a raven from the opposite shore.

As I left, admiring the chunky little sea spleenwort ferns in the stout outer wall, two fishermen brought their small craft into the steps on the inner wall and made it fast for the night among a huddle of others. No big fishing boats plied from here now and a vigorous growth of nettles had effectively anchored the discarded green fishing net at the pierhead to the grass beneath.

It was on another day, after dinner in the island cafe, that I strolled onto the oldest of the three piers – the one furthest from the open sea and in the shallowest water. Off the end on both sides were maternal eider ducks exercising their broods of newly hatched ducklings on the benignly calm surface. The five families each contained three to five chicks, these able to race across the surface at high speed, literally 'walking or running the waters' and leaving puny, splashy wakes when they got left behind the orderly cohort lined up behind their dam.

When they deemed their offspring sufficiently initiated into the sea-going life, the ducks took them ashore, climbing onto a wrack covered reef where the little ones disappeared from view, so good was their camouflage. A heron alighted with a loud scrawtch where some pale-winged hoodies were scavenging and embarked on a statuesque fishing vigil, while another , shoulders hunched in

197

meditation, seemed half asleep. A ewe had brought her twins down to nibble at the mineral-rich seaweeds.

These and the salt marsh plants helped to give that special flavour to the local lamb that delighted our palates on the first night at Tigh na Mara. Hens, too, fed among the wracks in places, taking in iodine and producing breakfast eggs with bright orange yolks.

A grebe-like bird was diving and surfacing offshore, low of body and thin of neck, in size between a great crested and a little. Was it Slavonian or red-necked or, indeed a red-throated diver? It was still there when we strolled along to the main new pier in the late gloaming, the long, wailing call wafting across the water suggesting a diver or loon. Red-throated divers nest on the inland lochs of Tiree and possibly here too.

Wheatears and meadow pipits perched on the wire fences and a wren bobbed along in front of us, appearing and disappearing from perches on Erica and eared sallow, with the same aplomb as the stonechat, also spotted.

Here were hard ferns, male ferns, pale-flowered cow-wheat and tormentil – also midges –

124. *Cow-wheat and Tormentil*

our only experience of these voracious dipterons throughout our stay, but one to be remembered. They were most persistent where I took the narrow path through tall heather, lousewort and heath bedstraw to get above the whalebone arch for a photograph. It was around ten pm and I needed the sun behind. Later I learned that the original jawbones were safely lodged in the Scottish Museum in Edinburgh and that these were casts.

I also learned that the midges appearing at the beginning of June are the non-biting males. The army of females needing human blood to render their eggs fertile, emerge around mid June and continue their attacks for about twelve weeks. Maybe we had beaten most of them to it, for we did not suffer again before our departure in mid June.

Or was it simple that it was too dry? The larvae need moisture to develop and we had no difficulty walking through Iris marshes which we would have expected to be much wetter underfoot. Or then again, it could have been the high light intensity. Strong light deters the adults, cloud and mist encourage them. Nor were we usually roaming the moor so late, or experiencing cloud cover by day, so escaped almost scot free.

From the least inhabitants to the greatest, we returned to Tigh na Mara to find our fellow guests discussing the basking sharks seen recently off this same pier. We were too late this time – and the next – but saw two exemplary sets of fin and tail before we left.

As soon as we stepped outside on our first morning we had been aware of the fussing of house sparrows and warbling of starlings. Both flocked around buildings and gardens as they did on the mainland before numbers fell off so drastically. Sparrows were not confined to the village. Any of the widely spaced houses might have their quota of these birds, once so urban as to be referred to as 'cockney sparrers'.

Sitting in our garden we could watch a feisty cock sparrow astride his mate, conjuring up the next brood or carrying contributions of dry grass to the nest behind the clinging honeysuckle. Strolling down "main street" we were subjected to the warbling trills and masterful mimicry of the starlings. One churring and chortling from a TV aerial atop a tall white chimney had clearly learned some vocabulary from the gull perched on a marker buoy offshore.

Another, based near the village store, had learned to imitate a corncrake, that elusive symbol of these islands that is so much easier to hear than to see. Many visitors come hoping to hear just that call. The starling was an unwitting tourist asset, sending folk home well satisfied. This little intrigue was not a complete hoax because *Crex crex*, the corncrake, must have been around for the starling to learn its scientific epithet and was, indeed, to be heard legitimately if one sallied forth in the right place in the late dusk.

Starlings were to be seen throughout the island, often associated with livestock, but those in the village had plenty of sheep to serve as tick birds to supplement their protein intake and allow them to use their fleece to warm their naked feet in cold weather.

Pied wagtails trotted jauntily across mown and sheep-nibbled lawns and swallows skimmed round the barn-like building at the head of the municipal pier as though nesting within. Skylarks hovered over the houses and wheatears watched for flies from garden fences, reminding us that the primal heath was only just beyond their bounds.

4. COLL. ARINAGOUR, BUTTERFLIES AND FLOWERS

The spreads of Irises between our house and the sea were sufficiently robust to exclude almost all other plants, but in one embayment they were replaced by the silky plumes of many-headed cotton grass. Knolls emerging from the counterpane of yellow blooms or wispy fruits were home to English stonecrop, hugging the sparkling rock and gentian blue heath milkwort among sheep nibbled fescue.

The air above the Iris beds trembled with butterflies, mostly green-veined whites, but it was the heftier, furry bumble bees rampaging through like overdressed dowagers, which seemed to be pollenating the Irises. Only they could lift the stiff, strap-like style with the sensitive stigmatic flap to reach the pollen and nectar in the heart of each bloom legitimately.

I was on the lookout for great yellow bumble bees – national rarities, known to exist on Coll and cherished on the RSPB reserve there, but those I saw were too well endowed with black stripes to be known by any such name.

This must surely be the same as the all yellow carder bee, *Bombus muscorum ssp, smithianus*, pointed out to me on Inisheer in the Irish Aran Islands twelve months before by an entomologist. My reference reads "Almost confined to Aran, although seen also in the Hebrides". (*Gillham, "This Island Life", Halsgrove, 2007.*) Another Hymenopteran rarity on Coll is a mining bee, *Colletes floralis*.

A few painted lady butterflies were zooming past at speed, seeming to the fluttering white philanderers as swifts are to robins. Not for them were the lazy, meandering flaps of those petal-like morsels that abounded throughout the village but were less often seen elsewhere. Green-veineds are often colonial like this in Scotland, where they are commoner than both large and small whites, although more often solitary in the South, where the other two are more wedded to domestic cabbage patches and are more often seen.

The painted ladies, although not in flocks here as sometimes when migrants arrive en masse, could be spotted wherever we went on the island, always in the same hurry and as active at ten o'clock at night as throughout the torrid days.

Featherlight bursts of colour, their wings were yet uniformly faded compared with the glowing hues seen on the second and third home-bred broods of summer. This was scarcely surprising. These individuals would have flown all the way from the desert fringes of North Africa to reach our shores and, not content to remain in the South, had continued all the way to Scotland, a journey that had taken us the whole day by rail.

A painted lady was the only butterfly recorded on St. Kilda in a recent survey, implying a marathon flight for so fragile an insect, unsuccoured by a nectar source over miles of sea.!

The species is well able to withstand the exposure prevalent on islands and mountains, where winds are too strong for most other butterflies apart from their migrant counterparts, the red admirals. We did not see those here, but they have been recorded, along with graylings.

125. Painted Lady Butterfly

The painted ladies were encountered inland with small heaths, both keeping close to the heather tops. The only other butteflies seen were a single common blue at Ballyhaugh and a large white over a cabbage patch on Tiree.

Since 1997 a few painted ladies have been recorded staying to overwinter in Britain, but it seems unlikely that they would do so this far north. Indeed, the modern *Millennium Atlas of Butterflies in Britain and Ireland, 2002,* shows very few records at all in the Highlands or in Ireland, compared with the dense coverage throughout England and Wales, so it is remarkable that we saw them so regularly on both Coll and Tiree. This, perhaps, is another reminder that these islands have the record for hours of sunshine in Scotland.

The peak of painted lady immigration occurs in June, so these must have been new arrivals so early in the month, possibly wafted up the coast from Spain to the Hebrides without making landfall en route? The above-mentioned tome reports that individually marked painted ladies flew from Africa to Northern Europe at speeds of about 150km per day in 1996 – a phenomenal performance and one hard to credit – even though wind-assisted. Little clumps of thistles, Scotland's national flower, occurred throughout the islands, these a favourite food of the caterpillars, so further broods were likely to materialise through the summer.

Small heath butterflies are mapped in the national record as almost as common in Western Scotland as in England and Wales – no doubt helped by the distribution of heathland – but they thin out in the far North and are seldom seen on the Outer Hebrides. My one common blue comes between the last two in distribution density.

While the butterflies and bees were enjoying the unprecedented sunshine, the ewes, as yet unshorn, were obviously finding their heavy fleeces a burden. They lay, sometimes panting, sometimes just looking jaded (what other way does a sheep ever look?) in any shade they could find. Groups were huddled behind buildings or vehicles or, more comfortably, under the curved hulls of grounded fishing boats. Their lambs, wearing less bulkily knitted woollens, strayed, as youngsters will, but returned at intervals to their dams.

The free range flock did a good job of cropping the grass of unfenced seaside swards, which were as neat as mown ones alongside. One of the gardens stretching back up the hummocky slope towards the school was as Nature made it, and no less attractive for that. Clumps of Irises and ferns grew in strategic sites among the more unruly, while a few shrubs defied the worst that winter could bring among sparkling rock outcrops and rabbit lawns.

Each time I passed no. 1 in the neat row of low-built, lime-washed cottages along the landward side of "Main Street", someone was out with a watering can tending plants liable to wilt in the unaccustomed heat. The dwellings, like the rows of Welsh miners' cottages that they reminded me of, had no front gardens, but their inmates made up for this by cultivating the gently rising land behind.

I spoke with one elderly gardener who told me that he was born here and returned every summer, first with his children and now with his grandchildren. Like many others in these affluent days, he owned another house on the mainland for winter, when conditions were less salubrious and the ferry service to the mainland weather-dependent and spasmodic.

Only ten to fifteen infants and juniors attended the little school up the hill, pupils boarding in Oban by the week after the age of eleven, It was different on Tiree, where the much larger, modern school took youngsters up to their university entrance year,

Perhaps the finest garden of all, which came second in the last annual gardens competition and aspired to be first this time, was that of the guest house where we were staying. The gardener who tended this quite spacious plot so meticulously, was also our waiter. He waxed lyrical when speaking of his plans for the colourful borders around the central lawn, which was neatly manicured, yet liberally sprinkled with the buttercups and daisies geared by generations of grazing to flower on truncated stems throughout the machair grasslands.

Half Spanish, he had created a Mediterranean gravel garden with a range of Mesembrianthemums, stonecrops, thyme, blue-eyed grass, creeping phlox and much more. This was a fine place to sit, protected by sun hats and sun cream, in contradiction to all that might be expected of a Hebridean holiday. In this fine spell the elegant statuette by the bird bath carried a parasol rather than an umbrella.

It was not ever thus. Rills pouring off the heathery bog behind to the Iris marsh in front, had necessitated major drainage operations, diverting the streams into a

channel beyond the garden wall. A number of shrubs had
been nursed through their vulnerable sapling stages and
propagated by cuttings, Escallonias from South
America, purple Hebes, prickly Olearias and Senecio
daisy bushes from new Zealand, *Rosa rugosa* musk roses
from Eastern Asia and rowan from the Highland hills.
Representatives from the four corners of the world had met
up here on this little Scottish island, where star-of-the-veldt

126. Rosa rugosa

daisies bloomed as prolifically as in South Africa's Namaqualand beside the
Hydrangeas so popular in rainy Scottish gardens.

Tall Canterbury bells and yellow day lilies, red and yellow Mimulus from the
Americas, Antirhinums and Petunias mingled with native bloody cranesbills. An
attractive feature in the far corner was an old rowing dinghy with lobster pot,
posed among yellow Cypress spurge and tansies. An important theme was to be
blue and white to evoke the cross of St. Andrew. Blue Lobelias were already set
out alongside the path, the white Arabis and snow-in-summer had arrived on the
last ferry. Back towards the holiday cottages an array of plastic plant trays were
lined up, containing goodies yet to be planted out – Begonias, Impatiens and
many another – freight charge thirty eight pounds!

5. COLL. EXPLORING THE SOUTH-WEST COAST

At fourteen miles long and three miles wide, tapering to a narrower section in the
south-west, there is much more to Coll than the village of Arinagour. We set off
early in our stay to explore the 7,400 hectares (18,278 acres) which once supported
1,440 souls but now had a population of only 201, most of these living around the
village.

With a thinner sand cover than Tiree, the hard Lewissian gneiss shoulders its
way through the thin skin of earth and peat clothing the rounded outcrops, which
sometimes show the scars of glaciation. This last is responsible for the dumped
erratic boulders of foreign rock and a number of raised beaches, some occurring
near the village.

The imperviousness of the underlying rock is demonstrated by the amount of
surface water held up, particularly in the north-east – in no less than seventy five
lochs and lochans. Some of these boast ancient, Bronze Age crannogs or fortified
lake dwellings. No hill rises higher than 340 feet.

The one single track road makes an incomplete circuit around the island
centre, the loose ends connected by sandy byeways, and sends an offshoot out
to the far north-east point. We set off to the south, around the main loop clock-
wise.

A little beyond the triangular war memorial garden dedicated to the fallen of
two world wars, we came upon a herd of Eriskay ponies, roaming over the
heather. This is a rare breed and Coll's is apparently the largest herd anywhere.
There are said to be about sixty here, out of a world total of some hundred qualifying to be recognised as the pure breed. A few of the mares were suckling fluffy
foals, one particularly new, weak and wobbly on unsteady legs. These were the

issue of the white stallion who lorded it over the harem. Most of the foals are born black and fade gradually through grey to white.

The originals came from the tiny island of Eriskay off the south end of South Uist, better known for the popular "Eriskay Love Lilt" and the 1941 wreck of the "SS Politician" bound for New York with 243,000 bottles of good Scotch whisky on board – the incident that inspired Compton MacKenzies' novel "Whisky Galore". The ensuing film was made on nearby Barra Island. As if this was not enough for so small an island's claim to fame, it was the spot where Bonnie Prince Charlie first set foot on Scottish soil on his journey from France to the Scottish mainland in 1745.

127. Highland Pony and Foal

A little further along the road, we found ourselves confronting a cluster of dumpier Shetland ponies, looking expectantly over the fence, waiting for something to happen. Too much had happened to them in the past, when their toughness and small stature, forty two inches at the withers, put them in great demand for work in coal mines as well as on crofts. Offspring of those underground slaves, working in pitch darkness, are now more likely to be the little darlings of some littler missie.

There was a full blown woodland nearby, affording some shelter, many of the trees alien, including the wind-worthy sycamore, grey alder as well as the native, and aspen. Others which have got away here but not on lower, windier Tiree, are pedunculate oak, beech, ash and two conifers. These are Norway spruce, the usual Christmas tree, and Sitka spruce, which does so well on the most exposed mountains in Wales.

Who knows what the indigenous trees might have been before Mesolithic tribes moved in 6,500 years ago to leave their standing stones at Totronald? By the time the Beaker Folk were making their pots at Sorisdale around 2,000 BC, it is likely that most of the woodland would have succumbed to climate change and clearance by burning and browsing livestock.

Coll was part of the Norse kingdom of the Isles from round about the eighth century until 1266. Until 4,000 years ago, in the early Holocene, trees growing on the Outer Hebrides were oak, ash, birch, elm, aspen, alder, hazel, rowan, willow and Scots pine.

Dairy Loch, seen on our left, was a former source of drinking water. Two others closeby are prized for their freshwater fishing. Scars of former peat digging were to seen hereabouts and Gordon MacDonald was still extracting peat in the traditional way. Most houses now had central heating, the power reaching the island by under-sea cable from Tiree. It was the other way round in the past, sandy Tiree obtaining fuel for heating from peaty Coll. Despite the usual prevalence of wind, we saw almost no wind veins being used as sources of power.

Grindstones of the old Acha Mill had been silent now for more than eighty years, the old water wheel hidden round the back. Acha House, which formerly housed the laird and then a school, had been converted to holiday homes. Bees nested in the roof of wooden shingles according to "Mike", our knowledgeable driver and guide, who dissolved into a beguiling smile on the least provocation.

Hailing from Skipton, Yorkshire, he had chosen Coll as his permanent abode and was shortly leaving for Australia to visit the rest of his family who had opted to emigrate even further. Several other residents encountered were Geordies, replacing some of those "Collachs" who had emigrated to the New World.

Dun an Achbaidh on a knoll near the mill was an old Viking Fort. A remarkable vein of white quartz surfaced on our left near a track leading off to Friesland Bay, where lie the remains of a wrecked ship, her spars still reaching defiantly above the sand.

Near Uig in the island centre, we were alongside the patch known as the Airfield, although this was largely wishful thinking. Scheduled as the landing field for passenger planes, it was currently the spot where helicopters landed when called in to an emergency.

From here on we were running along the boundary of the 1,221 hectare (3,017 acre) RSPB Bird Reserve, bought in 1991 and working in conjunction with neighbouring farmers for the welfare of the precious corncrakes. Still within the designated area, we headed south to visit two of the island's coastal beauty spots, Breachacha and Crossapol Bay

Built decoratively just back from the shoreline at Breachacha are two castles, claimed to be the finest in the Inner Hebrides. The more elegant "Old Castle" dates back to the fifteenth century and has been restored by descendents of the MacLeans, who built it as their private home. The "New Castle", built closer to the sea in 1773 for the twelfth chief of the MacLeans, is also now a private home. Way back in time it afforded hospitality to Johnson and Boswell on their famous tour.

The stream flowing into the so peaceful looking Breachacha Bay is known as "The stream of the heads" in memory of one of the many Highland massacres in the bad old days of 1593. A local reporter of the time wrote: "Ducks swam in Duart blood and the stream was choked by Duart heads."

If the ancient MacLeans had time between their wars to appreciate scenic beauty, they could scarcely have chosen a more delightful spot to settle over the centuries. Away to the left a lone gull lorded it over a wide expanse of white sand patterned with an assemblage of low wrack-covered outcrops and islets and fringed by the bluest of seas. To left and right dimpled hillocks rolled down to the water, dipping gently into the blue mirror beneath a border of inksplash lichens. Rock-strewn grassland undulated into the distance like the waves of a more turbulent sea, the grazing animals fetlock deep in tufty grass. The steadings on this land by the castles were formerly famous for their cheese.

Standing sentinel out at sea was the little island of Soa. Crossing the base of the adjacent headland, which held an ancient burial place, a crannog and a standing stone, we followed a sand track to the bigger Crossapol Bay. This headland is largely covered with sand which crosses the entire, but small, width of the island to link Crossapol Bay in the south with Feall Bay in the north. We were near the west end of the island here, with almost the whole of the west coast sand covered.

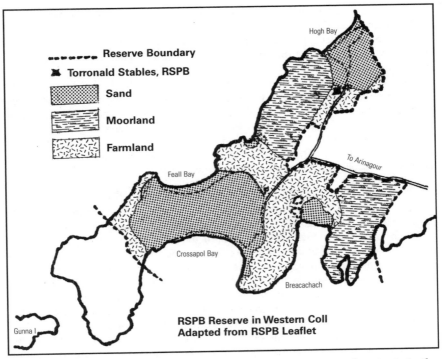

Hogh Bay

To Arinagour

Feall Bay

Crossapol Bay

Breacachach

Gunna I

RSPB Reserve in Western Coll
Adapted from RSPB Leaflet

Just out of sight was the little island of Gunna, stepping stone for giants to the altogether sandier island of Tiree.

Beaches were spacious at both Crossapol and Feall Bay, ideal for summer cricket matches if one could muster enough players in this land where we saw almost no other mortals after leaving the village. Both were backed by high dunes, some here in the west said to be over a hundred feet high, piled against rising rocks behind and slipping away in front to form little sand cliffs undermined by rabbits in places.

At Crossapol there was also a level area of saltings turf, the halophytic plants processing minerals from sea water to contribute to the lambs' delicious flavour that went so well with mint sauce. We would fain have lingered, but time moves on.

Mike's land rover bumped its way over more rutted lengths of track to Feall bay, where a big flock of gulls shuffled over the wet sand, preening and just loitering on the great curve of beach at the end of the bay. The sea glistened like the rolled steel seen at Margam Steelworks in South Wales, mirroring the sky and recording the shadow of every passing cloud in its polished sheen.

128. Great Black-backed Gulls

Tall marram clad dunes rose a short way back from the driftline. Their seaward face was unprotected from wind and tide but the ridge held firm, topped by a fringe of deep-rooted grass in parts and pierced by no major blowouts that we could see. Upper parts of the sliding seaward face had been partially colonised by stabilising vegetation.

With such a broad, almost flat beach to seaward, it is likely that waves would have lost much of their power by the time they rolled in to suck at the base of that potentially mobile ridge. In addition there is known to be an offshore underwater reef in the west, breaking the main force of Atlantic swells.

Green "Iona marble" has been found in the next bay to Feall Bay, beyond the intervening Ben Feall. This is a marble, as ancient as the gneiss itself. We did not visit here, but Gil found a few sea-worn green pebbles later on the Tiree shore.

6. COLL. BIRDS AND PLANTS OF THE NORTH-WEST

The accompanying map shows how much of Western Coll lies within the bounds of the bird reserve, the RSPB being the largest land owner on the island. It embraces approximately equal amounts of the three major island habitats: the indigenous moor, bog and hillside, areas inundated by wind-blown sand remaining in their natural state and the same which have been converted to farming.

It is the lime-rich sand which makes profitable agriculture possible. Lime does not feed plants directly but it strengthens their cell walls and makes other soil minerals more readily available to be taken in. This is largely by encouraging the growth of helpful, almost mycorhizal; but free-living soil bacteria.

Livestock, as often in wildlife sanctuaries, are managed in a way that helps the natural ecosystem. They are brought off the land most sought after by nesting waders before the eggs are laid, to prevent trampling and to allow the herbage to re-grow and provide cover and invertebrate life suitable for the eagerly searching chicks.

There were plenty of sheep about still, both black and white, these attended by crowds of starlings, which lined up along the wire fences when not busy food-finding. Some were tick-picking, like cattle egrets, others dung-probing like choughs (which were not seen here).

Potatoes were the only crop we saw other than grass but turnips were grown in times past and were commented on by Dr. Johnson. In 1852 almost all the crofters were removed during the clearances, not for sheep but for dairy cattle. Farmers from Ayrshire and Kintyre, keepers of the Ayrshire cattle prized for the suitability of their milk for cheese making, were encouraged to settle in their stead. Arable land has declined markedly in recent years – from 113 hectares in 1940 to 71 in 1960 and 61 in 1981.

During this period, from the 1950s and 60s, daffodils and tulips were grown for export. The bulbs were on the market a little before the Dutch varieties – but surely no earlier than those of the Scillies, which benefit from the same Gulf Stream but so much further south.

Coll bulbs were exported to Canada, which does not share this comforting warmth which flows obliquely from their side of the Atlantic to ours. With Coll lying at the same latitude as the southernmost tip of Alaska, at 56.5 degrees north, it was a plucky entrepreneur who ventured into the spring flower trade.

The next two decades of the 70s and 80s saw the rise and fall of a perfume and cosmetics factory, reminiscent of that run by the monks of the little Welsh Island of Caldey,

I was impressed by the unusual amount of cow parsley or Queen Ann's lace, occupying broad headlands in fields laid up for hay or put down to crops. These and the plentiful Iris beds provided the necessary cover for corncrakes while the hay grasses were gaining height. Haymaking was delayed until after the 10th August and cutting was from the centre outwards as on Islay, to give late chicks a chance to scuttle for the headlands instead of being chivvied into a central trap.

Corncrakes winter in South East Africa, remarkably, as they seem to fly as little as possible and apparently not very competently once they are here. They arrive in April but do not breed until some weeks later. Rare here – as everywhere where not already extinct – by the late 1980s, they have increased apace since measures were put in place to help.

129. *Corncrake and Yellow Iris*

Fewer than five hundred males were calling in the UK in 1993, just after purchase of the Coll reserve, most of these in the Outer Hebrides. The warden, Simon Wellock, records 2006 bird numbers in the Coll Magazine for 2007 as follows:

"There were 94 male corncrakes (in the reserve) with 38 on "RSPB Management Arrangements" and a whole island total of 171." Management agreements are hay:silage lets with four to five local farmers interested in corncrake conservation. They take their livestock off the fields by March or April and their rent is adjusted if this affects the return on the land adversely. Many are said to have a soft spot for their famous bird, despite sleepless nights caused by their raucous calls, which rise to a crescendo in the small hours.

Corncrakes, understandably, prefer rich farmland to poor hill country and can eat anything that this has to offer – worms, spiders, crickets, grasshoppers, beetles, flies, caterpillars and seeds. As relatively poor fliers, if they set out on the African journey on an empty stomach, they are unlikely to make it – this applying especially to the youngsters.

On the down side in 2006, the warden records "Terns and sea-birds that simply could not find enough sand eels to feed their young!" Specialities that he records for that year were two pairs of spotted crakes and three pairs of quail. 377 pairs of waders of seven species bred. Of these 80 pairs were lapwings and 65 redshanks, with 147 drumming snipe.

A series of skylark transects found 29 singing birds in 45 hectares of dune and machair, 7 in 15 hectares of late-cut meadow and species-rich grassland or 64 singing birds in 120 hectares (298 acres). My thanks go to Simon Wellock for assembling these figures.

We saw and heard curlews and a snipe perched conveniently on a post for our viewing, a grey wagtail on a fence wire. Plenty of lapwings were about this season, these preferring short grazed pasture.

We had fine views of a newly hatched lapwing chick trotting along the lane in front of us, unwilling to dive into the bordering undergrowth. Not entirely clad in the brown camouflage mottling of many wader chicks, this one already had the conspicuous black and white throat marking and white underside of the adult, both of which would be hidden when the chick crouched. Not long out of the egg, this scrap of life knew how to recognise danger and take avoiding action. A few more days, and possible admonition from a parent, and the value of imobility and camouflage might be added to its survival kit.

130. Lapwing Chicks

Little things done to help the birds were noticed. One was a letter box on a post with the orifice blocked by a sponge except for an inviting hole at either end and a notice with the reassuring information that there will be no collection today. It seemed that 'working' post boxes on the island got utilised as nest boxes without invitation.

Another was a lifelike scarecrow of a woman with a baby doll in a pushchair, accompanied by a wee dog. This last did not impress the sheep with its ferocity and had suffered as they got some of their own back for past canine chivvying.

Some unexpected sightings included in Simon Wellock's report for 2006 were as follows: A kingfisher (the first since the one that was shot in 1903. How could they?) a tree sparrow, (the first since 1937), a blue-headed yellow wagtail from Southern Europe and a nightingale, a southern bird with only four records for Aygyllshire.

As always where there are ornithologists skilled enough to recognise them, some obscure rarities had turned up. What most of us would have passed over as willow-chiffs or lbjs (little brown jobs) were barred, arctic and yellow-browed warblers, the last with goldcrests. Two others spotted on consecutive November days near the free church were a Blyth's reed warbler followed by a Siberian chiffchaff, another of which appeared in December. These sightings, as Simon remarks in his article were "A welcome break from trying to count almost 2000 barnacle geese on the reserve."

Unfortunately the warden was on leave during our visit, so we had to rely on our own inadequate bird sightings. Those inserted in my notebook as the land rover bumped over hoof-pocked, wheel-ridged tracks were largely illegible. I had neglected bird watching in favour of word botching!

We called at the RSPB Visitor Centre set up in the old sandy-floored Totronald Stables opposite a corncrake viewing platform, perhaps more appropriately a corncrake listening platform for use at night. There was open access to the interior to view the display of photographic posters illustrating life on the reserve. In tussocky grass outside the door was a small collection of whale bones, vertebrae and a shoulder blade.

The nearby Totronald standing stones were set where the lane humps up over a hillock, making them visible from afar. The names of the stones translate as "The teller of tales". Granite slabs aligned WNW -ESE, they must have been directionally significant. They date back to the Bronze Age and make handy scratching posts for itchy cows.

Before dropping us off with our packed lunches later in the day Mike drove us to a particularly fine viewpoint in the shadow of the upstanding Cnoc na Moine at the south end of Hogh Bay. There was no recognised track to this point but it was easy to follow the line taken by previous vehicles by observing the vegetation.

This was undulating machair country predominantly yellow with buttercups. The wheel tracks winding down over the brow of the hill were marked by short green grass. The strip between – and alongside on the steepest gradient – were white with field daisies. These traditionally oust the buttercups and much else as treading gets severe but succumb themselves if it becomes too heavy. It is gratifying to be able to read the signs of past land use in the vegetation, even to the extent of seeing how foot traffic spreads sideways on the more arduous stretches.

Rock exposures on the knob to the south behind the headland of Rubha nan Uan showed an unusually rich veining with glistening white quartz. The contrastingly dark heather and short grass between the outcrops gave way to bog cotton in a shaggy sward fenced off from the buttercup-spangled pasture backing the bay.

A line of tall marram dunes rose from the broad sandy beach to dip into the valley behind and rise again where blown sand had piled algainst the grey hill south of Totamore. Pale scars marked scattered blow-outs but there were remarkably few signs of the rabbits which usually have a ball in such easily excavated sites. It seemed that the rabbit eradication programme running since 2000 was having an effect.

As ever, it was hard to drag ourselves away, but we regained the narrow track and were dropped at the north end of Bay with instructions to walk on behind the next headland for pick-up later at Ballyhaugh, the site of the Hebridean Centre and Project Trust.

7. COLL. HOGH BAY AND BALLYHAUGH LAKE

The cosiness of our lunch spot, tucked in among grass tumps on a leeward slope, made up for the frugality of the fare. Afterwards we went our own ways, Gil seeking local specialities hidden among the more obvious and me following up the course of the local stream.

This was two partite, one branch tumbling down from Creag an Fhireoin, near more standing stones and cairns, the other pursuing a tranquil passage along the sandy valley from the lowland lake at Ballyhaugh.

As I moved round the headland to where the sweet water spread across the salty sands, the bulbous buttercups and bird's-foot trefoil of the piled sand gave way to pink centaury and downy, two-partite heads of lady's finger or kidney vetch. Flowers were only just emerging from the mats of bloody cranesbill foliage, whose stems and leaf tips were bloodier hued than the rich purple petals.

The gentler pink of sea milkwort, partially inundated by sand, marked the transition to a saltier habitat. Among the accompanying scurvy grass were the hoof prints of sheep which had strolled down to see what the tide might have brought in. Succulent clumps of roseroot on the backing cliffs kept well up, out of their reach.

On arrival at the beach top the rivulet lost its individuality, the water seeping away ignominiously into the sand. There was probably a different suite of invertebrate animals exploiting the changed salinity regime, but this remained hidden. – as did any pad marks or spraints of otters which might visit this so desirable habitat.

Sand sedge and the hoof shaped leaves of coltsfoot gave way to jointed rush and marsh horsetail as I returned along the water course. Soon there were thick banks of watercress good enough to eat and kingcups, still alight with the floral cups fit for an elfin king to sip from. This was but one of the spring flowers that southerners expect to see in March and April rather than June.

Where the runnel divided around seasonal islets, splaying rosettes of the rare early orache (Atriplex praecox) were spreadeagled across the sparkling sand. The radiating stems were crimson, the narrowly triangular leaves a deep vermilion. Apart from a small area around Berwick-on-Tweed in the East this species is confined to the western fringe of mainland Scotland and the offshore islands. We saw it frequently on Coll and Tiree, standing in for the more widespread Chenopods and making up in colour what it lacked in size.

Stands of yellow flags, rooted in pure sand, were present, as always here in the west. The banks of water mint were more familiar to southerners, their flowers not due until autumn. The scent that assailed my nostrils so pleasantly from this popular condiment is emitted throughout the plant's life: we do not have to wait for flowering time to savour it. The attraction of pollinating insects when their services are needed is not its only function. It also serves to repel grazing animals throughout the vegetative phase – as with thyme and other members of this family.

Scattered among the regimented stands of cone-topped spike-rush were delicate mauve blossoms of milkmaid or lady's smock that botanical pundits are urging us to refer to nowadays by the overworked vernacular name of cuckoo flower.

Above a sharp bend and the confluence of the two branches were some elegantly tall plants of water speedwell (Veronica anagallis-aquatica) There is a blank on the map of this handsome species through the West Scottish mainland, but it turns up again on the islands.

From here on the stream broadened into a linear marsh, the tall emergent plants so dense that I had to part them to see the bronzed mat of broad-leaved pondweed (Potamogeton natans) coating the water beneath. Fenced across where it left the lake that fed it, I had to deviate through two farm gates between the sand track and the tarmac lane. These led past the Coll Project Trust's headquarters and training centre.

Although the place seemed deserted on both visits here, it was the hub of training and selection of 17 to 19 year olds for their year of service in the third world. Around 200 student volunteers passed through here each year, preparing for their "gap year" overseas between school and college.

Since 1972 over 4,000 youngsters had entered its portals, benefitting by what the island has to offer in preparation for life in communities less complex than their own. Growing potatoes on lazy beds has more in common with earthing up yams on bamboo poles than does the mechanised farming of their homeland.

Outlying villages in the Tropics have much in common with outlying islands on the D I Y front. The "make do and mend" mentality so necessary in these is a far cry from the throw-away society that we have allowed ourselves to drift into – with the inevitable loss of the skills and initiative required for ensuring comfortable survival in less sophisticated surroundings.

Volunteers passing through Coll have served in twenty four countries around the world, these innovative, character-building years, fostering independence and adaptability and often influencing the direction of their subsequent careers.

The lake, which I explored forthwith, lay between Totamore to the north and Ben Hogh to the east, its placid waters as blue as the overarching sky. On my side it was fringed by a strip of bogbean with wispy white flowers, topping the rich green of trifoliate leaves. On the further side the mountain dipped its toes into the lake, the silvered, craggy toenails black with inksplash lichens where they dipped into the water, with a nail varnish of orange above – just as if they were dabbling in sea water rather than fresh. Patches of green beween were closely nibbled by sheep and diligently probed by wheatears.

A dilapidated board walk led out through the bog bean of the near shore, allowing some of the flowers to push through. As well as amphibious bistort and lesser spearwort there were club rush and wispy, widely spaced reeds. These were not too sparse to attract a handsome cock reed bunting, which stood out

131. *Reed Bunting and Common Reed*

in sharp relief instead of disappearing among the culms, as so often in reed beds.

Three families of grey lag geese sailed into view, each with goslings, 2, 3 and 5 respectively, these not much more than a few days old. More orderly than the sea-going eider ducklings, these youngsters followed in line ahead, the goose or gander leading the file and the other parent bringing up the rear.

The mute swan family, which sometimes converged but did not intermingle, consisted of the pen only, with six cygnets, these, too, not much more than a few days old. The previous day there had been seven. These were more adventurous, perhaps because the cob was skulking in the reeds on the further bank instead of curbing their curiosity.

My curiosity about the plants was curbed by the depth of water in the bogbean marsh and the barbed wire fence between me and the headwater marsh proper – with a handsome piebald pony beyond. Rarities in wet places such as this on Coll included the little bog orchid (*Hammarbia paludosa*) and Irish lady's tresses orchid

(Spiranthes romanzoffiana), but, most especially, I would like to have found the rare pipewort *(Eriocaulon aquaticum)*, which I had only ever seen in its native Ireland in much more acidic sites than this sandy loch.

Here too on Coll's eastern lochs were water Lobelia, shoreweed, pillwort *(Pilularia globulifera)* and quillwort in the stony depths, as in those on Colonsay. True bulrush, now common clubrush, grows with great fen sedge *(Cladium mariscus)*, which overtops other marginal emergents, as by turloughs on the Irish Burren and the East Anglian Fens -where it is still cut for animal litter, despite its national rarity.

Floating rafts of vegetation were all against the further shore – pondweeds or bistort, perhaps, even water milfoil or water starwort but frustratingly far off for identification. As I browsed. obviously botanising, another of this ilk, visiting from the Midlands joined me. He was most interested in the sedges and was plant recorder for his county. Intrigued to hear that Gil may have found a rarity, he set off with Jamie, his black Labrador, to intercept her, a little too late.

I joined his companion, and it was not long before we saw the two of them scrambling up the flank of Ben Hogh across the water in search of montane rarities. My own memories of this mountain, which I did not climb, are of the famous, ice-transported erratic perched precariously on its northern end, with the land falling steeply away below. Pale grey and decorated with wavy veins of white quartz, this great boulder is balanced on three smaller stones. The under-lying tableland has worn down to show patches of blue sky between the three supports as viewed from below, as between the stubby legs of a monster hippo.

On our road home through Grishipoll and Arnabost, we encountered several flocks of grey lag geese, each of twenty to thirty birds but with no nests. According to the rules non breeding flocks of grey lags are supposed to be on Coll during the winter, with the barnacle geese and others, and to return to the Arctic breeding grounds for summer. Maybe these were too young to breed. Our guide's explanation: "They just like it here". How very sensible!

A nice sighting was the snipe, which left its perch to fly across in front of the land rover to potter round the edge of a bog pool, affording good views of the disproportionately long beak and dark bars along the back. Then we were driving back alongside the seaweedy creek at the head of Loch Eatharna. First a Bronze Age cairn, thought to date from between 1700 and 1400 BC,

132. Snipe

lay close to the road, then a new hotel springing up on the site of a demolished school. We were close to the village here, the scene of centuries of historical change, much of it bloody.

8. COLL. BALLYHAUGH AND TOTAMORE

We returned with our new-found friends the next day. They had brought their car over on the ferry, to furnish their self catering accommodation – where we visited them after dinner one night. It was good to be able to share their transport on this occasion by day.

There seemed to be more heathland birds about that morning, but we looked in vain for the corn buntings which are reputedly part and parcel of the island's farmlands.We were compensated by more snipe and lapwings. There was the cheery chinking of a cock stonechat and four skylarks were seen taking off in vertical, fluttering flight to shed their silver notes across the rolling landscape.

An avian team scattered fairly evenly around the old football pitch, with its rusting goal posts, was of hooded crows. As we watched them at play the grey form of a cuckoo flew in quite close to the ground. It seemed to be the victim of a running tackle, the opposing team being of meadow pipits. Two were speeding along close on its tail and another five were jostling it from above.

133. Cuckoo

Did they mistake it for a male sparrow hawk or were they aware that they were the most sought after victims of its brood parasitism? The cuckoo, which had emerged from a spinney, escaped their attentions by perching on a telegraph pole near a cottage. Apparently it was the flying image that triggered the passerines' mobbing behaviour. A redshank flew past, flaunting white rump and wing secondaries, then another snipe and no shortage of lapwings, but these always as singles and uttering none of their so evocative calls.

A shaggy Highland bull standing contemplatively at the roadside brought us to a halt. There were not so many of these hereabouts and photographs were called for. The thick curtain of ginger hair dangling over his eyes but not obscuring the ring in his nose must have blinded him completely. There were no cows around to produce companionable moos or emit fruity bovine smells and his demeanour savoured of complete boredom. He showed less interest in us than did the farm cat just across the road, the pony at the farm gate and the amused farmer standing in his porch.

When we approached Ballyhaugh Lake two of the goose families were strolling along the road. The goslings were much more nimble and spritely than their flat-footed parents, with staid, swaying gait and who had further to go. Those were trapped on the road, too portly to get through the sheep mesh fence which proved no hindrance to their offsrping. The group re-assembled on their way down to the lake.

The rest of the party trekked off south to botanise. Not wishing to cover the same ground again, I headed north towards Totamore and the mild descent into the rocky valley south of Rubha Hogh headland. I was escorted throughout by a series of chinking wheatears as I passed from each territory to the next.

This was my first leisurely sortie into Coll moorland and I hoped to find bearberry (*Arctostaphylos uva-ursi*), juniper and black crowberry, all present on Coll, but there was no such luck. Among the dominant Scottish heather, fine-leaved heath and deer-grass were the usual heath subordinates. Most attractive were the short-stemmed heath spotted orchids and pink lousewort.

Generously branched almost white fronds of *Cladonia impexa* lichen cushioned trails of tormentil and bedstraw among the multitude of sedges and leaves of devil's-bit scabious. Black bog rush *(Schoenus nigricans)* increased as I topped a rise into a zone of blown salt spray.

A rectangular patch of reeds had been fenced off in a valley to landward, the denuded buff heads from last year's purple plumes wisping high above the new foliar growth. Interwoven through the margins were tall meadow buttercups and lesser spearwort, with little clumps of the rare marsh cinquefoil with their clashing puce and brick red flower heads.

A pair of reed warblers was in residence, the sparse reed growth insufficient to afford adquate cover. The cock bird sidled up his chosen culm to trill his scratchy little song, as though he expected it to carry further from greater elevation. Readily distinguished from sedge warblers by the lack of eye stripe and of streaks on the back and wings, these are much the rarer of the two this far north. A wheatear patrolled back and forth along the bounding fence wire.

The reed bed seemed set to form a sump for run-off water from a sizable new pond that was currently being dug on the coll above. This was on a minor watershed, with soggy seepages converging on the further slope to form a stream which became more deeply cut as the waters gathered.

A mechanical digger was at work on the low crest of land, shovelling out chunks of rock in a matrix of peaty brown earth and leaving ridges of displaced boulders reminiscent of a series of old raised beaches. Those being torn from the ground went straight into a trailer hitched to a tractor, which drove out along the winding track as lunchtime approached.

A brilliant pair of shelducks circled progressively lower over the already quite extensive body of water, as I approached, not tardy in sussing out possible new sites. As they failed to alight, I assumed they decided that it was not yet ready for them to move in. There was no sand cover round about to encourage the digging of nest burrows and the pool was too new to be a provider of food in competition with the rich rocky foreshore not far below.

The stream gathering from the quagmires beyond was very different from the one ambling gently across the flat sands into Hogh Bay. The heathers, all but the water-tolerant cross-leaved heath had given way to grasses, sedges and heath rush here. Water seeped through carpets of marsh pennywort threaded with star sedge and lesser yellow sedge, almost imperceptibly at first. As the gradient steepened it gained impetus, tunnelling under grassy overhangs and nurturing clumps of kingcups.

Here the contours levelled out, sometimes through a neatly grazed sward of sea plantain starred with white-flowered brookweed. It lingered in little pools roofed with the shining oval leaves of bog pondweed. Steeper gradients triggered little cascades, the silvered water collecting between rock outcrops stained a reddish brown, either from peat extracts or from ferric iron dissolved from the rocks. The burn side-slipped and slithered downhill, appearing and disappearing, winking mischieviously as it caught the sun.

Clovers and buttercups bore inundation with fortitude, but English stonecrop and scraps of pearlwort stayed above water level, where the lichens were crisp underfoot. In the sea milkwort and silverweed zone at the stream mouth foraging rabbits were scratching in a fine beige shingle, displacing white shell flakes up to half a centimetre across.

The hysterical calling of an oyster catcher by the Oxford blue sea was the only sound apart from the companionable tinkle of water gurgling over pebbles. Commuting shags were silent, as always. The floral gems of this little cove were undoubtedly the line of roseroot clumps following a horizontal rock shelf at head height in the backing cliff. Male and female flowers are borne on different plants, their yellow exceeded in brightness by the orange fruits which followed.

Butterflies here were mainly small heaths, with only the occasional painted lady and it was back at Ballyhaugh that I saw my only common blue. In addition to the three pairs of grey lag geese with chicks, another nine adults were grazing the sandy pastures bordering the loch, on a day that had evolved into a veritable scorcher. The swans, wisely, patrolled the waters in majesty, keeping their fluffy brood cool.

9. COLL, THE NORTH END

It was our first guide, Mike, who showed us around the north of Coll. As we set off seven herons were assembled in the upper arm of Loch Eatharna, these viewed at one point through the intricate aerial dance of green-veined white butterflies.

Conifers passed were said to be thirty years old although still quite small and the bared ploughlands in this region of many cattle grids were scheduled to be put down to grass rather than arable crops. Two entire fields were submerged under a froth of cow parsley, pierced by tall meadow buttercups, a perfect haven for those elusive corncrakes. Turning east at Arnabost, past Gallanach, we had superb views to the unmistakable Sgurr on Eigg, with Muck in front and Rhum to the left.

About half way to the north point was a snug little harbour that had been the centre of a thriving fishing industry until the 1880s. At that time rich harvests were taken from sub-marine banks within easy range of the currently used sailing vessels. By the time potato blight struck and a thriving fishery would have been most beneficial, these banks had been almost fished out and catches of eel and ling were reported as poor. Steam-powered trawlers had appeared on the scene by then – referred to by the old sailors as "Those engines of destruction". These were too big to dock in Cornaig Harbour and the trade there died.

From Bousd we were travelling across the north of the island through dramatic hilly country with steep-sided, partially bare but often smoothly rounded knolls rising abruptly from narrow valleys where sheep wandered among scattered Iris beds. It was very beautiful but would be hard work to cross on foot.

The road terminated at Sorisdale, near the island's north-eastern tip. Formerly a village of about fifty folk, there were now only three dwellings, one a holiday cottage, with a young woman playing with a child and a dog on the smooth greensward.

We walked past an old farm pond where black and white muscovy ducks dabbled, then a small, reed-thatched, grain or hay store to the final lookout.

Swinging northward we gazed on a complicated cluster of islets, the largest appropriately named Eilean Mor.

"You've just missed the basking sharks." This from a couple returning past the crumbling ruins of a former croft. Not again!

We retraced our wheel tracks, to be put down for a few hours near the Fishing Gate, where Angus kept his Orkney flock. It was there alright, not in a huddle but spread over the rock strewn grazings like Welsh Mountain sheep. The animals were black, with outsize armaments, but also well up among the rumpled hills. We did not call them down.

Inland of the road was a vertical sand cliff several metres high and penetrated by round holes much too small to be truncated rabbit burrows. Sand martins, quoth Mike, but we saw no birds.

The two attractions here were a soggy patch of mire, the acidity alleviated by blown sand and another delectable stream finding its way down a long sandy gully to the sea. Between them they constituted my favourite spot on the island – a little bit of heaven by the sea -where gneiss and shell sand, placid rock pools and rippling stream, grassy sward and flowery mire mingled in a perfect mix under a benign sun.

The mire was just this and no more when viewed from a passing vehicle: its charms had to be sought at close quarters among the dewy grass. Here were deep reddish-pink early marsh orchids and the nodding flowers of insectivorous butterwort, so like violets in both colour and shape but rising from more lethal leaves.

Most special for me were the pea-green, heart-shaped leaves of grass of parnassus (*Parnassia palustris*) which I have seen seldom and associate with sites like the sands of Holy Island in Northumberland rather than these western outposts. The species is widely distributed, although uncommon, in Northern Britain, ascending to 6,200 feet but is rare in the South.

134. Grass of Parnassus

The cup-shaped flowers have a ring of five fringed staminodes alternating with the pollen-bearing stamens, but were not yet open. Traditionally the only genus of its family this had lain between the Saxifrages and the Hydrangeas, but has recently been allocated to the former.

I succumbed to my passion for following streams to their mouth and was preceded most of the way by a common sandpiper, whose peevish whistle each time it moved on to make way made me feel like the intruder I was to this little Eden. "Little trotty wagtails" of the pied variety shared the foraging on the grassy tumps and seaweedy sand flats with the graceful little wader. A skylark sang so ecstatically that it seemed not to notice that its song was being broadcast into salty air over the foreign terrain of the ocean. A gull hung in the vacant sky off the adjacent cliff, supported by the updraught.

The watercourse meandered aimlessly over bare sandflats where not confined by rock outcrops. Sometimes it was broad, sometimes it divided around islands bonneted with cushions of almost ungrazed fescue. Some of these emergent patches were clad in pure sea milkwort, the short leafy stems buried in silver sand almost to the terminal flowers. Hopefully this washed away when the current ran faster than in this long dry spell, allowing the neatly ranked leaves to photosynthesise.

Dark red plants of early orache featured here, vegetative star bursts, having remarkable long white root tufts holding grimly on to the sand. The backs of the leaves bore a deep purple pigment. Thrift was surprisingly rare and sea campion not seen at all.

135. Early orache

The burn diversified as it meandered seaward, spreading in sandy pools and following sinuous creeks between low reefs. These last, with their different substrata were the richest in plant and animal life at this level.

Sea slaters, armoured like mini tanks, scuttled over the rocks, dwarfing the ginger hued springtails, *Petrobius maritimus,* which are one of the few true insects which can be regarded as wholly maritime. Firm sandhopper territory changed subtly to muddy lugworm territory and yellow and orange flat periwinkles crawled among the smashed remains of limpet shells.

From the plant angle the most remarkable feature was the abundance of the brackish water wrack *Fucus ceranoides* , an uncommon seaweed more often associated with estuaries, although quite at home at the mouths of small streams. Maybe in normal weather more fresh water would be tumbling down from the heights above to dilute the mixture here.

Fronds were from six inches to several feet long, somewhat narrower and more sparsely branched than those of the flat and bladder wracks among which they grew. Margins were undivided and apices more narrowly pointed. Their main feature, however, was their inflation, the two faces of the frond coming together only along the conspicuous midrib and the margins. The air or other gases thus stored, served in the same way as that in the specially shaped air bladders of some of the others, floating the fronds towards the surface to benefit from sunlight when submerged by the tide.

Reproductive bodies are borne at the tips of smaller fronds budded off near the plant base. These are shorter and narrower and turn black as the plant dries while the main frond remains a yellowish brown. The spindle shaped receptacles developing in twos and threes at their tips may contain eggs or sperms or both together, these shed into the water for external fertilisation.

A wide range of intermediate forms was to be found stranded on the sand or attached to rocks, the brackish wrack hybridising with the other two and those sometimes with each other, the offspring having characters from both parents. Dense swards of inch high wrack plants might have been youngsters of any of these, or of the chanelled wrack of higher reaches, and the soft felt of brown sporelings snuggled into crevices be an even earlier phase of germination.

A generous flotsam of both red and brown algae from greater depths had drifted in on the tide, but time was too short to unravel these intriguing taxonomic tangles, and we were soon hastening back upstream under the marram-clad sand bank piled against the eastern flank of its valley, for our pick-up.

There was one more call to make, this a bumpy ride across the grassed cliff at Killunaig near Toraston. Here were ancient cists and a medieval church, but a fun feature lightening memories of a harder past was a length of stout rope coiled into the name of "Coll" and snuggled comfortably into the greensward as though it had grown there.

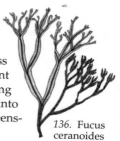

136. Fucus
ceranoides

10. TIREE, ISLAND OF SUNSHINE, SAND AND SEA

The table was laid for four at breakfast on our last morning on Coll – the free church minister, the policeman and ourselves. The minister and Gil were bound for the mainland, she to attend a conference in Stirling and return to rejoin me four days hence. The policeman, and I would be disembarking on Tiree. He told me not to worry about luggage.

"I'll put it in the police car and see you to your accommodation on Tiree."

This was reassuring. We had booked late, when only single nights were available on the island. My first four nights there were to be in four separate places and, without transport, transfers might be difficult. This was a good start.

My first billet was at Kirkapol House, my second at Tiree Lodge Hotel, my third in the Mill House Youth Hostel and my fourth at the Sandaig Guest house. The hostel might be a problem as they provided bed without board. I phoned ahead.

"I'm not travelling with food."

"No problem. Just ask the bus driver to take you to the shop and he'll wait while you buy what you need."

Islands have their problems, but lack of flexibility is not one of them. There are not so many folk about that a stranger can get lost in the crowd and their needs overlooked.

The "Lord of the Isles" pulled into Scarinish, Tiree's main township, whose Norse name implied Cormorant Headland, but we saw no cormorants.

I joined up with the policeman at the head of the long angled pier and we were soon turning into the drive of Kirkapol House, rattling across a cattle grid and temporarily flattening the kingcups pushing bravely through the bars from the gloomy depths. Mrs. Sweeney, chatting in the garden with a neighbour, showed consternation at the arrival of a police car, but was soon reassured. My driver introduced himself – he was new here – and told her she had infringed no laws.

The building was an old church, painted bright yellow. This was one of many such converted to other uses or allowed to fall into ruin when the population dropped from around 5,000 in the mid nineteenth century to around 700 as it was today.

Liquefying in the heat, I was led upstairs and shown into a room on the seaward side. Good, I should have a sea view, but not a bit of it. The sunshine flooding in came through a row of skylights in the sloping roof, too high for me to see out.

In this erstwhile holy place I was to lie in bed and contemplate the heavens, unmarred by earthly scenes. The only wings I saw fluttering past were those of late retiring or early rising painted lady butterflies, rather than members of the celestial hosts. Just a single chortle came from a perched herring gull which sounded suspiciously like "So there!"

Lying at latitude 56 degrees 30 minutes north, the same as Southern Alaska, Tiree is Britain's twentieth largest island. It is just over ten miles long at its longest and five miles wide at its widest. Kirkapol House is on the southern shore, where the island is at its narrowest, great sandy bays dipping in towards each other from opposite coasts. Twenty two miles west of the Scottish mainland, this island hosted a meteorological station set up in 1926 in the school yard, with the headmaster recording the weather three times daily.

During the war this was taken over by the R A F and moved to the airfield in the island centre. Twice daily weather reconnaisance flights penetrated eight hundred miles out into the Atlantic in planes of squadron 518. 1995 saw a new weather station and 2000 saw this automated. The annual average rainfall is a modest 35 to 40 inches, with few high points to check the rain clouds. Ben Hynish in the south-west rises to 460 feet (141 m), Ben Hogh in the north-west to 119 m. The flatness between made it highly suited as a military airfield on the region known locally as the Reef.

We were fourteen to eighteen miles due west of the Treshnish Islands and fourteen miles from the nearest point on Mull. Most lies less than fifty feet above sea level, lending itself to golf as well as aircraft. Although recognised as having more hours of sunshine than anywhere else in April, May and June, it is open to all the winds that blow, with gales on an average of thirty four days a year and up to 120 knots in autumn.

What must be endured may as well be exploited and islanders are recognising their potential as a centre for wind surfing, kite sailing and sand yachting. There may even be potential when swells roll in from the Atlantic for surf boarders to risk life and limb under the curving lip of those monster green waves that break in linear sequence as they roll along the flat beaches.

Such holiday water sports are a summer pastime, but weather can be too summery. During most of our short stay the gentle summer zephyrs scarcely ruffled the mirror calm of the sea and had insufficient force to propel the multi-coloured crescentic kites that were the motivating force of those seeking an adrenalin rush below. The fifteen mph easterly on our last day caused an expectant excitement in the surfing community based at Sandaig House.

The island's bedrock is Gneiss, 75% of this a raised tidal platform thinly covered with peaty gleys and podsols. Most has a superficial layer of fine white shell sand, the combination yielding fertile farmland regarded as the most productive in the Hebrides. Still, in modern times, the island is divided into 286 crofts, farmed by probably no more than 100 crofters. The thirty one crofting townships are administered by grazing committees. By the 1830s almost 4,500 people lived here, sustained by farming and the kelp industry

It has been regarded as a desirable place to live from earliest times. Over

137. Fourteenth and thirteenth Century Chapels at Kirkapol

twenty Iron Age stone circles and fortresses still survive, some with phenomenally thick walls, two of them brochs, the 'skyscrapers' of the Iron Age.

The Ringing Stone, a big rounded boulder inscribed with cup-shaped hollows, is a geological feature as well as a record of early man. It is an erratic of augite, thought to have been transported here by ice from Rhum, the carvings believed to have religious significance from pre christian times.

St. Columba, that great traveller among islands, is thought to have been here after his arrival on Iona in 563. He founded a monastery on Tiree, posssibly at the Soresby Graveyard but equally likely to have been where the old chapels stand at Kirkapol.

These lie a few hundred yards inland of the Tiree Lodge Hotel, the smaller thirteenth century chapel on a green knoll suggestive of an earlier pagan site. The larger fourteenth century one in the cemetery closeby had its highest point favoured by a carrion crow for the delivery of a brief but resounding corvine sermon.

A fascinating array of different coloured rocks contributed to the walls, a few smoothly rounded by the sea. Some walls were hidden by a cement coating, this painted orange with lichens. Fifteenth century grave slabs include one which may show the earliest known representation of a Scottish claymore.

In memory of the saint one gravestone bore a small carving of Columba, the dove, its shiny white marble also painted by orange lichens. It was furnished with an extra forelimb, with which it wiped a tear trickling from its beady eye to the delicate beak. This seemed a particularly apt and original motif.

When the Romans withdrew about 400 AD local war lords competed for power and lands were divided. Vikings moved in towards the end of the eighth century, first to raid, then to overwinter and finally to settle and intermarry, but there were five more centuries of turbulence from 1000 to 1500.

The main emigration occurred between 1848 and 1852, most emigrants headed for Montreal – to more frigid winters and hotter summers than those to which they were accustomed. Not all went by choice, but some were offered grants.

By 1886 the crofters act set security of tenure at fair rents, the ability to pass the property on to their successors and to be compensated for any improvements they had made if they left. By the start of the twentieth century some had emigrated to Patagonia (like the Welsh) and sang the praises of the money to be earned there by shepherding, but most of these returned in due course.

11. TIREE. BEACH COMBING ON TRAIGH MHOR, THE BIG BEACH

Traigh Mhor is named for being the largest stretch of sandy beach on Tiree. It borders Gott Bay, towards the eastern end on the south side, encroaching onto terra firma immediately opposite the two matching bays of Vaul and Salum dipping in from the north. Land in between is not much more than a mile wide.

The tide-washed expanse is backed by a sandy clifflet mostly less than a metre high and, because of the curvature, is some 4.5 km (2.75 miles) long, although the distance from point to point as the shag flies is only 3 km (1.75 miles). The headland with pier and monument in the west and the tidal island of Soa in the east close the arc still further, making the opening of the bay to the sea less than 2 km or little more than a mile across.

Waves pounding onto the sand are thus somewhat curtailed, although this was not possible to appreciate, as the water was as glassy calm without as within during my exploration. Sand dwellers below the surface would be less influenced by wave action than those exposed on the wave-smoothed rock outcrops intruding to the east of Kirkapol and at Carsamult along the sandspit connecting Soa. Investigation of the two was an enticingly gentle occupation for a sultry afternoon, with the heat untempered by any sort of breeze.

The driftline following the smooth curve of the beach consisted mainly of seaweeds torn from rocks elsewhere and ranging from the giant knobbly hemispheres at the base of furbelows (*Sacchoriza polyschides*), the largest of our brown kelps, to delicate red algae, filamentous or with fronds simulating the texture of a deflated balloon.

138. Furbelows (Saccorhiza polyschides)

Only the more buoyant animal remains had been deposited with this lightweight drift and it was here that I found fragile sea urchin tests. Flattened, penny bun shaped green sea urchins (*Psammechinus miliaris*), were likely to remain intact, with spines often adherent, whereas the more easily damaged sea potato urchins (*Echinocardium cordatum*), were usually in pieces, the spines worn away.

Fragments of pink tinged, intricately branched organisms resembling coral were to be found here. These were not the animals they simulate but heavily calcified fronds of one of the encrusting red algae, *Lithothamnion calcareum*. They were rare here, although so abundant at other sites as to form a major component of more shingly beaches.

139. Green Sand Urchin, Potato Urchin and False Coral

I padded along to the cluster of seaweedy rocks in the centre of the bay, the fluffy, half dry sand and rubbery driftweed resilient beneath my feet. At this state of the tide the sea seemed nearer, dappled by shadows and threaded by curls of sand-flecked bubbles. Shell fragments brought up short by the outcrop clinked and grunted underfoot as they talked back to me, the shattered relics of perfectly crafted natural symmetry.

The rocks were bonneted with a velvet sward of fescue grass and thrift, grading down through sea lettuce and its kin to golden brown drapes of common wracks. They had arrested the passage of longshore drift from far and near, this piled up along their flanks.

Most durable were the molluscs, two-shelled bivalves living under the sand and single shelled Gastropods crawling over the rocks. Largest of the former were the razor shells (Ensis spp.), named after the old long handled cut-throat razors that we used in biology classes to cut sections.

The largest grew to 8 inches (20 cm) long and about an inch wide, the discarded shells either shining white or with some of the brown outer membrane still adherent. In life they are orientated vertically, the two siphons opening at the sand surface when submerged by the tide. The muscular foot which extruded from the lower, actually the anterior, end, is immensely efficient at pulling the

140. Top: Rayed Artemis, Milky Lucina, Rayed Trough. Bottom: Common Whelk, Flat and Rough Periwinkles, Painted Top

animal down to safer levels when the vibrations of an approaching fisherman bent on digging it out for bait, or indeed for culinary use, are detected.

Next largest was the rayed artemis *(Dosinia exoleta)*, some 5-6 cm in both directions with a lop-sided apex. The concentric ridges are very close, crossed by three broad, radiating brown bands, these more sharply demarcated in smaller specimens.

Rayed troughs *(Mactra corallina)* had smoother, more brittle white shells, their apex more central and tinged purple, the concentric rings not etched into the surface as furrows. Small and equally delicate, but with raised sculpturing, were milky lucina shells *(Loripes lacteus)*. A few of these had a neat round hole bored through just below the peak, where some predator such as a dog whelk had sucked out the contents.

Much the commonest of the Gastropods or sea snails were the multicoloured flat or blunt periwinkles *(Littorina obtusata)* with no peak to the shell. These came in yellow, orange, chestnut, buff or grey. Rough periwinkles *(Littorina (saxatilis) rudis)* were more sombrely coloured, the shells rough with concentric ridges and coming to a sharp peak.

The painted top shells *(Calliostoma ziziphinum)* were perfect cones, as broad at the base as they were tall and named after the highly coloured tin spinning tops that children played with three generations ago. Larger than any were the

222

common whelk shells *(Buccinum undatum)* tapering to a sharp point. This is the species whose egg masses resembling fossilised frogspawn so frequently get washed up on the beach.

Traces of those other, more complex shelled organisms, the Crustaceans, were unusually common. Here were the pink and red carapaces of edible crabs *(Cancer pagurus)* with their neat 'pie crust' margins and the more spiky greeny-brown ones of shore crabs *(Carcinus maenus)* .

If undamaged these have probably been discarded during normal growth, in a process known as ecdesis. The old hardened skin splits and is pushed off by a younger one formed below. This absorbs water and allows the body to expand before it hardens into an effective armour.

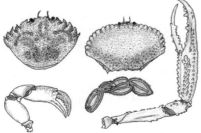

Chunky businesslike pincers were likely to be those of shore crabs. The elegantly flattened bristly hind legs were those of velvet or fiddler crabs *(Macropus (Portunas) puber)*. These are swimming crabs, showing the flattening of limbs into paddles as in unrelated groups such as sea turtles, seals and scuba divers. Most spectacular were the paired pincers of what must have been a fine Norwegian lobster *(Nephrops norvegicus)*.

141. *Left: Shore Crab carapace and pincer. Centre: Edible Crab carapace and Velvet Swimming Crab hind leg. Right: Norway Lobster claw*

More unexpected than any were the tangled mounds of sea dwelling plants which grow only on sheltered shores such as estuaries and tidal lagoons. My initial perplexing finds were of tightly spiralised, crisply dark brown or black ribbons a millimetre wide and a metre or more long. Some had been in the sea for long enough to support growths of hydroids or sea firs, the individual polyps fluffing out into the water on those few specimens caught up in pools.

Unravelling some of the tousled masses I found an end here and there emerging from a flattened sheath more typical of a grass or sedge than the large Dictyota type seaweed that it so resembled. Clearly this must be a flowering plant and the only British candidate this big had to be the eel-grass or grass-wrack *(Zostera marina)*.

Diligent search revealed a few fresher specimens, broader, flatter, more supple and green, with a complex, 20 cm long bunch of more durable white roots emerging from the base of the give-away sheaths. Held up to the light, the flattened leaves, some of which reached 150 cm (5 feet) revealed the compartmentalised interiors typical of underwater flowering plants. Although so different, they were

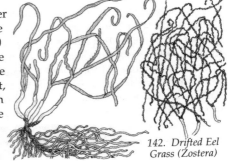

142. *Drifted Eel Grass (Zostera)*

obviously precursors of those brittle black, tightly coiled spirals with the texture of shrivelled algae.

Coll, Tiree and the smaller island groups round about seemed unlikely places for mudflats of any sort – apart from a few fescue-glasswort type saltings submerged only by very high tides. The pliant fronds of Zostera need to remain permanently submerged. Had these sea-borne deposits drifted across from a sea loch marsh on Mull or the mainland, I wondered?

No noisy gull flocks broke the stillness of the afternoon, but thin, sharp cries came from a little group of terns fishing offshore. The shrill, three-partite whistle of a common sandpiper drew my attention before it took off to make a beeline towards me and new foraging grounds beyond. A black and white ringed plover trotted jauntily across my field of vision, the movement negating the camouflaging effect of the good use of ground cover and colour harmony into which its distinctive pattern usually merged.

Scattered rock pipits scurried over the hotch potch of grass and algae, pecking at unseen morsels, to be joined by a pied wagtail. The resident skylark trilled its bubbling song over the bordering strip of golden buttercups and silverweed upshore, coupling seashore, land and sky.

12. TIREE, VAUL BAY BY THE NORTHERN GOLF COURSE

The morning that I hitched a lift from Kirkapol to Vaul Bay in the north, to explore the bay and headland and return afoot, was the one occasion when my winter woollies were appreciated. A keen, eye-watering wind whistled in from the west, making photography difficult but imperative because of the magnificent views across the gleaming silver sea patterned with black reefs and green islets.

Ominous black clouds hung over the northern land mass of Mull, where it must have been raining, quite heavily. Only the briefest spatter fell on Tiree before the sun broke through and I once more enjoyed the warmth to which I had become accustomed.

Vaul Bay is twinned with Salum Bay to its east, the two separated only by a slender peninsula terminating in a tumble of islets, the largest loosely attached at low tide by an expanse of yellow sand. Only gradually did the clouds lift from the mountains of Skye to the north and the mist reel in its tendrils to enhance the backdrop of these entrancing seascapes.

The approach lane had served a cluster of stone crofts tucked into the west end of the beach and now in ruins, with grass and nettles growing in the living quarters and yellow flags in the vegetable plots. In modern times the lane served the golf club house and a series of still inhabited cottages further inland.

No golfers were out today, but it would be hard to visualise a more attractive setting in which to pursue a little white ball, whatever the quality of the golfing hazards. I saw no artificial bunkers. Low, well grassed dunes backing the beach rolled away in an unbroken expanse of buttercup yellow, with humps and hollows all the way. I did not trepass to see if the greens were mown.

The sandy coloured animal watching me warily from the track ahead was not the expected rabbit but a hare, twitching each long black-tipped ear in turn, the better to assess the oncoming threat. There are no rabbits on Tiree and none are tolerated – that including pets confined to hutches, even if castrated. This island, farming the most fertile land in the Hebrides, was taking no risks.

Foxes, too, are absent, so the hares have things more or less their own way, taking their less drastic toll of grass and root crops. Otters are present and have been known to vary their usual fish diet with unwary poultry. Mice and voles scuttle through the herbage and rats were a problem when rubbish was being incinerated.

Conspicuous on the Vaul beach was a much larger than usual pure white gull. With no black on wings or tail it was quite distinct and kept aloof from the rabble of herring gulls preening round about.

Only two of our gull species are completely white, these the glaucous and the Iceland. The Vaul bird was indisputedly the glaucous, which is described as "obviously larger and longer legged than the herring gull" while the Iceland gull is "smaller and shorter legged than the herring gull." The glaucous is "more heavily built, with larger beak, small eyes below a sloping forehead and angled high crown, giving a mean, aggressive look."

It fitted the description but its behaviour towards the others was exemplary. Apparently some of these larger birds visit Tiree in winter and this one had failed to return to the Arctic breeding grounds with the rest of its kind so that by now, in June, the residents would have got used to it. It walked with a slight limp and showed no inclination to fly during the whole of my stay, so maybe it was unable to. There was no shortage of provender in the amply supplied driftline for a bird with no qualms about eating carrion.

143.
Glaucous Gull

Much more aggressive were the lapwings. One was describing a series of verti-cal oval flights to actually touch a hooded crow crouching among dried wrack on each downward pass. The quarry ducked at each swoop but gave no ground. Lapwings are more likely to nest on the golf course – where grazed a bull and his harem – than on the beach, to which another drove intruding herring gulls more than once. As the quarry in both cases were the better armed, the lapwings must have been exploiting the right of ownership.

Two skeins, each of six geese, passed over while I was watching a young thrush experimenting with ways of breaking snail shells on a handy knob of rock.

My own fossicking along the driftline yielded two interesting brown seaweeds. One was the elegant, beaded *Cystoseira tamariscifolia* reaching from a foot to half a yard long. Like a string of beads the main axis was 'threaded' with neat oval bladders providing buoyancy. In between these were multiple short brown spines, giving the feathery appearance for which it was named after tamarisk, the feathery leaved shrub so popularly planted on seaside promenades in the South. An associated species is named 'ericoides' for similar reason.

When submerged the fronds have a bluish-green iridescence resembling the lining of the big New Zealand paua (ormer) shells, *Haliotus paua*. Tufted repro-ductive bodies formed at the shoot tips.

The second brown alga, of unusual shape, was *Leathesia difformis*. This consists of uneven spheres, rather smaller than golf balls. They start solid and become hollow, with filamentous interiors, their texture rubbery and firm, their colour a fresh yellow brown. Although not particularly uncommon, they seldom come ashore in such good condition.

Here, too, was the uncommon green Codium, sometimes known as sponge weed. It reverts to its original form after the water is squeezed from it, like Sphagnum moss. Others were brown bootlace weed and thongweed and red pepper dulse *(Laurencia pinnatifida)* among the more mundane.

The collection of kelp and its processing was second in importance only to farming on Tiree as well as on Eigg and other islands. Gathering the tangle, often waist deep in water was desperately hard work, sometimes undertaken in the middle of the night to utilise the richest growths at low spring tide level. These big weeds grow only attached to rocks, the more easily negotiated sands unable to hold them, so there would be plenty of wave splash on the uneven surface and rough walking carrying the dripping load above the reach of the high springs, which followed as surely as the day the night. At least this was a summer harvest, taken in June, July and August.

Some of the stones on which the material was dried can still be seen at Traigh Bhi between the south-western sea-bird cliffs and Ben Hynish. The ash was burned for eight hours, pounded into lumps and covered with turves to cool, the product being used at first for glass, soap and linen bleaching.

As the industry expanded a factory processed the ash in big iron retorts, heated by coal. Iodine was extracted and the spent charcoal sold as fertiliser and deodorant for freshening up the standard earth privies. Coal was landed at Hynish Pier and carted to the factory in some of the six hundred horse-drawn carts used for haulage.

The factory closed in 1901 and was later demolished to make way for aircraft runways used during the second world war – when the charcoal might have been used as filters in the gas masks with which we were all equipped.

Following me along the narrow path towards the An Cnap headland and the dun at its seaward point was a flock of free range sheep. These were mostly ewes shedding ragged tufts of fleece, but they were led by two matronly figures with neatly upholstered twin lambs. One pop-eyed ewe of an indiscriminate brown colour had charge of two coal black, long-eared lambs. Others gave rides to some of the many starlings which foraged over the rocky foreshore with misplaced house sparrows. I sat on a rock to let them pass, twenty six adults plus offspring. With scarcely an exception, each jumped up on a broken wall section to look me over before risking the scuttle past. It was either that or turn back and they chose to stay together.

Returning along the lane I was filled with admiration for the colourful gardens of the few bordering cottages. Horizontal wooden slat fences, green mesh netting and piled rocks served as windbreaks, along with tattered withies, two metres high. These leaned wearily against each other and bore green shoots only on their lower halves.

Conserving precious pockets of quiet air were Escallonia, Hebe and a white-leaved shrub resembling a Senecio or a Griselinia. *Rosa rugosa*, a popular component, was known as the 'wild rose' here in the absence of the more usual dog and field roses.

Dame's violet or sweet rocket (a favourite also on the equally flat and windswept Irish Arans) was doing well along with bistort, fennel, giant poppies, garden Geraniums and Fuchsias. The prize specimen, and one I have not seen elsewhere, was a proud foxglove spike with deep pink flowers at the base grading to bright yellow ones in the upper half.

The prize for ingenuity must go to the gardener with a sense of humour who had built a snowman in the almost complete absence of snow. From the base upwards this was a large driftwood stump (no island tree would grow that big). Then came a black car tyre surmounted by a big white metal fishing float for the rotund body. A smaller yellow plastic float, painted with a beguiling smile, wore a terra cotta plant pot for a hat.

A resident met later in the day said that only once in her twenty years on the island had snow lain as a complete ground cover, drifting against the walls. "There were no cars on the roads then. Drivers couldn't guess where the roads were before the wire mesh fences went up. If fences showed, they wouldn't know where the ditches were, or how deep. Children, delighted at the opportunity, were sent out in gumboots to see if the old folk were alright."

13. TIREE; WHISTLE STOP TOUR OF THE EAST END

Half way along the Gott Bay highway was a notice depicting the back end of an elephant. This was "Elephant's End", with a long drive leading up to a building which did not advertise itself as a restaurant but where I had been told I might get something to eat.

Over what would have been called a Devon cream tea at the other end of Britain, I was offered a most welcome car lift around the local sites by Mrs. H., the proprietress' mother – a gesture typical of Tiree generosity. Thus it was that I was able to see something of the eastern end of the island.

We approached Salum Bay behind the dunes at the end furthest from Vaul, arriving at Fadamull with its generous scatter of tied or tidal islands. In that fantasia of scattered tumps and flats, my new friend had collected cockles from the sands and mussels from the rocks in her younger days.

"The freezer lorry would drive down and take our boxes to the steamer and the mainland hotels." She herself had been a cook at one such establishment in later years.

A thin ribbon of white cirrus cloud stretched the width of the bluest of blue skies, shredding and coagulating as the tiny ice particles melted and refroze in an insubstantial aerial ballet. Then the evocative call of a redshank wafted in from the now deserted beach – a lonely sound in a lonely place.

The main road ended at Caolas with branches north to Urvaig and south to Port Ban and a short detour to the beach at Port Ruath. The first showed an old daisy path across the yellow machair, the last fine views across Gunna Sound.

Gunna Island rose in green and brown humps. The south-western tip of Coll to its right was bordered by yellow sand, the higher land half hidden by the lower but nearer intermediate isle.

My driver's grandson had been a full time fisherman around this coast when fishing was more remunerative. He dredged scallops, the local clams.
"But the British won't eat them and he gave up on those. Mackerel became his mainstay – these caught around the island but taken to Oban for smoking. This fishery, too, dwindled, and now his mainstay is crabs and lobsters."

She extolled the quality of the fine salmon and trout that they used to catch in the rivers of Mull and Loch Etive. The nearby radio station where the undersea cable brought power to the island had employed many people in the past.

A short stroll at the end of the southern branch to Acarsaid an Duin and we were back inland, stopping to fraternise with two small herds of delightful Iceland ponies. Six were roaming over an expanse of rock and heather and another six grazing some fenced machair, but not too well fed to prevent them from coming to lean over the fence and beg a few titbits.

These friendly animals had been used for pony trekking until the year before when this activity ceased. More famous equines on Tiree had been the Clydesdale work horses, the island having its own breeding herd. Donald McIntyre was the last islander to keep these. He worked them until both he and they were too old and now there are no more to follow on – nor work for them to do in this mechanised age.

There remained one more road to be followed to the coast on this eastern arm of the island. This led south to Rubha Phuirt Bhig, where tidal sands reached out towards Soa Island. It was a favourite place for seals to haul out to bask and fluff their body hair from sleek darkness to downy buff.

My driver had generously tacked this eastern tour onto a routine shopping expedition for fresh fish and vegetables at Crossapol in the opposite direction. She dropped me off on the Reef, south of the aerodrome while she gathered her wares for the restaurant in stout wooden crates.

Most land outside the runways was pristine machair and I explored the ungrazed belt backing the high sand cliff that dropped steeply to the long beach of Traigh Bhaigh. As far as I could judge from the top the sand face was about five metres tall, with sand sedge, marram and fescue grass interwoven into a tough stabilising mat which overlapped the brink before breaking away in uneven slips.

In the current absence of grazing there were taller plants here. Ragwort, yarrow, hairy hawkbit and thistles crowded among the marram and tall oat grass. Kidney vetch, ribwort, a very robust eyebright and deep blue patches of particularly fine milkwort added colour among the bulbous buttercups. Shorter wavy hair grass, its tiny florets shining in the sun, gave sparse shelter to a less striking pink milkwort and tenuous sprays of fairy flax.

144. *Blown Sand on Hogweed leaf*

Legumes included kidney vetch and bird's-foot trefoil as well as red and white clovers. Yellow lady's bedstraw was just coming into flower among wild carrot, the most attractive of the umbellifers.

A suprisingly substantial layer of blown sand had been deposited on big flat leaves such as those of hogweed. More powerful winds would have blown this away as well as depositing it, but the even layer was an apt indication of how much sand there was on the move, even in calm conditions.

It was no wonder that the little land snails were crawling around in sand-abraded shells instead of the polished armoury that we expect. I started gathering shells of the two commonest – the flattened heath snails (*Helicella itala*) with the hollow umbo in the centre beneath, and the long, cone-shaped pointed snails (*Cochlicella acuta*), assuming the weathered ones to be empty.

145. Heath Snail and Pointed Snail

This proved not so when little horned heads popped out and trundled their sturdy homes away to freedom. Such wear is avoided by the bivalve shells which spend most of their lives buried in beach sand, emerging bright and shining above the surface only into the flooding tide.

Larger snails – garden and hedge snails (Helix and Cepaea) lived among more protective vegetation, often the nettles and cow parsley by old walls, and managed to maintain an intermediate polish. Slugs, with no shells to speak of, came out only during rain or after dew fall. They had to be searched for during the long days of sunshine, only the largest species of Agrion and Agriolimax likely to be found. Blown sand can be a problem in winter, when certain of the roads have to be cleared, but farmers harrow it into their grazings, glad of the extra fertility that it brings.

146. Slugs: Agrion and Agriolimax

A few oyster catchers and terns fequented the local beach and "The Reef" is one of the main areas for nesting waders – despite the incompatability of aircraft and flocking birds liable to cause air strike. The RSPB manages its Reef Reserve quite closeby, snipe, redshank and dunlin, as well as lapwing and oyster catcher accomplishing their courtship displays unphased by roaring aero engines. Ringed plovers breed on the runways, a local publication stating them to "breed here by the thousand".

New areas of open water are being created to provide more nesting sites for ducks. These also enhance the habitat for the whooper swans which fly in from Iceland in winter and the barnacle and white-fronted geese from Greenland. Tiree in 2007 was ranked as having the highest population of breeding corncrakes in the U K , equivalent to twenty per cent of those surviving in Western Europe.

Curlew and turnstones winter around the coasts where coastal shallows provide good pickings for arctic and little terns in summer, these shared with eider duck and shelduck. Like all other islands manned by competent ornithologists, Tiree adds its quota of rare migrants to the national list.

On her return my new found friend pointed out the radar station on the hill, assisting transAtlantic liners, the tall radio mast on the airfield and the upstanding monument. Indeed much more, from the O A Ps' home and the Doctor's surgery to the distant Paps of Jura, which I had failed to see for clouds when I visited there the previous year.

We explored something of the old port of Scarinish on foot, viewing the stark outline of the wreck of the "Mary Rose", of which little remained but the naked spars, curving defiantly up from their last anchorage in the sand. Moored by the outer jetty were some of the lobster boats, their decks colourful with the big red floats that we saw bobbing over the set pots offshore.

This little harbour, now frequented by seals, was where the old ferry boats had come in, landing passengers on the beach. Cattle had been driven down and swum out to other boats. Then came the old stone pier, at which a tourist boat was currently moored, and, later, today's huge "roll on – roll off" ferry bringing pantechnicans loaded with stores and other goodies, as well as tourists from all over, some with their cars.

14. TIREE; LOCH BHASAPOL

I was anxious to explore the shores of Loch Bhasapol, described as a "Shallow, fertile machair loch tucked between ancient acidic Lewissian gneiss rocks three thousand million years old" to contrast the plant life with the Lobelia, shoreweed, quillwort type of peaty loch more common on other islands.

With this in mind I accepted an early morning lift with a Kirkapol resident who taught in the school just north-east of the lake. She assured me that there were paths all round the lake and that I should easily make the circuit back to the school for a midday pick-up. Although she was a P E teacher, her P E obviously had not extended to walking the lake shore. All others consulted – too late – confirmed that this was not a possibility, even for the fittest mortal.

My map showed no footpaths and there were scarcely likely to be any when the entire shore apart from two points of access were included in the bird reserve nesting area and so not open to the public. The only road was set well back and securely fenced throughout. After a wide detour to the north-west, it turned south and petered out at Kilmoluaig west of the inlet stream from the southern smaller lochs which fed it. The map showed a wilderness of knolls stretching back from the south-east of the lake, with no connections to the north-south trunk road leading to the school beyond.

It was as well that I did not know how many miles of tarmac I should trudge and how few water plants I should see before the day finished. Nevertheless, it was by no means a wasted day, despite this misinformation and I saw quite a few birds, albeit in the far distance.

It looked promising where I was dropped off near the school. Not only was this one of the two points where the water could be approached, but there were a few moored boats, providing perches for the myriad starlings and a series of tourist information plaques. It seemed there was room for sailing and fishing as well as birds.

I read that the crannogs or ancient lake dwellings had a long history here as real or artificial islands. Boulders may have been floated out on rafts to the timbered dwellings, which might connect with the land along an underwater causeway. Jetties would have accommodated dugout canoes or coracles. So much for the theory. The real thing was not on view.

Visitors were informed that a system of cultivation involving six-row barley was undertaken during Neolithic times, ribwort and mugwort among the arable weeds identified by the standard pollen techniques. Excavated bones of red and roe deer were thought to be those of domesticated rather than wild animals.

My only contact with the real thing was within a few yards of this picnic area where a line of springs near the hut succoured a small reed patch before gathering force to supply the old mill wheel further down. Swallows hawked flies over the dewy grass and a cormorant passed over. Their roosting here was regarded as a warning of bad weather to come in the days of no weather bulletins.

I found no water plants in the sharply demarcated grass turf bordering the lake. Hay species ranged from yellow rattle, yellow pea and yellow bedstraw to lesser meadow rue, hop trefoil and a few marsh orchids. The transitions to sheep or cattle grazing was quite close here, but the monotonous acres of reedswamp between road and lake increased as I converged closer after following the road taking me progressively further away towards Carachan.

Here and there a runnel of water sneaked under the stock-proof fence into the roadside ditch, carrying a few less usual plants such as mud crowfoot or marsh arrow-grass *(Triglochin palustris)* among the ubiquitous kingcups. A few early marsh orchids shared the moisture with common spotted orchids and ragged robin, while yellow flags appeared, competing less well with the overall green of reed, rush and sedge than in its more usual saltier sites near the sea.

One Iris plant bearing three open flowers was covered with tiny thrips, while, to add insult to injury, garden snails browsed over its leaves. Thrips are tiny black flying insects of the order Thysanoptera, meaning 'fringed wings'. Each of the four wings is fashioned like a bird's quill feather, with a fringed central shaft – a little like a simplified plume moth's. Often to be found in flowers, I do not recall ever seeing such a heavy infestation as on this particularly fine specimen (see colour plate XIX).

They feed by piercing the epidermis and sucking up the sap through a hollow beak. One, the pea thrips, is an agricultural pest, the numerous punctures for sap extraction leaving the pea pods mottled with the silver of the empty, collapsed cells. Some may transmit disease, but their damage may be offset by their work as pollinators, though doubtfully in such a massive flower as the Iris. They are referred to as thunder flies when they take to the air en masse in sultry weather. This is when they are likely to get in the eyes and hair and cause irritation.

Frequently machair pasture intervened between road and lake carrying weaned heifers and steers being brought on as store cattle. Black and belted

Galloways were a popular breed, the few isolated, smart white cottages presumably those of the crofters who tended them.

Two clouds of white birds were spied over the distant waters on the west side of the lake. Their flight patterns suggested terns and black-headed gulls respectively. These were said to be breeding here, the gulls particularly lining up along the fence wires when not on nest duty. Otherwise the birds seen were isolated redshank and snipe, both with a habit of perching on posts, to make a late getaway as I approached. Lapwings were so numerous that they must have been nesting and the occasional oyster catcher was spotted.

147. *Black-headed Gulls*

Tufted duck and teal have bred on those hidden waters and Tiree is regarded as probably the sole place in the Hebrides where corn buntings still breed. Did I see some, or were these other finches – twites perhaps?

A man with binoculars slung over his shoulders pedalled past on a push bike and I caught up with him later in the bird hide – set well back from the lake behind acres of reeds. Visiting from Derbyshire, about as far from the sea as he could get, he had sat here for part of every day during the past week, passing the time after a disappointing and gruelling climb over the "seriously rough trek" to view the sea-bird colony in the South-west at Ceann a Mhara.

"And after all that effort you are fenced off fifteen feet back from the cliff edge and can't see a thing."

Tiree is definitely not an island for "bird spectaculars". He was here for ten days, listing all bird sightings in neat capitals in his notebook – the twitcher version of a train spotter. Sadly there was not much to spot at this distance. A big brown and yellow caddis fly with mottled wings, a pro-active hairy spider and a buzzing bluebottle failed to move him.

He had brought his push bike in the back of a capacious van, in which he had spent a frightening night during last autumn's hurricane on a neighbouring island.

"The van was rocking from side to side, with the wheels coming off the ground. Me, half naked at the wheel in the middle of the night, trying to steer her head on to the gale". – like a mariner nosing his vessel into the oncoming waves.

Two meadow pipits and a skylark dropped down among some nearby lady's smock and horsetail and some starlings rose from a clump of kingcups. We even managed to persuade each other that the faint grunts emerging from distant reeds came from a corncrake. A lone figure, presumably the warden, followed a lightly trampled line beyond the armoured fencing below. We wondered if he would come up to see if anyone was in the hide, but he did not look our way, intent on his bird count or whatever he was about.

I left the unfulfilled twitcher and pressed on, knowing that I would never make the midday rendezvous but still hopeful that there might be a way through eventually. Half a mile or so further on a car hove in sight with a red-faced farmer and a black and white collie in the front. Waving it down I tried to address the driver across the dog. He beckoned me round. "She'll eat you."

I asked if there was anywhere that I could get down to the lake to look at water plants and if I could get back to the school this way. The answer to the last was "No way." To the first he wasn't sure but tried to be helpful. The suggested possibility of a lake circuit was definitely not on.

"Even the fittest chap would have his work cut out. There's streams coming in, boggy stretches, impenetrable reeds in knee deep water and rocky bluffs."

He eyed me quizzically and a broad grin spread over his face.

"And for persons of a certain age...." His voice tailed away.

OK, Yes. It *was* sixty six years since I worked in the Women's Land Army, but there was life in the old girl yet!

Nevertheless, he indicated a couple of gateways with only a small stream between.

"If you go through that hay crop and along that wall, you'll come to a rocky headland. You might be able to get through there." He didn't sound too hopeful. "I'll be coming back this way in half an hour or so. I'll pick you up here and take you back the way you came."

I climbed the first gate. The second was a bit wobbly so I unravelled the complication of frayed binder twine and secured it temporarily behind me. The hay crop I was wading through was fully knee high and more colourful than any I had seen. Robust red bartsia and yellow rattle formed the bulk of the herbage, with sparser orchids, ragged robin and ox-eye daisies and big bushy eyebright such as I had never seen before.

White and painted lady butterflies, honey and humble bees were busy pollinating. I was doing far too much damage trampling this wonderful crop and it was a very long wall, with the plants along its base even taller. After a bout of photography I gave up.

I spent a long time securing the middle gate after passing through and finished off with a half bow to make things easier for the next user. It was as well I did because a bunch of black and brown store cattle had by now drifted down from the hillside and were queued up at the gate, dying to get their teeth into that burgeoning crop.

Only when I had pushed my way through to the road gate did I realise that the walking stick I had carried unused over all that tarmac had got left behind among my photographic subjects. I could have done with it now to poke the heifer who was assiduously chewing at the crucial nest of binder twine around the wobbly gate. The half bow had already been pulled loose and I was on tenterhooks that the rest might unravel. It held – and the returned farmer told me I'd made a good job of it.

148. Red Bartsia

He drove the cattle back up the hill and volunteered to collect my stick, following my tracks with no difficulty and waving it in triumph when found. Not bothering with gates, he returned to a hump and hollow crossed by the lethal looking fence, pushed the dog underneath where the land dipped and swung a leg over where it rose, his trews stout enough to repel the barbed wire. The collie was banished to the back seat.

He needed to go on to turn and soon after we set off he pointed laughingly at a small handwritten notice "To the lake".

"I never saw that before – in all the times I've been by here."

It indicated the headland he had suggested as a likely spot – if I could have got out of the hay.

On the return drive he pointed out a field with no flowers.

"That's what happens when you don't graze."

Of course, buttercups that are not eaten anyway, get smothered with grass growth and with them goes the colour of the machair.

He seemed amused by the whole incident and steadfastly refused to accept my tenner when he finally got me back to the school. This was yet another example of the goodwill of the Tiree folk towards ignorant strangers.

There followed an interesting spell looking round the big modern school and observing their projects, which ranged from profiles of the boys volunteering to attempt the Three Peaks Climb to the handiwork of girls furnishing a dolls' house.

I awaited rescue perched on a stone watching a little group of seniors making a film sequence for a "Western" by the netball courts with a young teacher. A harrassed cyclist peeled off from a passing group and came pedalling in with a big black dog trotting gaily behind.

"He's been following us all the morning. He'll be miles from home by now."

She was obviously more worried about this than Bonzo was.

He deftly avoided all restraining hands and scampered cheerily away over the cattle grid after his new found friend. After an enjoyable tussle with a group of senior boys, the miscreant sat back, grinning at all and sundry. The school caretaker was summoned. He brought a length of rope and I imagined him taking the culprit on an identity parade in front of the assembled school. With all those youngsters, from four to eighteen years old, somebody must know him. Or would they? Apparently a lot of tourists brought their dogs and big black retrievers were popular at the moment. This sounded like a job for the policeman and a public notice.

15. TIREE. THE OLD MILL HOUSE HOSTEL

I spent one of my last few hours at Tiree Lodge watching some recalcitrant sheep being rounded up, much against their inclination. Did they sense that this was for the last time – next stop the island abbbattoir? The operation involved five men and a sheep dog, who disgraced himself by chasing a bunch of sheep into the furthest corner of the outsize field and was kept on a leash during the rest of the operation.

The stock lorry described several figures of eight trying to back into a field corner where adjoining gates served three fields. To block all exits and make a sheep-proof joint involved complicated manouvres. The resident sheep crowded round initially in the hope of new arrivals or extra fodder, but dispersed when the empty van suggested they might be the targets. Freedom is precious. No animal likes to feel trapped.

A tempting trail of sheep nuts was laid along the wall where the flock finally bunched, this leading up the ramp to the dark interior, but the wily leading ewes were not falling for that after the first tentative sniffs.

The whole circus went round the field several times before about twenty sheep were closeted inside and the slatted doors slammed shut behind them. As the van drove off there was a bemused silence among the rest, then one, philosophically inclined, resumed grazing with an "Ah well, that's that" look and the others followed suit. But not for long.

In less than a quarter of an hour the lorry was back with another, weaving once more around the field corners. Other trails of bait were laid and the dog's exuberance quelled until all the rest were finally behind bars. Those five stalwort shepherds had certainly earned their lamb chops after several kilometres run, arms waving wildly.

The slaughter house, for cattle and sheep, was owned by an elderly lady and her daughter in law who was likely soon to take over. They ran their own livestock on the machair as well as killing for other farmers. Some of the island livestock had to go ashore for "finishing", as there was not enough nutriment in the closely grazed pasture to fatten them all to the desired weight.

Pigs were not kept. Nanny State law prohibited the feeding of swill and food leftovers from the thriving tourist industry because of the imagined danger of disease. All those valuable calories were destined to be part of our horrendous "throw away society", although much more nutritious than those that could have been spared for the crofters' pigs of old. Pork and bacon and all the other pig derivatives were off the menu for now, until someone sees sense or more frugal times demand a more prudent use of assets.

Mine host at the Tiree Lodge Hotel dropped me off at the Old Mill House Hostel after late dinner on my last night in Kirkapol, furnishing me with the wherewithal for a frugal breakfast. The building was brand new, smart and practical, but was surrounded by an expanse of large beach cobbles over which it was impossible to trundle a wheeled luggage container and which did nothing for those arriving on push bikes.

I found a slip of pink paper on the first door inside. It read "Mary. Your room is upstairs on the left. See you later. Judith." It proved to be a spacious dormitory containing six beds, each with green and blue duvet and pillow, bedside cupboard and a big storage box below. There were sloping skylights in the roof again, but these afforded pleasant views of the surounding landscape.

Tracey, a bespectacled lass with hair in a pony tail, sat cross legged on the furthest bed, reading a novel. She proved to be the current student helper, earning her keep in house and garden, and proceeded to show me round. Focal points for more normal weather were the laundry and drying rooms. Hot water was laid on in the showers for two hours in the evening and two in the morning. The door with the pink note opened onto the day quarters – a kitchen cum diner with three other inmates draped on sofas in the lounge section beyond. Another sat outside in the late evening sunshine. These had all booked early enough to have single rooms.

Judith, the owner, appeared later, for settling up, and one of the guests guided me in leaving a message on the bus company's answer phone. I expected to enquire if a pick-up was possible and at what time. Not easy on a recorded message. That was not the routine. The idea was to state what one wanted and expect it to happen, willy nilly. I baldly stated my desired pick-up time and destination.

My room mate was up at 6.30 am the following morning, pyjamas neatly folded, sitting in the garden in the sun, finishing her novel and starting another. I had the kitchen to myself and found that tea without milk was quite bearable, having forgotten when packing at home that powdered milk weighed no more than tea bags. Any fool can boil an egg!

True, when they have located the electric stove switches after a life of using gas.

I probed the mysteries but the outcome had the consistency of a sorbo rubber ball. I looked with distaste at the cold sausage salvaged from yesterday's gargantuan hotel breakfast, then had the bright idea of dunking it in the still boiling egg water to warm up. It served, after a fashion, lessening the stodginess.

A sinewy gent came in with a carton of drink and went out with a length of flex and a plug – from the electric kettle?

"Trying to steal some electricity for a shave. I'm not holidaying here but working. A solicitor, run my own firm. It's cheaper staying here."

Another came briefly to pick up his pack, then I had the kitchen to myself instead of the expected scrum to get at the stove. As I cleared my plates Tracey passed the window carrying my already laundered sheets to the clothes line. Another fleeting guest that passed in the night: gone without trace!

I got my baggage outside and explored the old mill site. All that remained apart from the mill pond was the butt end of the old stone building and half a huge renovated mill wheel protruding above the thick turf snuggled round its base.

This had been a corn grinding mill built in 1803 and serving a population which grew more cereals for domestic and animal feed. History tells us that more ancient crofters, armed only with sheaths of corn, repulsed marauding Vikings. It also goes further back to mark this as the site of the buried village of the six-fingered people.

Further back still, ten thousand years ago, the bank on which the Loch Bhasapol bird hide now stands was an Ice Age shoreline. Many of today's dunes are known to be of the same vintage, the millennias' loads of sand blowing in the wind masking the physical reality of the bones of the landscape below.

Water still gushed through the rectangular stone sluice into the mill pool beside the wheel replica, nourishing more aquatic plants here than I had seen during my day "by" Loch Bhasapol from which it flowed.

Here were regiments of soldierly, cone-topped stems of Eleocharis spike rush and hollow water horsetail axes bearing no lateral whorls of branches. Their backdrop was a yellow-green mass of branched bur-reed, backed in turn by great hairy willow-herb, yet to break into purple flowers. Reed and Iris were unusually sparse.

Spearing up from cushioning banks of edible water-cress and lesser water parsnip were sprays of Coll's elegant water speedwell *(Veronica anagallis-aquatica)* There was still space in the sparkling stream flow for the brackish water crowfoot *(Ranunculus baudotii),* all its pale green leaves of the feathery under-water type.

Rumour had it that this stretch provided a rich feeding ground for trout. The patient heron a little further downstream seemed to think so. The leat curved out to flow under the road and into a long straight dyke worthy of fen country. Currently this served a pied wagtail and a mob of polyglott starlings, with a redshank exploding from the dyke further down.

A ripple of sound between a gobble and a trill drew my attention to a skein of geese flying over in V formation. Below their flight path were the flickering black and white wings of a flock of lapwings tumbling across the tranquil sky.

With all the wind that was usually about, I found myself wondering why the islanders had built water mills instead of windmills. When I wondered later, in company, as to why *149. Water Speedwell* there were few if any modern wind vanes generating electricity, I was informed that salt corrosion, gale damage and general disintegration would shorten the lives of any such installations, adding both to their initial cost and subsequent maintenance.

Our host at Sandaig regarded solar power as a much more practical way of 'going green', with so much early summer sunshine, no ground frost to speak of and ground temperatures seldom dropping below four degrees Centigrade. He hoped to replace the whole guesthouse roof with Blackhouse type roof storage spaces served by solar panels connected with a turbine in the garden.

The community bus arrived on cue at 10.15 am, driven by an elderly lady, one of several part-timers, mostly O A Ps, who took turns to drive, planning their routes according to the nature of requests. I had the entire fourteen seater bus to myself for the whole of that pleasant journey across the western end of the island – at the frugal cost of one pound fifty.

16. TIREE. SANDAIG, CATTLE AND CROFTS

Sandaig proved to be no crofting village, but a few widely scattered residences on rolling buttercup-yellow pastureland hummocking down to the low west coast. The day was still young and Polly, my new landlady, was sorting out bedrooms, so I gathered what I needed and strolled forth to explore.

This was a cattle dominated landscape – not stores or fatteners as by the loch but nurse cows suckling calves of all ages. Chatting later with our landlord, Duncan, I learned that the Duke of Argyll owns all the land except plots like his own, which have been sold off freehold. The crofters pay their rent to him.

He or the Scottish Agricultural Board own most of the bulls, crofters paying for use as required. To avoid paying for each service, successful or otherwise, some of the crofters have banded together to buy a shared bull. The sires run with the herds and calves seem to be produced at least throughout the summer months. Unlike bulls chained up for most of their lives indoors, they seemed very placid.

I saw none of the Highland breed so popular on other islands although those are so much better insulated against winter weather than the smooth-coated, quicker growing varieties. This, I assume is because of the better quality pasture. On islands with more gneiss and less sand only the hardiest breeds could make a living. There had been problems with cobalt deficiency but these were easily remediable with the application of as little as two pounds per acre of cobalt salts. There are no cattle sheds.

"The animals remain out all winter. They don't like it and shelter from the wind behind any available building when they can. They just have to put up with it."

Bulls hereabouts seemed to be of the early maturing continental breeds which are so good at putting on flesh in all the right places at a relatively tender age. These were all beefers. There was no dairy industry, no cheese or butter making. The local Charolet bull, who eyed me curiously when I passed through his territory, merely wrinkled his nose in apparent distaste and turned his attention to more desirable females.

Not for these the constant nibbling on the hoof to get sufficient nourishment. There was enough for all on these lush slopes. Much of the day could be spent idling in the sun, sleek flanks sunk among the buttercups as they gently chewed the cud.

The ewes and lambs made more conversation than did this sleepy mob but they were fewer on these fertile rolling sandhills than on the rockier terrain of the North and East. Their bleating was often the only sound apart from wild bird calls. No murmur came from the waves, no swishing of shingle as the advancing tide crept gently among stony fragments and no flurry of wind.

Following the coast north, I settled above a big brackish pool at the top of the tide at a particularly fine viewpoint and very soon became intrigued by the well spaced out succession of four cows plodding past in the same direction. All had a bulging udder but none had their calf with them. It seemed they had abandoned those temporarily to go on some special mission.

It was soon apparent that they were intent on drinking salty water from just such upshore pools as this – despite the provision of freshwater troughs on their grazings fed by blue hose pipes snaking through the grass.

Having sojourned in Western Australia, I was well aware that cattle can drink much saltier water than we can, but I had not believed this to be a matter of choice. Rather was it a case of "needs must" as so much salt was drawn up to the surface by capillarity during evaporation in the long droughts.

The black cow which had selected the pool I happened to be overlooking was obviously anxious to reach it – by a path more suited to goats than cattle – but seemed dubious about the proximity of the seated human. After a spell of eyeing me to pluck up courage, she progressed a few steps at a time down the tricky descent, stopping to unload a very liquid cow pat – no shortage of liquid there.

Then her nerve failed. There was only one way out. She could be trapped down there and panic. She backed up and came tentatively along the top to get a closer look and sniff. Evidently satisfied she tried again, having set her mind on this particular site. Shying back as a pebble slipped underfoot, she finally made it and drank briefly from among the growth of green seaweeds and flotsam of browns.

Scrambling up she passed close by me to peer into another pool, but this offered no practical descent so she returned to the other to try again. Obviously this was a tried and tested site and this time she drank deeply. The other cows, passing on to more distant pools, also plodded back after her to the herd and their calves.

In a flashback to my farming days, I remembered how the wartime Ministry of Agriculture, Fisheries and Food encouraged farmers to put plenty of salt in their silage. We thought it was to give the cows a thirst and encourage them to drink more water and produce more milk. Perhaps there was more to it than that. The cows should know best. Plenty of other animals go to salt licks, natural and artificial.

I rose to take photos across Traigh Thodhrasdail to Telegraph Hill, with the path ascending Choc an Fhithich to the pylon and the 119 metre Beinn Hough rising behind. More cattle were down on the sandy beach to the north where there was neither food nor drink to be had, nor even flies to get away from on the adjoining land.

On my return I passed a more accessible pool, colonised by salt-loving plants such as sea plantain, scurvy grass and sea milkwort, but with a freshwater runnel trickling in from a sward permeated by the curving, succulent foliage of spring squill. The soil was pitted with the hoof prints of cattle. Why had those others bipassed this more desirable watering hole, I wondered.

There were similar pebbly enclaves inundated by high tides, which nourished living Petrobius and sand hoppers and discarded egg capsules of lesser spotted dogfish (Scyliorhinus canalicula). Common around these shores, the latter are usually referred to as mermaid's purses and when at sea they are most often attached to weeds by the tendrils sprouting from the four corners.

150. Dogfish egg case and Silverweed

Each would have contained a single embryo before the celluloid-textured sac broke free and drifted ashore. As members of the shark family, dogfish do not produce hundreds of eggs from the union of hard and soft roes, as do the bony fishes.

Staying as we were, close to the historic row of thatched farm dwellings preserved as a museum, a visit here was a must, and the diminutive old lady who acted as janitor and guide, happened to be on hand when we passed, so we saw inside as well as out.

These 'crofts with a difference' were in general use until the end of the second world war and were built to withstand the weather. The six foot thickness of the walls could be appreciated from the outside because the window glass was fitted on the inside, leaving a great whitewashed cavity facing outwards instead of the usual bay added to the room within.

In fact there was an inner and an outer wall, the space between filled, not with rubble, as in my own Welsh cottage, but with sand. Moreover the roof trusses were supported on the inner wall, allowing drainage from the roof into the infill, making possible the growth of grass and flowers, even rhubarb, on top and room for grazing sheep and sleeping sheep dogs. We could only wonder about the internal waterproofing, particulalrly as the dressed stones were set without mortar.

Thatch was not of the more usual cereal straw, reeds or heather but of marram grass from the dunes. Even when in the prime of flowering, marram does not lend itself to the neat, sheath-like trusses of the first two and it is laid on loose, a new layer applied every two years. As in other Scottish and Irish black-houses (which are usually white) the thatch is held on with netting and the netting weighted down all round with rocks on short tethers.

Our elderly guide, dressed the part in a long black gown, had lived here herself, and some of her family still did – in the larger house alongside which was not open to the public. She was more concerned with the family photographs of grandpas and uncles and ma-in-laws and their life histories than in the artefacts, but we got views of butter churns and the patterned tools used to imprint the butter pats before these became so aggravatingly concealed within tight-fitting silver paper.

Flat irons shared the cluttered dresser with outdated cooking utensils. How easily the mind flits back over a span of seventy five years or so to the sight of Mama lifting similarly heavy black triangles gingerly from the stove, using one of the many thick iron-holders, blanket-stitched around the edges by my school-girl fingers.

The word "recycle" was not part of our vocabulary in those days, but we knew a lot more about what it meant than do today's youngsters. The warp and weft of every pot-holder, tea cosy or rag doll had a history then in the family archives.

Black silk dresses with intricate fancy beadwork and hand crafted lace lay beside white cotton nighties and petticoats such as were worn by suppressed but rebellious Welshmen during the "Rebecca Riots". What we failed to see was any cupboard or closet in which all this stuff could be kept.

Next door in this same long house was the barn or cattle shed, where we noticed slabs of dried peat between the rafters or roof laths and the thatch. The pre-war and war-time farm implements brought other memories. For several centuries until the "Dig for Victory" upheaval of the 1940s, agriculture had barely changed. My post-war departure from such buildings had coincided with the start of the revolutionary change from horse power and man or woman power to the almost complete and unrecognisable mechanisation of modern times.

Livestock farming had changed less than arable, particularly here, where cattle were over-wintered outside and not subjected twice daily to mechanical milking in a specially built parlour.

17. TIREE. ROCK DOVES AND NESTING TERNS

As I followed the coast southwards on another occasion the sea was an Oxford blue, the horizon sharply demarcated against the paler blue sky as though etched by a razor blade rather than a pen. It showed the slight downward curvature at either end that we perceive from a liner on the high seas. This was the west end. The ocean I gazed upon was the vast Atlantic.

I enjoyed frequent sightings of cliff nesting rock doves, ancestors of the rabbles of London pigeons in our towns and parks. They came in one plumage pattern only, this typified by a conspicuous white rump and black wing bars and tail tip.

151. Rock Doves

Three eider ducks were exercising their newly hatched ducklings on the motionless waters of one of the many little inlets which punctuated this coast. A trio of dunlin flew a little way out to sea, calling the while, then turned about and returned. An oyster-catcher, pied piper of the shore, was spotted, alongside a youngster, prettily mottled in velvety dark brown and beige fluff. These chiselled limpets from the rocks as well as picking up ambulatory winkles and sedentary mussels and probing for cockles.

152. Author with Oystercatcher Chick in 1962

The real bird spectacle occurred when I reached the deep indentation of an old quarry, where sea-rounded cobbles had been removed for transfer to the R A F runways. The artificial declivity was separated from the sea by a piled storm beach of assorted boulders and this was the location of a tern colony.

The birds were mostly Arctic terns but with a fair proportion of little terns, which are only two thirds the size – nine to ten inches long as opposed to fourteen or fifteen inches. It was impossible to see if there were common terns among the arctics, but the latter are much the commonest this far north. Both have red legs and red bills, the arctics lacking the black bill tip seen in the commons. Little terns have yellow bills and yellow legs and feet with black toenails, so these delightfully spritelike birds were easily distinguished.

All was quiet as I approached, the pale grey birds merging invisibly with the pale grey pebbles. First to rise and sound the alarm were common or mew gulls,

241

suavely elegant, with yellow-green bill and legs. These hovered above me shouting abuse and turning me back.

The terns followed them into the air churring, squawling and dive bombing for the instant before I withdrew, to walk discretely round the back of the excavated hollow and settle on the landward slope with my biscuits and cheese to observe in comfort.

Things quietened down quite quickly, but every so often something spooked the birds and they rose in a shouting cloud of flashing white and silver wings. The nesting bank of loose stones was deeply scored with the wheel tracks of the heavy vehicles responsible for the hollowing out of the area within, but this seemed not to worry the birds. Sometimes a single tern would rise vertically above its nest and then descend, for no apparent reason, unless to check that the intruder was no longer on the move.

Occasionally two birds rose together to chase each other back and forth at a low level before settling, or an oyster-catcher rose briefly. These were the only indications that so large a concourse was present and anyone following the path round the back of the quarry where I sat might pass none the wiser that so much life crouched on the seaward pebble bank. It was impossible to see whether there were eggs or chicks in the colony at this distance. This is not the only place on Tiree where terns nest.

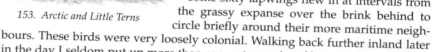

153. *Arctic and Little Terns*

Pairs of rock doves still passed over and some sixty lapwings flew in at intervals from the grassy expanse over the brink behind to circle briefly around their more maritime neighbours. These birds were very loosely colonial. Walking back further inland later in the day I seldom put up more than one or two pairs of lapwings at a time but it was evident that they were nesting over a wide area here. With them were skylarks and meadow pipits.

But there was more to watch than just birds. As I moved round the brink I became aware of two brown hares sitting erect and watching me – from a safe distance. I slid below the skyline and settled back under a low sand cliff. This seemed to calm their fears and they returned to their leisurely grazing of the lush hoof-pocked turf on the quarry floor. They found time for chasing and play. Finally they filed up the sand and pebble cliff, past a patch of nettles where shed sheeps' wool showed that the flock had been resting, and disappeared from sight among the lapwings of the hinterland. I left them my apple peel as a brief change of diet.

Hares eat much the same provender as rabbits, but a trait in their favour is that they do not dig burrows – an irresistible pastime for rabbits living on or in so much friable sand.

"Most of the Tiree houses are built on sand. Rabbits could undermine their foundations."

As I ruminated a small lobster boat followed along the coast close inshore, throwing the occasional pot overboard, marked by one of the big scarlet floats. Pots were laid inside the outermost offshore reefs, where tiny wavelets were rising a foot or so above the dark weed in white foam. The lobsterman left to the south, zig-zagging further out to sea and was last seen heading in the direction of the Skerryvore Lighthouse.

As I progressed towards Port Bharrapol I saw my first fulmar petrels. The auk cliffs were further on and I saw no sign of their inhabitants on the sea. Shags, razorbills and guillemots bred here, but not puffins. The three common gull species, great black-backed, lesser black-backed and herring gulls, also bred, along with kittiwakes, both these and cormorants to be seen over the sea, well away from those closely guarded cliffs.

18. TIREE. THE WORLD OF THE MACHAIR IN MINIATURE

Moving on through the sultry afternoon heat, I decided a siesta was called for. A depression where the greensward was grazed less closely fitted the contours of my body perfectly. I lay back, inhaling the scent of the few smoother knolls of purple thyme. A lark suspended in thin air added his liquid notes to the gentle hum of pollinating bees attracted by the heady aroma and I dozed off.

I opened my eyes after a suitable interval to find myself gazing out through a miniature world of meticulously crafted mini-blooms and sculpted seed pods. These were everyday flowers which make up the backdrop of our natural world, but which do not seem worthy of a second glance when viewed from five or six feet above ground. These I had first grown to cherish many decades ago through the more appreciative eyes of a child. Those memories are associated with later romps in the hay, which lay loose in even swathes or piled in haycocks instead of hard packed and unyielding in bales or rolls.

A sprig of grass from this angle became not just an integral part of the green counterpane but a living entity in its own right. I rolled over, the better to view this unfamiliar mini-world from a new angle. Soon I was propped on my elbows trying to transfer some of these symmetrical but infinitely varied shapes onto pages of my notebook.

Red fescue spikelets (1) really were red, or rather purple, reaching sideways at maturity to leave the main axis sinuous instead of apparently straight. Warm sunshine had encouraged anthesis and bright orange anthers dangled from the splaying inner bracts to release their pollen onto the minimal breeze. How often do we notice the two feathery white stigmas protruding from the tip of the grain within that trio of pollen dusted anthers, to waylay pollen from the neighbours?

The cylindrical spikes of sea plantain (2) were altogether more robust. Tiny symmetrical flowers were packed tightly together, the more rotund blobs of pale pollen extruded on the tips of wobbly hair-like filaments from tiny, four-petalled florets. They ripened from base to apex, a wave of primrose yellow moving up to the still green tip and leaving a spent, straw-coloured base.

In the more rotund heads of ribwort plantain (3) the pollen was white, held away from the darker brown head to exploit the gentlest of air currents. Here was

154. *Ten Small Components of the Machair Sward*

the same procession from base to apex to profit from a succession of different strength breezes carrying away the precious stuff of life.

Fairy or purging flax (4) bore flowers infinitessimally small and squat seed vessels. Each shoot terminated in the oldest flower which was ripening seeds while paired stems bearing younger flowers sprouted from the stem below to overtop it. The resulting elegant sprays bore pairs of tiny, blue-green leaves.

More robust were flowers of the common mouse-ear chickweed (5), the five white petals so deeply divided as to sometimes appear as ten. This adopted the same basic pattern of the dichasial cyme – the opposite of the simple spike – with the first flower terminating the main stems and later ones arising to left and right below. The ensuing seed capsule protruded beyond the sepals after petal fall, each with a characteristic sideways list. The tiny seeds shed through the neatly zig-zagged mouth of the container were capable of producing several generations a year.

Perhaps most elegant of all were the little 'silver pennies' borne by Danish scurvy grass (6) after the seeds have been shed – or picked off by finches, pipits or twites. These are the transparent inner partitions of the two-chambered, flattened seed capsules – miniature versions of those of honesty which we strip of their covering for dried winter decorations. So strong was the light that I found these casting a clear shadow on the page, producing so sharp an image that I could have drawn round them for an exact photographic reproduction.

The multiple flower heads of white clover (7) started as spheres but, as the individual flowers matured from the base up, they bent down towards the stem, creating the image of a dancer in a balet skirt, constricted amidships.

Another of the mighty legume fraternity was the bird's foot trefoil (8), its yellow and orange pea flowers sometimes referred to as bacon and eggs. But why bird's foot? The radiating seed pods provide the answer, splaying out like a bird's foot, sometimes with more than the requisite number of toes.

There remained the machair pasture's two dominant colour components, the buttercups and daisies. – small in themselves, but transforming acres by their multidudinous presence.

Although tall meadow buttercups occur in the hay crops, those of the grazed pastures are predominantly bulbous buttercups (9) with reflexed or back-turned sepals. The petals fall to reveal a neat cone of single-seeded achenes, too solid to be wafted away by the wind but breaking apart under trampling hooves and becoming incorporated in the soil for another blaze of colour a year hence.

The multiple flower heads of field daisies (10) produce seed from both the central yellow disc florets and the surounding white ray florets, but only the disc florets produce the pollen to fertilise the ovules. The one-seeded fruits are loosely attached to the enlarging central cone and easily brushed away to ensure subsequent generations.

This mini jungle had its quota of animal life, including scurrying spiders, green flower bugs, resident grass moths and visiting butterflies. Most in evidence were the long-legged dune craneflies (*Tipula juncea*). They resembled the common craneflies (*Tipula paludosa*) that erupt in huge swarms in autumn – causing great excitement among the birds which converge to feed on them. Those are geared to emerge from underground and lay their eggs in the turf in September and October, the dune craneflies were several months ahead.

A mating pair, flying tail to tail, alighted on a nearby nettle, the lower one hanging head down and swaying gently in a rising air current. This species lays eggs in May in Central Europe and two to three weeks later in Northern Europe, so this was the transfer of sperm, seen more often in dragon and damselflies.

When the female broke away to lay or oviposit, she inserted her long abdomen far into the sand, so that her legs and wings were spreadeagled on the surface – almost like a pressed specimen. In damp dunes eggs may be deposited slightly more than two centimetres below the surface where there is ample food for the larvae. The presence of nettles on the chosen patch here automatically indicated an increase in local soil fertility. Are the larvae called leather jackets, like the more pestiferous ones of the common cranefly, I wonder?

Associated with the nettles was the uncommon woolly thistle. A young flower head dropped onto the sand simulated the image of a green sand urchin, the spines sharper and closer but the whole uncannily similar in size and shape.

19. HYNISH AND THE SKERRYVORE LIGHTHOUSE

The Skerryvore Reef lies some ten miles out from Tiree's south-west corner. Two counter currents meet there, swirling over the intruding outcrops and creating dangerous turbulence. It is a focus for undersea life and a fishing boat works in the vicinity in suitable weather catching pollack, saithe and whiting, with mackerel in summer. Lobsters, edible and devil-velvet crabs are also trapped, but few spider crabs now. Sand eels, the primary food of sea birds, were thought to be still present in reasonable numbers.

Trading ships were plying between West Scottish ports and the New World during the nineteenth century and these waters became vital to food-carrying convoys and naval vessels during World War II. Important submarine exercising grounds were in use around Skerryvore while there was no doubt naval traffic to and from Scapa Flow, that great inland harbour with the Churchill Barrier across one entrance, tucked in among the Orkney Islands to the North.

The Ministry of Defence owns the Airport area of Tiree Reef and Crossapol Beach to its south, this an area of strategic importance in wartime and in a more politically stable locality than might otherwise have been sought in Northern Ireland.

Hynish on the southern tip of Tiree, is the land base from which the Skerryvore Lighthouse was contructed in the early part of the nineteenth century and it had been developed as a Heritage Museum to celebrate this achievment in the latter part of the twentieth century

` The name Skerryvore comes from the Gaelic 'Sgeir', a rock, and 'mhor', big. The question most of us want to ask when gazing upon the immovable solidity of a lighthouse perched on an offshore rock is "However did people manage to build it, get the materials there, fix them firmly enough to withstand the batter- ing of ocean swells and – most importantly – recruit enough men willing to risk their lives in such a hazardous and comfortless project?"

Work started in 1837, a century before its services were needed by the Royal and Merchant Navies in World War II and before the massive sea-going craft and mechanical aids available by then were even thought of.

I had seen the light winking away through the short, starlit June nights from Sandaig Guest House. Having stayed in sundry manned lighthouses during my sea-bird island researches in the Southern Hemisphere in the 1950s and 60s, before they were all automated, I was especially glad to be able to find out more about this one, if only at a distance.

The day of our visit to the Hynish Heritage site on the northern shore of the Am Barradhu Headland, was the one on which Gil returned from the mainland. Duncan gave me a lift to the ten o'clock ferry boat, with two departing guests, so no time was lost before setting off.

Her luggage safely on the way to the guest house with Duncan, we boarded the island bus which habitually meets the ferries. It was a male driver this time, who was happy to take us to the Scarinish general store and wait while we bought the wherewithal for lunch. We thought this unduly generous of him but, nevertheless, appreciated the fact that a twenty minute break for a cigarette, or shopping of his own in this quiet backwater where he no doubt knew almost everybody, was a vastly preferable situation to that of a London bus driver trying to quell the hooliganism of young trouble makers on board or having to leave legitimate passengers on the kerb to prevent a gang from boarding. Someone had wistfully remarked to me on Coll.

"The world seems to have passed us by here." How lucky they are!

Our driver took us along the twelve miles or so of sunwashed coast to Hynish and arranged for us to be picked up in mid afternoon for return to Sandaig.

At the time of building, in the 1830s and 40s, there was a brisk trade of sailing barques between Glasgow and North America, going west laden with manufactured goods and machinary and back home with the already much coveted tobacco from Virginia. Each vessel could make two return voyages annually and the hazardous Skerryvore Reef had claimed hundreds of lives over the years and much valuable cargo by the time the Northern Lighthouse Board decided in 1837 that a light must be installed to mark this hazard in the Hebridean Sea.

This was to be the tallest lighthouse in Scotland and Alan Stevenson was appointed as chief engineer. Over the next sixty years others of his family became involved in the work. The exception was novelist and poet, Robert Louis Stevenson, Alan's nephew. He trained as an engineer in the family tradition and also as a lawyer, but worked instead on novels such as "Kidnapped", "The Master of Ballantrae". "Dr. Jekyll and Mr. Hyde", "Treasure Island" and many more.

Robert's name has become a by-word for the generations that followed, but few have heard of Alan. Which of the two, one wonders, did the greater service to mankind? Robert has given many armchair-bound folk hours of pleasuarable leisure. Alan has averted impending disasters, saving an unknown number of human lives and much property, and he worked in much more exacting and dangerous conditions to achieve this goal.

The uncle lived a life of real adventure, with the liklihood of being stranded in temporary barracks on the reef for weeks at a time. The nephew fabricated fictitious adventures for characters who existed only in his own mind. Alan was the man of action, the master artisan at the cutting edge of one of the most remarkable engineering feats of the nineteenth century. Robert sat quietly in his study inventing situations which might never happen, to titivate the imaginations of those who came after. Are we honouring the right man?

We, of course, saw only the shore station, which had been decommissioned by the Northern Lighthouse Board in the 1890s and was in a parlous state of dereliction when the Hebridean Trust set about restoring the buildings, pier and harbour as an important feature of Tiree history.

Black stone from a local quarry had been used for the base of the mighty tower, which rose to a height of 138 feet (42 metres). The next few layers were of the beautiful rose pink gneiss so well seen at Fionnphort. This and other granites used were shipped in from quarries on the Ross of Mull twenty five miles away.

Bathed in warm sunshine, we strolled out along the massive stone pier on which imports had been landed, sorted and shipped out to the construction site. Somewhere along the line each granite block had been so perfectly shaped by master masons that no mortar was needed to hold them together against the fury of the Atlantic. This could be an important advantage, as mortar or cement was likely to get dissolved out by lively waves and lead to possible instability.

The neatly tooled blocks of the pier were remarkable botanically in hosting better clumps of thrift than I had seen anywhere on either Coll or Tiree. This species, usually abundant on such islands, seemed quite rare here.

To leeward of the pier was the harbour where smaller craft had lain at their moorings. This was floored with sparkling yellow sand, moved by every tide and now banked up against the hindmost wall. It had sanded up before, barring the entry of boats. Hand shovels and wheel barrows are poor implements to pit against the all powerful moon dominated tides.

Nothing daunted, the engineers raised an embankment to create a freshwater reservoir on the rising slope to the north-east. Once filled, the 'plug' was withdrawn and the contents rushed down the connecting conduit to flush the sand from the harbour and allow work to continue. Simple in theory, but arduous in the achieving.

The Ordnance Survey map shows a stream heading to the coast through this site, from a lochan between the museum and Ben Hynish to the west, this obviously used to feed the reservoir and augment the natural run-off of rain. Well below the flat top of the dam, which lay above the road opposite the Morton Boyd House Old Smithy and Workshops, was a rusted iron cogwheel which probably controlled the flow through the stone sluice.

There was no through flow of water at present, any overspill being piped away underground. Nevertheless, water still lay under the lower arched stone culvert, this choked now with watercress and other herbs. Some soaked away through the soil, nurturing yellow Irises, which showed no signs of being eaten by the sheep which lolled on sward and stonework. Very likely the final section had always been piped to maintain pressure at the lower level of the banked sand, rather than allow an untamed flow to spread harmlessly over the top.

The row of cottages above the cowsheds, presumably used by the workers during construction, were converted into lighthouse keepers quarters, where men could join their families during off duty spells. Those, too, have been renovated and are now in service as holiday cottages.

After a fascinating spell absorbing the well set out information in the central museum buildings, we ambled up the slope past the cylindrical lookout tower, from which relatively low elevation the lighthouse could be viewed. We settled among the sheep on a rocky knoll overlooking the walled garden for our picnic lunch.

Food had been grown in the shelter of those lesser but still sturdy walls for the workers and it was still being grown in 2007. We looked down upon neat ranks of potato plants and rows of tiny seedlings. A man was progressing slowly along a row on hands and knees, apparently thinning carrots or the like. White butterflies coursed back and forth, seeking out the Brassicas to establish nurseries for their voracious but attractively ornamented caterpillars. The faded, much travelled, painted ladies still zoomed around, their vigour undiminished.

As we rose to go our separate ways, we became aware of a particularly striking cloud formation – a satin-smooth white ellipse with several smaller outliers. Almond or lentil shaped heavenly bodies such as these have been reported by past observers as flying saucers. In scientific circles where cloud formations are accorded a genus and a species, they are known as *Altocumulus lenticularis*.

These are orographic clouds, ones which form when air is forced upwards over an obstacle – such as Ben Hynish and the higher Carnan Mor over which these now sailed. As they rise they expand and cool, causing some of the contained water vapour to coagulate into droplets, giving substance to the formation and rendering it visible. As they pass on to leeward they dissolve into apparent nothingness or, more accurately, into invisible vapour form. Gavin Pretor Pinney, author of the "The Cloud Spotters' Guide", 2006, p. 117, writes:-

"Altocumulus lenticularis is one of the most dramatic and beautiful species there is. It has a smoother, silkier surface than the crisp mounds of convection clouds. They just come to remind us that clouds are Nature's poetry, spoken in a whisper in the rarified air."

Nicely put!

We came back to earth, Gil striding off along the cliffs towards the fort above Eilean an Aodaich to shake off the aftermath of much public transport on the mainland, and me dropping down to the east facing shore around Cul Sgathain.

This was not one of those glamorous sandy beaches that lend themselves to shell collecting and sun bathing, but an amalgam of rock outcrops separated by pebble-floored gullies choked with rotting seaweed, which no recent waves had been strong enough to disperse. The lack of disturbance had allowed time for kelp fly eggs to hatch and hoppers and other crustaceans to emerge – these a draw for birds of the hinterland as well as the shore.

A concourse of about seventy starlings had converged to join the resident rock pipits and wagtails. The amalgam of sound drifting from the busy throng was wheezy, as from a distant band of discordant melodions or squeeze boxes. An earnest hooded crow stood, tarsus deep in the black sludge, tossing fronds aside with a hefty black bill designed for more demanding tasks.

Redshanks were about and several ringed plovers trotting blithely over a substrate better fitted to bear their featherweight forms. Two clusters of eider ducks had appropriated inshore pools as exercising grounds for their chicks, but the main diversion for me here was the shelduck family. So far I had only seen adults, but this Hynish pair escorted a brood of eight ducklings.

155 Shelduck Family

The little ones were boldly striped and blotched in black and white – small replicas of their handsome parents. Unlike eiders, where neither ducks nor ducklings could be more effectively camouflaged than they were and the striking black and white drakes kept well out of the way, shelducks, grown or young, displayed themselves, unafraid, to the world at large.

Both duck and drake were gaudily garbed in chestnut and luminous green as well as black and white, embellished with crimson bills. The male was as fitted a baby sitter as the female and, thus supported, this family did not skulk on inshore pools but braved the open sea beyond the outermost of the weed-draped reefs.

The water was glassy calm there, but the drake held station at a little distance to seaward, while the octet of juveniles clustered round their dam. As I watched, this outer surface began to ruffle up. Was this the turn of the tide? The family responded by moving shoreward up a channel into stiller water among the quietly sucking kelps.

Our return bus drew up outside the Hynish Old Smithy on time, with a lady driver, and whisked us away north and west for further wanderings on our 'home' shore.

Dinner was a rowdy meal that night, in the nicest possible way. The other guests, a party of wind and kite surfers, had had enough wind at last to get themselves water-borne and their adrenalin flowing and had worked up a steam that needed release now that they were warm and dry again.

Outside the natural world was settling into the daily withdrawal of the human presence. A few passing sheep peered in through the all round, low set windows and brown hares engaged in their evening frolics, undisturbed. Lapwings invaded the sunset sky at intervals in bursts of twisting, tumbling flight and a pair of pied wagtails was accompanied by a youngster,

This indulged in rushes at imaginary prey, ending abruptly with a bout of animated vertical tail wagging like an overworked pump handle. Parts that would later be black were a faded grey, parts that would be white seemed not to have fully lost the pale grey fluff of the nestling.

Expertly balancing a tray of crockery, Duncan indicated the wall beyond the garden where the corncrakes could be heard at night but that, unfortunately, was the nearest we got to those elusive island symbols. Next morning we were away, back to the mainland.

A couple of basking sharks came to see us off, each displaying no more than parts of dorsal and tail fins, but at least we had glimpsed them in the flesh. There was a meagre gannet escort. Birds flying just above the waves were easily outpaced by the McBrayne's boat, but those flying overhead outpaced us just as easily in the less obstructed medium, plus help from our slipstream.

We arrived eventually in Glasgow to find gatherings of hooded crows splashing in rain puddles as we passed the time of day in a local park. North East England was suffering severe flooding and there was much more to come in the Midlands as far south as Tewkesbury and Gloucester.

The next few weeks were dubbed "The wettest July in Britain since records began." We had been so lucky weatherwise in this strange year of April heatwave and midsummer fall. My mind went back to a scrap of conversation once heard when disembarking from a small boat after an island trip.

Passenger: "It's been a wonderful day".

Boatman" "Every day is a wonderful day".

Is it all the luck of the draw, or are such sentiments spawned deeper down?

VII

Two Northern Isles: The Shiants and Handa

THE SHIANTS

1. THE SHIANTS, THE MIGHTIEST COLUMNAR BASALT OF ALL

Moving on northwards, fourteen miles beyond the northern tip of Skye, the next personable island group between the west Scottish mainland and the Outer Hebrides is the Shiants. Probably not included in the Inner Hebrides, we visited these on one of our tours of the Outer Island Chain.

They rise in perpendicular majesty from the turbulent waters of the Northen Minch, twelve miles south of latitude 58 north at 57 degrees 51 minutes and seventeen miles east of Tarbert, where the West and East Tarbert sea lochs almost divide the Island of Harris into two parts.

They have a character of their own, quite different from the ancient Lewissian Gneiss which forms the bulk of the Outer Hebrides. While their larger neighbours to the west are the worn down remains of those ancient rocks – a land of rounded hills and deeply indented coastlines – the newer rocks of the Shiants

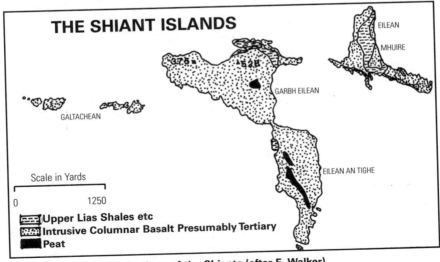

Geology of the Shiants (after F. Walker)

251

156. Parallel Columns rise 350 feet from the sea in the North Shiants

stand four square to the winds, boasting no sea lochs nor rock outcrops other than those too steep to hold more than a scanty covering of soil. Comprising three grassed islands and a cluster of smaller ones, they cover approximately five hundred acres and reach to 523 feet

We sailed from Carnach on the promontary north of Loch Tarbert East, following the northern shore of Scalpay Island and coming first to Galtachean, the line of reefs reaching out to the west. Some of these had disappeared beneath the tide on our return, but were exposed in full as we first saw them at the ebb, draped about with giant kelp; a hauling out place for seals and a resting site for off duty shags.

From here we sailed along under the sheer northern cliffs of Garbh Eilean, tallest of the islands, to land on the pebble storm bank of the narrow neck of land linking this to its sister island of Eilean an Tighe. Away to the north-east of our landing beach brooded the third island of the group, Eilean Mhuire, its black cliffs crowned by a sloping greensward. We circled around this on our return voyage to see some of the staggering numbers of sea-birds which thronged wherever suitable niches interrupted the bland face of the impregnable rock walls.

We were back here among the Tertiary Basalts and columnar jointing that we marvelled at on Staffa and the Treshnish Isles. These volcanic outpourings are associated here with comparatively recent Jurassic strata, as on Eigg. Those beds are shaly and appear at the surface on more than a third of Eilean Mhuire and in a few places on the two larger, joined islands. The meeting of the liquid laval flow with the Liassic rocks occurred several miles underground here, so there was no overwhelming of living trees as on the Sgurr of Eigg.

The more ancient matrix was of 120 million year old fossil bearing rocks formed from compressed accumulations of sand, silt and mud of an ancient sea floor. Molten rock rising beneath them, much later, some 58 to 60 million years ago, opened fissures, the incandescent material destroying and pyritising the fossilised marine creatures. The hot magma rose in pulses, cooling more rapidly when in contact with cold mudstones, to form a smooth, fine-grained rock.

Once again, we are on the great divide here, where the Atlantic Ocean was born, the rifts opening as the Earth's crust stretched to become partly plugged by upwellings from below. Some of the old Jurassic sea bed was pushed aside to crumble into the fertile soil on which humans not yet evolved, would grow their corn and potatoes.

Liquid lava welled out in four main flows, so the two rock types are interleaved. The dolerite surfaces are topped in parts by a narrow reddish band due to atmospheric weathering and possible deposition of volcanic ash – like those red bands we had seen on the shores of the "Small Isles" further south.

As it cooled segments of lava pulled apart, leaving perpendicular cracks and creating columns taller than any of those on the islands further south. The two larger Shiants are formed essentially of a single sill of dolerite, some five hundred feet thick and inclined at an angle of ten to fifteen degrees to the south-west. Thus the western side of both islands slope at a comparatively gentle gradient in contrast to the five hundred foot vertical columnar cliffs of the north and east whose base we followed during our sea passage to the landing beach.

These columns are far greater in size than those of Staffa, which are so much more photographed for their patterning and precision, with most extraneous matter cleaned away by the sea. Those of the Shiants, although predominantly straight, curve slightly towards their tops and individual columns are as much as three hundred and fifty feet high. Although the average diameter is five feet, some are as much as eight feet across and, while hexagonal is a common shape, the number of lateral faces varies.

Fraser Darling regards the colonnades as the most impressive examples in all Scotland, but also points out in his New Naturalist volume *"The Highlands and Islands"*. "Although the steamer from the Kyle of Lochalsh to Stornoway in Lewis passes within four miles of the Shiants, these islands are seldom visited and the tremendous columnar architecture remains almost unknown."

It was an awesome experience gazing up at that half mile long, five hundred foot high curtain of columns from our tiny open boat riding the gentle swell at their foot. Black and impassive, they cast a dark shadow over an apparently bottomless sea, the true opalescence of which could be appreciated only when we were afoot on the sunlit side.

Subsequent earth movements have contorted some which twist obliquely. Yet others have slewed at right angles and appear on the cliff face in transverse section like a monster honeycomb, the hexagonal 'cells' of the jigsaw coloured bright green by guano-nurtured algae, probably Prasiola.

2. THE SHIANT'S MYRIAD SEA BIRDS

Where the jointing is perfect there is foothold for neither plant nor animal. Where columns break off few of the resulting shelves and cracks seemed to remain unoccupied. We saw nothing like the neatly stepped recession on Ailsa Craig in the Firth of Clyde where almost every alcove of the giant staircase is occupied by a pair of gannets. The Shiant cliffs are too perpendicular. Larger niches afforded nest sites for fulmar petrels, smaller ones sufficed for kittiwakes. Lines of broken columns produced ledges thronged with guillemots. Shags tucked themselves into anywhere that would accommodate their gangling extremities and bulky nests.

Larger ledges below high water mark formed the reefs and offshore rocks which enabled hundreds of seals to sun themselves during the period of low water. The Galtichean Reefs are habitually crowded with their somnolent forms, but the boatman exclaimed that he had never seen so

157. *A gentler Shiant cliff on South-west Garbh Eilean*

many scores gathered along the foot of the Garbh Eilean bastions as those which we witnessed on 31st May, 1985. They included none of the common seals that frequent the eastern sea lochs of the Outer Isles, only grey Atlantics. Four eiders, two drakes and two ducks, drowsed on a higher ledge, to which they could scarcely have scrambled unless left there by the falling tide, seal fashion.

A lone gannet towered incongruously in the midst of a mob of guillemots, like Gulliver in Lilliput, in the spot where it had been seen two days earlier. Was it experiencing the lordliness of its height or the lonliness of its plight? One could not but equate it with the black-browed albatross that had spent so many years, unmated, in the gannet colony of the Bass Rock in the Firth of Forth, a loner seeking solace with the nearest substitute for companionship that it could locate – but finding no mate.

These tertiary lavas erode into terrace-like formations, said to correspond with the actual flows. Where these occurred on the northern cliffs, the soil had slumped across their surfaces to give a sloping greensward, pin pricked with the inumerable burrows of an immense puffin population.

The scale was so vast that, even from directly below, binoculars showed the horde of puffins as a swarm of gnats. They milled to and fro across the surface in alternating drifts of black and white as they twisted and turned, wader fashion, to avoid collision. Waves of birds surged out over the sea, whirring past our cockleshell craft in clouds, mixed with guillemots and razorbills, whose crevice nest sites were easier to locate than the specks of puffin burrows.

When scuttling runs across the sea surface close to the boat failed to get them airborne, they dived, in panic. We had fine views over the gunwhale of their underwater 'flying' through the sapphire depths, with half furled wings functioning as paddles.

Those scrambling ashore at the foot of the cliff would fold their 'hands' behind their backs and gaze quizzically across at our little craft, so ignominiously dwarfed by their mighty 'high rise apartment block'.

This was a tapestry of bird life that only a few selected corners of the world's oceans can produce. The Shiants form the hub for countless thousands, which fan out over the sea to feed. Most are highly vociferous, their wild calls evocative of some of our most spectacular wilderness areas. Only the phlegmatic shags, airing themselves in black phalanxes on the lower rocks, had little to say. Others seemed to be shouting in a demented effort to make themselves heard above the clamour.

` No other puffin breeding sites occur northwards until one reaches the Torridonian Sandstone of the RSPB Reserve of Handa Island. The Lewisian gneiss, with its uncompromising rock faces and glutinous peat, along the coast of Wester Ross, Sutherland, the Summer Isles and Outer Hebrides does not suit them. Basaltic cliffs such as appear again on Fladda, Chuain and Ascribes off Skye and the Treshnish provide good friable soils for burrowing and a sound skin of turf to hold the honeycombed ground of the puffinries in place. These are the islands which the puffins select as their summer homes. To quote Fraser Darling again. "The number of puffins is legion but the restriction of their breeding sites should be remarked."

Several hundred pairs of great black-backed gulls nest on the southern tip of the island where we walked, but there was too little time to assess what effect these were having on the vegetation. Skuas are not known to nest here, but four great skuas or bonxies were present, frequenting the high ground along the eastern clifftop. Fibrous pellets of goose dung scattered on the sward showed that wild geese fly in to share the grazing in winter.

No doubt this was also a haunt of white-tailed sea eagles, which ceased to breed on the Shiants about 1890. They became extinct on Skye and the North-western mainland at about the same time, having already disappeared from Mull, Jura and Eigg by 1879.

Recently this species was reintroduced to Rhum and birds are now seen from Uist to Lewis. The first chicks flew successfully from a nest in 1984 and two more in 1986. They feed on bait and offal discarded by fishermen and are said to gorge themselves until quite unable to fly. We were told of one seen north of Stornaway, so bloated that the feathers of its distended crop projected perpendicularly, the grounded bird drooping like a satiated vulture, which, in a way, as a scavenger, it is. Such birds are grounded until digestion and dispersion of the booty.

Other gourmets, a threat to the living but not above consuming the dead, were the ravens, whose insistent honking came slicing through the thin atmosphere at intervals. Snipe were twice flushed from a lowland marsh and the usual comple-ment of piping oyster catchers frequented the shore, but there were no sandy beaches and we saw no other waders. A rock pipit perched closeby as we lunched atop the pebble ridge. It was of the dark Hebridean subspecies (*Anthus spinoletta meinertzhageni*) – which differs from the shorebound *A. S petrosus* of the mainland by penetrating further inland to the moors (when there are moors to penetrate).

There was no shortage of insect life for them. Flies ranged from gangling craneflies and the fat, legless tipulid larvae from which they emerge, to creatures the size of small stable flies. Pale moths fluttered over the grass surface, round-bodied harvestmen or daddy longlegs ranged across the inland cliffs and a green crab spider was seen awaiting prey on a flower head, well above the scuttling horde of black and grey ground spiders below. There were medium sized black Carabid or ground beetles and smaller bronze Chrysomelid or leaf beetles. Most elegant of this group was the slender skipjack or click beetle *Corymbites cupreus* or *C. pectinicornis* -*a* male with strikingly pectinate or comb like antennae. This member of the Elateridae has a northern distribution and is on the wing from the beginning of June, pupating in July or August and spending the winter thus. Beautifully iridescent, the thorax was bottle green, the elytra a coppery hue.

3. SHIANTS, THE LAND AND ITS POTENTIAL

The basalt terraces are more extensive on the southern flanks of Garbh Eilean and the western ones of Eilean an Tighe. They are stepped down, with lines of low inland cliffs running lengthwise and separating a series of grassy slopes which bring the land surface gently down to sea level. Their soil is a rich brown earth, their sward is lush and there is no obvious peat accumulation, so former inhabi-tants were probably denied this source of fuel.

No-one lives permanently on the Shiants today, though an old homestead stands on the western shore of Eilean an Tigue, with the ruins of others in the nettlebeds alongside. Four families found a livlihood here – one of their living legacies the small tortoiseshell butterflies frequenting the nettle patch, which romped across patches fertilised by their residual nutrients.

The islands are still prized as sheep walks, in spite of transport problems, and are able to support others beside the hardy blackface longwools of the peaty hills. Black faces were present but the white Roman noses of others sugested Cheviot or Border Leicester blood. Many of the ewes had well grown twin lambs, a rare achievment on the barren hills of Lewis and Harris. On Skye these basaltic lava soils are regarded as cattle country, and might be here if it were not for the even greater difficulty of getting cattle water-borne than sheep. It is illegal to butcher on site, as even free range cattle cannot be regarded as game.

The inevitable rabbits were present and were no doubt a valuable food source in times past, but not in the numbers that habitually live in sandy machair country. A recently dead brown rat was spotted, reason enough for there to be no puffins burrowing on accessible slopes.

Soil fertility and height above sea level contribute to plant diversity and ninety five species of flowering plants and ferns were recorded on our late May visit – a very incomplete count but a considerable one for an island of this size. (Only Eilean an Tigue was included in our brief exploration, as there was scant time for exploring across the connecting isthmus.)

The overall community was one of mesophytic grassland, i.e. within the middle range, neither as acid as the moors nor as alkaline as the limestones and shell sands. At the eastern summit it graded into grassy heather moorland: at the western shoreline into rushy Iris marsh, with the inevitable maritime element marginally. Inland cliffs gave plants the opportunity to escape grazing pressure, coastal ones sometimes gave the added growth incentive of liberal helpings of guano.

Bracken occurred on the deeper soil around the steading, but was represented by a few pathetically dwarf fronds on the upper slopes, so isolated that, unless a relic population, they must have arisen from spores rather than the normal rhizome growth below the surface.

Mosses ranged from shoots of bronze-tipped *Polytrichum juniperinum* on dry outcrops to sodden beds of Sphagnum in depressions. The thick sward allowed scant space for Cladonia and other soil lichens but rock faces were shaggy with salt tolerant Ramalinas. A splendid orange sheet probably of *Xanthoria parietina* extended half way up the eastern cliff of Garbh Eilean near the landing beach.

Lazy beds had been constructed by earlier inhabitants, drainage, at least at these lower levels, being evidently as important as on the peatlands where this farming system evolved. Those on steeper north-facing slopes at the southern end were atypical, being a series of very much higher round-topped ridges and furrows, and they may have served an additional purpose. By lying across the contour lines to effect good water run-off, they also lay athwart the prevailing winds and may have been effective in providing shelter for the patient, long suffering sheep. Such cover is not afforded by the natural contours as the intersecting inland cliffs all seemed to face into the teeth of the westerlies.

Although the Shiants have been virtually unlived on since the end of the nineteenth century, they were owned by the author Adam Nicolson for the two decades of the 1980s and 1990s. He fell in love with them and produced *"The Story of One Man, Three Islands and Half a Million Puffins"*, Harper and Collins, 2002. Here he escaped into another dimension and probed among the ruined bothies left by past residents for the elusive spirit of the islands. Though the last of the residents left a century before, Adam Nicolson brings the place alive again for those of us seeking to escape, if only temporarily, from this frenetic world of the New Millennium. In 2005 he was to pass them on to his son Tom. Perhaps he too, will record his impressions of this magic place that we peeped at so briefly.

4. A GLIMPSE OF SHIANT'S FLORA

After putting us ashore to grub among the plants, our two boatmen busied themselves amassing a collection of "Bottom fish frae the tangle." These were extricated from the jumble of submerged fragments from broken columns enclosing a labyrinth of dark crevices where crabs and lobsters lurked and prey fish found sanctuary from predators in the tortuous passages.

The men referred to their catch as lythes, which may have been local terminology. The fish resembled coley or coalfish *(Pollochius virens)*, which are the northern counterpart of the pollack of the South. Lugubrious looking fourteen inchers, they had low set mouths, down-turned at the corners, as befitted their mode of feeding among the tangle.

We divided our wanderings between the north-facing sea-bird cliffs rising directly from the sea and the inland, west-facing cliffs scarcely affected by grazing animals, leading down to more regular slopes accessible to livestock. A fourth habitat embraced the wetlands.

158. Lythe caught off the Shiants

Subjected to no grazing, little treading and a generous rain of smelly white macro-nutrients from above, plants of the bird cliffs were rank in the extreme, their softness enhanced by the lack of sunshine on these north and east faces, Tall red fescue fringed the ledges between clumps of flowering thrift and feathery-leaved sea mayweed daisies. Soft sprays of common sorrel stood out against the dark, nitrogen-boosted background of outsize leaves. The pale blobs of sea campion and Scottish scurvy grass flowers added to the general whitewashing effect, but the red campion, a typical bird cliff plant here in the north (and one which some folk take into their gardens) was quite local.

I failed to reach the summit of these cliffs but observed the lush flora grading into straggly heather which, at that height, avoided much of the input of guano from flying birds and salt from flying spray. Some of its contemporaries might have been more at home in woodland – among them some fine clumps of primroses and violets tucked into crevices among more plebian dandelions. In sunnier climes these two benefit from the shade of trees and hedgerows, but this is scarcely necessary in the cooler, damper north.

Potential woodland here was manifested by the shiny, bronze-tinted leaves of aspen saplings sprouting from niches in the rock. More generally distributed was creeping willow, larger than usual in the absence of nibbling livestock, its low-slung canopy pierced in places by hawksbeard and wild golden rod. Low thickets of wild rose were looped about with honeysuckle, both yet to flower.

Fine clumps of succulent-leaved roseroot splayed out from crevices, their chunky stems bearing mopheads of nectar-laden blossoms, almost as bright as the spreads of bird's foot trefoil on more open patches between. Common in the North, roseroot is absent from most of the South. Diligent search is necessary to find any of the very few specimens venturing as far from its centre of distribution as the Brecon Beacons in South Wales. Slender St. John's wort occurs there as well as on the Shiant cliffs, the Scottish lovage does not. Although able to withstand the stock grazing at lower levels, the cushions and curtains of wild thyme were more strikingly colourful on these protected heights,

159. *Roseroot and Fulmar Petrel*

Less precipitous rocks accessible to sheep bore humbler plants, such as English stonecrop, a plebian relative of the nobler roseroot, with fruiting heads of fairy flax and leaf rosettes of cat's-ear and hawkweed. Tiny, but unusual and attractive, were the neat flowers of awled pearlwort (*Sagina subulata*) punctuating shining mats of silky annual hair grass (*Aira praecox*). False brome grass, a woodland species in the South, was tucked away in shady crevices. There were subtle differences in the main greensward with decreasing height above sea level, affected locally by the intermittent lines of clifflets deflecting wind and blown spray.

Soil slip as well as downward seepage of minerals in rain run-off depletes the plant medium of the upper slopes and adds to the lower ones, which bear grass heath. This is typified by purple moor grass, Nardus hard grass and splaying tufts of heath rush. Upstanding among the tormentil, milkwort and heath bedstraw were bog asphodel and heath spotted orchids.

Percolating drainage seepages scarcely worthy of the name of stream, might be paved with the discs of marsh pennywort leaves and brightened by the pink of lousewort and bog pimpernel. Watercress could have furnished the crofters with some valuable vitamin C. Golden orbs of kingcups or May blobs were abundant in marshes close to sea level, giving way to the subtler shade of yellow Iris as the summer advanced and the less pushy gold of silverweed flowers winding about their margins.

Only locally were the quagmires typically those of acid moorland with wiry deer-grass and fluffy bog cotton splaying out of soggy Sphagnum moss. This is where we found the insectivorous butterwort and, more excitingly, the diminutive net-leaved willow *(Salix reticulata)*, an arctic-alpine, mat-forming shrub. The circular leaves were characterised by conspicuously curving main veins on the dark green upper surface and a fine network of smaller ones on the silvery white undersides. The result is a wrinkling of the leaves, as in the pointed, more oval leaves of the common eared sallow *(Salix aurita)* with its green 'ear' stipules instead of smaller brown ones.

The net-leaved willow is one of the dwarf species so common in Scandinavia but is very rare in Britain and confined to Scottish mountains, not necessarily near

160. Net-leaved Willow

the sea. Its headquarters are in the West, well to the south of the Shiants, but with a small outlier on the north-west corner of the mainland near Cape Wrath. Catkins are borne late, concurrently with the leaves in June and July. They are small and oval, like those of the much more widespread creeping willow which occurs with it on the Shiants in an apparent hybrid swarm of plants bearing both rounded and narrow leaves.

There is no real mouth to this rivulet. After nurturing water starwort and Eleocharis clubrush, the water just seeps away among the sea-rounded cobbles of the beach, which can be highly mobile when bowled around by the waves.

HANDA ISLAND, SUTHERLAND

1. THE BACKDROP TO HANDA ISLAND

Geographically Handa does not fit comfortably with the rest of the Inner Hebrides but, in our passage north along Scotland's scenic west coast from Islay in the south, it would be wrong to omit this island in the far north which is, arguably, the most dramatic of them all, the dot on the i in the chain of fragmented scraps of Mother Earth.

It lies some eighteen miles south-west of Cape Wrath, the most northerly point of the Western Highlands and at approximately the same latitude as the northern tip of Lewis in the Outer Hebrides. Way out to the north are the tiny outposts of North Rona and Sula Sgeir, famous for their large colonies of gannets, fulmars, leach's fork-tailed and common storm petrels. Those are largely inaccessible and were viewed only from the sea on our International Ornithological Conference circumnavigation of Scotland in 1966. Orkney, Shetland and that bird watchers' paradise of Fair isle between the two are away to the east, north of John o' Groats.

It was mid June in 1983 when I first viewed the grandeur of Handa during a tour of Scotland's Far North. Those few magical weeks on the mainland produced botanical gems such as pink bird's eye primrose, white mountain avens, cloudberry and stone bramble. These failed to make it to the island, or failed to persist if they did, but Handa makes up for the floral deficiencies in ample measure with its fifty six thousand pairs of sea-birds and stunning cliff scenery. Low mounds of pink on cliffs at Cape Wrath were not all of the expected thrift but of moss campion *(Silene acaulis)*. Very likely this occurred on Handa too, but we failed to spot it.

Great rocky bastions rebuff the fury of the North Atlantic in the north and west, of the island, the land sloping away eastwards towards the mainland, which is only a mile away, so that it is spared the worst that those ocean spawned swells can wreak. Handa translates as "Sand Island" and there are some fine sandy beaches, but the impression as one follows the coast path is of massive precipices, vertical sided stacks and the great blow hole of Poll Ghlup. We saw more sand on the mainland coast.

My log of the day before, starting in the cod and haddock fishing port of Kinlochbervie reads: "To machair of gneiss at Bal-chreik and walk to the most remote and beautiful beach in Britain across four miles

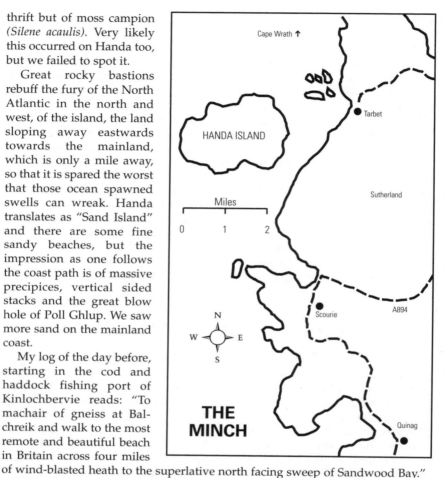

of wind-blasted heath to the superlative north facing sweep of Sandwood Bay."

We drooled over massed kingcups in rippling burns, roseroot and black spleenwort ferns in stony recesses and the rare spotted cats-ear *(Hypochoeris maculata)* before lunching above the lobstermen's stone jetty, destroyed in a storm and undergoing repair. Gangling fledglings reached scrawny necks from three shags' nests just below and a hoodie crows' nest within a stone's throw was bulging with chicks, well grown but still in down.

Our attention was captured by a rare view of a stoat trotting over grassy clifflet and beach boulders while being mobbed by two wheatears and two rock pipits. It made towards us, its bright beady eyes fixed challengingly on ours, afeared of neither bothersome birds nor static humans. An exclamatory rasping call emanated from a nearby nettle bed. *Crex crex,* invisible, as usual, but with a few yellow billed twites for good measure.

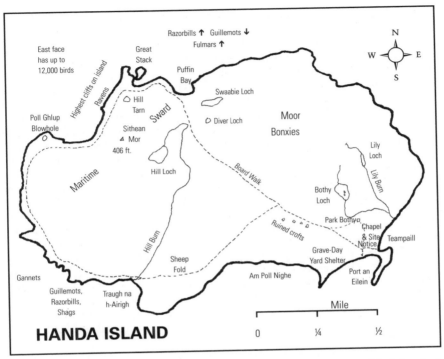

Razorbills ↑ Guillemots ↓
Fulmars ↑

East face
has up to
12,000 birds

Great
Stack

Puffin
Bay

N

W ⊕ E

S

Highest cliffs on island

Ravens

Swaabie Loch

○ Hill
Tarn

Sward

○ Diver Loch

Moor

Bonxies

Poll Ghlup
Blowhole

Sithean
⊿ Mor
406 ft.

Lily
Loch

Lily Burn

Maritime

Hill Loch

Board Walk

Bothy
Loch

Park Bothy

Chapel
& Site
Notice

Teampaill

Hill Burn

Ruined crofts

Sheep
Fold

Grave-Day
Yard Shelter

Port an
Eilein

Gannets

Guillemots,
Razorbills,
Shags

Traugh na
h-Airigh

Am Poll Nighe

Mile

HANDA ISLAND

0   ¼   ½

The track to Sandwood Bay passed a lochan, noisy with great black-backed gulls. Near where part of the path had washed away a red-throated diver dozed, its head tucked in among the shoulder feathers. It was still there, on negligent 'nest duties' perhaps on our return.

A plaintive call drew our eyes to a golden plover wearing the black belly of summer, trying to keep track of a small bundle of fluff, scuttling hither and yon among the peat hags. Two red grouse, a cock and a hen, showed themselves where the heather had been ripped out to leave gullies three feet deep and mushroom shaped peat hags reminiscent of undercut saltings in a tide rip.

161. Golden Plover and Chicks

And then came that wonderful sweep of beach. This was Handa's hinterland, the wild backdrop. What would the sea-bird citadel have to offer on the morrow?

2. HANDA, THE BASICS

Handa has no permanent residents, just a fleeting population during the summer nesting season. The parish of Durness had 2.4 persons per square mile – in 234 square miles -in the mid 1980s and is still the most sparsely populated in Great

Britain. This is wilderness indeed – a rare phenomenon in our crowded land. The RSPB wardens who 'hold the fort' for birds and bird watchers during the more kindly months need to have the right temperament to withstand the siege when Atlantic swells, divided by the massive cliffs, meet round the 'back' of the island, effectively barring the way to the mainland. One was assailed by the worst sort of a gale during his first few days alone on the island and was said to have been brought off a broken man, resolved never to return!

My experience of Handa in June 1983 was very different. We boarded a little open boat at Tarbet for a nominal fare and handed over twenty five pence a head landing fee, for furtherance of the RSPB's efforts for wildlife in Britain and beyond. It is easy to wonder at this miniscule amount twenty years later, but it meant something in those days – after the twenty shilling pound had been converted to an amount having only ten 'shilling equivalents' with inflation greater before than since. Twenty five new pence bought a pint of milk in 1987. Twenty years earlier, in 1967, our 'pinta' cost just four pence – eight times less. Twenty years later in 2007, it costs thirty seven pence, only half as much again, but the equivalent of nine pints twenty short years before. But I digress.

Beyond the almost glassy calm of Tarbet Sound the rising brown moorland fringed with golden machair sand lay bathed in sunshine, with mackerel clouds playing in the blue above. The new warden reported fifty two days without rain and wondered why the path across the island was paved with raised duck boards, when all around was so crisply dry. All Britain had a drought that year, but northern Scotland was ahead. The rest of us had savoured little of the dry spell as yet.

A couple of red plastic milk crates were dropped into the sandy shallows of the landing bay, to ensure that we stepped ashore dry shod, so calm was the sea today.

One and a half miles from east to west and about a mile across, Handa occupies 766 acres and, with Oldanay, is the largest of several uninhabited islands along this north-west coast. Its north-western cliffs tower to four hundred feet and are red, like the Devonian Old Red Sandstone and Triassic New Red Sandstone of further South, but are vastly older. Like them, these Torridonian Sandstones were laid down as horizontal beds under desert conditions, but these are pre-Cambrian. At some seven hundred million years old, they are more ancient than any but the Lewissian Gneiss, which juts out as Cape Wrath where the coast of Scotland turns to face the Arctic.

Torridonian rocks weather to a miserably poor soil, capable of supporting only acid moorland, but this is transformed to a bright green turf where Atlantic spray is hurled across the seaward edge, mitigating the inherent acidity. The hardy sheep are as aware of this as any. When not relegated to the shelter of the leeward sloping moor by insupportable gales, they are out there on the greensward, eating their fill.

The naming as Sand Island is not so inappropriate as it seems, much sand having been deposited along the sheltered southern shore. This resembles the West Hebridean machair but bore a less spectacular floral display. Its productivity was such, however, to entice men to farm, and the remnants of their lazy beds still show clearly, low down on the sunniest of the southern slopes.

Seven families wrested a living from land and sea, subsisting on potatoes, sea-birds and their eggs, fish and shellfish. Life proved intolerably hard at the time of the potato famine and the last of these inhabitants left in 1848, mostly for America. Now the sheep, like the warden and the ornithologists, were here only in summer. Even the machair is regarded as too spray-drenched for survival in winter and the whole flock was taken ashore. The absence of the wolves, which might have preyed on them during the hungry season, is commemorated by the graveyard, to which deceased mainlanders were brought for burial, to save their remains from the carrion-eating carnivores still at large in mainland Scotland.

Other creatures manage to overwinter, but these can tuck in underground during the worst of the storms, as the sheep cannot, for all their propensity for scraping out shelters under overarching peat banks. Also their appetites are smaller. Rabbits, brown rats and pygmy shrews find a year-round living here and otters sometimes visit from sea bays on the mainland.

162. *Pygmy Shrew and Pyramidal Bugle*

The lochans, peaty pools and streams provide breeding sites for palmate newts, smooth newts and toads. Common lizards are the only reptiles and there are, of course, the birds, birds galore, mostly sea-birds finding sustenance beyond the bounds of the unproductive ecosystem.

3. HANDA, A SEA-BIRD CITADEL

Almost without exception these birds, too, leave in winter, although the fulmars and kittiwakes are back by March – with no intention of laying their eggs until May. The fulmars will stay on until October, when most of the rest have left – sailing round on the autumn gales, which help them back to precipitous cliff perches difficult to attain when there are no lively air currents to be exploited.

Some fifty seven thousand pairs of birds nested in the mid 1980s, mostly on the steep north-western cliffs, from which they must depart before the onset of winter, when oceanic swells beat themselves to a halt as walls of green water against the rock face, making life there imposssible. Most head out to sea for a life on the ocean wave – the guillemots northwards, to waters off Norway, some west, some south. The moorland birds follow suit, giving southern sea-bird watchers the chance to see skuas pirating gulls and terns for their newly caught fish as they move south.

White-tailed sea eagles, by then extinct in Britain, except for occasional visits, as to Berkshire in the winter of 1983-84, bred on these cliffs until 1877 and may hopefully return since the recent introductions in the vicinity. Peregrines ceased to do so in the 1950s, in accordance with their decline in Britain as a whole, but were expected to try again in the 1980s with the banning of more lethal pesticides. Other birds of prey turned up spasmodically. Most frequent were buzzards, but merlin, hen harrier and even golden eagle might be seen.

The northern touch is imparted to the moorland by the wheeling, screaming skuas, both great skuas or bonxies and the light and dark phases of arctic skuas. These are relative newcomers, their numbers building up quite slowly, so that they are jealously guarded by the wardens and visitors were discouraged from straying into their territory. The bonxies nested first in 1964, the arctic skuas in 1968. By 1979 there were a dozen pairs of the first and half a dozen of the second.

163. Great Skua and Juniper

There is a long way to go before they become the dive bombing hazard that they are on Fair Isle, but it is a start. Skua photos of nests and chicks included here were taken during a three week stay on Fair Isle when I was doing the rounds with Peter Davis, the warden, ringing the youngsters.

Well over a hundred thousand nesting sea-birds cannot fail to be an impressive sight and the Handa cliffs are sufficiently dissected for these to be viewed from projecting headlands or the sides of gullies in all their majesty. Where they are too far off to be picked out individually their presence is indicated by the swathes of 'whitewash' coating and dripping from their ledges.

The guillemots, estimated at some twenty five to thirty thousand pairs, were particularly magnificent as they jostled each other, six to eight deep, on the spacious shelves. We assume that they are only ashore for the four summer months, from April to July, before the still downy chicks tumble off the ledges and paddle out to sea, but we may be wrong. Few people look at guillemot cliffs in winter. Someone who did – on Copinsay off Orkney – found thousands of guillemots crowded on the ledges for at least a week in October 1977.

There is an increasing tendency for guillemots and fulmars to come ashore in winter on Fair Isle, where the cliffs may be deserted for only a few weeks after the breeding season and in very rough weather. Like other auks and diving ducks, guillemots are very likely to fall foul of oil spills and the increasing presence of oil rigs and tankers in Scottish waters could pose a threat.

Other contributors to the grunting cacaphony of sound surging up from the Great Stack, Needle Rock and neighbouring cliffs are the razorbills, some nine thousand pairs in all. Puffins are represented by a mere three to four hundred pairs scattered along cliff brinks where there is sufficient depth of soil for them to burrow. Black guillemots are down to a few couples and were seen only on the sea during the boat crossing from Tarbet.

Second commonest are the thirteen thousand pairs of kittiwakes, with nests plastered to the merest irregularities of sheer rock faces. The constant ripple of sound wafting up from the crowded colonies is as evocative as any in our rugged West. Once this was also true of the more strident calls of our commonest gulls, the herring and the black-backed, which now conjure up no more romantic scenes than that of the local town rubbish tip. Kittiwakes are truly pelagic and would not demean themselves by exploiting our leftovers for a living.

Lesser black-backs are seldom found on vertical cliffs, preferring to nest among bracken on more level plots, and Handa does not cater for their needs. Herring gulls are no more numerous than puffins, although they make a great deal more noise and were beginning to learn about ornithologists' lunch packets, so brought themselves to notice more readily.

Great black-backs, always more solitary, were present to the tune of some fifty pairs. One had knocked down a kittiwake and was tearing it to pieces on the sea, while its gawky mottled chicks padded back and forth on the flat summit of Great Stack, dwarfing the fully grown puffins alongside. Terns and waders may also fall victim.

Fulmar petrels, familiar to us now in the South, are traditionally birds of the North and three thousand five hundred pairs are scattered over the cliffs of Handa, often only just below their brinks among the thrift and roseroot, so that they are easy to observe. Here they benefit from the full force of the cliff updraught, sailing effortlessly away as soon as their webbed feet lose contact with the fragmentary nest. They do not relinquish their patch readily and too close an approach may result in a douching with smelly orange crop oil.

Three hundred pairs of shags rear their young on the island, off duty birds occupying communal roosts on flat slabs near sea level, where the feathers of spreadeagled wings soon dry in the brisk onshore breezes so long as they are above wave splash.

4. PLANTS AND BIRDS OF MOOR AND LOCHAN

Handa, about a mile offshore from Tarbet and three miles from Scourie, boasts three main plant communities. The main block is occupied by moorland, bleak, featureless and forbidding – windswept and dotted with peaty pools and lochans.

The rugged eastern cliffs are not included in the circuit for day visitors, but the northern ones which are must be as dramatic as any. The duckboard path leads to the comparative seclusion of Puffin Bay in the north, from where folk make sinuous progress past the Great Stack alongside its headland and down the western cliffs, with the spectacular blowhole and more grandiose cliffscapes and islets.

The third habitat is lower and sandier, verging on machair inasmuch as it was the part where past inhabitants had established their lazy beds to wrest a meagre living from the land. Only the south-eastern corner is afforded minimal shelter from the prevailing south-westerlies by the opposing mainland coast, so life was tough, even on this lower ground.

The hammerhead shape of the promontary in the south-east offers the choice of two landing places, depending on which way the sea is running, the more deeply indented inlet being Port an Eilean facing south on its western flank.

Here, thoughtfully, a day shelter hut has been erected beside the graveyard for shorter stays by those arriving in inclement weather. Inland of the flagpole and noticeboard and to seaward of Bothy Loch were other features, a 'park', an old sheepfold and a cluster of ruined crofts.

We set off past these across dry, humpy heather to follow the boardwalk through skua territory. This had been an unpeopled wilderness between the exodus of the seven crofting families in 1848 and the establishment of the RSPB Bird Reserve in 1962.

This main block of the island sloping down from the seaward cliffs is spared the worst of the wind-borne spume and is clad in the sombre brown of moorland plants. The dominance of deer sedge, complemented by purple moor grass, was a legacy of years of over-grazing by sheep and frequent fires. Both are palatable only when young, so that other plants are taken in preference, and both have well protected buds hidden in their fibrous bases, so that they survive fire better than most.

Since the island came under the management of the RSPB in 1962 grazing pressure has alleviated and some of the species hitherto repressed were beginning to recover. Already showing among the twiggy heather in 1983 were the blue of heath milkwort, the pink of lousewort and the yellow of tormentil. Heath spotted and northern marsh orchids were flowering ahead of the bog asphodel which spatters the Sphagnum beds with gold in August.

The sandstone and conglomerate bones of the land, some pink and some grey, poked out through the skin of peat where this thins. Erosion gullies and peat pans cut into it where it thickens. Drainage ditches dug to lead off excess water were dry that summer, their channels choked with the severed, faded leaves of the moor grass to appear as white streaks across the brown.

Thirty nine species of flowering plants, excluding those of transition zones to machair and maritime turf, included black crowberry and various sedges among the velvet bent grass (*Agrostis canina*), sweet vernal grass and mat grass. Hard fern sprouted from beneath rocks and round-leaved sundew trapped unfortunate insects in the bog moss beds. Stunted devil's bit scabious occupied moist peat with cross-leaved heath, while mountain everlasting preferred the drier peat favoured by fine-leaved heath.

Skylarks, meadow pipits and wheatears are an accepted part of the moorland community anywhere in Britain. More special here are the occasional red grouse and golden plover and snipe of the rush and sedge beds. Golden plover chicks hatch in June and we watched little balls of mottled, gold-flecked fluff on long and spritely legs, a joy to see as they sprinted across the heather after their gleaming, golden-backed guardian. The dumpy grouse chicks were more secretive until able to fly, when the sudden whirring of many little wings startled the disturber more than the disturbed.

The water of the peaty pools and lochans is clear, yet stained a dark brown by tannin seeping from slowly decaying remains. Many are innocent of vegetation, their black beds sprinkled with stones. In others the bottom is hidden by floating polished bronze leaves of bog pondweed. Suspended strands of flote grass invade the raft and the edges are embroidered with a succession of lesser spearwort flowers.

Some pools were choked with the flowing, rusty orange leaves of the lake version of bulbous rush (*Juncus bulbosus var. fluitans*), its stems and leaves combed into undulating sweeps by water movements. Towards the shallows growths became shorter, but, only when land bound by recession of the water do they flower and produce the brown nutlets beloved by seed-eating birds. Yet others hold soft growths of moss, *Drepanocladus fluitans,* another with that 'fluid' name, along with blanket weed where fertility has been enhanced by sheep droppings. Drainage runnels leading out to the cliffs hold water starwort bordered by the green discs of marsh pennywort and starry white flowers of water blinks.

A few pond skaters scudded across the surface film and red and blue damselflies have been recorded, but the pools are oligotrophic (poor in nutrients) so that the level of life, both plant and animal, is low. Frogs have not yet discovered them so the toads and two species of newts have things their own way.

None of the lochans are big enough for black-throated divers to nest, but a few pairs of red-throated divers do and both species fish, summer and winter, in the waters of Handa Sound between island and mainland. Great northern divers nest away to the North and are seen only in winter, some of the younger, non-breeding birds lingering until May.

Red throated divers are mainly tundra nesters too so, bleak though Handa seems, it is a sinecure compared with the breeding grounds of some. Few nest on the Scottish mainland, the northern and western islands

164. *Red-throated Divers and Bog Cotton*

being their chosen terrain, where the pools occupied are sometimes as little as ten metres across. They fly up from their winter sea fishing grounds as early as March to busy themselves with courtship and home making while their more northerly contemporaries linger on in the Scottish sea lochs, knowing that their frozen homelands will not be ready for them for several weeks yet.

5. THE HARSH GRANDEUR OF THE NORTH-WEST CLIFFS

Approaching the north-west cliffs beyond Swaabie Loch there is a sharp change in the composition of the sward – a steady brightening from brown to green. This belt of maritime grassland where the path debouches at the head of Puffin Bay in the North is quite narrow. It broadens as the cliffs dip towards the prevailing winds so that more of the land rising behind has its acidity mitigated by blown sea spray.

The transition is typified by twiggy growths of creeping willow permeating the turf and the wiry tufts of heath rush huddling closer together. The willow, so familiar on southern sand dunes, flowered later here, the oval catkins, both male and female, still in the silken 'pussy' phase among the shining leaves in mid June. Only here did we see much of the salt-tolerant black bog rush, more conspicuous among the green and growing here with attractive mauve swards of flowering butterwort. The rarer pale butterwort was also here.

More creeping willow occupied the transition zone between moor and machair on the opposite side of the island, but its associates were different there and less wind resistant, the main examples being bracken and bluebells – an ensemble well developed on the less spray douched islands of Wales.

It is the black crowberry scattered throughout that marks this maritime turf off as different from those equivalent communities further south, where crowberry is essentially a mountain plant. Another manifestation of this shiny-leaved Erica mimic is well seen among the spectacular pink gneiss outcrops of Fionnphort, the port of embarkation for Iona.

Common to Handa and the Welsh islands are the dwarf rosettes of sea plantain, tightly packed in glistening mats. Buck's horn plantain seems rarer in the North and does not approach some of the southern varieties in leaf succulence. The bent-fescue matrix of the clifftop sward, with depauperate Yorkshire fog, is common to both. Thrift, as so often, increases progressively to dominance as the cliff edge is approached but sea campion, its common associate, is relegated by sheep grazing mostly to inaccessible faces. Paths are marked by strips of pearlwort and annual meadow grass, which may be bordered by daisies.

West along the north coast the cliff decreases in height, so that more spray sweeps over the edge and the green maritime belt broadens. It was here that we saw most of the sheep, which not only like their greens salted but which enjoy their more succulent texture. When they are withdrawn in winter a small flock of barnacle geese takes over, leaving only their droppings to apprise summer visitors of their sojourn.

Rabbits, too, prefer the fine grasses of this turf, which they help to make hummocky by their burrowing, thereby providing local shelter for unpalatable species. As often in island populations, a fair percentage are black. Sheep scrape out 'lairs' behind bosses of thrift, removing the peat to the bedrock in places, while some bed down in the hollows at the entrance to rabbit warrens.

Where sufficient soil remains the chickweed waxes lush with generous helpings of dung and urine. Similar often horseshoe shaped hollows occurred around the windward side of projecting boulders, as on tidal sandy beaches. Too wet for sheep to shelter in, these are the product of physical forces, wind scour, water drip and even, sometimes, frost heave.

There is 'waved heath' on the most exposed corner, the grass whisked up into little peaks by the wind to produce turbulence at ground level and reduce overall wind speed. Miniature field daisies and hairy hawkbit (Leontodon taraxacoides) nestle in the depressions with mouse-ear chickweed, while stunted marsh thistles braved the salty air stream above.

Naturally we lingered and lunched where we could enjoy the extraordinary panorama of the jostling hordes of sea fowl on the Great Stack and adjoining faces. Fulmars and razorbills might be quietly incubating only a few feet below us under the very brink, but we were static enough to see something also of the more cryptic insect life that eked out a living here, despite all the hazards on the accommodatingly irregular surface.

Like the Tundra, the whole area comes to life in summer. Downy black Staphylinid beetles more than an inch long scuttled across the turf, wearing short gingery wing cases like waistcoats. The wasp like yellow bars across the protruding abdomen with its dorsal line may be a warning colouration, persuading would-be predators to desist.

Grey caped hoodie crows dropped in from the sky to take medium sized black Carabid beetles. Rock pipits ventured quite close to snap up the little brown grass weevils and oystercatchers moved in from the southern sands to probe the turf for grubs and worms, giving variety to their diet of sea foods.

White-tailed bumble bees zoomed ponderously among the inviting pea flowers, sipping nectar to sustain their broods in underground nests. Among the myriad flies that nourished the spiders and other predators were scorpion flies, he with tip-tilted, bulbous red tail simulating a sting, both he and she with long-beaked jaws the better for holding prey.

Caterpillars of oak eggar and heath beauty moths found a living in the sward. When wind strength allows there are butterflies about, the expected meadow browns, common blues and small tortoiseshells and unexpected large heaths are said to occur. Painted ladies and red admirals manage to get this far in good summers, the latter particularly adept at remaining airborne in seemingle impossible winds.

There were pools in this maritime grassland too, their surfaces often strewn with feathers from moulting and preening gulls. Their acid waters soaked into the salt sodden banks to produce a marked, though localised change in the bordering plants by stimulating acid lovers such as bog cotton and even Sphagnum. Common sorrel and buckler ferns arched out over the beer coloured water.

Roseroot is a special feature of the sheer walls of Poll Ghlup, the great blowhole cut into the island's highest cliffs, where the sea enters around both sides of a massive supporting pillar of rock. This says much for its tolerance of douching spray, the chimney housing a veritable fount of rising water at high tide in rough weather. No birds nest on its walls. Disregarding the spray and the bitter updraughts, the space is probably too confined for all but the most nimble to find space for take-off.

Because of the parallel cracks between bedding planes of the Dalradian sandstone, the roseroot hereabouts sometimes grew in long narrow lines, uncannily like those plants along the grikes of the very different limestone rocks of the Irish Arans, but here the backdrop was dark red rather than silvery grey.

Scottish lovage, with dark, polished compound leaves, was just beginning to flower in June, well behind the Scottish scurvy grass alongside, but flowers of this last on into midsummer. Sea plantain here, free from pressure of grazing, can aspire to the heights that it usually attains only on salt marshes, although flowering is proportionally not much more prolific than on the stamen-peppered swards close cropped by rabbits and sheep.

6. WESTERN ROCKS AND SOUTHERN SANDS

Red campion, a leggy woodland plant in the South, is often a chunky cliff plant in the North, with flowers opening in mid June among guano stimulated cocks-foot and sea mayweed. Others find sanctuary among the ungrazed thrift and red fescue, including the rare but unspectacular pyramidal bugle. This needs protection but is so small that it is all too often likely to be overwhelmed by its protectors. Only one small clump was known on Handa at the time, in an obscure grassy rift of the cliffs, so we were fortunate indeed to spot it. No more than two inches high, the purple flowers crouched among downy leaves in a little fairy-land of flowering primroses and lesser celandines.

This rare bugle is more at home in the mountains of Central Europe, its British distribution being restricted to a few Scottish counties, Orkney, Westmorland, Clare and Galway. Its presence on Handa is all the more remarkable in that it is said to prefer basic rocks, which the Torridonian sandstones are definitely not. Perhaps sea salt and guano stand in with the necessary minerals here.

South of the western shag roosts the clifftop dips seaward to disappear in a great tumble of boulders piled as a storm beach considerably above the level of the land behind. To seaward of the beach is a slabby wave-cut platform; to landward is a linear freshwater pool fed by natural run-off and the Hill Burn. Smaller boulders and driftwood had been thrown up onto the backing, heather clad peat, where the seashore grades quickly into the general terrain.

Shaggy buckler fern, creeping willow and black crowberry have invaded the back of the storm beach, lesser spearwort and marsh pennywort occupy the pool, which the coast path crosses by stepping stones. Eider ducks lead their ducklings to sea here and we saw family parties in the wrack-choked gullies where the great oarweeds surfaced at low tide.

Circling on eastwards beyond the abandoned sheep fold and the ruined crofts, the sere moorland grades gently into machair, its austerity mitigated by

the covering of wind-blown sand, rich in the limey remains of pulverised sea shells. Here the milkwort flowers are pink, white and mauve as well as the rich gentian blue of the moor. They share the more open patches with creeping cinquefoil, dovesfoot cranesbill and field woodrush.

165. *Barnacle Geese and Ammocalamagrostis balthica*

Eared sallow is invading the abandoned fields and lazy beds, the bushes afforded a boost since the alleviation of grazing in 1962, but still reaching not much more than a metre high in this first twenty years. Massed silky seeds were bursting from the flask shaped capsules in June, in both the eared and the creeping species, so more bushes may be forthcoming, seed eaters and seedling nibblers permitting.

Tinies of the dry shallow sand over rock included wild thyme, common speedwell and heath violet. More robust growths in wet runnels were meadowsweet, marsh willow herb and common horsetail. Half way species among bracken and bluebells were typified by black bog rush, glaucous sedge and slender St. John's wort.

The real star here is the hybrid marram grass *(Ammocalamagrostis baltica)*, arising as a cross between marram grass and bush grass *(Calamagrostis epigejos)*. This is not just an intraspecific cross, but an intergeneric one, so it is not surprising that the progeny are sterile, with imperfect pollen produced in permanently closed anthers.

The miracle does not have to keep happening. Once in existence the plants are as capable of vegetative conquest of the sands by creeping rhizomes as is the marram parent, which they resemble the more closely. I had met this hybrid on dunes in Holland, but only two other sites are known in Britain. Both are on the east coast, nearer to the Baltic ones which give the plant its name, and they cleave more closely to that parent. Ross Links in Northumberland and Caister to the Horsey dunes in Norfolk are the other British outposts.

Towards the landing place at Port an Eilean rabbits keep the sward trimmed to a standard to suit the most fastidious gardener and the nesting wheatears, which need short tutrf to feed over. The lime content of the sward ensures the wherewithal for dune snails to build their multi-coloured shells.

Oystercatchers, ringed plovers and terns breeding on the offshore islets flip across to feed and rest on the sandy beaches of the Sound and eider chicks find an easier passage to the sea here than through the great rocks of Traigh na h Airigh. Spring and autumn passage migrants likely to join the residents along the tide line are curlew, redshank and greenshank and the ubiquitous dunlin.

At low tide, when the long reef of rock rose from the waters of Port an Eilean alongside the perforated peninsula of Toll a Choin, the scene was magical. Mountains rose tall and bleak to either side of Tarbet's sheltered glen on the mainland and grey Atlantic seals disported themselves among the swaying kelp which foots the eastern cliffs. Given the right weather, there can be few places more beautiful.

166. Boat at Handa. Homeward bound

List of Illustrations